I0801357

## Praise for *Double Exposure*

"The plays in *Double Exposure* insist that we examine the injustice, insanity, and despair wrought by the occupation of Palestine. This diverse mix of dramatic styles and voices is a brave, passionate, and collective call, a theatrical catalyst for investigation and resistance."
—Eve Ensler, Obie Award–winning playwright of *The Vagina Monologues*

"The powerful and dramatic situations from the plays in *Double Exposure* transported me into the West Bank, Jerusalem, and Gaza and placed me side by side with three-dimensional characters struggling to keep their hope, their humanity, and their moral compass amidst the brutalities, large and small, of the most intractable of conflicts. I became not an observer, but a participant in their lives. Essential reading."
—David S. Craig, 2016 Helen Hayes Award–nominated playwright

"'Blessed are the storytellers, for they shall interpret the earth.' My biblical revisionism notwithstanding, this beatitude shapes my view of the world, and I see it playing out in this extraordinary collection of plays penned by some of our most courageous and compassionate playwrights. Beyond the dictates of 'balance,' 'level playing fields,' and 'moral equivalencies,' we see the grinding, persistent injustice of Israeli occupiers brutalizing occupied Palestinians. With *Double Exposure* we begin to imagine a way out: we encounter glimmers of healing, transformation, and equality that not only give us hope, but provide us narratives for renewed commitment to justice."
—Jamil Khoury, Artistic Director of Silk Road Rising

## Praise for Hannah Khalil

"[*Bitterenders*] is thought-provoking, and attempts to give us an up-close look at everyday life in a world of imperfection. . . . The dialog here is sharp, heart-wrenching."
—*Stark Insider*

"As a Palestinian-Irish dramatist, Khalil writes with feeling about homelessness, migration and a culture in which masculinity is equated with ownership."
—Michael Billington, *The Guardian* on *Plan D*

## Praise for Arthur Milner's *Facts*

"Taut and volatile, a powerful piece that digs deep."

—*Financial Times*, London

"Hard-hitting, gritty, instructive and provocative; absolutely riveting."

—*Vancouver Courier*

## Praise for Natasha Greenblatt's *The Peace Maker*

"Greenblatt . . . writes agreeably pointed dialogue, and carefully balances her twin narratives and the pains and paradoxes they engender."

—Robert Cushman, *National Post*

"Greenblatt has taken the thorny, unsettling, upsetting subject of Israeli/Palestinian relations, and written a wise, thoughtful, prickly, and ultimately glorious play about that heartbreaking subject."

—Lynn Slotkin, *The Slotkin Letter*

## Praise for Ismail Khalidi

"Perhaps playwright Khalidi's greatest triumph is that somehow glimmers of the truth and the absurdity of human existence emerge from *Tennis in Nablus*. In a corner of the world with complex and seemingly unsolvable problems, he shows us human beings whom we wish we knew better."

—Manning Harris, *Atlanta INtown*

"Khalidi expertly mines rich elements of tragedy and comedy."

—*Stageworks/Hudson*

## Praise for Stephen Orlov's *Sperm Count*

"Full marks to Orlov for linking the personal and the political."

—*Time Out*, London

"Where many plays suffer from a woeful lack of ideas, this one takes on so many that by the end the head is spinning. . . . Orlov writes rather well on marital anxiety, on Jewish memory, and on the desire of a Palestinian doctor who 'chose the scalpel not the sword' to escape the revenge cycle."

—Michael Billington, *The Guardian*

**Praise for Samah Sabawi's *Tales of a City by the Sea***

"[A] nuanced exploration of the myriad ways the occupation affects Palestinians at home and abroad. . . . This gripping play is an act of resistance that implores its audience to take heed."

—Rebecca Harkins-Cross, *The Age*

"Sabawi has created an enthralling landscape and peopled it with believable characters. It looks beyond the political to examine the effect of war on those who cannot leave the battleground. It's a gripping piece of theatre that begs to be seen and heard."

—Tony Busch, *Adelaide Theatre Guide*

**Praise for Abdelfattah AbuSrour, Lisa Schlesinger, and Naomi Wallace's *Twenty-One Positions***

"AbuSrour, Schlesinger, and Wallace have written a brilliant, unsettling, searing, tragicomedy about the meaning and consequences of violent dispossession and military occupation on generations of human beings."

—Robin D. G. Kelley, UCLA Professor and Guggenheim Fellow

"*Twenty-One Positions* brilliantly explores the issues of the Wall separating Israelis and Palestinians and opens a dialogue of immense political and religious importance through a theatrical lens. It imagines a reality in which both sides learn to see one another. It is indeed a 'cartographic dream of the Middle East'."

—Matthew Maguire, Director of the Theatre Program
of Fordham College at Lincoln Center and
Co-Artistic Director of Creation Production Company

# DOUBLE EXPOSURE

EDITED BY
STEPHEN ORLOV
SAMAH SABAWI

# DOUBLE EXPOSURE

## PLAYS OF THE JEWISH AND PALESTINIAN DIASPORAS

Playwrights Canada Press
Toronto

LIBRARY AND ARCHIVES CANADA CATALOGUING IN PUBLICATION
Double exposure (Toronto, Ont.)
Double exposure : plays of the Jewish and Palestinian diasporas / edited by Stephen Orlov, Samah Sabawi.

Contents: Twenty one positions : a cartographic dream of the Middle East / Abdelfattah AbuSrour, Lisa Schlesinger & Naomi Wallace -- Sperm count / by Stephen Orlov -- Facts / by Arthur Milner -- Tales of a city by the sea : a play / by Samah Sabawi -- The peace maker / by Natasha Greenblatt -- Sabra falling / by Ismail Khalidi -- Bitterenders : a short play / by Hannah Khalil.
ISBN: 978-1-77091-562-6 (paperback)

1. Arab-Israeli conflict--1993- --Drama. 2. Jewish-Arab relations--Drama. I. Sabawi, Samah, editor II. Orlov, Stephen, author, editor III. Title.

PN6120.A76D69 2016 808.82'98924 C2016-905457-8

Playwrights Canada Press staff work across Turtle Island, on Treaty 7, Treaty 13, and Treaty 20 territories, which are the current and ancestral homes of the Anishinaabe Nations (Ojibwe / Chippewa, Odawa, Potawatomi, Algonquin, Saulteaux, Nipissing, and Mississauga / Michi Saagiig), the Blackfoot Confederacy (Kainai, Piikani, and Siksika), néhiyaw, Sioux, Stoney Nakoda, Tsuut'ina, Wendat, and members of the Haudenosaunee Confederacy (Mohawk, Oneida, Onondaga, Cayuga, Seneca, and Tuscarora), as well as Metis and Inuit peoples. It always was and always will be Indigenous land.

We acknowledge the financial support of the Canada Council for the Arts, the Ontario Arts Council (OAC), Ontario Creates, the Government of Ontario, and the Government of Canada for our publishing activities.

*To our young grandchildren, Emad and Salem, and Taylor,*
*who inspire our work and offer us hope for the future.*

## CONTENTS

# PREFACE

How do two strangers, a Boston-born Jew in Canada and a Gaza-born Palestinian in Australia, come together to choose seven plays for an anthology about the Israeli-Palestinian conflict?

The starting point for us was trust, something we felt from the moment we read each other's plays about the issue. What made our process work was mutual respect, honest exchange, and guiding principles.

*Double Exposure: Plays of the Jewish and Palestinian Diasporas* is the first anthology of its kind. Diaspora writers outside the conflict zone offer a distinct viewpoint. Many of us live in multicultural societies that accord us both privilege and perspective, enough that we view the conflict through a more diverse prism and experience its impact differently.

We categorically reject the notion expressed by some that writing from the safety of our homes, far from the heat of battle, negates our right, our reason, or our ability to address the issue in public. The Diaspora journey from page to stage is marked by the cultural footprints of our ancestors and the emotional, material, and familial ties of so many to the conflict. And this is an issue for all humanity, not solely for Jews and Palestinians.

*Double Exposure* challenges one of the last remaining thematic taboos to permeate much of Western theatre from North America to Oceania. We make that bold claim with humility and regret, for we wish it were not the case. Despite the fact that the Israeli-Palestinian conflict is one of the world's longest and most inflammatory ongoing regional hostilities of the past seventy years, most major theatres in Canada, America, Australia, and Europe have not commissioned, solicited, or produced plays on the subject, many for political more than artistic reasons. This silent de facto boycott has not been a conspiracy; it has been fuelled for decades by prejudice, ignorance, and timidity.

This is true of scripts written by progressive playwrights of both ethnic descents who dare to criticize Israel onstage. Few companies produce such plays, but most theatres, especially those run by mainstream Jewish cultural institutions, stamp the scripts, particularly those written by Diaspora playwrights, "non-kosher." In 2011, the board at City University of New York rescinded an earlier decision to grant an honorary degree to Jewish Pulitzer Prize–winning playwright Tony Kushner because of his criticism of Israel; public outcry erupted, however, prompting trustees to grant him the degree. And in 2014, Washington DC's Theater J fired its long-time artistic director, playwright Ari Roth, one of the few heads of an American Jewish theatre to showcase plays critical of Israel, including a stage-reading festival of scripts penned by Arab-American playwrights. Both controversies were instigated through intense lobbying by pro-Israeli zealots.

Closer to home, Montreal's major English and French theatres have never portrayed on their mainstages a single Palestinian character in plays of their subscription seasons. And the Australian branch of the largest international Jewish membership organization, B'nai Brith, recently instigated unsuccessful attack campaigns in the press against *Tales of a City by the Sea*, triggering a debate in the Victorian State Parliament, with some opposition MPs condemning the play's inclusion in Victoria's recommended high school drama curriculum. The controversial censorship campaign backfired, however, and the play has remained on the recommended curriculum list. Its subsequent three-city tour received solid reviews of sold-out shows.

The price we pay scaling hurdles to mount this conflict onstage is minuscule compared with the death and destruction that so many face in this seemingly endless war over birthright and homeland.

Beyond navigating through the political complexity of the conflict, our work as editors was artistically challenging, for both of us faced some different but equally complicated obstacles in our search for submissions. We both knew that not many playwrights of either Diaspora had tackled the conflict onstage, partly due to limited chances of production, but we were surprised to find during our research so few produced plays to solicit for publication consideration.

Despite the high number of Jewish playwrights residing in their global Diaspora, you can almost count on your fingers and toes how many of them have written such plays produced at professional theatres. Some Jewish dramatists consider the topic to be overly complex, polemical, or angst-ridden to pen for stage, but too many avoid it for partisan or career reasons. While proportionally more Palestinian Diaspora playwrights address the issue directly, not all write in English. And we knew that some playwrights of both descent would balk at participating in a dual-Diaspora anthology.

Some excellent plays considered but not chosen were worthy of publication. The most common weakness of other submissions written by both Jews and Palestinians was their stereotypical depiction of the "other" characters. The plays in our anthology do not shy away from portraying the "other" side as the enemy, and a few secondary characters are limited to unidimensional roles. However, we have tried to offer you a collection of dramatic works that turn the political into the personal with universal themes delivered through authentic characters, time, and place. We have sought variance in genre between drama and comedy, in aesthetic between reality and the surreal, in setting between the Diasporas and Israel/Palestine, in playwrights (with three plays written by Jews, three by Palestinians, and one a collaboration by both), and in characters' political opinions.

Since we began working on this anthology project over two years ago, we have noticed that more Diaspora playwrights are now addressing the issue and a few more theatres, especially in England, are producing such plays. Their success highlights the growing demand for compelling theatre that calls for a just peace, however distant in the horizon. Dramatizing that onstage is not merely a pipe dream of fiction. The brutal Israeli bombardment of Gaza in 2014 and its ongoing siege have furthered a shift already in the making of global public opinion toward a more balanced stance on the conflict. The publication of this anthology is very much a reflection of these changing times.

We believe theatre should be a visionary art that dares to shine a light on what blinds us with fear, and the stories we pen as dramatists should expose the dark shadows of the past and the firestorms of our present to help us create a world that is more just and more peaceful for generations to come.

Samah Sabawi and Stephen Orlov
Melbourne and Montreal, July 2016

# ACKNOWLEDGEMENTS

We first extend our gratitude with deep respect to our outstanding playwrights—Abdelfattah AbuSrour, Natasha Greenblatt, Ismail Khalidi, Hannah Khalil, Arthur Milner, Lisa Schlesinger, and Naomi Wallace—whose extraordinary plays have so greatly augmented our own script contributions to make this anthology worthy of its goal as an historic literary collaboration of high artistic merit by Jewish and Palestinian dramatists dedicated to peace and social justice. We thank them for inspiring us with their artistry, their dedication, and their collegiality.

We equally thank the fabulous staff of Playwrights Canada Press—Annie Gibson, Blake Sproule, Mandy Bayrami, and Stephanie Nuñez—without whom this project would never have been realized. Their publishing expertise, wise counsel, and literary vision have been a constant source of professional support and emotional encouragement from beginning to end.

We are so fortunate that acclaimed playwrights Karen Hartman and Betty Shamieh both agreed to write introductions to this publication. We thank Karen for her insight on the importance and challenges of such an anthology and her comprehensive commentary on the specific plays. And we thank Betty for her perceptive reflections on the need to open ourselves to a multiplicity of Diaspora voices and narratives that deepen our mutual respect and understanding.

We also express our appreciation to the fine playwrights who submitted plays for consideration that we were ultimately unable to include in this anthology.

We are grateful for the suggestions, contact recommendations, and encouragement that we have received from some of our contributing playwrights and from other theatre practitioners, including acclaimed dramatists Eve Ensler and Playwrights Guild of Canada President, David S. Craig; former Artistic Director of New Dramatists and current Executive Director of University of Washington's School of Drama, Todd London; theatre critic and professor Alisa Solomon; and Founding Artistic Director of Silk Road Rising, Jamil Khoury, among others.

Lastly, we thank with gratitude and love our dear spouses, Monir ElRayes and Karen Kaderavek, for blessing us with their valued feedback and unconditional support throughout our journey of the past two years.

# INTRODUCTION
## BY KAREN HARTMAN

The twin pitfalls of writing about Israel and Palestine are: 1) nobody cares, and 2) everyone is offended. It's a beastly subject for discourse, so my hat goes off to Stephen Orlov and Samah Sabawi for gathering this moving, significant anthology of plays. Even in Diaspora (or perhaps especially in Diaspora), conversation about Israel and Palestine quickly becomes simultaneously polarizing and numbing. It is one of the few subjects upon which the politically Left will virulently disagree.

Even a comradely gesture like inviting a Jewish and a Palestinian writer to write introductions might suggest a false equivalence, as if "Israel" and "Palestine" are peer nations, with similar resources and parallel points of view. I'm pretty confident that my friend and colleague Betty Shamieh would object to that image. I would too. (A few years ago I started sketching out an Israeli/Palestinian *Romeo and Juliet*, but quickly realized that Shakespeare's play hinges on the premise that the families have equal status with no real reason to fight—in other words, it can't transpose.)

Beyond the political quicksand of even the word "both," and despite the engaging title *Double Exposure*, what's so satisfying about this collection is that each play is not binary, but prismatic. Each writer presents a multiplicity of characters who tangle with questions of perspective: How does one make definitions, and in what language? How does one delineate space, time, names of places, foundational myths? Each play asks such questions differently, framing new stories in the way it draws the line and shutters the lens.

Taken together, the plays ask in rich profusion, "How shall we in Diaspora converse about Israel and Palestine?" What boundaries, what layers, what maps, what historical events form the given circumstances? What terms are used? More than a double exposure, the collection offers multiple exposures, many points of light.

When Naomi Wallace won a MacArthur "Genius Grant" Fellowship in 1999, she used some of the money to bring five American playwrights to the West Bank. *Twenty-One Positions* is a collaboration between Wallace, another of those American playwrights Lisa Schlesinger, and Abdelfattah AbuSrour, a playwright and director who grew up in Bethlehem's Aida Refugee Camp and founded its Alrowwad Cultural and Theatre Society. As Robin D. G. Kelley explains in his introduction to the actor's stage performance publication of the play: "The genesis of this play was itself a bold cartographic dream."

Discourse across boundaries forms the very bones of *Twenty-One Positions,* which lays out cruelly uncrossable lines, but also the human capacity to leap through imagination and formal shifts. On a theatrical level, the play moves fluidly, with shifts of time and place, of reality, even as the characters within the play can hardly move at all. A little girl Rund sings "Song of the Necessary Permit," concluding:

*If you want to pass through the wall,*

*Go to the hospital or swim the sea,*

*If you want to die, and be buried at all!*

*You gotta have a permit.*

I was fortunate to see what seems to be (maddeningly) the only production so far of *Twenty-One Positions,* directed by Lisa Peterson at Fordham University in New York in 2008, in association with the Public Theater. Onstage, the play's multiple narratives and modes of storytelling compound even as they compete, as if the urgency of the tale requires every possible tool for telling.

The divisions and questions of ownership in this play not only cover the land, but dig into its depths. An Arab-born Jewish Israeli archaeologist looks for proof of Jewish civilization under Palestinian soil, hoping the right kind of discovery will lead to a university job. He claims, "The Davidic Empire, the United Monarchy, Solomon's Temple. That is where it all begins. The rest is prehistory." When Rashid, an American-born Palestinian, says, "Before David and Israelites. The Canaanites," the archaeologist answers: "Oh them. We conquered them." In his reckoning, only certain layers count.

Arthur Milner's *Facts* wrestles differently with the question of what lies under the soil. The play begins as a political whodunit:

an American archaeologist has been killed in the West Bank, and to solve the murder, an Israeli inspector (Yossi) and a Palestinian police chief (Khalid) first need to discover the motive. Both men are secular moderates parsing the actions of an extremist. Yossi says: "If you tell me he was digging in an ancient burial ground and one of our many fanatic sects beat him to death with the jawbone of an ass like what's-his-name, I'll believe you no questions asked . . ." but Khalid shocks this urban liberal by explaining that the dead archaeologist was gathering evidence to support what is now a "mainstream view": that the Biblical Exodus never happened, and the Israelites were never in Egypt.

As they attempt to find this vigilante murderer, the Israeli and Palestinian colleagues come up against physical as well as historical differences. Yossi invites Khalid for coffee in Tel Aviv, but Khalid won't cross the green line, even if Yossi gets him a permit: Yossi: "Is that a point of principle?" Khalid: "Yes." Due to literal and philosophical blocks, the partnership frays.

Although *The Peace Maker* also takes place in the West Bank, Natasha Greenblatt's main concern is the legitimate role of those in the Diaspora. A naive Jewish Canadian woman purposely overstays on her free, American-Zionist-sponsored Birthright trip to Israel in order to give music lessons to Palestinian youth, but then blithely leads them across boundaries she doesn't truly understand.

Greenblatt has a light touch here; the reader sees Sophie's limits but can't fault her motives. She is a good-hearted Westerner in her own earnest, privileged picaresque. When an angry Palestine teenager, Haneen, lists American injustices, ending with "Go Back to America. GO HOME," Sophie answers, "But . . . I'm Canadian."

By the end of the play, Haneen begs Sophie to take her across the border for real. Again Sophie is out of her depth:

HANEEN You bring us from Palestine to Jerusalem. This is a big thing.

SOPHIE A stupid thing.

HANEEN But a *big* stupid thing. And it is so big that it opens me, it cracks me open and now I feel big too, like I can make things change.

SOPHIE Well, I'm glad. I'm glad you feel like that—

HANEEN I want to come with you.

Sophie backpedals, and Haneen responds with disappointment and rage, wishing Sophie had been killed long ago instead of his mother, and ending, "You make me big with your ideas and now I have nothing."

It's the ultimate accusation against Diaspora individuals—that they are tourists in a crisis where others are bound. Samah Sabawi's *Tales of a City by the Sea* escalates the lines between Diaspora Palestinians and Gaza residents into a compelling romantic tragedy, pushing a complicated question of who stays and who goes from Palestine, who belongs and why.

Sabawi creates her story entirely among Palestinian characters—that too is a different frame from the other plays in the collection. The effect is of a photograph, cropped so that you see a universal love story, then widened to explore the political circumstances. Rami, an American doctor of Palestinian origin on a humanitarian mission, falls in love with Jomana, a Palestinian journalist and Gaza native. She is wary:

> "You know . . . your type. Palestinians with international passports . . . they come here on a feel-good adventure to see the poor people of Gaza. They take photos, make promises, and then they run back home to their comfortable lives where once in a while, they talk about the plight of their people over polite dinner conversations . . ."

In a gripping twist, and in part to prove he is not toying with his Palestinian identity nor with Jomana, Rami sheds his privilege and crawls through underground tunnels to enter Gaza and treat the wounded. By the time he crosses those boundaries, he knows the stakes and danger of the borders. He makes himself less free, for love and for country, and he pays the price.

In *Sabra Falling*, Ismail Khalidi starts the conversation further back in time—1982, in a different place, Lebanon. He also blurs the boundaries in a more intimate way: in the opening, an enemy soldier falls through the ceiling of a Palestinian refugee home. The most basic boundary—the roof—collapses and crumbles, and the family is exposed.

Even more disturbing, the identity of the trapped pilot comes into question. The middle-aged Sofyan seems to recognize him and asks, "Eyad?" Is the trapped man a foreigner, Eyal (an Israeli name) or the long-lost son who has somehow catapulted back into the family home, Eyad?

Yet Khalidi isn't setting up some fantasy in which it doesn't *matter* who's who, in which the point is that we are all human beneath the skin. He rather foments a blurred discomfort—is this my son or my enemy? Furthermore, *Sabra Falling* catalogues the treatment of Arab Jews by European Jews, suggesting, subversively, that the conflict between Jewish Arabs and Palestinian Arabs can be framed as a civil war.

Stephen Orlov's serio-satirical work, *Sperm Count*, also looks at politics through the paternity question—are we related and why does that matter? Orlov, however, takes a comic perspective on how boundaries commingle in the most intimate possible way.

A Palestinian fertility specialist helps a Jewish couple conceive, and their desperation to be parents pulls them into risky science and a new set of moral questions. The staunchly Zionist grandfather-to-be reckons with his moral and biological legacy. *Sperm Count* is a comedy of interdependence, presenting zany cooperation for the sake of the future. It's the only play set in North America and the most optimistic of the collection, because in Orlov's Diaspora world, human borders can be breached without tragedy.

Hannah Khalil's *Bitterenders* draws its line starkly, formally, potently. She begins:

> "We are inside a house in East Jerusalem. There is a visible line drawn in chalk on the floor. One side of the line is empty of people, but furnished. On the other side of the line is a basic kitchen and a family."

Within the family's side of the house, the grandmother Sitti cradles a hairless, broken doll. Khalil literalizes the arbitrary, ugly line of division. At one point, Sitti's son Ahmed cautions his wife Selma not to cross the line.

SELMA What would happen if I went over?

AHMED Don't do it.

SITTI There might be guards—a sniper, a watchtower.

SELMA There's no alarm.

AHMED You can't, Selma. We've been over this—you can't.

When the daughter Maha loses patience and throws her grandmother's doll to the other side, all three adults panic:

SITTI MY BABY!

*She cries.*

SELMA AHMED, AHMED!

AHMED *comes in.*

AHMED What's the matter? Why are you shouting? I go out for one minute and—why is mother crying? Maha?

MAHA *points to the doll on the other side of the line.*

AHMED Oh shit.

These adults are not crazy. They are accommodating a warped reality. They are grieving. The other side of the room might as well be the other side of the moon. The family's effort to recover the doll, and hold the line against further destruction, shows how very intractable such divisions have become.

Why would we in the Diaspora even engage these difficult questions and unsettling images, beyond the beauty of the language and imagery presented on the pages? I return to *Twenty-One Positions.* Rashid speaking from Palestine says, "This is the centre of the earth . . . What goes down here will go down in Cincinnati, will go down everywhere."

From these plays, we gather the will to sustain engagement with Israel and Palestine, easy to avoid from afar. Too often, audiences feel simultaneously inundated and confused. Yet Orlov and Sabawi have gathered plays that, through the clarity of individual voice and the tangle of collected characters, create layers of conversation: buried, adjacent, and exposed.

Again I respectfully expand the title of this collection, and invite the reader to see each of these plays as a prism, and the collection like gems strung together—a compounded multiplicity.

I would call such abundance a celebration but that would belie the circumstances. In their diversity of voices, these plays cry for justice, for help, for alertness and change and (in some cases) for peace. These works are written for all, though they speak particularly to us of the Diaspora, who are not right now in the extremis of Israeli and Palestinian soil. Whatever their differences—and the beauty of the work is in the differences—in the act of creation, the authors convey a shared wish to broaden conversation and humanity. They increase exposure.

# INTRODUCTION
## BY BETTY SHAMIEH

It is so strange how one word can have two hauntingly different meanings. Such is the case with a word like "exposed." Do we really want our communities, ourselves, and our children to be exposed?

If you think of exposure as possessing a deep understanding of the perspectives of other kinds of people, yes. But if you think of exposure as being unprotected and physically vulnerable, probably not.

You might assume that most "learned" people wouldn't be bothered by the fact that their minds are exposed to other ways of seeing the world. You could argue that we are only precarious about putting our physical bodies in places where others can gain access to them.

This is a false assumption. Most of us are deeply, even savagely, invested in preserving our own worldview. We are taught to insist that our own version of history is the most important story, usually in the blind and instinctual way that we are sure—as children—that our parents are the only ones capable of protecting us. Even when they do not.

I was lucky enough to return as a Playwriting Fellow to spend a year at the university where I was once an undergraduate. I attended a debate by Noam Chomsky and Alan Dershowitz at an event named "Israel & Palestine After Disengagement: Where Do We Go From Here?"

Rather than simply allowing myself to be reactive to the points the speakers were making (or failing to make) about my people's history, I decided to try as much as possible to observe the theatrical aspects of this kind of political discussion. Why? It was a trying event for me to attend in the first place. As a Palestinian-American, I was nonplussed that there was no professor deemed worthy enough from our community to represent "our" perspective at the John F. Kennedy School of

Government. But that did not seem to matter to the audience, which appeared to be largely composed of Jewish and Arab undergraduates.

It felt scarier than debates I remembered attending as a student. There was no pretense of politeness. Before the speakers began, the students were glaring at one another. Perhaps the fact that Chomsky was arguing for the human rights of people that were different from himself was much more destabilizing (and therefore more dangerous) than if a Palestinian intellectual like Edward Said had done the talking. I felt grateful to Chomsky, and then I felt weird about feeling grateful. I began to put myself in his shoes. I had always seen myself as an activist. But was that because I was raised to believe they were the only kind of people who might help "save" mine? Was I truly an activist, a humanist, and an idealist at my core? Or did I just figure out those kinds of folks might be useful to have on my "team"? No one else seemed to care a whit about what happened to my family and people like us.

If I was raised by Jewish parents, would I have the courage and/or inclination to stand up for Palestinian rights in the way that Chomsky did? I had to face the fact that I could not know for sure.

But I did know something else. I had worked abroad and travelled enough by that point to realize that, as a playwright, I had more in common with a playwright from *any* other culture than a person who did not care for words from my own ethnic background. I realized that we theatre artists make up our own tribe. That fact is unacknowledged and ultimately unimportant to most of us, at least when it comes down to the brass tacks. We might sign a petition if playwrights were being persecuted in another country, but would we put ourselves in harm's way for them? If there was an army to protect them, would we join it? Or even contribute significant dollars to arm that army? Probably not. The only tribes that truly matter—in that way—are the ones that we were taught to defend since our days in the cradle.

As the debate continued, I watched this very privileged group of highly accomplished students turn into a seething, angry mob. Some of them were wearing T-shirts identifying their ethnicities. These T-shirts were like costume pieces which indicated their "role" and prevented them from being confused for a member of the "other" side. As the speakers made their opposing arguments, the mostly teenage sneering crowd began to mutter furiously under their breath or cheer with manic frenzy when a point was "scored." It did not feel like a political debate. It felt like a sporting event and not a friendly one. The audience seemed, in short, on the verge of becoming completely unhinged. Murderous. I think, if they could have punched each other without repercussions, several of them would have been delighted to take a shot. What I had read about the teenage brain not yet being fully formed made sense. They lacked the impulse control required to sit in their chairs without fidgeting like toddlers. They didn't seem capable of physically handling the emotions that were stirring within them while continuing to act appropriately in a professional setting.

I thought to myself, "I'm so glad no one in this group has a gun!" Then, I realized our world's armies are filled with kids about that age, all armed with guns.

When our beliefs are questioned, particularly about a subject that involves whether our kind is more sinned against than sinning, we often react as if being physically threatened. The fight or flight instinct takes over. This is particularly true of people who don't recognize tribes that are distinct from (and perhaps more meaningful than) their ethnic ones, the identities that they would need the courage to select for themselves rather than the ones that were chosen for them.

Some argue that our deep need to divide ourselves into separate tribes at all is an evolutionary by-product—our ancestors who stayed in herds tended to fend off predators and fared better than those who didn't adhere to the structures of a group mentality. So, the loners or happy-go-lucky, generous-to-all folks got eaten early on and unfortunately did not have the chance to live long enough to procreate. Thus, we have evolved into a species that feels hysterically threatened by the telling of stories from ethnic perspectives, especially when these stories contradict the ones we were taught as children. We believe the act of even entertaining a tale about a different person's experience of our shared history is a betrayal. Betraying our tribe means we can be thrown out, which for so long meant almost certain death.

Yet still there are those of us who attempt to have the heart to hear each other's experiences. There are those of us who even try to place them side by side. That is what makes *Double Exposure*—with its multiplicity of different urgent voices—very important. Alongside the playwrights included in this collection, we must insist on the ability to listen. We must affirm the need to expose ourselves to more than what feels safe, to have the courage to believe that another's insistence upon equal coexistence is not a coded way of manipulating the "other's" self-destruction. The first step to that kind of coexistence, the hardest step, is to give dignity to both of our stories.

# BITTERENDERS
BY HANNAH KHALIL

*For my family near and far, especially my husband and mother who enable my writing through their practical and emotional support; and to my daughter who reveals the world to me anew every day.*

# ACKNOWLEDGEMENTS

I must firstly thank Sandpit Arts for running their Bulbul playwriting competition—it was the impetus for me to pen this play that had been brewing in my mind for so long. The play enjoyed many short performances and readings, in Brighton, London, and Dublin, and I'm deeply grateful to all the producers, actors, and directors for their work and dedication, especially Alia Alzougbi, Chris White, Donal O'Kelly, Eleanor Methven, and everyone at PalFest Ireland. I must also thank the A.M. Qattan Foundation and the Mosaic Rooms in London for their continued support. Finally my gratitude to Torange Yeghiazarian, Evren Odcikin, and Golden Thread Productions in San Francisco who selected the play to be programmed as part of their 2015 ReOrient Festival.

After a staged performance at the Nightingale Theatre in Brighton, UK, as part of Sandpit Arts' 2013 Bulbul playwriting competition, the first full production of *Bitterenders* was as part of Golden Thread Productions' 2015 ReOrient Festival at Z Below, San Francisco, from September 10 to October 4, 2015, with the following cast and creative team:

| | |
|---|---|
| Selma | Nora el Samahy |
| Ahmed | Lawrence Radecker |
| Sitti | Bella Warda |
| Maha | Roneet Aliza Rahamim |
| | |
| Director | Manijeh Mohamedi |

## A NOTE ON THE TEXT

A slash (/) indicates the point at which speech is overlapped.

## CHARACTERS

| | |
|---|---|
| Ahmed | Father, fifty. |
| Selma | Mother, forty-five. |
| Sitti | Grandmother, sixty-eight. |
| Maha | Daughter, twenty-five. |

## PART ONE

*We are inside a house in East Jerusalem. There is a visible line drawn in chalk on the floor. One side of the line is empty of people, but furnished. On the other side of the line is a basic kitchen and a family:* AHMED, SELMA, *and* SITTI.

AHMED *is sitting on a chair at the table, looking at his mobile phone.* SELMA *washes some dishes in the sink.* SITTI *is sitting on the floor with her back to the audience. We cannot see what she is doing.*

AHMED She's not back yet.

SELMA I know that.

AHMED She should have been back by now.

SELMA I know.

AHMED She missed the food.

SELMA I know.

AHMED Do you think something happened to her?

SELMA I don't know.

*A beat.*

Sitti, get up.

*Silence.*

Ya, Mama . . . Umi . . . Get up. You'll get a sore leg again and I'll have to massage it all night. Come on. Stand.

*A beat.*

AHMED She was going to bring me cigarettes.

*A beat.*

I haven't had one all day . . .

SELMA Is that what you're worried about? I thought you were worried about your daughter, but turns out you just want a smoke.

AHMED No—no I am worried about her. She normally texts if she's going to be late.

SELMA If you're so desperate for a cigarette, go out and buy some yourself. You're not a cripple, are you?

AHMED Go out? Are you mad? And leave you two alone? After what happened? Never again.

SITTI *(whispering)* "I'm already drowning so why should I fear getting wet."

AHMED What?

SITTI *(to* AHMED*)* "I'm already drowning so why should I fear getting wet"—it's what you always say.

SELMA Sitti, get up off the floor, come on, I'll make some tea. Sit at the table, yallah.

SITTI Oh, help me up then. I'm not a young woman.

*SELMA helps her up and to a chair at the table. SITTI is holding a baby doll. It's very ugly with no hair and only one leg.*

Poor baby is crying.

AHMED I don't blame her. She's probably worried about Maha too.

SITTI Don't be stupid. It's a doll.

*AHMED sighs and goes back to his phone. SELMA boils the kettle.*

AHMED Maybe she got stopped. I told you you packed too much in that bag.

SELMA It was just food. Nothing else. Food.

AHMED Enough to feed an army.

SELMA Enough to feed my boys. I don't know what they give them in there.

AHMED There are only two of them. You've only two sons.

SITTI I've two children.

AHMED No, you've only got one son, Sitti—me.

SITTI And the baby girl.

AHMED No, just me. *(to SELMA)* They probably won't be able to eat it all— I told you there was too much— It's a waste— They'll probably give it away.

SITTI Don't say that!

AHMED You spent so much money and time on it, and they'll give it away—I could be eating that makloubeh, instead I'll be living on oil and za'atar all month.

SELMA So what if they give it away? They're all my boys in there, doing time, for what? They all deserve a bit of love—a bit of home cooking.

AHMED It won't be the other prisoners who'll eat it—it'll fill the belly of an Israeli soldier, give him the energy he needs for his next interrogation.

SELMA Shut up! Don't say that!

SITTI Ahmed! Don't say that to a mother! Don't worry, Selma, the boys will get it.

*A beat.*

AHMED Sorry. I'm just worried.

*Pause.*

SITTI They're out again then, they're always out, that lot.

SELMA Good. I hate it when they're in. I hate listening to them talk.

AHMED You just wish you could understand them.

SELMA What could they possibly say that is of interest to me?

SITTI After all the screaming they did to get in you'd think they'd stay home a bit more. *(to the doll)* I don't think they like us—do they, baby? Your crying keeps them up at night too. We all hear you crying, *(softly)* we all hear you crying.

*SITTI continues to speak in hushed tones to the doll.*

SELMA I'm glad they go out. We can pretend it never happened.

AHMED "Better a thousand enemies outside the house than one inside." When they're in it's impossible to ignore them, all the noise they make.

SELMA And the smell of their food—it's so strange—it smells like . . . like—hospital food.

AHMED It smells all right to me. Where's that tea?

SELMA It's coming.

*SELMA doesn't move.*

I think their daughter's pregnant, you know.

AHMED Why do you say that?

SELMA Haven't you noticed the way they're all looking at her nowadays? Different. And she doesn't do so much housework.

SITTI She's eating a lot—getting fat.

AHMED Are you sure?

SELMA They all look so pleased with themselves. I'm sure. Soon she'll start getting round.

*A beat.*

It'll kill Maha.

AHMED Why would she care if those people have a baby?

SELMA Use your brain, Ahmed. *She* can't after what happened to her—can she?

AHMED Maha's not even married though.

SELMA Sometimes you are so stupid, do you really think Maha will get a husband? Everyone around here knows what happened to her, that she can't have a child. So to have to watch that woman grow big and flaunt it—it'll be so painful for her.

AHMED If you're right—but she might not be—

SITTI She is—she's pregnant. Her colour's changed. And the husband's behaving like the prize bull.

SELMA Maybe we should send her away.

AHMED Who? Maha? How can we? Where to?

SELMA Your cousin in Jordan. I've that money from my jewellery—she could take that.

AHMED We need that. Emergencies. And anyway—who'd run all our errands?

SELMA I can.

AHMED No—no there needs to be three of us here at all times—two they could overpower but three . . . there's safety in numbers.

SELMA Don't be ridiculous—Maha deserves a fresh start. And as for that lot, they've got what they want. A roof over their heads.

AHMED You think they want to share with Arabs . . . They're biding their time, waiting, and as soon as we get complacent they'll attack again and we'll be out on the street. I don't want to live in a tent like a refugee. This is my house.

*A beat.*

SITTI It's mine, actually.

AHMED Besides—if Maha left who'd go and visit the boys?

SELMA They won't be in prison forever. And when they come out everything will be different. If they'd been here none of this would have happened in the first place.

AHMED I did my best. I'm an old man.

*A beat.*

At least we got half the house.

SELMA Why "at least"? It's all ours.

SITTI It's mine, actually.

SELMA Exactly. So why are they confident enough to go out all the time. We should go over there and take their stuff and throw it out of the window. And change the locks.

AHMED We can't do that.

SELMA Why? Why can't we do that?

AHMED Because a court ruled that we have to share with them.

SELMA What court?

AHMED The court.

SELMA An Israeli court—I don't recognize an Israeli court. I'm in Palestine. They have no business being in our house. I'm going over there and throwing all their stuff out.

SITTI Yallah, go!

AHMED Be reasonable. Don't make a fight—we're at a compromise now.

SELMA What bloody compromise? We're the ones compromising. They just came in and took what they wanted.

*SELMA gets up and approaches the line.*

SELMA What would happen if I went over?

AHMED Don't do it.

SITTI There might be guards—a sniper, a watchtower.

AHMED There might be an alarm.

SELMA There's no alarm.

AHMED You can't, Selma. We've been over this—you can't.

SELMA Why?

AHMED Always "why"—you know why: because if you don't respect their space then they won't respect ours. We are being forced to live together, we have to make it work . . . We have to be mature. We have what we need here. Come on, darling. Come away from there. Forget about it. Come back.

*She sighs and turns back.*

Make me some shay bil n'ana—my favourite—you make it the best.

*She nods and goes to reboil the kettle.*

*MAHA appears at the door.*

SITTI She's back!

AHMED I didn't hear you come in.

MAHA Following your proverb, Dad: "Go softly come softly—"

AHMED "—So the cat doesn't get you." My girl.

*He kisses her.*

*She hands him a pack of cigarettes.*

Thank you! I've been dying for one of these all day. Can I—?

SITTI It's bad for the baby.

SELMA Go outside.

AHMED I don't want to leave you alone—in case.

SELMA Go outside.

*He gets up and goes outside to smoke.* MAHA *sits at the table and sighs.*

SITTI She looks tired.

SELMA Of course, she's been travelling all day. She went to another country you know.

SITTI The Land of David.

SELMA How are they?

MAHA I only saw Firas.

SELMA What—why? Only Firas? What about Hussein?

MAHA They said there'd been a mistake. That I could only see Firas.

SITTI One is better than none.

MAHA Yes. And he's okay, Mum. He seemed okay. A bit quiet—

SELMA You gave him the food?

MAHA Yes, of course.

SELMA You told him I made makloubeh—and that there were pastries too.

MAHA Yes. He was pleased.

SELMA How did he look? Did he look thin?

MAHA Not really. He looked tired.

SITTI Maybe the baby's crying is keeping him up too.

SELMA Why is he tired? What else is there to do in prison but sleep?

SITTI And dream.

MAHA I don't think it's relaxing—they make them do jobs in the day. Work. And at night I don't think it's peaceful.

SELMA Of course it's not peaceful.

SITTI The baby cries.

*SITTI begins whispering to the doll.*

SELMA What did he say about Hussein?

MAHA Not much.

SELMA He's not getting himself in trouble in there, is he?

MAHA I don't think so.

SELMA He just needs to keep his head down—they both do, not get involved in anything stupid, just get through it and get home.

MAHA There's hardly room for them to come home now.

SELMA There's always room for them. This is their home.

*A beat.*

SITTI Is Firas the handsome one?

SELMA Both my boys are handsome.

SITTI No they're not—one is handsome the other has a big nose.

MAHA Yes, Firas is the handsome one, Sitti.

SITTI We like him, don't we, baby?

*Once again she whispers to the doll.*

*A beat.*

MAHA Why do you let her carry that thing around everywhere, Mum?

SELMA It keeps her calm.

MAHA It's weird. I hate it—it's ugly—it's got no hair. Where did she even find it?

SELMA I don't know.

MAHA Look at it—it's missing a leg and it's falling to bits. She's an old woman—she's got no business carrying a doll around.

SELMA Leave her alone.

SITTI She's not ugly.

MAHA It's embarrassing. What do people think?

SELMA What people? We never go out anymore after what happened—unless you are talking about them? The people who live in our house? Do you care what they think of us? / Because I don't

MAHA Of course I don't—why do you always bring "them" into everything?

SELMA How can I avoid them? They're here, in my house.

SITTI Don't you call her ugly, she's beautiful. The most beautiful baby you have ever seen. With auburn curls and slate blue eyes—look closely and you'll see there are yellow flecks—she doesn't look like an Arab at all—her skin is white and smooth like marble and she has lips like rose petals. She's perfect. You're just jealous because she's more beautiful than any child you've ever seen—jealous because she's more beautiful than any child you'll ever have—jealous because you can't have a child—because a black bullet burrowed its way into your stomach where your baby would have lived and now you are scarred and ugly and dry and you'll always be / empty—

SELMA That's / enough, Sitti.

MAHA Give me that thing.

SITTI NO! Get off.

SELMA Leave her—

*MAHA grabs the doll from her grandmother.*

SITTI My baby! My baby—she's got the baby.

SELMA Give it back.

MAHA I'm going to pull her head off.

SELMA Don't, Maha, don't—

SITTI She's crying, please don't hurt my baby!

MAHA Ugly bloody thing.

SELMA Give it back.

SITTI Please!

MAHA If you want her, go and get her.

*MAHA lobs the doll across the room and it flies over the chalk line into the area on the other side.*

*A beat.*

SITTI MY BABY!

*She cries.*

SELMA AHMED, AHMED!

*AHMED comes in.*

AHMED What's the matter? Why are you shouting? I go out for one minute and—why is Mother crying? Maha?

*MAHA points to the doll on the other side of the line.*

Oh, shit.

## PART TWO

*The family sit around the kitchen table.*

SITTI I can't bear to hear her crying.

AHMED Why would you do that?

MAHA You didn't hear what she said to me!

AHMED You are an adult, Maha.

MAHA So is she!

SITTI How can you sit there and listen to it?

*She covers her ears.*

AHMED Your granny needs that to keep her calm.

MAHA Why can't she just take tranquilizers like everybody else!

SELMA Maha didn't mean it—she had a tough day. What's done is done. Now we have to get it back, before they come home.

AHMED What do you mean?

SELMA Look at her, she's so distressed. She needs it back.

SITTI My baby.

AHMED We will wait until they get back and ask them to pass it to us.

SITTI What if they take her prisoner? Kidnap her? Interrogate her? She doesn't know anything! They might kill her, she's just a baby!

MAHA What if they won't give it back out of spite?

AHMED I'm sure they'll be reasonable.

SELMA REASONABLE? Were they reasonable when they forced their way into our home?

MAHA We need to go over there and get it before they get back. It's just over there. It'll only take a second.

AHMED It's a bad idea.

SITTI Please, please, don't leave her there; to be attacked by the wild animals.

AHMED What if they've put booby traps over there, or an alarm on the line.

SELMA We'd have seen them if they'd done that—one of us is always in this room.

AHMED I don't know. It seems dangerous. What if they find out? They'll think, "They haven't respected the line." And if we cross the line, they could do the same.

MAHA How would they know? We just go over there, pick up the doll.

SITTI Baby.

MAHA And bring her back. End of story. They'll never find out.

AHMED You might knock something over. Break something by accident.

SELMA She won't.

MAHA I won't.

SITTI Go on, go on, you—you caused this problem.

MAHA I did not cause this problem!

SITTI You heartless thing—you threw her over there, listen to her.

MAHA This is stupid, I'm going—

AHMED No!

SELMA Go on—do it quickly.

*MAHA gets up and approaches the line.*

AHMED Darling, please!

MAHA Dad, I spent the best part of my day today waiting at Israeli checkpoints where there were soldiers—with real guns, itching to shoot people. I think walking across a room to pick up a doll should be a piece of cake.

SITTI Go on then, hurry up.

SELMA Yes, go on, Maha, before they come home.

MAHA Okay. I'm going.

*A beat.*

*She is about to step over the line but AHMED stops her.*

AHMED NO! No, don't do it.

MAHA DAD!

AHMED Don't—I don't want to lose you—you're my only daughter. You're young. We need you. I'll go. If something happens to me it doesn't matter. I'm an old man—I'm good for nothing.

MAHA On that reasoning Granny should go—she's the oldest

SITTI Get lost! I'm not going over there. Who knows what could happen to me. You go, Maha. This is your fault. You go.

MAHA Fine. I'll go.

SELMA Just do it quickly, stop talking about it—I keep thinking I can hear them coming.

*A beat.*

SITTI Go on!

SELMA Yes, quickly!

MAHA Dad?

AHMED I'm not happy about it.

SITTI Stop talking and go—I can't listen to that crying anymore, my head will explode—go!

*MAHA steps over the line and stops still, waiting to see if anything is going to happen. A beat. She turns around to her family and laughs.*

MAHA SEE! I told you nothing would happen.

SELMA Hurry up.

SITTI Get the baby!

MAHA Now I'm here, I might just take a look around.

AHMED Come back—quickly!

MAHA I'll see them out of this window—remember it has a view of the yard . . . Don't worry.

AHMED They're good at sneaking up on people—that's how we got into this position—remember: "He who peeps at his neighbour's window may chance lose his eyes."

MAHA Well it's our window, isn't it! They've put a nice window box outside actually—with herbs.

SELMA Hurry up.

MAHA There's parsley—mint —sage—do we need any for dinner, Mum?

SELMA Leave it, come back.

SITTI Pass me the baby.

MAHA All right, all right, calm down.

*MAHA goes to the doll and picks it up.*

SITTI Is she okay? Is she hurt?

MAHA She's still only got one leg.

SITTI That's okay—a birth defect. Be gentle with her.

AHMED Come back, Maha.

MAHA I'm coming.

*She approaches them and is about to cross over the line when something on a table catches her eye.*

SITTI Why have you stopped—give her to me.

MAHA There's a letter here, Dad—it's addressed to you.

AHMED What? It can't be.

MAHA It is—look.

*She picks it up and holds it up for him to see.*

SELMA It's addressed to them.

MAHA And Dad—afterwards, see?

SELMA That's strange.

SITTI Come back—bring me my baby.

AHMED Are you sure?

MAHA It's open. I'm going to read it.

AHMED Don't—it's not for you.

MAHA No, it's for you, Dad.

AHMED Exactly. Bring it to me. Come here.

*MAHA crosses back to her family's side of the house. There is a sense of relief. MAHA gives SITTI the doll.*

SITTI My poor baby.

*SITTI takes the doll to a corner, rocking and whispering quietly to it. AHMED takes the letter and reads it.*

SELMA *(to MAHA)* Are you okay?

MAHA Yes. That was quite exciting, actually.

SITTI Poor baby. What a trauma.

*A beat, then at the same time MAHA and SELMA address SITTI, overlapping:*

MAHA Sorry, Sitti. I didn't mean it. I've just had a hard day—a long day.

SELMA Baby's okay, isn't she, Sitti? She's a tough old thing, been through much worse than that.

SITTI Been through the wars.

*Meanwhile,* AHMED *has been reading the letter and his face has paled somewhat. He quietly places the letter back in its envelope and approaches the line. The women suddenly notice.*

MAHA What are you doing, Dad?

*A beat.*

AHMED *crosses the line and puts the letter back on the table where it came from.*

SELMA Omri? What are you doing?

*Very slowly,* AHMED *sits in a chair and smooths his face with his hands. The women gather at the line staring across at him agog.*

SITTI Son! Quick, what if they come back?

MAHA Dad?

AHMED "I complained because I had no shoes, until I met a man with no feet."

*Pause.*

SELMA What does that mean? Ahmed!

MAHA He looks strange, Mum.

SELMA What did the letter say?

*Silence.*

Habibi?

*Silence.*

Go over there and get him, Maha.

MAHA Shall I?

SITTI AHMED! This is your mother speaking—get back over here this instant before I tan your hide. I'm not joking. I've a wooden spoon and you know I'll use it.

MAHA Dad!

SELMA Ahmed—they might come back—taala hone, habibi.

AHMED Shut up, you harpies!— Let me think for a minute.

*Silence.*

SELMA But what if they / come back

AHMED They're not coming back.

MAHA They're not?

AHMED No.

SELMA How do you know?

AHMED The letter.

MAHA They've really gone? For good!

*He nods.*

SITTI Does that mean it's my house again?

MAHA Yes, Granny!

SITTI Mashallah! *(to doll)* Baby, do you hear that the Yehuds have gone home!

SELMA I can't believe it!

*The three women proceed to dance around on the chalk line, scuffing it up as they do, laughing and ululating and singing joyously.* AHMED *sits in the chair, defeated, with his head in his hands.*

## PART THREE

*Three large laundry bags stand in the room. The chalk line is all but gone.* MAHA *and* SELMA *are filling the bags with things as* AHMED *sits at the kitchen table looking at his mobile phone.*

AHMED "If you know—it's a disaster. But if you don't know, it's a greater disaster."

*Pause.*

"Only three things in life are certain: birth, death, and change."

*Pause.*

"If a wind blows, ride it."

SELMA ENOUGH! Enough with your bloody proverbs! When did you start this incessant proverbing! MY GOD—you didn't do it when I met you!

MAHA Don't take it out on him, Mum, it's not his fault.

*A beat.*

Besides—I like them. They're comforting. How do you remember them all, Dad? Were they something your father said to you?

AHMED Oh no—my father was a modern man, he didn't believe in such things. I read them on Twitter.

MAHA You're kidding me? You have a Twitter account?

SELMA Twitter?

AHMED *(indicating his phone)* Yes—not many followers—I don't say much but I like to read others. There's one called Arabic Proverbs.

SELMA *gives him a look.*

What? They're helpful.

SELMA How—how are they helpful?

AHMED They help to keep me positive.

SELMA Positive! Put that phone away and get the bedding.

AHMED Okay.

*AHMED gets the bedding and puts it in one of the laundry bags.*

MAHA We'll never fit everything in here.

AHMED We can't bring everything—just the things we can't live without.

SELMA One bag each. It's all we can manage.

MAHA It's hard to know what to take and leave.

AHMED Us Palestinians should be good at this by now.

MAHA What will happen to the things we leave behind?

SELMA What do you mean?

MAHA Will they come and clear the house first? Perhaps give everything we leave to the needy . . .

SELMA The needy? We are the bloody needy! Do you think those people care about "the needy"? If they did they wouldn't do this to us!

MAHA Really? They won't even come and look inside?

AHMED I doubt it. Just start the engine and / drive—

SELMA Don't—let's not talk about it. I can't think about it.

*A beat.*

Just as well your mother has gone ahead. I don't

think she'd be able to cope with seeing this—it's better she doesn't know. After all it took her to buy it.

MAHA Tell me the story.

SELMA You've heard it a hundred times.

MAHA Please.

SELMA Your father will—Ahmed?

AHMED You tell it.

SELMA Fine. *(as she continues to pack up)* That poor woman. What a life—'48, Nakba, refugee camp, married. Had him *(indicating* AHMED*)*. Then '67, only in her twenties. And it happened all over again. Lost everything, even her husband.

Everyone else left Palestine. Not her. She came here. To Jerusalem. Took the Israelis to court. For what happened to her husband. Shot. In cold blood. No reason. But there were witnesses. Proof. So she sued them. Took years, worked as a cleaner, slept with your father in one room, in the basement of a house she cleaned. And eventually she won. WON! They admitted they'd made a mistake. Of course the financial sum that they put on his life was laughable. Yet after she'd paid all the lawyers and the fees she had enough to buy this—this small house.

Bought from the blood of her husband. So for this to happen . . . it's sacrilege.

*A beat.*

MAHA It's so inspiring, Mum. She's so brave.

SELMA Shame her courage didn't pass to her offspring.

AHMED What would you have me do? Lie down in front of the bulldozer?

SELMA You know that's not what I'm talking about.

AHMED I've seen enough of Israeli courts to last me a lifetime.

SELMA It's one thing to roll over and die, but to pay them? To pay them to finish you off! Come on, Ahmed—I thought you had some blood left in you?

AHMED Selma—we agreed.

SELMA I didn't.

AHMED We agreed—not in front of / Maha.

MAHA What does she mean, pay them?

AHMED Nothing.

SELMA She's not a child—tell her!

MAHA Tell me what, Mum?

AHMED You really want me to do this? You don't think it's humiliating enough for me? You want me to spell it out to my daughter? Fine. You're right. Maha—listen up—not only is your father a coward who can't provide for his family, can't protect them—now he's paying for the enemy to destroy his home—with money he doesn't have—

MAHA Paying? What do you mean?

AHMED The letter said—either we bulldoze it and bill you, or you do it yourself— How am I supposed to do that?

MAHA So the Israelis are making us pay them to bulldoze our house?!

SELMA I've told him to take them to court, fight—like his mother. But he wants to roll over and die. Where are we supposed to get this money anyway?

AHMED We'll have to use your emergency jewellery fund.

SELMA What? No way—you know I wanted that for Maha.

MAHA Me? I don't want any money.

SELMA She needs a fresh start—to get away from here—it's my money.

AHMED I bought you that jewellery.

SELMA Don't you dare! It's MINE!

AHMED ENOUGH! I need a cigarette.

*AHMED exits.*

SELMA *(to herself)* That's right—smoke. Leave us to sort this out.

MAHA I don't need money, Mum, honestly—

SELMA We'll talk about it later, come on, quickly, let's just grab the last few things, put them in the bags and take them out. Quickly. Like ripping off a Band-Aid.

MAHA Except the Band-Aid's on a mortal wound.

*The women try to zip up the bags as they look around the room.*

I don't feel as sad as I should.

SELMA You're brave.

MAHA No. It just hasn't felt like home since those people moved in.

SELMA That was the beginning of the end for us.

*A beat.*

SELMA I wanted you to go to Jordan.

MAHA Jordan?

SELMA To his cousin. More opportunities for you there. People don't know you, us.

MAHA I'm happy here.

SELMA Happy?

*MAHA shrugs.*

I wanted better for you—better for you than me or your father or your brothers . . . but now they want to take what little money we have too . . .

MAHA I don't want to leave anyway—they'd probably never let me come home again.

*The women struggle out of the door under the weight of the three laundry bags.*

SELMA Concentrate on the bags. Don't look back. Come on, Maha.

*They exit.*

*We can hear them talking to AHMED offstage.*

You take this one—it's the heaviest.

AHMED Okay—oh it's very light!

SELMA That's because you are stronger than us. You're the man.

MAHA Come on, let's go before I get upset.

SELMA Yallah!

*They shuffle away, dragging the laundry bags with them.*

*Pause.*

*In the distance we hear something that sounds like a baby crying.* SITTI *enters.*

SITTI I can hear you.

*A beat.*

Where are you? Habibi?

*A beat.*

Don't hide—not now . . . come on . . . Where are you?

*She looks around—then finds the doll.*

There you are! Were you hiding from me? *(whispering to the doll)* What were you doing behind there? Did you hear what they were saying—about me? About my life? Did you believe it? It was true you know. All of it—the truth. Just a few facts were missing. A few. Vital. Facts.

*A beat. Through the following,* SITTI *begins by speaking to the doll but gradually starts talking to the audience.*

I was three. 1948. When It happened. I don't remember much. Just a sea of people. Running away.

*A beat.*

The second time I remember though, baby. The second time I remember it all. The morning. Cold. The baby was crying. Had kicked off her blankets, silly thing.

*A beat.*

Strange. It was really peaceful. Once you stopped crying. I put the blanket on you, and it was really peaceful. Your father was already at the garage working, he was coming back for breakfast any minute. Your brother was still asleep. I made myself a tea—with n'ana—and the smell of it—the mint—was peaceful, even with the bitter edge of the tea. But then in a second everything changed. The noise, the shouting, the blood, the noise—getting closer . . . It was a nightmare—crazy. I grabbed your brother—I grabbed you, we ran—outside—with nothing. Just us—the most precious things to one another. And all around us the buildings falling—those wispy homes we had built in haste—went up quickly, came down quicker, all around us in a flash. Like paper.

*A beat.*

Your father didn't have a chance. Found himself face to face with a gun. And that was it. The black bullet burrowed its way into his stomach. And he was gone.

*A beat.*

But we escaped—ran and ran out of the town into the woods, through the woods, and gradually—as we got farther away we managed to catch our breath a little—but we didn't stop. No—not until we got to the olive grove. That was far enough—to be safe—to be sure. And then we stopped—exhausted—the three of us—I was beside myself . . . What had happened to your father? But I had you two—my babies. I held you both. My son—so brave—he'd held on to me, my hand—so tightly. And I held you—my baby—fiercely—close. I wanted to look into those beautiful, calm eyes of yours—but when I loosed my arms—nothing—blankets—you'd disappeared. Where? Where? Still in bed? Fallen— No, not fallen—not dropped—a mother never drops her child . . . She can't—it's not possible. Still in bed then. Please, God, still asleep. Peaceful. Not knowing. Oblivious.

*A beat.*

I went back. I went back for you. I searched and

cried out for you—my daughter—with perfect auburn hair—your grey eyes with yellow flecks.

*A beat.*

But I never found you, my baby, did I? You still elude me—still hide from me. Were you inside that house? Inside your bed? Under the covers? Behind the pillows? Under the rubble? I'll find you, my girl . . . I promise to come and find you—I'll just close my eyes here for a minute and you hide, then call me when you're ready and I'll come and find you.

*She sits in a chair.*

Don't worry—I won't cheat. I won't look. Hide wherever you like.

*A beat.*

I'll count to ten.

One,

Two,

Three—

I'm not looking I promise.

Four,

Five,

Six—

Hide wherever you like. I'll find you.

Seven,

Eight—

Make it as difficult as you want, I won't give up.

Nine—

Even if it takes forever.

Ten.

*She stays seated.*

*We hear the sound of a bulldozer engine starting up.*

*Blackout.*

# REFLECTIONS ON *BITTERENDERS*

## INSPIRATION, CHALLENGES, AND EXPERIENCES IN WRITING AND PRODUCING THE PLAY

Sadly the idea for *Bitterenders* came from real-life happenings in Jerusalem that I read about and watched online. This situation—of a Palestinian family forced to share their home with settlers—seemed like such a dramatic and ripe topic for a piece of theatre. I also loved the image of a line splitting our characters' house in two. It reminded me of a very funny episode of a British sitcom that my father used to enjoy when I was a child called *Steptoe and Son*. It tells of the bleak, destructive, codependent, but ultimately funny relationship between a father and son who are rag-and-bone men in West London. In this particular episode they fall out so badly that they divide the house in half to great comic success. What struck me on reviewing it as an adult is that they use the term "apartheid" to describe the division, a word which is being used more and more to describe the situation in Israel and the Occupied Territories today.

I wanted my play to have the same dark humour of the TV show, to represent characters in existential crises reminiscent of many of Samuel Beckett's hopeless souls who are condemned to hope. It's no accident that Beckett's work, and the absurd situations his characters find themselves in, is often cited when talking about the Palestinian experience. The whole idea of the house being shared also felt like a neat metaphor—a microcosm of the situation in Palestine.

The title *Bitterenders* is taken from the name of a faction of the fighters in the later stages of the Second Boer War—the Bittereinders, as their name suggests, were the last men fighting. They'd go on and on no matter what, willing to fight to the bitter end. It struck me that all Palestinians are Bitterenders by another name, fighting in spite of everything, against all the odds: for their nation, for equality, for dignity, and for humanity—for their very existence.

# FACTS
BY ARTHUR MILNER

Facts *is dedicated to my daughter, Sabina, and to my grandchildren, Anna, Miller, Kailey, and Dakota.*

## ACKNOWLEDGEMENTS

I would like to thank the following individuals and institutions for their advice and support: Samer al-Saber, Sam Awwad, Robert Bockstael, Jennifer Brewin, John Brewin, Naomi Campbell, Vince Chetcuti, Martin Conboy, Barbara Cuerden, Kamel Elbasha, Richard Greenblatt, Lise Ann Johnson, Kris Joseph, Peter Larson, Barbara Linds, Sam Kalilieh, Diana Kirkwood, John Koensgen, Patrick McDonald, Henry Milner, Diana Ralph, Rory Runnels, and Ulla Ryum; and the Manitoba Association of Playwrights, the New Theatre of Ottawa, the Great Canadian Theatre Company, the Canada Council for the Arts, the Ontario Arts Council, and the City of Ottawa.

*Facts* premiered at the Great Canadian Theatre Company (GCTC) in Ottawa, Canada, on April 15, 2010, as a GCTC/New Theatre of Ottawa co-production, with the following cast and creative team:

| | |
|---|---|
| Danny | Kris Joseph |
| Khalid | Sam Kalilieh |
| Yossi | John Koensgen |
| | |
| Director | Patrick McDonald |
| Set Design and Lighting | Martin Conboy |
| Costume Design | Sarah Waghorn |
| Assistant Director | Patrick Gauthier |

An earlier version of *Facts* was workshopped by the Manitoba Association of Playwrights and produced at the 2005 Winnipeg Fringe Festival by Rory Runnels and Who Knows Productions, under the direction of Ulla Ryum.

| | |

*Facts* premiered in Arabic at Dar Annadwa Addawliyya in Bethlehem, Palestine, on September 26, 2012, in an Alrowwad Cultural and Theatre Society/New Theatre of Ottawa co-production, with the following cast and creative team:

| | |
|---|---|
| Danny | Amer Khalil |
| Khalid | Abdelfattah AbuSrour |
| Yossi | Kamel Elbasha |
| | |
| Director | Samer al-Saber |
| Translator | Kamel Elbasha |
| Design | Martin Conboy |
| Technical Director | Ramzi Alsheikh-Qasim |
| Associate Producer | Dan Daley |

*Facts* premiered in Europe on February 26, 2013, at the Finborough Theatre in London, UK, produced by Worn Red Theatre, with the following cast and creative team:

| | |
|---|---|
| Danny | Paul Rattray |
| Khalid | Philip Arditti |
| Yossi | Michael Feast |
| | |
| Director | Caitlin McLeod |
| Set and Costume Design | Georgia Lowe |
| Lighting | Elliot Griggs |
| Music | Tegid Cartwright |

| | |

*Facts* premiered in Turkish at Çevre Tiyatrosu, Istanbul, Turkey, on March 19, 2014, produced by Semaver Kumpanya, with the following cast and creative team:

| | |
|---|---|
| Danny | Serkan Tınmaz |
| Khalid | Hakan Atalay |
| Yossi | Mustafa Kirantepe |
| | |
| Director(s) | Volkan M. Sarıöz and Serkan Keskin |
| Translator | Philip Arditti |
| Set Design | Zeki Ilyas Kızılısık |
| Lighting | Cem Yilmazer and Mustafa Karakoyun |
| Costume Design | Merve Isık Kızılısık |

Thank you to Ani Haddeler Pekman and Selen Senay.

## NOTES ON THE TEXT

*Language*

This play is presented in English, but the languages actually spoken by the characters are either Arabic or Hebrew. This is most apparent in the scenes with Danny. Since he does not speak Arabic, one can tell which language is being spoken by whether or not Danny understands what is being said.

Biblical quotations are from *The New Jerusalem Bible*, Standard Edition (Doubleday, 1998). Quotations from the Quran are combinations of several online editions. See, for example, the Online Quran Project at http://al-quran.info.

*Background*

On January 19, 1992, Dr. Albert Glock, an American archaeologist at Birzeit University in the West Bank, was shot dead. That unsolved murder is the starting point for this play. Any other resemblance to actual events or persons, living or dead, is entirely coincidental.

Anyone interested in pursuing the actual story of Dr. Glock's murder should read Edward Fox's excellent *Sacred Geography: A Tale of Murder and Archaeology in the Holy Land* (Metropolitan Books, 2001).

## CHARACTERS

| | |
|---|---|
| Danny Rakoff | West Bank settler, thirty-five years old. |
| Khalid Yassin | Police Inspector, Palestinian Authority, forty-five years old. |
| Yossi HaCohen | Detective, Israeli Police, sixty years old. |

## SETTING

A meeting or interrogation room in an Israeli army facility in the West Bank. There is a table, three chairs, a telephone, and a source of drinking water. If the exterior, right-hand door frame is visible, there should be a mezuzah at shoulder height.

*A mezuzah is a small wooden or metal box containing a prayer that traditional and especially religious Jews affix to their doorways.

## SCENE ONE

*West Bank, Palestine. A small meeting room in the Israeli army (IDF) offices.* YOSSI *is sitting, waiting. He looks at his watch, makes a call on his cellphone. No answer. He waits. The door opens.* KHALID *enters, carrying a briefcase.*

KHALID *(angry)* I'm late. Please excuse me.

YOSSI A checkpoint?

KHALID Yes.

YOSSI I left your name.

KHALID They tricked you. You left my name at the Arashi checkpoint. It was closed. No warning, no signs. Half-hour drive to Nefesh and, of course, it's jammed. I sit in my car for forty-five minutes. A young soldier looks—

YOSSI . . . who's a prick, I know.

KHALID He's polite. Looks at my identification, listens to my story, speaks to a superior, and returns to tell me, politely, "I'm sorry, Inspector Yassin, I can let you through, but your car must be searched."

YOSSI Are you done?

KHALID I refuse to accept this as a normal life.

YOSSI Good. Hold on to that resentment. Let it eat away at you.

KHALID It's forty degrees. I am allowed to pass ahead of people in wheelchairs and I step over mothers and infants.

YOSSI If you don't mind, how long will it be before we can get to work?

KHALID You wanted to talk about Philips.

YOSSI Why are you speaking Hebrew?

KHALID I don't know. Habit. From the checkpoints. I'm polite. You're my guest.

YOSSI You're my guest. I asked you to meet me.

KHALID We're in the West Bank. You're my guest.

YOSSI All right. But let's speak Arabic.

KHALID As you wish. So. Why the sudden interest in Philips?

YOSSI I was in America and I met with—I went for a conference on police technology. I brought back this gun that when you squeeze the trigger lights your cigarette. They have wonderful weapons. A system that soon I will be able to enter a part of a fingerprint or a piece of your cheek into a receptacle on my desk and, in forty-five seconds, search the whole world for a match.

KHALID Which will work if everybody's fingerprints are on file.

YOSSI And I would need a working computer on my desk. Americans love machines. They love facts. They think the world, crime, evil, everything is only about facts. They think if you have enough technology, you can solve all the crimes, and if you solve all the crimes, there won't be any more.

KHALID And you?

YOSSI There will still be corruption and moral indignation and rage and broken machines. I told them: facts are facts but nuance is more important.

KHALID What did they say?

YOSSI They assured me of the validity of my oriental approach. They've all taken courses in cultural sensitivity. Speaking of which—how is your wife?

KHALID Fine, thank you.

YOSSI Give her my regards. Mine is gone.

KHALID I'm sorry.

YOSSI Not dead.

KHALID I'm still sorry.

YOSSI When did we work together?

KHALID Two years ago.

YOSSI The butcher?

KHALID The clarinet player.

YOSSI That was a bad time. Was I difficult?

KHALID Very.

YOSSI That's a relief. I was afraid my depression had made me agreeable. So. Philip Gordon.

KHALID The archaeologist who was killed.

YOSSI Yes.

KHALID Gordon Philips.

YOSSI Him.

KHALID Why?

YOSSI Interest at the highest levels.

KHALID You mean . . . *(points up)*

YOSSI Higher. The American administration. Gordon's family is apparently connected. He was some kind of fundamentalist Christian, and they are—

KHALID No.

YOSSI No?

KHALID It's in the file.

YOSSI *(indicating a thin file)* I read it.

KHALID This is what I sent. *(takes out a thicker file)*

YOSSI What was he?

KHALID He was a Christian when he came to the Holy Land, twenty years ago, to walk in the footsteps of Jesus. But he went through a . . .

YOSSI Epiphany.

KHALID A conversion on the road to Damascus.

YOSSI To what? Marxism? Islam?

KHALID Science.

YOSSI Science. Instead of Christianity. Are they incompatible?

KHALID For Philips, after his conversion, yes. Archaeologists used to come here to find out where Abraham sacrificed Isaac and God sacrificed Jesus. Someone said, "Let's assume we don't know what happened here. Let's work from the evidence to the history, instead of the other way around." So they did that and what they found was controversial.

YOSSI Big surprise.

KHALID It required a whole different way of looking at the world.

YOSSI Science instead of God.

KHALID Discovery instead of revelation. I can figure out who committed a crime. Or I can let God tell me.

YOSSI In Philips's case?

KHALID I'm waiting for a revelation.

YOSSI What about hunches and intuition? Where do they come from?

KHALID Mine are usually wrong. So, is there new evidence?

YOSSI Not that I know of.

KHALID Why are we meeting?

YOSSI We have to show the Americans we made an effort.

KHALID That's it?

YOSSI In two weeks or two months we'll write a report and the prime minister can tell the Americans that—

KHALID Thank you for thinking of me, but I'm not interested.

YOSSI Why not?

KHALID I don't have time. *(starts to leave)*

YOSSI It won't take time. We'll meet. We'll talk.

KHALID A man was killed—

YOSSI Is this your first case?

KHALID A man was killed, a university professor, an almost-retired archaeologist, an American, maybe connected to the troubles here, maybe not—none of that matters. But it was in al-Khalil. In the West Bank. If it was in Israel, you wouldn't be saying, oh, let's pretend to find the killer.

YOSSI Of course I would. We fail all the time. If the case isn't going anywhere and somebody wants me to put in a few more days, I don't have a fit.

KHALID I went to your army for assistance—right here—

YOSSI I didn't know that.

KHALID I get delay upon delay. I send fingerprints for identification, they have better things to do. You ask for the file, they send you that—what's in it, his name and address? Now you offer to put in a little work—

YOSSI I didn't know.

KHALID If the victim is a Jew, the investigation is aggressive and thorough. If it were an American in Israel, no stone would be unturned, order must be restored, reputations upheld. Here, well, we'll tell the Americans it's the jungle, they have no respect for life. In your jurisdiction you can decide which failures will be tolerated. *(puts his papers away as he prepares to leave)*

YOSSI I was looking forward to practising my Arabic.

KHALID It's beyond help.

YOSSI I was looking forward to working with you again.

KHALID *(indicates the larger file)* Call when you've read it. *(goes to leave)*

YOSSI Wait. *(takes out his cellphone and dials, puts it to his ear)* . . . Avram, it's HaCohen. I'm sorry, I need to talk to your wife . . . Thank you. *(to* KHALID*)* You have become very sensitive. *(on the phone)* Dalit, I need a favour. The IDF has a file on . . .

KHALID Gordon Philips.

YOSSI *(*YOSSI *is preoccupied.)* I apologize for disturbing you at home . . . Never. I'll never do it again. *(opens the file)* Write this down. IDF number 4-8-6-W-B-D-4-4-J. Read it back to me . . . An army file, yes. In this file, you will find fingerprints, well, you should find, but you will look. There is a request from our colleagues in Ramallah for . . . Palestinian colleagues, yes, a request for fingerprint indentifi— . . . Of course he can wait, he's been waiting four months, but I can't . . . Yes, I apologize. *(to* KHALID*)* Did I not say that? *(to* DALIT*)* What? . . . Oh. Philip Gordon.

KHALID Gordon Philips.

YOSSI *(checks the file)* Sorry. Gordon Philips. Gordon Isaiah Philips . . . the American, that's right, the archaeologist . . . If he leaves you, you can marry me . . . There's no reason to be insulting. But look, Dalit. Right away. I'm not leaving until you call. *(hangs up)* These reversible American names are impossible. Are you in a hurry? My trip to America— Listen. Europeans are a modern people. They appreciate facts, but know their limitations. Americans worship facts, like peasants. They idolize facts. We're all supposed to be Judeo-Christian, but Americans are peasants. Well, half are peasants, who don't accept facts. And then there are the artists who transcend facts.

KHALID How do you transcend facts?

YOSSI You can't. It's bullshit. But listen. A peasant, if it doesn't rain, prays harder or whips himself or sacrifices a virgin.

KHALID Or circumcises his children.

YOSSI Exactly. To a peasant, if a man is different, he's, uh . . .

KHALID The devil.

YOSSI To an intellectual who has transcended facts, the difference—skin colour, culture, religion—is celebrated, and proves he is untainted by Western civilization.

KHALID In both cases facts are ignored.

YOSSI This is how you transcend facts.

KHALID The peasant is pre-fact, the artist post-fact.

YOSSI Exactly.

KHALID And us?

YOSSI You and me?

KHALID *(gestures)* Us.

YOSSI We are peasants. Speaking on behalf of my people. We Zionists had ambitions, we embraced socialism and science. But Israel is full of peasants who worship and idolize. And Palestinians?

KHALID We were on our way.

YOSSI To what?

KHALID Modernity?

YOSSI What stopped you?

KHALID You said "Judeo-Christian."

YOSSI When?

KHALID Before. You said, "We're all Judeo-Christian."

YOSSI Oh, I see. Well, Islamic-Judeo-Christian is too long. Did I offend you?

KHALID If you use "Judeo-Christian" to mean "modern" . . .

YOSSI I apologize.

KHALID Judeo-Christian is about sacrificing goats and gods impregnating virgins. The modern world begins with Greeks and Romans.

YOSSI Gordon Philips?

KHALID Yes.

YOSSI Where did the fingerprints come from?

KHALID *(with precision)* We went house-to-house in the neighbourhood of the murder. A woman said a man knocked on her door that evening, asked to use a phone. There were prints from sisters and nephews and one set we couldn't trace.

YOSSI How close?

KHALID Five hundred metres.

YOSSI Five hundred metres from the murder to the woman with the phone? It means nothing.

KHALID I know.

YOSSI Did he run out of gas half a kilometre from the scene of the crime? Some murderer. What did he look like?

KHALID Thirties, Ashkenazi, nervous, wearing a light—

YOSSI Ashkenazi?

KHALID Yes.

YOSSI A Jew. Walks up to a Palestinian home in Hebron—sorry, al-Khalil—and knocks on the door. I bet he was nervous. You think a Jew would do that? You think a Jewish murderer would do that? And they let him in. What did he say on the phone?

KHALID They left him alone.

YOSSI Did he speak Arabic?

KHALID English.

YOSSI Accent?

KHALID They wouldn't know.

YOSSI Was he wearing a kippah?

KHALID Knitted. Black.

YOSSI A man in a kippah knocks on a Palestinian door in al-Khalil. I would guess that doesn't happen every day. That's it? Any other suspects?

KHALID Thousands.

YOSSI Name six.

KHALID Who don't hate archaeologists?

YOSSI Of course, but . . .

KHALID Who?

YOSSI What?

KHALID Who hates archaeologists?

YOSSI Farmers, peasants, me . . .

KHALID Why you?

YOSSI Me? Someone finds a potsherd in a ditch, they close the road for a month. Traffic is bad enough without stupid archaeologists.

KHALID Why peasants and farmers?

YOSSI The Department of Antiquities throws a fence around your field, you can't plant.

KHALID Who else?

YOSSI Religious fanatics.

KHALID Why?

YOSSI Archaeologists defile sacred ground.

KHALID If you object to the desecration of sacred ground, does that make you a fanatic?

YOSSI I suppose not, but if you kill someone for that . . .

KHALID Why else? What other reason do religious fanatics have for hating archaeologists?

YOSSI I don't know—they drive on the Sabbath.

KHALID What about when they dispute what's in the Bible?

YOSSI You mean like when they say that God didn't make the world in six days?

KHALID For example.

YOSSI I've been known to shout "God doesn't exist" in a crowded restaurant. Nobody killed me. If you catch an archaeologist digging your olive patch or your father's grave, but Philips was killed— He wasn't digging up relics, was he?

KHALID Leaving a friend's home.

YOSSI In al-Khalil. There's a lot of relics there. Was he digging up relics?

KHALID No.

YOSSI So who hates archaeologists enough—archaeologists in general, not our specific Mr. Philips—to select one and lurk outside his home and . . .

KHALID His friend's home.

YOSSI Am I making sense?

KHALID *(takes a book from his briefcase)* Are you familiar with this book?

YOSSI The Tanakh?

KHALID The Old Testament.

YOSSI Sure, a bit.

KHALID There's a difference.

YOSSI Between what?

KHALID The Tanakh and the Old Testament.

YOSSI Is there?

KHALID Protestants and Catholics have different Old Testaments, different combinations of—

YOSSI All right.

KHALID The Tanakh is the Jewish version of the Old—

YOSSI And it's different?

KHALID The book of Tobit, for example—

YOSSI Never heard of it.

KHALID Or Judith—

YOSSI I've heard of her.

KHALID They're in the Old Testament, but not in the Tanakh.

YOSSI Fascinating.

KHALID And the books are in a different order.

YOSSI Does it matter?

KHALID To millions of people, yes.

YOSSI My family are devout atheists for three generations.

KHALID This is from what the Christians call Deuteronomy and the Jews call Words. The last book of the Torah. *(begins reading Deuteronomy 34)* "Then, leaving the plains of Moab, Moses went up to Mount Nebo, the peak of Pisgah, opposite Jericho. And Yahweh showed him the whole—"

YOSSI Excuse me. I thought you weren't supposed to say that word.

KHALID *(teasing)* What word?

YOSSI That word.

KHALID Yahweh?

YOSSI Yes.

KHALID The Catholics say Yahweh.

YOSSI And nothing bad happens to them?

KHALID They get everlasting life.

YOSSI It doesn't seem fair.

KHALID Say it.

YOSSI Why do you have a Catholic Bible?

KHALID Say it.

YOSSI What?

KHALID Yahweh.

YOSSI *(uncomfortably)* Yahweh. Yahweh. Yahweh. All right?

KHALID And Yahweh showed Moses *(continues reading)* "the whole country, Gilead as far as Dan, the whole of Naphtali, the country of Ephraim and Manasseh, the whole country of Judah as far as the western sea, the Negeb, and the region of the Valley of Jericho, city of palm trees, as far as Zoar. Yahweh said to him, 'This is the country which I promised on oath to give to Abraham, Isaac, and Jacob, saying: I shall give it to your descendants. I have allowed you to see it for yourself, but you will not cross into it.' There in the country of Moab, Moses, servant of Yahweh, died . . ." It's sad, isn't it? Moses leads his people out of Egypt, there have been many victories and many losses, they have wandered in the desert for forty years, and now, on the eve of entering the Promised Land, and maybe, finally, getting a bit of rest under the palm trees of Jericho, God takes him up Mount Nebo—even if we leave God out of it, and it's simply Moses leading his people out of slavery—and he's about to enter this land he's dreamed of all his life but has never seen, and now he sees it, spread out beneath him, but he's old and he knows he's not going to make it, he will never enter.

YOSSI So?

KHALID It's sad.

YOSSI Yes.

KHALID And beautiful.

YOSSI Khalid . . .

KHALID According to Dr. Philips, it never happened.

YOSSI I see where you're going.

KHALID Good.

YOSSI If you tell me he was digging in an ancient burial ground and a member of one our many fanatic sects beat him to death with the jawbone of an ass like what's his name, I'll believe you, no questions asked. But Philips was a writer, and these fanatics only read the Torah, over and over and over . . .

KHALID The whole of Exodus.

YOSSI What about it?

KHALID It didn't happen.

YOSSI The Exodus?

KHALID None of it. No slaves. No Egypt.

YOSSI No slaves.

KHALID According to Philips, the Israelites were never in Egypt.

YOSSI He said this?

KHALID He wrote it in books. Your father was a Zionist.

YOSSI Yes.

KHALID A leading Zionist.

YOSSI Yes.

KHALID And the story of the Exodus . . .?

YOSSI What?

KHALID Inspired him?

YOSSI Yes. Passover was the only holy day he observed—in a secular way. But he didn't believe that God . . .

KHALID . . . gave Palestine to the Jews.

YOSSI Parted the Red Sea.

KHALID He was an atheist.

YOSSI Yes.

KHALID But he did claim that the Jews, the Zionists . . .

YOSSI What?

KHALID . . . were returning home.

YOSSI Yes.

KHALID To what had been their country.

YOSSI Yes.

KHALID The Land of Israel.

YOSSI Yes.

KHALID Not just where his ancestors lived, but their country, of which David was king.

YOSSI Yes.

KHALID Your father was an atheist.

YOSSI A Marxist atheist.

KHALID Better still. He appealed not to God but to history.

YOSSI Yes.

KHALID History.

YOSSI Khalid.

KHALID Mr. Philips says it never happened.

YOSSI What didn't?

KHALID King David.

YOSSI He's a historical figure.

KHALID Not according to—

YOSSI *(irritated)* So his name wasn't David, it was Uri or—

KHALID No David, no Solomon.

YOSSI According to Gordon.

KHALID Philips.

YOSSI *(angry)* Philips!

KHALID *(hard)* According to Philips—no united Judea and Samaria. No Kingdom of Israel.

YOSSI It's nonsense. Everyone knows that King David—

KHALID They don't.

YOSSI *(accusing)* What do you know about him?

KHALID King David?

YOSSI Philips. An American who chooses to work in the West Bank.

KHALID Which makes him an anti-Semite.

YOSSI Did you check him out? Why is he so interested in the history of Israel?

KHALID He's an archaeologist.

*YOSSI doesn't respond.*

His co-author is an Israeli Jew.

YOSSI Proves nothing.

KHALID There's a stela in Tel Dan that mentions a "House of David." Some say it's a reference to King David, but if it is, it's the only one outside the Tanakh. If he had been king of a powerful nation . . .

YOSSI There would be more.

KHALID Among archaeologists, this is now the mainstream view.

YOSSI So the question is, would someone kill him over that? Would someone plan and carry out a murder because he objected to certain stupid ideas?

KHALID If there never was an Israeli kingdom, what is the justification for Zionism?

YOSSI You're right. We'll leave.

KHALID I'll help you pack, but it's not my point.

YOSSI Why don't you get to it?

KHALID You're a liberal Israeli.

YOSSI Until two minutes ago.

KHALID It's very deep. It's about habits and traditions. It's about identity. You're not a fanatic, but you are very angry. If people are told that what they take to be their history is . . .

YOSSI Lies.

KHALID Or stories.

YOSSI And you think that could provoke someone—

KHALID I'm saying it's a sensitive subject and there are many people who deeply resent the work Philips and his colleagues are doing.

YOSSI It's easy for you.

KHALID What is?

YOSSI Why would you care if Moses never existed?

KHALID Because I—

YOSSI Because you are Muslim.

KHALID The Quran, sura 3, verse 84. *(recites)* "We believe in Allah and what has been revealed to us; and what has been revealed to Abraham and Ishmail and Itzhak and the tribes, and what was given to Moses and Jesus and to the prophets . . ."

YOSSI The Quran?

KHALID They're all Muslim prophets.

YOSSI Abraham, Moses, David . . .

KHALID Yes.

YOSSI Do you believe that?

KHALID I have my beliefs.

YOSSI Do you believe what Philips says? No Moses, no David.

KHALID He has his beliefs.

YOSSI What about you? What do you believe yourself?

*KHALID doesn't answer. A standoff. YOSSI's cellphone rings. He waits for an answer from KHALID but then looks at his phone.*

It's Dalit. *(answers)* Speak . . . Is that why you called? . . . Well, keep looking. Just a second. *(to KHALID)* The fingerprints. Who were you dealing with?

KHALID A captain . . . Katz—Katzman.

YOSSI Motti Katzman? *(to* DALIT*)* Dalit. Call Colonel David Segev. Tell him I sent you, it's an international incident. Tell him the fingerprints were sent to Captain Motti Katzman . . . Because Dudu and I served together and because Katzman's an idiot . . . Dalit, I'm still waiting. *(hangs up)* She couldn't find the—

KHALID I heard.

YOSSI Do you play bridge?

KHALID What?

YOSSI The card game. You know, like Omar Sharif.

KHALID The actor.

YOSSI He's a world-class bridge player.

KHALID I don't play.

YOSSI He's one of your people.

KHALID Bridge players?

YOSSI An Arab. He was in *Doctor Zhivago.*

KHALID And in *Lawrence of Arabia.*

YOSSI Of course. So. In all card games, you play the odds. But in bridge sometimes you play against the odds. You look at your cards and you say to yourself, "The only way I can make this hand is if east is holding a doubleton Queen of Diamonds and west is void in spades."

KHALID I have no idea what you're talking about.

YOSSI It doesn't matter. I'm saying, if our mysterious caller rowed a boat from Cyprus, walked across the Negev, et cetera, killed Philips, and returned home in an invisible space ship, we'll never find him. But, if we make certain assumptions, that he's a settler from or near al-Khalil, and he drove his car, we have a chance.

KHALID Go on.

YOSSI What else do we need to assume? What do we know? He shoots Professor . . .

KHALID Philips.

YOSSI I was going to say Philips—and he—shoots him from his car?

KHALID No.

YOSSI He jumps into his car, and he drives . . .?

KHALID West.

YOSSI *(indicates the file)* Is there ballistics? What kind of—

KHALID Forty calibre.

YOSSI Of course.

KHALID And damaged beyond—

YOSSI Of course, again. So he drives west, five hundred metres.

KHALID Yes.

YOSSI And he stops to make a call.

KHALID Why didn't he use his mobile phone?

YOSSI He doesn't own one.

KHALID If he's a settler, he owns a mobile.

YOSSI His battery is dead. I don't like it. He kills Professor Philips—

KHALID Bravo.

YOSSI . . . jumps into his car, drives five hundred metres, his car breaks down. He tries to make a phone call, and his mobile's dead. He gets out of the car and his pants fall down. It's a bad movie.

KHALID We're playing bridge.

YOSSI I still don't like it.

KHALID All right. His car didn't break down. He got lost.

YOSSI He lives there. Near there.

KHALID In H1?

YOSSI No, of course not.

KHALID The murder and the phone call were in H1. It's in the file.

YOSSI Okay. H1 is the Palestinian sector.

KHALID They're both Palestinian. There are a hundred thousand Palestinians in H1. In H2, there are thirty thousand Palestinians and eight hundred settlers.

YOSSI I stand corrected. Both sectors are Palestinian, all right? And the Jewish settlements are in H2.

KHALID Yes.

YOSSI Now. To get into H1, he'd have to go through a checkpoint.

KHALID No problem. He's Jewish.

YOSSI So it makes sense. He would know H2, but he's never been in H1.

KHALID Do you know al-Khalil?

YOSSI No. I've heard it's quiet.

KHALID There's a joke. al-Khalil used to have a nightlife but—

YOSSI We tell the same joke about Jerusalem.

KHALID Where did she move to?

YOSSI Haifa.

KHALID Wait.

YOSSI What?

KHALID The phone call was at seven o'clock.

YOSSI And the murder . . .

KHALID Twenty minutes before.

YOSSI Twenty minutes to drive five hundred metres?

KHALID Wait. You kill someone, you start driving, and you realize you're lost . . .

YOSSI Go on.

KHALID What do you do? You just killed someone. You don't stop and ask a person by the side of the road—you keep driving.

YOSSI But he did stop. He knocked on a door . . .

KHALID But maybe first he drove, for five minutes, or fifteen minutes . . .

YOSSI So he's lost, and he drives in circles, and twenty minutes later he gives up. And he's right back where he started? I'm getting a headache.

KHALID We assumed he was lost, which means he doesn't know the neighbourhood, which means he doesn't go there.

YOSSI So?

KHALID If he was there only once, we won't find him.

YOSSI You should play bridge.

KHALID We're back to his car breaking down.

YOSSI He's been there before. His car breaks down. What else do we know?

KHALID He spoke English.

YOSSI There are eight hundred settlers.

KHALID In the old city. And another eight thousand in Kiryat Arba to the east.

YOSSI How many of them are men between twenty-five and forty years old?

KHALID Two thousand? We're down to two thousand suspects.

YOSSI How many speak English?

KHALID Most.

YOSSI Did he try to speak Arabic?

KHALID No.

YOSSI Maybe he's American.

KHALID Maybe he isn't. In bridge, does this ever work?

YOSSI You only do it when you're desperate.

KHALID We had to assume he often came to H1.

YOSSI Yes.

KHALID And we assumed his car broke down.

YOSSI You did.

KHALID You agreed. But what if his car wouldn't start?

YOSSI What's the difference?

KHALID It means he was parked in the area, not just driving through. If we also assume he often parked in the area . . .

YOSSI What?

KHALID There would perhaps be parking tickets.

*YOSSI takes out his cellphone and dials.*

How many people with yellow license plates get parking tickets in H1?

YOSSI *(on cell)* Dalit? Listen— . . . Okay, you first . . . Really. *(to KHALID)* They found the fingerprints. *(to DALIT)* Just a second. *(to KHALID)* Get a pen. *(to DALIT)* I love you. *(to KHALID)* Not you.

*KHALID begins writing.*

*(to DALIT)* Rakoff. Daniel. Kiryat Arba. Excellent . . . Yes, of course. Whatever you can find. Everything. Here's another— Look for parking tickets . . . In H1, yellow plates . . . Yes, in H1. Yellow plates, Israeli plates. *(hangs up; to KHALID)* I'll teach you bridge. You can be my partner. (*stands*) Can I take the file?

KHALID Of course.

YOSSI We'll meet tomorrow at my office in Tel Aviv. We can go to Shenkin for a coffee.

KHALID No.

YOSSI Have you been to Shenkin Street? It's the new Dizengof.

KHALID I won't cross the green line.

YOSSI I'll get you a permit.

KHALID I won't cross.

YOSSI Is this a point of principle?

KHALID Yes.

*YOSSI looks at KHALID impatiently. They exit.*

## SCENE TWO

*The next day. As before. KHALID is waiting. YOSSI enters with two cups of coffee.*

YOSSI How were the checkpoints?

KHALID Perfect.

YOSSI They let you in ahead of the cripples?

*KHALID doesn't respond.*

Okay, it's not funny. But look, I don't like having to cheer you up every time we meet.

KHALID Did you bring sugar?

*YOSSI gives sugar to KHALID.*

This is very nice but tea would be better. What did you find?

*YOSSI slides him a piece of paper.*

*(reads)* Parking tickets.

YOSSI Five.

KHALID Over six months.

YOSSI Three before the murder and two after.

KHALID And then they stop.

YOSSI What does it mean? Does this make it more or less likely that he's our murderer?

KHALID It means we found the man with the fingerprints.

YOSSI He's out there.

KHALID Where?

YOSSI There. Here.

KHALID Here? Were we right?

YOSSI He's a settler, he lives in Kiryat Arba, and he's from America.

KHALID Not bad.

YOSSI *(uncomfortable)* Philips was killed outside the home of his friends, the Shehadehs.

KHALID Yes.

YOSSI . . . who have a daughter—Huda—who was a student at Birzeit University. A student of Gordon Philips's.

KHALID That's right.

YOSSI Huda has a doctorate in archaeology from Oxford. But when the university hires an archaeologist, they hire a foreigner.

KHALID A Swede.

YOSSI How am I doing?

KHALID With blond hair and blue eyes.

YOSSI There's anger at this insult to a local star—demonstrations, denunciations of the hiring committee, calls for the administration to overturn the decision. Six months later a member of the hiring committee is dead.

KHALID Those are the facts.

YOSSI Why didn't you mention this?

KHALID When?

YOSSI Yesterday. Instead, you were making speeches from the top of Mount Sinai.

KHALID Nebo.

YOSSI What?

KHALID Mount Nebo.

YOSSI Don't you think this is a little more important than your theory about the missing King David? This is an actual suspect. This is a woman who has a—

KHALID Speaking of which, we have an actual suspect waiting.

YOSSI He can wait.

KHALID The theory of King David is not in the file. On the other hand, every detail of your brilliant summation of the case against Ms. Shehadeh is.

YOSSI The file is not complete.

KHALID For example.

YOSSI Were there threats against Philips?

KHALID Yes. Against all the members of the hiring committee.

YOSSI How many?

KHALID It's in the file. We investigated them. They led nowhere.

YOSSI Did she and Philips have professional disagreements?

KHALID Small ones.

YOSSI Among academics there are no small disagreements.

KHALID It's a matter of emphasis. Her generation, my generation, doesn't need to disprove the Bible. It's been done.

YOSSI Her area of research is . . .?

KHALID Thirteen centuries of Arab culture.

YOSSI A good pair. He erases the history of the Jews and she scribbles in the history of the Arabs. She has an obvious motive. The whole family has motive. Philips visits the Shehadehs to make excuses, tempers rise, Philips leaves, an angry brother follows—

KHALID She doesn't have a brother.

YOSSI An angry cousin follows Philips outside . . .

KHALID I never thought of that.

YOSSI *(unpleasantly)* What did you think of?

KHALID *doesn't respond.*

What was your relationship with her?

KHALID We're friends.

YOSSI Did you sleep with her?

KHALID She's a very good friend of my wife.

YOSSI You didn't answer the question.

KHALID Don't talk to me like this.

YOSSI Like what? Like you're a suspect? Like you avoided certain lines of investigation because you had a personal—

KHALID Like you're my superior officer.

*YOSSI is silent.*

Huda and I are from old al-Khalil families. It would be unlikely for us not to know each other.

YOSSI I'll want to talk to her.

KHALID She's at the Sorbonne.

YOSSI Thank you.

KHALID In Paris.

YOSSI I know where the Sorbonne is.

KHALID She's not suffering.

YOSSI I will try to be polite. She and her family had motive and opportunity. You dropped the investigation. Did you decide she's boating on the Seine so she must be innocent?

KHALID New information came to light.

YOSSI *(indicates the file)* Show me.

KHALID It's not there. It's personal.

YOSSI *(makes a rude gesture)* So. You and her?

KHALID Stop this. Don't treat her like that. We were not sleeping together. But you're right. There is something missing from the file. Philips and Huda agreed it would be better for her to look for a post abroad.

YOSSI But she applied for the post here.

KHALID Palestine can be a difficult place to leave. One disappoints a great many people.

YOSSI I am familiar with the phenomenon. You're saying she wanted to leave.

KHALID Yes.

YOSSI Do you think about leaving?

KHALID I lived in America for two years.

YOSSI Why did you come back?

KHALID I wanted to come home.

*The office phone rings.* YOSSI *picks it up.*

YOSSI *(to* KHALID*)* I have fantasies about living in Paris, among the violins in the Place des Vosges. But I can't. I'm addicted to my wonderful life in Israel. Unless—this Huda, is she good looking? Maybe I'll call her. *(into the phone)* Yes . . . Really? Tell him he can sit there until the Messiah comes—Liebnitz, put him on the line . . . Mr. Rakoff . . . Mr. Rakoff . . . *(interrupting)* Of course, you're busy, who isn't? Would you—would you—please. Write out what you remember of the evening of last April 17 . . . Do your best. It will speed things up . . . As soon we can. *(hangs up)* So who killed Philips?

KHALID My guess? A Palestinian student with political and romantic fantasies.

YOSSI To avenge her honour.

KHALID Yes. But even then. Philips lived in Ramallah. Every

day he walked from his home to the university. Why would our heartbroken student follow him to al-Khalil?

YOSSI He didn't. He went to proclaim his love to Huda. He's about to enter, sees Philips leave the house, it's too much. Bang.

KHALID Huda was in Paris by then, and before that she lived in Ramallah.

YOSSI I knew that.

KHALID Here's something else. Huda's parents didn't know about her plan with Philips and they blamed him when she didn't get the job. When Huda found out, she told her parents the truth. Her parents wanted to apologize to Philips. They invite him to visit, on April 17.

YOSSI Very bad timing. Or . . .

KHALID Or they set up the whole thing.

YOSSI Yes.

KHALID Your case against the Shehadehs was built on motive. Where's the motive?

YOSSI *(picks up the office phone)* Except for that it's airtight. And you still had the fingerprints of a mysterious Jew in an Arab home in H1.

KHALID Wait a second. What does it mean that he got five parking tickets in six months? Even if he killed Philips . . .

YOSSI He only killed him once.

KHALID So why does he keep going there? For the falafel.

YOSSI For a prostitute. For a prostitute with falafel. Settlements? You think they want to put settlements in

Hi now? All right. I hate to keep settlers waiting— Was Philips involved with the settlements?

KHALID No.

YOSSI I mean against the settlements.

KHALID No. We asked. Everybody said—

YOSSI Settlers are always claiming that Joshua brushed his teeth here and slept there before he blew the shofar. Philips could be an expert witness. You be the good cop.

KHALID What?

YOSSI You be the good cop.

KHALID Me?

YOSSI Why not you?

KHALID He's a settler. I'm Palestinian.

YOSSI What is this? A professional puts aside his personal feelings. You fake it. It's called acting.

KHALID He'd know. He'd never trust me. Why not you?

YOSSI I hate settlers— Okay, I'll do it. *(into the phone)* Liebnitz. Send in Mr. Rakoff, please. *(hangs up)* Watch this. Just like Omar Sharif.

*YOSSI opens the door. DANNY touches the mezuzah and puts his fingers to his lips before entering.*

Mr. Rakoff. I'm so sorry you were kept waiting. Please, sit. Can I get you a coffee?

DANNY I don't speak Arabic.

YOSSI I'm sorry. We'll speak Hebrew.

DANNY Thank you.

YOSSI I'm Inspector HaCohen. Can I get you a coffee? Please sit down.

*DANNY remains standing.*

Or stand if you prefer.

DANNY This is the statement you asked me to write.

YOSSI Statement? No, nothing so formal. Read it. Please.

DANNY *(referring to KHALID)* Who is he?

YOSSI I'm sorry. How rude of me. Mr. Daniel Rakoff, Inspector Yassin of the Palestinian Authority.

DANNY I won't speak to him.

YOSSI It's all right, he speaks Hebrew.

DANNY I don't recognize his authority.

YOSSI This is a very serious matter, Mr. Rakoff. We all have the same objective—to clear up a murder and a misunderstanding and to go home to our loved ones.

DANNY *(reads)* "On the seventeenth of April, in the city of Hebron, in the Land of Israel, my car broke down."

YOSSI It's a bureaucratic problem, Mr. Rakoff. The city you call Hebron, the Palestinians call al-Khalil, but that's a detail. The point is, whatever you call it, it's not in Israel. *(to KHALID)* I'm just explaining that a week from now some junior bureaucrat in the Department of Public Security will read "Hebron, in the Land of Israel" and return it with forms to be completed in triplicate. *(to DANNY)* Make my life simpler, Mr. Rakoff. Just say "Hebron, West Bank." Or leave it out. Just say "Hebron."

DANNY *(continues reading)* "I went to a nearby home, where I was permitted to use a telephone. I called my office. They gave me the number of a mechanic. I called, he arrived and repaired the car. I left Hebron." End of statement.

YOSSI Concise. To the point. Well. I have no further questions.

*DANNY prepares to leave.*

Excuse me. Do you have any questions, Inspector Yassin?

KHALID What were you doing in Hebron, Mr. Rakoff?

*DANNY doesn't answer.*

YOSSI Inspector Yassin asked you a question.

DANNY I told you. I don't recognize—

YOSSI My colleague spent many hours this morning waiting at a checkpoint. You know how it is. He's not entirely sympathetic to our security needs. It left him bitter. I suggest you answer his question.

DANNY Arabs don't tell Jews what to do in the Land of Israel.

YOSSI *(to KHALID)* Ask him again, politely.

KHALID What were you doing in Hebron—sir?

*DANNY doesn't answer.*

YOSSI *(to KHALID)* You can hit him. Feel free.

*KHALID doesn't move.*

*(to DANNY)* Have you heard of Arab rage, Mr. Rakoff? He's restraining himself now, but once he gets started, I don't know if I'll be able to stop him. I suggest you co-operate.

*DANNY turns to look at KHALID. YOSSI grabs DANNY.*

Inspector Yassin is a police officer on police business. You will answer his questions like a human being or you will answer them handcuffed to the table and with my foot on your throat. Is that clear?

*DANNY tries to answer but YOSSI has an arm on his throat.*

I'm sorry. I can't hear you.

*DANNY tries to answer but can't.*

KHALID Yossi—

YOSSI What?

KHALID Omar Sharif.

YOSSI I forgot.

*YOSSI throws DANNY at a chair. DANNY sits.*

*(politely)* Please. Tell Inspector Yassin why you were in Hebron.

*DANNY can't talk.*

Don't rush. Can I get you a glass of water?

*YOSSI fills a cup of water. DANNY goes to reach for it, but YOSSI drinks it instead.*

DANNY *(with difficulty, to YOSSI)* I work there.

YOSSI Address Inspector Yassin.

DANNY *(to KHALID)* I work there.

KHALID In Hebron?

DANNY Yes.

KHALID Your office is in Hebron.

DANNY No. In Kiryat Arba.

KHALID Where you live.

DANNY Yes.

KHALID Your work takes you to Hebron.

DANNY That's right.

KHALID How often?

DANNY Two, three times a week.

KHALID What do you do?

DANNY I manage property.

KHALID You buy property.

DANNY No.

YOSSI You steal property.

DANNY I manage property. I see that broken windows are repaired and swastikas are painted over.

KHALID What were you doing that day—the seventeenth of April—

DANNY I had two appointments in the afternoon.

KHALID Write down their names please.

*DANNY writes.*

Where did you meet them?

*DANNY is silent.*

Which part of the city?

DANNY (*to* YOSSI) A murder was committed. It's natural you blame a Jew.

YOSSI Is this more of your official statement?

DANNY I will make a formal complaint.

YOSSI The world will come to a stop. You were asked a question. Where did you meet them?

DANNY On Al-Shuhada Street.

YOSSI Both? Both appointments?

DANNY Yes.

YOSSI (*to* KHALID) Do you know it?

KHALID It's a main street in the old city.

YOSSI In H2.

KHALID A Jewish-only street.

YOSSI And there's a settlement.

KHALID A small one. A few buildings.

YOSSI (*to* DANNY) Is that where you met them?

DANNY Yes.

KHALID What's it called?

DANNY *doesn't answer.*

YOSSI What's it called?

DANNY Beit Hadassah.

KHALID What time were your appointments?

DANNY Five.

KHALID Until?

DANNY Six.

KHALID And the second one?

DANNY Both. Five, then five thirty—

KHALID And you left at six.

DANNY Yes, about six.

KHALID *(looking at the statement)* Then your car broke down and you called your office and a mechanic, who came and fixed the car. Is that correct?

DANNY Yes.

KHALID Are you sure? You can change it.

*DANNY doesn't respond.*

Then you went home to your wife and . . . *(checks file)* six children.

DANNY Seven.

YOSSI Congratulations.

KHALID The mechanic you called—does he live in Kiryat Arba?

DANNY He's an Arab.

YOSSI You didn't answer his question. He asked, "Does he live in Kiryat Arba?" You answered, "He's an Arab."

KHALID Yossi. *(to DANNY)* Why didn't you call him directly?

DANNY I don't know him.

KHALID So you called your office and they called . . .

DANNY Yes.

KHALID Write down his name and number. Please.

*DANNY glares, takes out his cellphone, finds the information, and writes as YOSSI continues.*

YOSSI Why didn't you use your mobile?

DANNY The battery was dead.

YOSSI And you don't have a charger in your car.

DANNY I had forgotten to—

KHALID If your mobile was dead, why do you have the number now?

*DANNY doesn't respond.*

YOSSI *(to DANNY)* It's a good question.

DANNY I put it in later.

YOSSI Good answer. So your car breaks down. Your phone is dead. You don't have the name of a mechanic. It's a lot of bad luck. I'm not even including the very bad luck that on that day a famous professor of archaeology happened to be murdered near where you made the phone call. So I can see, at this moment, two camel-size holes in your story. *(to KHALID)* Two?

KHALID Two.

YOSSI *(to DANNY)* Guess.

*DANNY doesn't respond.*

Your meeting was in H2, in east Hebron. You made the phone call from west Hebron.

DANNY Big hole. Brilliant, Detective. I was lost.

KHALID You crossed into H1.

DANNY So?

KHALID There are checkpoints.

DANNY I pass checkpoints all the time. They wave me through.

YOSSI You were lost.

DANNY Yes.

*YOSSI makes changes to DANNY's statement.*

YOSSI And then your car broke down.

DANNY Yes.

YOSSI Where?

DANNY I don't know where, I was lost.

KHALID You work in Hebron.

DANNY I go for meetings.

KHALID How many times have you been there?

DANNY Many.

KHALID A dozen?

DANNY A hundred.

KHALID And you didn't know where you were.

DANNY I don't know that part of—

KHALID You had two meetings on Al-Shuhada Street in east Hebron. You live in Kiryat Arba, further to the east. The home from which you made your phone call is in H1, directly to the west.

YOSSI What happened, Danny? You travel between Kiryat Arba and Beit Hadassah twice a week, but that day you got in your car and instead of going east, you go—

KHALID Do you know a shortcut from Hebron to Kiryat Arba that takes you one hundred and eighty degrees in the wrong direction?

YOSSI And through a checkpoint and you didn't notice? Or maybe you had an appointment you forgot to mention.

DANNY I was lost.

YOSSI You weren't thinking. You made a turn.

DANNY Yes.

YOSSI And then another. And another. And soon you were lost. Even though you've been to Hebron a hundred times. And then your car broke down.

DANNY Yes.

KHALID It broke down.

DANNY Yes.

KHALID Did it run out of gas?

DANNY No.

KHALID It wouldn't start.

DANNY It broke down and it wouldn't start.

KHALID Not the other way around?

DANNY What? I'm sorry—

KHALID There's a difference. In one case, you're driving and your car breaks down. In the other, you park your car, you go for an appointment, and when you come back it won't start.

DANNY I was driving, it went pt-pt-pt-pt, and it died.

KHALID When you stick to a stupid story, it doesn't help. But it's your story. Here's the bigger camel. You said your meeting at Beit Hadassah ended at six. According to the Palestinian woman who allowed you to use her phone, the phone call was a few minutes after seven. So it took you sixty minutes to get lost.

DANNY So?

KHALID Most people can get lost faster than that.

DANNY Maybe I left Mr. Tamir at six thirty. Maybe she got the time wrong.

YOSSI *(indicates the report)* It's in here, Danny. She was sure of the time because she was listening to a news report on Ajyal Radio when you arrived. As for Mr. Tamir, don't worry, we'll ask him.

KHALID Do you normally come alone?

DANNY What?

KHALID Do you come to Hebron by yourself?

DANNY Why wouldn't I?

KHALID Aren't you afraid?

DANNY I can protect myself.

YOSSI Do you own a gun?

DANNY Of course.

YOSSI Did you have it with you?

DANNY Yes.

YOSSI Did you carry it in your hand? Big American cowboy, walking through the fields, bringing truth and justice to the . . .

KHALID Indians.

YOSSI Did you have a horse?

*DANNY doesn't answer.*

Where was your gun? Where did you have it?

DANNY *(indicating a holster under his jacket)* Here.

YOSSI The gun?

DANNY Yes.

YOSSI *(realizes DANNY has the gun)* Open your jacket.

DANNY No.

YOSSI Open your jacket.

DANNY You don't have authority. I have a permit from the army.

*YOSSI is furious but restrains himself. KHALID gets into position, ready to disarm DANNY. YOSSI stops him, picks up the phone, and dials.*

YOSSI *(into the phone)* Liebnitz. Please instruct Mr. Rakoff to surrender his weapon . . . Why? Because there happens to be a protocol with respect to the entry of civilians into facilities of— . . . Liebnitz. I'm going to pretend you didn't say that. I'm going to—I am going to pass the phone to Mr. Rakoff and you will command him to surrender his weapon. Failing that, I will make a phone call to my first cousin the general who I'm sure— What's that? . . .

*He offers the phone to DANNY. DANNY takes it.*

*(to KHALID)* He said . . .

DANNY (*into the phone*) Yes, Shlomo.

YOSSI (*to* KHALID) He said, "Why should I ask for the gun?"

DANNY (*into the phone*) It's okay. What choice do you have?

YOSSI (*to* KHALID) He said, "He's one of us."

DANNY (*into the phone*) Her sister is visiting.

YOSSI (*to* KHALID) "He's one of us."

DANNY (*into the phone*) The whole month. It's not worth it to come for just—

YOSSI *snatches the phone and hangs up.*

YOSSI Where is she from?

DANNY *doesn't answer.*

Your sister.

DANNY *puts his gun on the table.*

You know what? This is very suspicious. This is our most common gun. Everybody has a Jericho 941.

DANNY It's a good gun.

YOSSI There are other good guns. If I was planning to use my gun for illegal activities—murder, for example—this is the kind of gun I would use.

YOSSI *puts the gun in his briefcase. He slides a paper to* DANNY *and holds out a pen.*

I revised your statement.

DANNY (*reads*) "I, Danny Rakoff, have absolutely no explanation for what I was—" I'm not signing.

YOSSI It's what you said.

DANNY I said I got lost.

YOSSI So write that down. Write down that you got lost.

*DANNY pushes the paper over.*

DANNY I'm not signing anything else. And you should treat me with respect in front of an Arab. *(stands)* Am I under arrest?

YOSSI No.

DANNY Then I'm leaving.

YOSSI Sit down. This isn't America. This isn't even Israel. Sit down.

*DANNY sits.*

You're lying about something, Danny. There's a missing hour.

KHALID What car were you driving?

DANNY My car.

KHALID You always come in your car?

DANNY Why shouldn't I?

YOSSI Write down the licence number, make, model, year.

*DANNY writes. YOSSI watches.*

Colour.

*DANNY writes.*

KHALID Let's finish up and go home, Mr. Rakoff. Your explanation is that you became lost and your car broke down.

DANNY It's in my statement.

KHALID (*checks the statement*) Let's be precise. (*amends the statement*) You didn't mention getting lost. And your car broke down while you were driving. Is that correct?

DANNY Yes.

YOSSI Swear to God?

*DANNY is silent. KHALID slides the paper over.*

KHALID Please sign.

*DANNY signs.*

Thank you. Perhaps now you would tell us about the parking tickets.

DANNY Parking tickets?

KHALID There were five parking tickets in a part of Hebron you claim you never go to.

YOSSI Do you know why you're here, Danny?

DANNY Parking tickets?

KHALID There was a murder.

DANNY I forgot.

KHALID Do you know who?

DANNY Was the victim a Jew?

KHALID No.

DANNY Why should I care?

KHALID An American.

DANNY I repeat. Why should I care?

KHALID Do you know who was killed?

DANNY I forget his name. The archaeologist.

KHALID Gordon Philips.

DANNY They should all be dead.

KHALID This one is.

DANNY They deny the Torah. They should be condemned.

KHALID And killed?

DANNY They desecrate sacred soil.

KHALID You're a modern man, Mr. Rakoff. You have a car, a mobile phone. Do you use a computer?

DANNY Of course.

KHALID You press a button, and in a moment your letter is delivered to your father in America. The same knowledge that brings you these miracles now tells you that the founder of your nation never existed.

DANNY *(laughs)* Let's see. Archaeologists crawl in the dirt while our Lord lives in heaven. Who should I believe?

KHALID The Tomb of Abraham, this holy site you think justifies your destroying a Palestinian city, is empty. Abraham isn't buried there because, according to modern scientific investigation, he never existed. Not him or Sarah or Isaac.

DANNY *(to YOSSI)* Do I have to listen to his lies?

YOSSI Not lies, Danny. Fairy tales.

KHALID No pillar of salt. No sacrifice of Isaac. No slaves in Egypt.

YOSSI You know what the children ask on Passover?

KHALID No Moses. No plagues. No Red Sea. No wandering in the desert.

YOSSI "Why is this night different from all other nights?"

KHALID No Exodus.

YOSSI "Why is this night different from all other nights?"

KHALID You know what that means?

YOSSI Because nothing happened.

KHALID You know what that means? It means God didn't give you this land.

YOSSI Get it? It never happened.

*DANNY doesn't answer.*

He says there was no King David.

*DANNY doesn't answer.*

It doesn't bother you?

*DANNY doesn't answer.*

It bothers me.

DANNY Why would it bother someone who isn't a Jew?

YOSSI *(furious)* You know what, Danny? You don't get to decide who is a Jew. I'm a Jew. I am a descendent of Jews. My mother was Jewish and her mother before her and her mother before her. And I'm circumcised. So even in your archaic, tribal bullshit rules, I get to be a Jew.

*YOSSI exits.*

KHALID Is he right?

*DANNY doesn't answer.*

Is he a Jew?

*DANNY doesn't answer.*

Technically?

DANNY There is no technical way to be a Jew. Circumcision and a Jewish mother are necessary but not sufficient. What your colleague thinks and what I think and what our government thinks doesn't matter. It's what he says. And he did us a favour. He said it to Moses. And now it's written down word for word in the Torah, so you have to read the Torah.

KHALID So what does it take to be a Jew?

DANNY *(laughs)* You have to read the Torah.

KHALID Did you know Dr. Philips?

DANNY I never had the pleasure.

KHALID Did you know his work?

DANNY I am familiar with his type.

*KHALID shows DANNY a photograph.*

KHALID Have you seen this man?

*DANNY puts the photograph aside.*

DANNY Is this your Mr. Philips?

KHALID Yes?

DANNY Our Lord gave us the Land of Israel and he commanded us to keep it. There are many who would take it from us. The Arabs, but you are weak. There are other devils—I will not say their names—who would drown us in the sea. Do you know who is Israel's most dangerous enemy? Israelis. Like your colleague HaCohen, or archtraitors like a former prime minister, who will give away the Land of Israel, for peace or so that the world will like Jews. But our Lord says no, he is not interested in peace and friendship, he gave us the Land of Israel and commanded us to keep it. Compared to the traitors among us, compared to devils who will drop a nuclear bomb on us, are archaeologists dangerous? Why should I lift a finger against Mr. Philips?

KHALID Here is why. You work to acquire Palestinian property.

DANNY Me? No.

KHALID And Mr. Philips was an expert on Arab and Jewish history in Palestine.

DANNY And?

KHALID He would appear in court as an expert witness.

DANNY I see. We would say that Abraham our father grazed his sheep on this hilltop and Philips would say he didn't.

KHALID Something like that.

DANNY Where do you come from?

KHALID Excuse me?

DANNY Where is your family from?

KHALID Look at the photograph. Have you seen this man?

DANNY Did you know that HaCohen's father was a Zionist? We learned from them. This is what we do, Mr. Yassin. Our movement establishes ten new settlements. The army says, "Five are illegal." We go to court.

The court decides, "Settlement number nine is illegal and is to be evacuated." The television cameras gather, the army drags out children, pregnant mothers yell "anti-Semite" and "Nazi" at Israeli soldiers. It is heartbreaking. And the whole world sees that the government opposes illegal settlement activity. The final score? Nine to one for my team. Everybody wins except you. So I repeat, why should we kill your expert witness?

KHALID Look at the photograph.

DANNY This is where my family comes from. Right here, we have nowhere else. We don't want a hilltop, we want the whole land. God owns everything and he gave this land to us. Every inch of it is Jewish land.

KHALID Mr. Rakoff, have you seen this man? We can find out if you were ever in the same place. Look carefully. One lie, and your story will collapse.

*DANNY makes a show of inspecting the photograph. YOSSI enters with three cups of coffee. He glances at the photo as he distributes the coffee and a large pile of sugar packets for KHALID.*

YOSSI Does he look familiar?

DANNY Now I recognize him. He is the man I was standing over after I shot him in the heart.

YOSSI Yes. One shot to the heart.

DANNY How else do you kill a man?

KHALID We need research.

YOSSI I'll call Dalit. *(YOSSI dials; to KHALID)* What do you want?

KHALID Tell her—

YOSSI You tell her. *(into the cellphone)* It's me. Our colleague, Inspector Yassin, has some questions.

*YOSSI hands the cell to KHALID.*

KHALID Can I call you Dalit? . . . Thank you. I need you to look into records of settler protests and court— . . . No, not criminal. Newspapers, radio. Maybe there's a picture or a story— Show his picture to— *(to YOSSI)* Who wrote that book on the settlers?

*YOSSI doesn't know.*

*(into the cellphone)* No, it's a woman, but check with him, too . . . That's all I can ask.

*YOSSI takes the cellphone.*

YOSSI *(into the cellphone)* Dalit. It's me. Quickly. He's moments away from confessing. *(hangs up; to DANNY)* You're not drinking. *(to KHALID)* The Israeli army has a rabbi to approve everything that is served here. But that's not good enough for Mr. Rakoff. He and his friends have their own special rabbi, and if he doesn't approve it, they starve to death. It's a big problem.

DANNY *(to KHALID)* Your colleague is polite.

*DANNY takes a cup of coffee.*

YOSSI Really?

DANNY You can have a reasonable discussion with him.

*YOSSI passes him sugar. DANNY adds it, stirs.*

YOSSI I haven't found that.

DANNY You think he's modern like you.

YOSSI We're all Greco-Roman.

DANNY Do you know the fifth commandment?

YOSSI "You shall not kill"?

DANNY That's number six. Number five is "Honour your father and your mother." What does this mean? It means that the prohibition against murder is to be obeyed only after your father and mother are properly honoured. Your colleague understands this. He remembers every day where his forefathers lived.

YOSSI *(to KHALID)* I don't like where this is going.

DANNY He remembers every olive tree that grew and every slaughtered goat. And his father will be properly honoured only when every Jew is driven from the land of his ancestors.

YOSSI *(to KHALID)* There we are. Do you want to respond?

KHALID Why?

*KHALID prepares to leave. He finds his cigarettes and a lighter as YOSSI continues.*

YOSSI *(to DANNY)* I agree with you, Danny. Be careful, he could explode at any moment. Did you know that in 1948 Inspector Yassin's father was expelled from a beautiful home in Jaffa and ever since— Wait, no, our army suspected that his mother's twice-removed second cousin on her uncle's side once knew the nephew of a terrorist so they demolished her house and ever since then—or maybe he grew up in a stinking refugee camp in Gaza and spent sixteen years squinting through a fence at rich Jews almost naked in their swimming pools. Still, he educated himself and became a decent man. But as we know, Danny, civilization is very thin, and every time he's humiliated at a checkpoint his resentment festers and the veneer is stripped away to reveal the worms eating the heart of a suicide bomber.

*KHALID leaves.*

Now, back to our business here. According to you, it was an hour between the end of your meeting with Mr. Tamir and the phone call in H1. Unless you are detained at a checkpoint, this is a drive that takes a few minutes. You told us you were lost. Do you expect us to believe you?

DANNY *is silent.*

Of course you don't care what I believe. You think there is one God, and he is your God, and he picked your little tribe and your little tribe is allowed to lie to us because we don't count. And in this case, it's true, what we believe makes no difference. But the judge is a different matter. And when he asks you what you were doing during those sixty minutes, if you sit there like a wart, you will end up in jail for a long time. It's not like killing an Arab, which of course they would call self-defence and for which all you would get is congratulations from your friends. This is a well-connected American. You may think him some variety of pig flesh but he has a family who loves him, and that family is like this *(crosses his fingers)* with the president of the United States. Which means there will be journalists in court every day from *The New York Times*, writing down every word, keeping a close eye on Israeli justice. Which means, I can practically guarantee, a life sentence, unless they manage to extradite you to America, where they fry people, in which case you will roast like a goat on a spit. Make my life easier, Mr. Rakoff, by telling me a story that makes sense, that can't be disproved by an idiot, and I'll do my best to help you. Maybe you have a real alibi, and are ashamed to tell. Or maybe you saw Mr. Philips walking down the street and were overtaken with nausea and an uncontrollable rage. Who would not sympathize with an act of passion? Or maybe God came to you as a burning bush, and said unto thee, "Danny, take this man unto a high mountain, or unto an alley if it's more convenient, and slaughter him for me, as a sign of your love."

KHALID *returns.*

DANNY *(stands)* You can insult me all you like, but I won't listen to disrespect for our Lord. *(begins to leave)*

YOSSI No.

*YOSSI pushes DANNY back into the chair.*

KHALID Mr. Rakoff. Here is our theory of the crime. You finished your meeting in the Old City. You drove west passing easily through the checkpoints. You went to the home of Mr. Philips's friends and waited outside for more than half an hour until he came out. You shot him, and drove away. Your car broke down. You knocked on a Palestinian door. The rest we know.

DANNY It's a good theory.

KHALID What is your theory?

DANNY I already told you.

KHALID You became lost and your car broke down.

*YOSSI's cellphone rings.*

DANNY Yes.

KHALID You became lost.

DANNY Yes.

KHALID So this was your first time, your only time in H1.

DANNY Yes.

YOSSI *(looking at his cellphone)* It's Dalit. *(answers)*

KHALID *(to DANNY)* Are you sure?

YOSSI *(into the cellphone)* What did you find?

DANNY *(stands)* Yes, I'm sure. I told you. I wrote it on—

YOSSI *(to DANNY, loudly)* Quiet. *(into the cellphone)* Say that again? *(a long silence as he listens)* Anything else? . . .

Dalit. Thank you very much. *(hangs up; to* KHALID*)* Hand me the file.

*KHALID does.* YOSSI *opens the file.*

*(to* DANNY*)* Sit down.

DANNY — What did she say?

YOSSI — *(sternly)* You want to sit down.

*DANNY sits.*

Your father was from Latvia—a lawyer.

DANNY — An accountant.

YOSSI — *(checks file)* You mother was—your mother lost her family at Treblinka. *(looks at* DANNY *for a reaction)* She studied law. She was the lawyer. They married in 1954, lived in Park Slope—Park Slope?—Brooklyn. Nice neighbourhood?

*DANNY is silent.*

They went to synagogue on the High Holidays. They attend the ballet, the most boring art form ever invented. They came twice to Israel, once in—who cares? They never got in trouble, Danny. They were modern people who accept the compromises necessary to live beside your neighbour. Then you came along. Nothing about your childhood. At university, you studied literature and look at this, anthropology, which is interesting because our victim was also a professor of anthropo—

KHALID — Archaeology.

YOSSI — Oh, that's right, archaeology. And this is where the trouble begins. You join groups. Militant groups, religious groups, militant religious groups. Now I read somewhere that many young people become involved in political organizations in order to have sex. But you, did you really believe that that schnitzel with the funny hat was the Messiah? God tells you: "Go study the Torah twenty-four hours a day." Then God changes his mind and says you should cut your hair and reclaim Jewish soil. And then he tells you "Go east." So on the nineteenth day of October 1995, you arrive in the Promised Land and, as far as anyone knows, you go right to Kiryat Arba, because, because, here it is, you have a sponsor, a friend, a certain Rabbi Schmuel Wineberg. And this is where our file ends. No trouble. No arrests. A quiet life in the land of milk and honey. *(closes the file)* Do you remember Baruch Goldstein, Danny? An American settler like you, except a doctor, who walked into the mosque at the Tomb of Abraham with a machine gun— *(to KHALID)* You remember.

KHALID Yes.

YOSSI *(to DANNY)* February 25, 1994. Dr. Goldstein killed twenty-nine people, injured one hundred and fifty, all busy at prayer. You know this part, Danny. Outside Hebron, a wondrous marble tomb was raised in the killer-saint's honour. Holy rabbis blessed his remains, idolizers came in multitudes to thank him for his act of Jewish kindness, infertile women came to pray for little Baruch Goldsteins of their own. It took five years—it was five years before the government of my country sent bulldozers to strike down this new Sodom, and even then the settlers rose up in righteous anger to protest the desecration of their hero's name. And among them, detained, so we know he was there, but never charged, fresh from America, Mr. Daniel Rakoff. The Lord's gift to the Holy Land. *(to KHALID)* This is what Dalit found. *(to DANNY)* Do you repent? Let this be your personal Day of Atonement. I will give you five seconds. *(counts silently)*

DANNY "He sacrificed himself for the sake of Israel, the Torah, and his land."

YOSSI I am familiar with the inscription on his tomb. This room is not a free country. I won't discuss it.

*YOSSI slides a sheet of paper to KHALID.*

KHALID What do you want me to do?

YOSSI Interrogate him. Please.

*KHALID hands the sheet to DANNY.*

DANNY What is this?

KHALID Read it.

DANNY *(looks)* It's Arabic.

KHALID Parking tickets.

DANNY Parking tickets.

KHALID Five parking tickets, starting January 30th—

DANNY I confess. Take me away. Lock me up.

KHALID Five tickets on your car, in west Hebron, within two hundred metres of where you claim your car broke down. Where you said you were lost. Where you just said you had been only once. We know you were there six times. You—

YOSSI Five tickets. You were there at least six times. You went back to west Hebron over and over and over. What were you doing?

*DANNY is silent. YOSSI slams the desk.*

What were you doing? What explains six visits to H1? Stealing Palestinian property? Did Professor Philips get in your way?

DANNY Other people drive the—

YOSSI *(with rising anger)* Or you were visiting a prostitute? That's the only—

DANNY Other people—

YOSSI —thing—that's a reasonable explana— What?

DANNY Other people drive the car.

*YOSSI finally understands. He and KHALID are stunned.*

YOSSI *(desperate)* What were they doing there?

DANNY You'll have to ask them.

YOSSI *(desperate)* What are their names?

DANNY I don't know. I don't keep track. The keys sit in the car. If somebody needs the car, he takes it.

YOSSI *(desperate)* I will come to Kiryat Arba and I will interrogate every one of you until I find out who was in west Hebron and on what days and what they were doing there.

DANNY I look forward to it. Can I go?

KHALID Go.

YOSSI *(with rising anger and frustration)* Let me tell you, Danny. I have decided you are guilty. Mr. Philips was executed in west Hebron. We can prove you were nearby. And motive? A settler? No problem. Unless you come up with another reason to explain why you were in west Hebron six times. A prostitute makes a good alibi. That would explain why you spent an hour in west Hebron on your way to nowhere. So if you confess to visiting a prostitute, and provide us with his name, you can go. I know this is embarrassing for you. We won't tell your wife. Or your rabbi. We're not like that. We won't tell God either. He's the jealous type. Your secret is safe with me, Khalid, and the newspaper of your choice.

KHALID Yossi.

YOSSI *(with rising anger and frustration)* Was it lust, Danny, or did you fall in love? You're among men. We understand these things. Say to us, "Look, it's a delicate situation. He's a nice Arab boy, I don't want to cause him trouble." And we know how it is after a few years of marriage. Who doesn't get bored? Who doesn't go looking for a little action on the other side of the ghetto? If you appeal to us as men, as human beings who laugh and cry and bleed, just like you—if you appeal to us as equals—you can go. Which is the bigger sin, Danny, to cheat on your wife or have sex with an Arab? Is it an extra sin to cheat with an Arab? Which commandment is that? Or maybe it doesn't count—because they're not of your tribe, it's more like bestiality than adultery. Is that what the Torah teaches? *(to* KHALID*)* You know what? I don't think it was love. What happens is, he goes to see his Arab lover, and he gets on his hands and knees . . . *(to* DANNY*)* . . . and he whips you, and you ask for this because you know you deserve punishment, and in this way, you live out your fantasies of divine retribution.

KHALID His or yours?

DANNY Can I go?

YOSSI No.

KHALID You can go.

YOSSI No.

KHALID Go.

DANNY *(waits to see if* YOSSI *reacts)* It's been a pleasure.

DANNY *exits.*

YOSSI It's not over.

KHALID Good. Let me know how it goes.

YOSSI Your problem is you care too much about facts. An artist would understand a man can be guilty in essence.

KHALID My problem is we have no evidence he committed the crime we know about, and a strong suspicion he did something we don't know about.

YOSSI Maybe we should have another look at Ms. Shehadeh.

KHALID Good idea. Let's waste some more time.

YOSSI He was in the right place at the right time. He has the right gun. He lied to the police. As for motive, everyone knows, Zealots hate archaeologists.

KHALID It's not enough.

YOSSI It's enough for me.

KHALID You talked about nuance? What are your feelings telling you?

YOSSI That he's guilty.

KHALID I'm sorry. I used the wrong word. Not your feelings—we know what they're saying. Your instinct. What is your cop instinct about Rakoff?

YOSSI That he's guilty of something.

KHALID Exactly.

YOSSI There will be a meeting with the Americans, the ambassador if he wants, a few of our people. I will tell them Rakoff did it, and have him arrested.

KHALID You won't.

YOSSI I will list the evidence and I will paint the picture and he will be charged with murder.

KHALID Two weeks later it will be thrown out of court.

YOSSI Two weeks? What country are you in?

KHALID And you will lose your job.

YOSSI I'll get a pension, I'll go to Paris, and sit in a café with your friend. You can visit.

KHALID Is this your contribution to the Palestinian struggle?

YOSSI These people want to go back three thousand years.

KHALID They're fascists.

YOSSI Yes.

KHALID Just so we're clear, they didn't take my country. It was people like you. I have to live here. I can't arrest people because I don't like them.

YOSSI He celebrated the mass murder of Palestinians.

KHALID I know people who celebrate the mass murder of Jews. Do you want me to arrest them?

YOSSI Our army already does that.

KHALID Yossi. I told you, al-Khalil is a small city. My family has been there for many generations. Among those killed by Doctor Goldstein were my mother's brother and his son, my cousin, my closest friend. Do you want to get serious with Rakoff? A false charge of murder against him? What does that accomplish? Nothing. It's symbolic. Do you want to find out what he's really up to? Do you want a confession? Let's bring him back. We'll torture him. I'm ready. I'll help. If he were a Palestinian in the hands of your army, that's what they would do. They'd keep him in jail for years without trial, and they'd destroy his relatives' homes. Are you looking for some equality of abuse between Jews and Palestinians? Here's your chance.

*The office phone rings.* YOSSI *answers.*

YOSSI *(into the phone)* What? *(to* KHALID*)* He wants his gun. *(into the phone)* Send him in. *(hangs up)*

*YOSSI takes the gun out of his briefcase and is about to remove the clip as DANNY enters.*

DANNY You see, Mr. Civilization. This is why we win. You shout, you threaten, you insult, and then what? "You can go." Your father was a real Zionist. They did what they had to do. They maybe compromised when they shouldn't have—who doesn't? They were pioneers. They remain a model for us. You? Your type?

*DANNY spits.*

YOSSI Here.

*YOSSI offers the gun. DANNY takes a step forward.*

DANNY Thank you—

*YOSSI lifts the gun, aims at DANNY. DANNY flinches. YOSSI moves the gun and fires, missing intentionally. DANNY reacts. YOSSI removes the clip and puts it in his pocket. He places the gun on the table, and walks upstage, his back to the audience.*

*The phone begins to ring.*

*DANNY takes the gun, exits.*

*Blackout.*

## REFLECTIONS ON *FACTS*

### INSPIRATION, CHALLENGES, AND EXPERIENCES IN WRITING AND PRODUCING THE PLAY

*Facts* was inspired by many things. First of all, my parents were Polish Jews who narrowly escaped the Holocaust. They survived the war in Uzbekistan, working in a textile factory. When the war ended, they headed west, to Europe, to search for relatives—without success. They ended up in a displaced persons camp in the American sector of Germany. A few years later, they were accepted for immigration to Canada, and in 1951 we arrived in Montreal. My brother was five; I was one.

My father had been a Zionist from an early age. In Montreal, he was a fundraiser and organizer for Herut, the right-wing Israeli political party led by Menachem Begin. Begin was to become a prime minister of Israel, but he was then better known as a leader of the terrorist gang that had blown up British soldiers and Arab and Jewish civilians in the King David Hotel. In my youth, Begin was an occasional visitor to our home.

In my twenties, I started writing plays, almost always on political subjects. Eventually I decided it was my responsibility to write about Israel/Palestine. I wrote *Masada* in 1981.

Sometime later, I became interested in Biblical archaeology. When I read about the unsolved murder of an American archaeologist teaching in the West Bank, I thought: I can write a play about this.

Writing the Jewish settler was tough. I don't know people like him, it's very hard to imagine how their brains work, and I have absolutely no sympathy for them. Still, a playwright has to try. The Palestinian cop came easier, but I had no confidence in my ability to get him right. I got great advice from Palestinian friends. The Jewish cop is, in a sense, me. At least he's the kind of grumpy Ashkenazi Jew I've known all my life. He flowed from my pen.

It was hard to get a production. I distrust it when playwrights say,

"People are afraid to do my work," but I think Canadian (and American) artistic directors are gutless when it comes to doing plays critical of Israel. *Facts* is a mystery story with a lot of comedy, a three-person (i.e., cheap) play—and audiences have loved it; but North American theatres won't produce it. The Manitoba Association of Playwrights (where it was workshopped), GCTC and NTO in Ottawa, and Vancouver's United Players are notable exceptions.

People at the Palestinian National Theatre read it and immediately wanted to translate and tour it, so that part was easy. But the actual production process, essentially raising money for a Palestinian-Canadian co-production, was arduous. A generous grant from the Canada Council for the Arts helped tremendously.

*Facts* has been very well received. I did quite a few talkbacks after performances in Ottawa and Vancouver, and in several cities in Palestine and Israel. Overall, audiences loved it. In Canada, audiences really liked the relationship between the two cops. Palestinians, though, are suspicious of official relationships between Palestinians and Israelis. The questioning was a bit tough at times. Still, it got standing ovations everywhere.

Informally, I've received a lot of positive feedback from Canadian theatre professionals, but not much where it really counts, i.e., in getting productions. On the other hand, it's had productions in Palestine, England, and Turkey. That's pretty positive feedback. I got to go to openings or galas in Bethlehem, London, and Istanbul. What could be better? And I wrote a play about an event in Hebron that was translated into Arabic and performed for the people of Hebron, and I was there, and afterwards a young woman asked me: "How do we learn to write plays like this?" What could be more exciting? What could be a greater honour than that?

# THE PEACE MAKER
BY NATASHA GREENBLATT

*For Luke, who wanted to see the world.*
*And for Alan, who gave us the maps.*

# ACKNOWLEDGEMENTS

I am deeply indebted to Andy McKim, Aviva Armour-Ostroff, and Kendra Fry at Theatre Passe Muraille for programming *The Peace Maker* as a part of their Buzz Festival multiple times, giving the play an audience, and giving me feedback and encouragement. I am grateful to all the actors who have been involved in the many workshops: Hrant Alianak, Sascha Cole, Eric Craig, Vivien Endicott-Douglas, Sara Farb, Susanna Fournier, William Greenblatt, Richard Greenblatt, Melissa Haddad, Natasha Hall, Sina Madahamiri, Jordi Mand, Lisa Norton, Adam Paolozza, Alex Poch-Goldin, Kaitlyn Riordan, Ben Sanders, and Richard Young.

The music in *The Peace Maker* could not have evolved without the miraculous talents of Ronen Segall and Mike Landoni, nor would the words have taken root without the guidance and support of the magnificent ladies from Nightwood Theatre's Write from the Hip Program: Jordi Mand, Aisha Sasha John, Meghan Swaby, Audrey Dwyer, and Anna Chatterton. I could not have finished this play without the challenging questions of Christopher Morris, Razi Shawahdeh, and b.h. Yael, the brilliant insights of Alisa Palmer and Richard Greenblatt, and the detailed workshop direction of Aviva Armour-Ostroff.

The Next Stage Theatre Festival production was blessed with the dedication and talent of Jennifer Brewin, Samuel Sholdice, Glenn Davidson, Lindsay Code, Raha Javanfar, Terrence Duraisami, Sarah Trachsel, Vivien Endicott-Douglas, Rebecca Auerbach, Jeff Irving, Sam Kalilieh, Michael Rubenfeld, Harveen Sandhu, Razi Shawahdeh, Emma Burke-Kleinman, Luc Mandl, James Plouffe, Maryem Tollar, Arie van de Ven, and Lauren Willis. I am forever grateful for the amazing fundraising committee: Orlando Buonastella, Celia Chassels, Kate Lushington, and Joyce Mason who brought the Island Feast to life. And to Kelly Straughn and all the hard-working people at the Next Stage Theatre Festival, thank you for helping make that production such a success.

Thank you to Emma Tibaldo at Playwrights' Workshop Montreal and Micheline Chevrier at Imago Theatre for asking me to keep digging.

And finally, deep love and gratitude to my fellow traveller, Amy Siegel, who has held my hand, dried my tears, made me laugh, and made me think again and again.

*The Peace Maker* was first performed at the Factory Theatre Main Space as part of the Next Stage Festival in Toronto on January 3rd, 2013, with the following cast and creative team:

| | |
|---|---|
| Sophie | Rebecca Auerbach |
| Ronen | Michael Rubenfeld |
| Wael | Sam Kalilieh |
| Haneen | Harveen Sandhu |
| Saif | Razi Shawhadeh |
| Oran | Jeff Irving |
| The Band | Emma Burke-Kleinman, Luc Mandl, James Plouffe, Samuel Sholdice, Maryem Tollar, Arie van de Ven, and Lauren Willis. |

| | |
|---|---|
| Director | Jennifer Brewin |
| Musical Director | Samuel Sholdice |
| Set and Lighting Designer | Glenn Davidson |
| Costume Designer | Lindsay Code |
| Projection Designer | Raha Javanfar |
| Stage Managers | Terrence Durasami and Sarah Trachsel |
| Assistant Director | Vivien Endicott-Douglas |

## NOTES ON THE TEXT

Acts 1 and 2 can be broken up by an intermission or played through.

A slash (/) indicates that the next line of dialogue begins, overlapping the current speaker.

English translations of Arabic and Hebrew text are included in square brackets for the benefit of the reader, where appropriate. These translations should not be spoken in performance.

*"What about identity? I asked.*
*He said: It's self-defense . . .*
*Identity is the child of birth, but*
*at the end, it's self-invention, and not*
*an inheritance of the past. I am multiple . . .*
*Within me an ever new exterior."*

—Mahmoud Darwish,
from "Edward Said: A Contrapuntal
Reading," translated by Mona Anis

## CHARACTERS

| | |
|---|---|
| Sophie | A young Jewish-Canadian woman travelling in the Middle East. |
| Ronen | An American-Israeli tour guide with Birthright. |
| Wael | A Palestinian man who runs a music centre in the West Bank. |
| Haneen | Wael's daughter, a musical prodigy and a teenager. |
| Saif | A young Palestinian man who volunteers at the music centre. |
| Oran | An Israeli Soldier who accompanies the Birthright trip. |
| The Band | Musicians who play both Israeli soldiers on the Birthright trip and Palestinian youth who attend the music centre. The actor playing Oran doubles as a member of the band when they are the Israeli Soldiers. The actor playing Haneen doubles as a member of the band when they become the Palestinian youth in the music centre. |

If the actors who are cast as Haneen and Oran play different musical instruments than those noted in the script, other instruments can be substituted and the text can be altered to reflect that change. Most importantly they should both be musically gifted, especially Haneen. The actor cast as Sophie should also be a strong musician and singer.

Musicians in the band should include those who play accordion, clarinet, violin, and ideally, a qanun. They should also be comfortable playing Klezmer and traditional Arabic music.

# ACT ONE

*Lights rise.*

## *CANADA*

*SOPHIE is alone onstage holding a guitar. She looks out at the audience. She opens her mouth as if to sing, but nothing comes out. A sound pulls her into the past. The space transforms. The band enters or is revealed. They are dressed as soldiers. They tune their instruments. There is a flurry of movement and sound. SOPHIE watches, remembering . . .*

## *ISRAEL*

*RONEN enters wearing a kippah.*

RONEN *(to the audience and the band)* Is everyone here? Good. Good. Welcome home!

*The band explodes into the first verse of "Ammunition Hill," which morphs into the Palestinian version of the Islamic Call to Prayer, sung by one male voice.*

## THE MUSIC CENTRE, NABLUS, THE WEST BANK

*SOPHIE and WAEL are in an old stone building with large windows.*

WAEL You play?

SOPHIE I played piano for years. Now I play in a band. It's kind of an Indie–Rock–Afro–Beat–New Folk sort of thing. And I love kids.

WAEL This is good. There is many children in need of teaching, many instruments in need of using.

SOPHIE I see that.

WAEL These were all donated in '74, before the Intifada.

*She goes to touch the instruments.*

WAEL I wouldn't touch, if I were you.

SOPHIE Why not?

WAEL Asbestos.

*Sophie looks at her hands.*

A joke. This is funny?

SOPHIE Right. Yeah. Sorry.

WAEL Before the Intifada we are innocent victims. After we are terrorists. What are we now?

SOPHIE I—

WAEL You know what this means, Intifada?

SOPHIE The uprising, right?

WAEL The shaking off.

SOPHIE I read about it before I came. I did a lot of research.

WAEL It is one thing to read, it is another to see.

SOPHIE I am so excited to see everything.

WAEL This is good. It has taken many years to bring this music centre to life.

SOPHIE It's beautiful.

WAEL You will have one class to begin. You will be teaching teenagers. Boys and girls.

SOPHIE That's great.

WAEL You will have a translator, of course. His name is Saif. He does not play, but his English is very . . . strong. He will show you around the city.

SOPHIE Thank you / so much.

WAEL You read our dress code policy?

SOPHIE Yes, is this . . .?

WAEL Your collarbone.

SOPHIE Oh, I—

WAEL It is not I who think—it is for the more . . . conservative elements of our society. We are not here to challenge, we are here to teach music.

SOPHIE And I totally get that.

WAEL If you are a . . . homosexual, it is better not to talk about this.

SOPHIE I—

WAEL I do not want to know.

SOPHIE Okay, but—

WAEL Or if, for sake of argument, you are Jewish. It would be best to keep to yourself.

SOPHIE But—

WAEL You are not here to teach them how you think back home. We have had other volunteers who wish to tell about gay parades and good Jewish people. If they ask you if you believe in God, you will say yes.

SOPHIE Of course, I just want to help.

WAEL This is good. We need friends from the outside. It has been a long time we have been closed. It is time to open. We need musicians, we need writers, we need artists. I myself am very busy with business matters, so I will leave it to you to make the curriculum.

SOPHIE It's an honour.

WAEL And please, no swearing.

SOPHIE Of course.

WAEL Do you have any questions?

SOPHIE Do you know where I can find balls?

WAEL Balls?

SOPHIE Yeah. I meant to bring some with me in case there wasn't . . . I have a warm-up game I play. It's a get-to-know-you kind of thing. I didn't know if I could get any—

WAEL You mean to throw?

SOPHIE Exactly. Do you have anything like that?

WAEL Yes. We have balls.

SOPHIE Great. Thank you.

WAEL I have found for you our best musicians—

SOPHIE Oh, they don't have to be good. I just want them to learn. I believe in the healing power of music.

*Beat.*

I'm sorry. That sounds so cliché.

WAEL No, I agree with you. You will meet my daughter?

SOPHIE I would love to.

WAEL Haneen! Tali! Haneen. She plays well, but she does not always listen. Haneen!

HANEEN *enters the room. She is wearing a hijab.*

I will take your passport and find Saif. This is good?

SOPHIE Great.

WAEL Haneen, Sophie. Sophie, Haneen. Hadi mutatawi'a jdeedeh e'ena. Koono latifeen. *[This is our new volunteer. Be nice.]*

WAEL *leaves.* SOPHIE *and* HANEEN *stare at each other.*

SOPHIE Hello.

*Silence.*

So . . . what instrument do you play?

*Silence.*

*(miming)* You. Play. What. In-stru-ment?

HANEEN I play the clarinet.

SOPHIE You speak English!

HANEEN Go home.

SOPHIE What?

HANEEN Go. Home.

SOPHIE But, I just got here.

HANEEN We don't need your help.

SOPHIE Your father—

HANEEN He needs you for the money.

SOPHIE I just want—

HANEEN When I see US AID written on the parks, on equipment, I feel sick. With one hand you give us swings, the other you give bombs to our enemy. We do not want your aid. Go home. Go back to America. Go. *Home.*

SOPHIE But . . . I'm Canadian.

*WAEL comes back into the room with SAIF.*

WAEL So, you have become friends? Haneen, you are nice with our guest?

HANEEN Yes, Yaba.

WAEL I speak to her in English since she was born. She is good, yes?

SOPHIE Quite good.

WAEL I introduce you to your translator. Sophie, meet Saif.

SAIF I hope to be of very help. I am very . . . uh . . . happy to be with you. And I am very touch to be your Arabic voice. I will learn much from this uh . . . connection with the world. Your class will open my eyes to the bigger—

WAEL Khalas, Saif. Khalas. He talks.

SOPHIE That's great.

WAEL You will see the city?

SOPHIE I'd love to.

WAEL Saif will take you. Haneen, it is time for homework. We will see you at dinner.

*WAEL and HANEEN leave.*

SAIF Yallah.

*SAIF gestures to SOPHIE to follow him. She does, but is stopped by a sound. We are back in Israel, on a Birthright tour.*

*The band plays "Ammunition Hill" underneath RONEN's speech.*

RONEN *(to the audience)* Ladies and gentiles, goys and girls, welcome to the Holy Land. Welcome to the land of your ancestors. Welcome to Israel.

*The band plays a burst.*

I'm assuming you're all Jews? Or halfers? You've got to have a grandmother or great aunt kicking around, or you wouldn't be here. Unless you're a faker, and let me tell you we can smell you from a mile away.

*He gives the audience a suspicious look.*

You are lucky. You are one of almost three hundred thousand lucky, lucky people. We have flown you all, at incredible expense, to the land of olives and figs, beaches and deserts, hummus and falafel, lemons and sexy girls with guns! But this is your right. Your *birthright*. And so this is what we call the trip. Birthright. And now, let me introduce the soldiers. They will be staying with us for the duration of our trip, and let me warn you, they love to party.

*The band plays a burst.*

On violin we have Oran Zayev *(ORAN plays a violin solo.)* . . . hailing from just outside of Tel Aviv, Oran is an old-school kibbutznik. But they're not communists anymore, so don't try and take a bite of his shawarma. On trumpet we have Olga. Originally from Russia, Olga moved to Israel when she was fifteen. She may look like an Aryan youth, but she's a Jew and she can prove it. *(OLGA plays a trumpet solo.)* And, let's not forget Alon! *(ALON plays an accordion solo.)* A medic from Jerusalem, Alon is a traveller, an artist, and a vicious poker player. Don't touch his gun, ladies, he has a girlfriend . . .

*The band plays a burst, and then softly under the beginning of the next scene, the music morphs into a Palestinian folk melody. It sounds like it could be coming from a shop window.*

## NABLUS

SAIF This is it. The Old City! Do you like?

SOPHIE It's beautiful. Helweh, right?

SAIF *(laughs)* Helweh, yes.

*He takes her through the stone streets, past overflowing carts of lemons and tomatoes, cucumbers and garlic. Past coffee stands and nut shops, into small alleyways with arched entrances. The stone is crumbled, turned into rubble. A sign reads: "Never forgive, never forget." Pictures of men with eyes of fire line the walls. Some of them are holding guns.*

SOPHIE Are these posters . . . are they pictures of suicide bombers?

SAIF No, no. They did not make the suicide bombs, these. These were killed by Israelians. These are Martyrs.

SOPHIE Then why are they holding guns?

SAIF Well, sometimes they use, you know this program, Photoshop?

SOPHIE You mean they *Photoshopped* the guns in these pictures?

SAIF Some, yes. For the family. To make proud.

SOPHIE I see.

SAIF Some are freedom fighters. This was where they studied to defend the city. Many fought the Israelians here in the invasions.

SOPHIE Invasions?

SAIF Please, don't be scared—

SOPHIE I'm not, / I was just wondering . . .

SAIF It's been a long time since any bomb. Everything is quiet now, since one year.

SOPHIE Is it okay to go out on my own?

SAIF Of course, everything is safe now. Like my name. Saif. I am Saif. You like this joke?

SOPHIE Right, yeah, but seriously. Can I walk around by myself?

SAIF It is just a bit—uh, how do you say . . . complicated. I do not, we do not want you to get lost. You just call me. I will take you to all the places you want to go.

SOPHIE Thank you.

SAIF You are welcome, Soapy. What kind of name is this, Soapy?

SOPHIE Sophie. It comes from Sophia. It means "wisdom" in Greek. But you can call me Sophie.

SAIF Sophie. Helweh. Helweh kteer. Sophie, don't worry. When you are with me, you are Saif! You want Arabic coffee? *(to a coffee vendor)* Quahweh! Quahweh!

*SAIF disappears. The band plays the soldier's theme.*

ORAN I can sit here?

SOPHIE Uh, sure.

*Beat.*

ORAN What are you reading?

SOPHIE It's a book about politics.

ORAN I don't like politics.

SOPHIE Oh?

ORAN You should read something more exciting. You are on vacation, no? This is your Birthright. Relax.

SOPHIE I think it's important to—

ORAN Do you like poetry?

SOPHIE Sometimes.

ORAN Canada, right?

SOPHIE That's right.

ORAN Leonard Cohen.

SOPHIE He's one of my favourites. You know him?

ORAN He is a Jew.

SOPHIE Right.

ORAN I would like to see this Canada.

SOPHIE Which part. It's kind of big.

ORAN Where are you from?

SOPHIE Toronto.

ORAN This is the part I would like to see.

*The lights dim as the soldiers transform into Palestinian youth.* HANEEN *joins them. They tune their instruments noisily, making annoying, ugly sounds.* SAIF *is trying to get them to behave.* SOPHIE *stands beside* SAIF. *Lights rise.*

## THE MUSIC CENTRE

SOPHIE *(in a hushed tone)* I think I'm going to be sick.

SAIF Oh, my dear. There is a washroom if you need—

SOPHIE No. No. I'm just. I'll be fine. *(She takes a deep breath.)* Hello, everyone, my name is Sophie.

*She looks at* SAIF *to translate.*

SAIF Ahlan Wa Sahlan. Belferqa eljdeedeh, ahlan w allah eywaffeqom, hadi mo'allemetkom, Soapy. Wu Heyye musieqiyeh mashhura kteer, kteer fi Canada, wa ajat min hunak la hone a'ashan ta'allemkom, wu law samahto koono muhtarameen wu bala za'araneh. *[Hello to the new band, welcome and God be with you. This is your teacher, Soapy. She is a very, very famous musician in Canada and has come all the way to teach you, please show her some respect.]*

*The class laughs.*

SOPHIE What? What did you say?

SAIF I introduced. They will play for you? Yallah. E'ezifu!

*The students start to play "The Ants Go Marching One by One." They are terrible. Slowly, as they play, they improve, transforming into the Israeli soldiers, playing "Ammunition Hill."*

RONEN *appears. The band plays softly while he speaks.*

RONEN (*to the audience*) Who here still celebrates Shabbat? Anyone? Our day of rest? Here in Israel, it is a National Holy Day. The city shuts down. Businesses close, busses stop running. We all . . . stop. Some say that Israel does not keep Shabbat, Shabbat keeps Israel. What days do businesses close where you live, huh? What holidays do you get from school, from work? You are living in a Christian state, never forget this. But here, here we have rugelach in every bakery, mezuzahs on every door, and matzo in all the supermarkets. And every Friday evening . . . Shabbat. Here, we are the majority. Doesn't it feel good?

*The music stops.*

## NABLUS

SAIF It went great!

SOPHIE What are you talking about? It was a disaster! The boys were talking the whole time and the girls wouldn't look me in the eye for fuck's sake. Sorry.

SAIF They love you, I can tell this.

SOPHIE If by love you mean they thought I was full of shit, sorry, then yeah, they really, really did. I'm sorry, I keep—

SAIF They are just nervous. Here boys do not spend time with girls before they marry. We do not, how do you say, uh, hang out.

SOPHIE But how do you find a girl you like? How do you fall in love?

SAIF When I see her, I will know.

SOPHIE Love at first sight?

SAIF Yes, but uh, more physical. This is the woman who Allah has picked for me. They say you lose your mind. You cannot speak for days. They say your hands are hot and your face is red. They say you cannot breathe.

SOPHIE That sounds like love at first sight to me.

SAIF May I ask, I do not wish to be rude, but, uh . . . have you ever been in love?

SOPHIE I, yeah, of course, you know . . . you know . . . I don't really want to talk about it.

SAIF You are sad.

SOPHIE It's just not something I'm interested in right now. I think there are more important things.

SAIF There is nothing more important than love.

SOPHIE Right. Saif, do you know where I can buy a lamp? These florescent lights are killing me.

SAIF A lump?

SOPHIE Yeah, you know. Like, a small light bulb, with a hat, that I could put near my bed to read.

SAIF Ahhh. Perhaps my mother, she has something.

SOPHIE Oh, no. I'd be happy to / buy one or . . .

SAIF You must come for dinner!

SOPHIE I would love to—

SAIF You must meet my family. My new baby nephew! He is just born.

SOPHIE I would love to—

SAIF I am so happy! My little nephew. My little Jihad.

SOPHIE Jihad?

SAIF This is his name. Jihad. You don't like this name?

SOPHIE No, it's just—

SAIF Oh. I see. You think this means violence. No, no, no. Jihad, this means struggle, the struggle to be better person. This word is a beautiful word, not an ugly word. I see. You think it means holy war. You think it means bombs and towers falling. No, that is just the little Jihad. The big Jihad, Mohammad says this, the big Jihad is within.

SOPHIE Right.

SAIF I understand. We will call him Juju. This is better for you. Juju, the most perfect little big Jihad. You will come and visit?

*The sound of a clarinet brings us to . . .*

## *THE MUSIC CENTRE*

*One week later.*

*HANEEN is playing "Autumn Leaves." She plays beautifully. SOPHIE enters. She stops at the door and listens. Suddenly HANEEN sees SOPHIE. She stops playing abruptly.*

HANEEN What you are doing?

SOPHIE I didn't want to disturb—

HANEEN You are spying.

SOPHIE No, I—I didn't know you played jazz!

HANEEN You think Palestinians play only Arab music?

SOPHIE You're really good.

*Beat.*

Where did you learn?

HANEEN My mother.

SOPHIE Oh, is she—?

HANEEN She is dead.

SOPHIE Oh god. I—I didn't know. I'm sorry.

*Beat.*

So . . . where is everybody?

HANEEN Picnic.

SOPHIE But it's our class time!

HANEEN They like picnic.

SOPHIE Well, it would be nice if someone told me these things. Where's Saif? He's late again!

*Beat.*

So, you like jazz?

*Beat.*

I did my master's thesis on the influence of African slave music on the lineage of American folk music and how it continues to inform the independent rock scene to this day . . . .

*Beat.*

I brought my guitar.

SOPHIE *brings her guitar out of the case while she talks.*

I play cello in this band, but recently I've been making my own music. I've been experimenting with peddles, looping my voice. I've been working with some standards . . .

*SOPHIE starts to play Gershwin's "Summertime." HANEEN pretends to ignore her. SOPHIE starts to sing. For a while it is somewhat uncomfortable. HANEEN lets her suffer. But finally she can't help herself and she starts to play, following SOPHIE's lead. Eventually HANEEN gets lost in her own world. SOPHIE stops playing and just stares. HANEEN plays with the spirit of something else, as though she can't stop. She stops.*

HANEEN I know what you are doing.

SOPHIE What do mean?

HANEEN You try to be my friend so you can say, "I met this little girl in Palestine and she was so smart and she play so pretty, let me show you her picture, oh and here is an olive tree and a donkey cart and some chickens." I help you make a good vacation, yes?

SOPHIE No!

HANEEN Then why do you care?

SOPHIE Okay, look. You are pretty fucking good. Sorry. And . . . and . . . that makes me excited because I think music is . . . powerful. So why don't you give me a chance? And maybe, just maybe, you might learn something. Or don't. But—but I think—I think you love music as much as I do.

*Beat.*

HANEEN You know nothing of me.

SOPHIE So help me get to know you.

*Beat.*

HANEEN What it is you want to know?

SOPHIE If you could be any animal, what would you be?

HANEEN This is a stupid question.

SOPHIE You're right. Okay, okay. Do you want to be a musician when you grow up?

HANEEN When I grow up?

SOPHIE Like a career. I mean it's hard. Like very, very hard. But I think you could do it. You would have to go to school, of course. Maybe not here, maybe not in Palestine, / but you could be . . .

HANEEN This is my country.

SOPHIE I know that, I just mean, if you want to be good.

HANEEN I cannot be good here?

SOPHIE Of course. But if you want to be a professional.

HANEEN You are professional?

SOPHIE Sometimes.

HANEEN Saif, he says you are famous.

SOPHIE He did? I—well, I guess you could say that. In my . . . community.

*Beat.*

HANEEN I will go to live in America. Minneapolis.

SOPHIE I thought you hated Americans.

HANEEN I have a fiancé. He lives there.

SOPHIE A fiancé? How old are you?

HANEEN I am seventeen. This is not so young.

SOPHIE That's exactly what I thought when I was seventeen. Now I'm twenty-seven and I feel like a baby.

HANEEN Here you are too old to marry.

SOPHIE Fuck. Sorry. So who's the guy?

HANEEN My cousin. He move to America when he is a child.

SOPHIE You mean your second cousin, like—

HANEEN My mother's brother's son.

SOPHIE Oh.

HANEEN You think this is bad, right?

SOPHIE We just don't really do that where I come from. I think there's even a law or something.

HANEEN Here, this is normal.

SOPHIE I don't judge you. I think it's important not to bring my own cultural bias—

HANEEN I meet him once. He bought me a pizza and he says he is in love with me. He is a big man, very rich. He has a job and he wears a nice suit. This is lucky?

SOPHIE Do you think it's lucky?

HANEEN It is easy where you are. You pick someone out and then you say, I do not want, I will return. My father and mother, they fall in love. It is not possible for me. My father, he wants I leave, to go to America.

SOPHIE But what do you want?

*Soldier's theme.* ORAN *appears.*

ORAN If you could be any animal, what would it be?

SOPHIE What?

ORAN This is a serious question.

SOPHIE Sorry. Okay, any animal? Does it have to be real?

ORAN What other animal is there?

SOPHIE Well, it could be, like, a magical animal, like a unicorn or a griffin.

ORAN This is up to you.

SOPHIE I don't know. Maybe some sort of fish. I've always wanted to be able to breathe underwater. What about you?

ORAN I want to be a grasshopper. He lives in the grass, but every so often he leaps up and gets to sees the world from another perspective.

SOPHIE A grasshopper? Huh.

ORAN A grasshopper and a fish, they do not meet so often.

SOPHIE They don't have a lot of common ground.

ORAN Then I will just have to learn how to swim.

*The sound of a woman singing an Arabic melody brings us back to . . .*

## THE MUSIC CENTRE

*HANEEN is sitting, listening to the voice. She starts playing and singing along. WAEL enters. He listens until she stops.*

HANEEN Yaba?

WAEL Haneen . . . How are you, hayati?

HANEEN Tamam, bas—

WAEL English, Hayati.

HANEEN Yaba—

WAEL Haneen. English. You must be prepared.

HANEEN Yaba, I don't want to go.

WAEL We talk about this.

HANEEN This is my country. I want to fight for my country like you and—

WAEL Haneen.

HANEEN Like you did before. You fight before, why not me?

WAEL It was a different time.

HANEEN I want to go. I want to go on Friday. I will be careful, I promise, I—

WAEL No.

HANEEN Please—

WAEL NO. I forbid you. Look at me! I forbid! I cannot afford to lose you too, you know this.

*Beat.*

Khalas, Hayati. You have work to do. It is exams soon, this is right?

HANEEN Yes, Yaba.

WAEL I will be proud of my Hayati when I hear how good she does in school, yes?

HANEEN Yes, Yaba.

*HANEEN exits.*

## *SOPHIE'S APARTMENT, NABLUS*

*SOPHIE is playing and singing a song that she is writing, using the melody of "Yerushalayim," a Hebrew folk song. It isn't going very well. A knock at the door.*

SAIF Ding-dong.

SOPHIE Come in!

*SAIF enters with a lamp behind his back.*

SAIF Hello, little Soapy! It is I, your translator! I have a gift to make your house warm!

SOPHIE A lamp! Saif, you shouldn't have.

SAIF I ask my mother where to find and she looks into her closet and says, "Aha!" She says it is for you.

SOPHIE It's beautiful.

SAIF You must come and tell her yourself.

SOPHIE I've been meaning to come.

SAIF You are welcome.

SOPHIE Oh, sorry. Thank you.

SAIF When I say you are welcome, I mean you are welcome in my home, you are welcome in my country.

SOPHIE Saif . . . would you like to come in?

SAIF I should not, it is not—uh, proper—

SOPHIE Okay.

SAIF —but maybe . . . to help you put in the light?

SOPHIE Right, I might not be able to figure it out.

SAIF Then I must come in!

*He walks in, holding the lamp.*

SOPHIE I haven't really decorated or anything.

SAIF It is very good.

SOPHIE Would you like some tea?

SAIF Shukran.

*SOPHIE leaves to get the tea. SAIF looks around the apartment, finds a plug, and plugs in the lamp. He turns off the lights. SOPHIE comes back, holding the tea.*

SOPHIE Oh, it's dark!

SAIF I am ready with the light. One, two, three . . .

*The light turns on.*

SOPHIE It's lovely.

SAIF This light is a very, very beautiful light.

SOPHIE Thank you, Saif.

*She pours him some tea. There is a slightly awkward pause.*

So. What do you do? Besides translating.

SAIF Me? Well, it is, uh . . . how do you say . . . uh, I have never told anyone before.

SOPHIE That's okay, you don't have to—

SAIF No, no, no . . . I want for to tell you. Of course I want. I will make a business. A tourist business. Taking tourists on, uh, tours around the city. I will show them my Palestine. Not weapons and fighting. No! I will show them delicious food, tea and coffee, olive trees, orange trees. Beautiful things. Beautiful places.

SOPHIE This place is so beautiful. You know, sometimes I don't want to leave.

SAIF You will live here forever?

SOPHIE No. I mean. I have a life back home. Work. Stuff. You know. But sometimes, I imagine.

SAIF You are welcome.

SOPHIE Do you ever want to run away, Saif?

SAIF Run away? I do not understand.

SOPHIE Just, you know, leave your home, start fresh. Anywhere in the world. Paris, or—or India!

SAIF I would love to go to Jerusalem, one day.

SOPHIE You've never been? It's so beautiful!

SAIF We're not allowed.

SOPHIE Right. Sorry.

*Beat.*

SAIF I would like to see where you are from.

SOPHIE It's not all that interesting.

SAIF It must be. One day I will see this Canada!

SOPHIE You are welcome.

*Soldier's theme.* ORAN *enters.* SAIF *disappears.*

ORAN You see those people? This is a bar mitzvah they are having for their youngest son. These people are very beautiful. They are religious, but they fight.

SOPHIE Why does that man have a gun?

ORAN — Last year an Arab, he walks into a yeshiva, a school with young men, and shoots. Now these men, they always carry guns.

SOPHIE — And they're just allowed to / walk around . . .

ORAN — When I was in training, I always used to sit with the Orthodox at meals. They sing when they eat. They are very beautiful, very good people. Listen.

*The band softly hums "Yerushalayim."*

Eze yofi!

*Someone in the band replies in Hebrew. The humming continues.* ORAN *laughs.*

They think we are . . . in love.

SOPHIE — Us! That's funny! I mean / . . .

ORAN — They are congratulating me. East meets west, they say. I would be so lucky.

SOPHIE — What are they singing?

ORAN — It is a song about Jerusalem.

*The humming stops.*

## THE MUSIC CENTRE

HANEEN *enters, distressed.*

HANEEN — I cannot attend your class any longer.

SOPHIE — What?

HANEEN — It is not what is important.

SOPHIE — What do you mean?

HANEEN School, this is important.

SOPHIE Okay, but—

HANEEN I do not have time to waste on music. Soon we have exams. They read our marks on the radio. I have to study. I have to concentrate.

SOPHIE I'm sure you can do both, I—

HANEEN There is no time, I have to work. I have to work!

SOPHIE I don't understand. Why are you so upset? Haneen, what's going on?

*Beat.*

HANEEN There is a protest today. In a village nearby.

SOPHIE What protest?

HANEEN They build a wall through the village. The Israelis. Families cannot visit. Farmers lose their land. I will go.

SOPHIE What does Wael think?

HANEEN Do not tell my father. Please.

SOPHIE Is very dangerous?

HANEEN No. Yes. But I will go.

SOPHIE Right now? By yourself?

HANEEN Yes. You will come?

*The band plays "Ammunition Hill." RONEN enters. The music quiets down as he begins to speak. Throughout this speech, we see SOPHIE and HANEEN at the protest.*

RONEN All right, c'mon, everyone. Off the bus! C'mon. I want you to see something. This, my friends, is "the wall." At least, that's what it's called by people who hate us. The Wall. But we, we call it a security barrier. Since it was built we have had no more suicide bombers and much less violence. Do we want this barrier that separates us from our brothers and sisters in Judea and Samaria? And if I say West Bank, you will be scared, no? So I will call it by its proper, ancient name: Judea and Samaria. Do we want this barrier? Of course not! But until the terrorists can admit that we have a right to be here, a right to this land, until then we will continue building this barrier to keep the good guys safe and the bad guys out.

## *SOPHIE'S APARTMENT, NABLUS*

*SOPHIE and HANEEN are washing their faces. SOPHIE looks at HANEEN, she is shivering. SOPHIE takes the towel and starts to wash HANEEN's face.*

HANEEN You see how it is?

SOPHIE Yes.

*Beat.*

I—I couldn't see. That stuff, they sprayed—

HANEEN It is tear gas. They shoot tear gas.

SOPHIE I couldn't breathe. My face was burning.

HANEEN Yes.

SOPHIE They didn't have to do that. We weren't doing anything wrong. We were peaceful. Why did they spray us?

HANEEN Because they can. Last week a man, a Palestinian, he is shot with a tear gas canister. He is killed. But I think they do not shoot the gas at internationals. I think if you are there . . . I did not think they would shoot this at you. I am sorry.

SOPHIE Your father—

HANEEN My father, he forbid me to go. But how can I not see this wall? How can I not see this occupation? And if I see it, how can I not go?

*Long pause.*

SOPHIE Can I try?

HANEEN What?

SOPHIE Your scarf. Can I try it on?

HANEEN You want to wear?

SOPHIE Can I?

*Beat.*

HANEEN But this means you are my friend.

SOPHIE I hope so.

HANEEN *takes off her hijab and starts to put it on* SOPHIE.

HANEEN Because we unveil our heads, we unveil our hearts. We must tell a secret.

SOPHIE Okay. Well. I can't think of one. You go first.

HANEEN You are going to think I am silly. You can not tell anyone, but . . . I love black men. Dark black, like American black. It is terrible, but I am in love with LeBron James.

SOPHIE That's your secret?

HANEEN It is terrible, isn't it?

SOPHIE No, it's not terrible.

HANEEN There, like that.

SOPHIE How do I look?

HANEEN So pretty.

SOPHIE I think you are pretty.

HANEEN No, I look too brown.

SOPHIE But, you just said you like / black . . .

HANEEN It doesn't matter what I like, it matters what my husband likes.

SOPHIE No. It matters what you like.

*Beat.*

HANEEN It is your turn for a secret.

SOPHIE Oh god. Okay. I don't know! I don't have any secrets.

HANEEN That is impossible. Everyone has secrets.

SOPHIE My secret is . . . I think you could be a great musician.

HANEEN That is not a secret—

SOPHIE I'm serious! How much could you accomplish if you became known? You could be an ambassador, a spokesperson!

HANEEN What is this?

SOPHIE You could do so much more than that protest. We were just . . . cattle getting gassed, with no power, no impact! But if you became good, like really, really good? Like famous? You would have power. You would have a platform to tell the world what's really going on here.

*Beat.*

HANEEN You do not have to be here. You are safe and free where you live. Why do you do this? Why do you come here?

SOPHIE Because . . . I don't think it's right. I don't agree with what's going on. It makes me ashamed—

HANEEN Ashamed?

SOPHIE And I know some Jews—

HANEEN You are friends with Jews?

SOPHIE Everyone's friends where I come from, Jews, Arabs—

HANEEN They kill my mother. You saw them. They think we are animals. They treat us like dirt to be swept aside.

SOPHIE Not all Jews—

HANEEN You see those lights over there? Those are the settlements. They build on top of us. It is better to be more high, more powerful. Last week in the village, they come down and burn twenty olive trees. They piss in the well.

SOPHIE I am so sorry.

HANEEN Why are you sorry? It is not you who do this.

*Beat.*

SOPHIE I have never seen anyone with as much talent as you without formal training. You could really—

HANEEN Khalas. Come. Look at yourself.

*HANEEN leads SOPHIE to the mirror.*

Kifek, ya helweh? *[How are you, beautiful?]*

SOPHIE Il Hamdilella. Ou inti? *[I'm good, God willing. You?]*

HANEEN Tamam. Shukran. *[Good, thank you.]*

SOPHIE Inti sababa? *[You're cool?]*

HANEEN Sababa! Yes, yes, I'm cool.

*The girls giggle.*

Today, this is our secret.

## THE MUSIC CENTRE

SOPHIE *is now leading her much-improved class in a fairly decent performance of "When the Saints Go Marching In."*

SOPHIE One, two, three, four. Good. F sharp, Ahmed! Louder, Roula, I want to hear you!

*The song ends.*

Good. Good! You have all improved a tremendous amount! You know, I think we need a name.

SAIF A name? I do not understand.

SOPHIE A name for our band. I think we need a name, so that if we play in front of people we can say we are . . . you know, like the Beatles.

HANEEN Like . . . the Rage Against Machine!

SOPHIE Exactly! What should we be called?

SAIF *explains in Arabic. There is a flurry of conversation.*

HANEEN They say we could be Al Talib. This means the Students.

SOPHIE Could it be . . . something in English? Just so if we, you know, if we played for people who aren't Arab they could understand.

SAIF What about the Explosions of Light from Allah?

HANEEN Stupid! They will put us in jail!

SAIF Maybe—uh . . . Sophie and the Palestinians?

SOPHIE No, no. I want it to be about you guys, not me.

HANEEN I know, I know. We should have the name the Horns of Freedom. You see it is a joke yes, the horn like the trumpet and the horn like the bull. We are playing for freedom.

SOPHIE That's great! But how about the Horns of Peace?

HANEEN No. I do not think that is very good. Freedom, they will like this.

SAIF This is very good name.

*He tells the students. They all nod in assent.*

SOPHIE Well, Horns of Freedom it is.

HANEEN We will play for people?

SOPHIE What do you guys think? Would you like to play a concert?

SAIF *translates. They all talk amongst themselves.*

SAIF Yes, but they are nervous. They say they are not ready.

SOPHIE Well that's why we have to practise. Let's do our favourite.

SAIF *translates.*

Yallah. One, two, three, four . . .

*They play "The Ants Go Marching One by One." As they play, the music transforms into one of the songs of the Israeli soldiers.*

RONEN *appears.*

RONEN You see, back home, we have it all wrong. We think of ourselves as weak. Before I made Aliyah, before I moved to Israel, I was from a small town outside of New York. I was bad at sports, beaten up, the clown. This is what we are back there. A nebbishy scholar who never gets the girl, or to get the girl we gotta be a doctor, or a lawyer, or a psychiatrist. A neurotic writer. Look, I came here and I found my people. No tame house cat Jews in Israel. Wild Jews. Fearless Jews.

*The music stops.*

## *WAEL'S OFFICE*

WAEL *is working.*

SOPHIE Do you have a minute?

WAEL Yes?

SOPHIE The kids are doing really well. I wanted to tell you that. The improvement in just a few months . . . it is really incredible. We can actually play some songs now, and they actually sound good. So, I was wondering if you had any access to music, Arabic music. I want the kids to play songs from their own background.

WAEL I will see what I can do.

SOPHIE Thank you. And . . . I want to extend my stay.

WAEL Walla?

SOPHIE If you don't mind.

WAEL How long?

SOPHIE Another two months.

WAEL This is good.

SOPHIE I know! And I'd really like to have a goal for the students. I think it would give them a sense of accomplishment. I heard about this big event in Israel called the Good Deeds Day. They sponsor different groups, different projects.

WAEL Projects?

SOPHIE Peace projects.

WAEL I see.

SOPHIE I was thinking maybe we could propose a concert. In Jerusalem. Somewhere where people could meet and start a dialogue.

*Beat.*

WAEL Did you know that it is illegal in Israel to publicly commemorate the Nakba? The disaster? On the anniversary of Israel's independence we have a different memory; a memory of over a million of people turned into refugees, a memory of massacres, a memory of pain. This is the Nakba. But can we hold a vigil?

SOPHIE If Israelis could meet these kids, they might not find it so easy to label them. If they could hear the music / they might . . .

WAEL My dear. You do not know these people. They have to hate us, they must fear us. Otherwise they would have to give up their privilege. And people do not like to give up privilege.

SOPHIE People live up to the expectations we set for them. Like children, if you expect the worst, then that's exactly what you'll get.

WAEL My wife was like you. An optimist. But that was a different time. Now we have seen what happens when we compromise. It is not the time to roll over, to kiss feet. It is time to fight. Not with words, not with music. With actions.

SOPHIE People respect a diplomat.

WAEL No, my dear, they despise a diplomat. They respect power.

SOPHIE There's money involved.

WAEL You think I would betray my people for money?

SOPHIE It's not a betrayal, it's a concert. It can't do any harm.

WAEL It is not an option. You may extend your stay for a month. We will see how it goes. Do you understand?

SOPHIE I understand.

*She goes to leave.*

WAEL Haneen, she tells me you are doing a good job. She is happy. I am very . . . happy to see her like this.

SOPHIE She is very talented, you know. She should have the opportunity to perform.

*Beat.* WAEL *laughs.*

WAEL Yallah, go. I have work to do. Yallah.

*She goes.* WAEL *mutters under his breath, shaking his head.*

Hemarah ras'ha nashef. *[Stubborn little donkey girl.]*

## TEL AVIV

*SOPHIE and ORAN stumble out the back door of a club. They are very drunk. The band plays a Eurodance beat loudly as the door opens, continuing faintly when the door closes.*

SOPHIE Oh my god, / oh my god, that was—

ORAN Sophie, Sophie . . .

SOPHIE I've been to clubs before, but that—

ORAN Come here.

SOPHIE Grinding, hands all over—

ORAN You are very—

SOPHIE And those . . . They were all over you.

ORAN Who?

SOPHIE Those . . . girls.

ORAN I did not notice. I was watching you.

SOPHIE You were?

ORAN Of course.

*Beat.*

SOPHIE What?

ORAN Come back with me.

SOPHIE But—

ORAN I need to take off all of your clothes.

SOPHIE Oh god, oh god—

ORAN — Now.

SOPHIE — Okay.

*ORAN disappears.*

## SOPHIE'S APARTMENT, NABLUS

*SOPHIE is playing the last verse of Bob Dylan's "Don't Think Twice, It's All Right" on the guitar. SAIF is listening.*

SAIF — Huh.

SOPHIE — It's one of my favourites. You know, I think I put it on all of my breakup mix CDs.

SAIF — It is sad. I do not like this.

SOPHIE — Yeah, it's sad, but it's true, you know?

SAIF — Ah. Yes. Do you know the Ace of Base?

SOPHIE — Ace of Base!

SAIF — Now that is a band! They are my best band. All my friends, we listen to the Ace of Base.

SOPHIE — I used to listen to them when I was in grade six. I used to love them.

SAIF — See, we are the same. We have the same best bands!

SOPHIE — What's your favourite song?

SAIF — I like the one, it is about life is beautiful.

*SOPHIE sings the first line of the chorus of "It's a Beautiful Life" by Ace of Base. SAIF joins in with the first line of the chorus of "All That She Wants." SOPHIE joins him and they finish the line together. They laugh.*

Now that's a band.

SOPHIE Yeah, I guess you're right. They are pretty good. Hey, you have a good voice! How come you never sing with the band?

SAIF No, I cannot sing.

SOPHIE First of all, everyone can sing. And second of all, you *can* sing. I just heard you.

SAIF I am a translator, not a musician.

SOPHIE Do you know any Palestinian folk songs? I've been trying to track some down, but Wael is so busy.

SAIF My mother, she sings me songs since I was born.

SOPHIE Will you sing me one?

*SAIF makes a "tsk" sound with his tongue on his teeth.*

Losamaht? Pretty losamaht?

SAIF Khalas.

*She begs and he finally relents. He sings her "Al Dalo'ona."*

SOPHIE Saif. I can't believe you've been holding out on me. What does it mean?

SAIF It is very hard to translate. In Arabic when you say air, it could mean breeze, or it could mean love. It talks about this air, this breeze, this love that comes from the north. In this song he says how this wind, this love, she changes all my life and she continues to torture me. But in a cute way.

SOPHIE Saif! You have to teach it to me. It's so beautiful.

SAIF You are beautiful.

SOPHIE Saif.

SAIF No, let me say this. You are good to come to Palestine

and help us. And you are very beautiful and sing very sweet. You are very good.

SOPHIE Well, thanks.

SAIF But don't worry, I won't eat you.

SOPHIE What?

SAIF Well, if we say this meal is good, this means we want to eat it. But I say, you are good. But don't worry, I won't eat you. I promise!

SOPHIE Thanks?

SAIF You will come to see my family? They want to cook for you.

SOPHIE Oh god, I'm sorry. I completely forgot. I've just been so busy with the students and—I will come soon. I promise.

SAIF Inshallah.

*Beat.*

SOPHIE I'm trying to organize a performance for the students.

SAIF This is wonderful.

SOPHIE I want to bring them to Jerusalem to play!

SAIF We are not allowed to go to Jerusalem. I have never been in my life.

SOPHIE I think I can make it happen.

SAIF How do you do this magic?

SOPHIE I got in touch with this organization, this peace organization, and they would be willing to help us get the permits. Saif, the Horns of Freedom!

SAIF Wael, he knows about this?

SOPHIE This is an amazing opportunity, Saif. We can play in front of other people, show them how wonderful Palestinian kids are.

SAIF Who will we play for?

SOPHIE The concert would be at a home for old people. Israelis. It would mean so much to them to hear young people play music. It is so important for people to meet, to realize that we're all just human.

SAIF There are people here . . . they would not be happy / if we . . .

SOPHIE What if we played for Arab-Israelis?

SAIF Well . . . maybe this—

SOPHIE So what if we just say that we're playing for Arab-Israelis?

SAIF A lie?

SOPHIE A small one. Imagine for one second how amazing it could be. Palestinian kids who've never met Israelis before, except soldiers, meeting Israelis who've never seen these kids except in the news, throwing stones. Don't you want everyone to know how beautiful these kids are? It's like an advertisement for Palestine.

SAIF I thank you, but—

SOPHIE Don't you want everyone to see your Palestine? What if, instead of waiting for the world to come to us, we brought Palestine to the world?

*Beat.*

I need you. I can't do this on my own.

*Beat.*

SAIF I do not know if this is a good idea.

SOPHIE I'll talk to everyone myself. You'll have to help me, of course. But we can do it. I know we can. It's basically just a field trip! Why does it matter *who* we're playing for? Don't you want to go to Jerusalem?

SAIF You are truly a magician if you can bring us there.

SOPHIE Trust me, this is going to be great!

*The band plays "It's A Beautiful Life" by Ace of Base, klezmer style.*

RONEN *appears.*

*The music stops.*

RONEN *(to the audience)* Smell that air! Ahh. We have climbed Masada. This is where a small group of Jews fought the Roman Empire for seven years. For seven years we held them off from the heights of this mountain. It is better to be up high. But nothing lasts forever. When the Romans finally took Masada, what did they find? Nine hundred dead Jews. They had killed themselves before becoming slaves in their own land. They preferred death to defeat. We are an insistent people. And we will die before we give up our land.

*Beat.*

When young soldiers finish their training, this is where they come. And do you know what they say, at this moment? Masada will never fall again.

*Beat.*

Let's try out the echo, shall we?

*He yells the following, listening for the echo after each word:*

I!

Love!

ISRAEL!

*Lights dim to black.*

# ACT TWO

*Lights rise.*

## *INSIDE A SMALL TAXIBUS*

*SOPHIE, HANEEN, SAIF, and the students are on their way to the concert. Arabic pop music (played by the band) is blasting.*

SOPHIE I am so excited. Saif, are you excited?

SAIF WHAT?

SOPHIE ARE YOU EXCITED?

SAIF INSHALLAH!

*Beat.*

SOPHIE How are you feeling, Haneen?

HANEEN WHAT?

SOPHIE CAN YOU ASK HIM TO TURN IT DOWN?

*SAIF asks in Arabic. Nothing happens.*

ARE YOU EXCITED, HANEEN?

HANEEN I HAVE NEVER SEEN JERUSALEM BEFORE THIS.

SOPHIE I CAN'T BELIEVE THAT. YOU LIVE SO CLOSE.

HANEEN WHAT?

SOPHIE SUCH A SHAME!

*HANEEN yells very loudly at the driver in Arabic. The music stops.*

Well, that's better.

SAIF I do not believe they let us cross the checkpoint.

SOPHIE I can't believe you've never been to Jerusalem before, it's so close!

HANEEN You see? They do not treat us like human beings. They treat us like animals, to be kept in their cage.

SOPHIE They are very scared, you know. If these Israelis really see you they will be forced to look at you as human beings. If they hear you play—

HANEEN I thought we play for Arabs.

*Beat.*

SOPHIE We're playing at an old folks' home. For Jewish Israelis.

HANEEN But you tell me—

SOPHIE I know. But this was the only way to get us all here.

HANEEN Saif?

*Beat.*

SOPHIE I'm doing this for you. So people will hear your music. Don't you see? This is the first step.

HANEEN I—I cannot do this.

SOPHIE Please. We've come this far.

*Beat.*

HANEEN The others, they will not like this.

SOPHIE Let's ask! Let's take a vote and see. Saif, let's ask them.

SAIF If you think it is right.

SOPHIE Everyone! Can I have your attention? *(to the driver)* No, not you, please, keep looking at the road. Saif, will you translate for me? Tell them they are going to perform for Israelis. Tell them they are going to perform for old men and women who survived the Holocaust.

SAIF They do not know what this is.

SOPHIE The Holocaust?

SAIF They are from the camp.

SOPHIE Okay. Um. Just say what I say. Everyone, I have something to say! Sixty-five years ago a terrible thing happened in Europe. The prime minister of Germany decided he didn't like the Jews and tried to kill them all. Six million Jewish people died.

HANEEN Is it that we kill them? Why we have to suffer for this six million?

SOPHIE You shouldn't. But that's why, sometimes, the Israelis, the Jewish Israelis, are so emotional.

HANEEN So because they are emotional, they can take our land?

SAIF Do not listen to her. We do not like this man, Hitler.

SOPHIE Saif, will you try to explain to them? I want them to know, before we go. So no one says anything . . . inappropriate.

*He starts speaking Arabic to the students. The soldier's theme begins to play.*

## *SOPHIE'S HOTEL ROOM, TEL AVIV*

*SOPHIE and ORAN are in bed.*

SOPHIE East meets west. Not a bad line.

ORAN It is not a line, Sophie. It is truth.

SOPHIE Yeah, sure. So . . . here we are. East and west. I guess. Hello.

ORAN Hi. Sophie.

SOPHIE I don't like it when you use my name.

ORAN Why?

SOPHIE I'm just not used to people saying my name a lot.

ORAN Do most people call you "hey you"?

SOPHIE We just don't use names that much. We just talk.

ORAN All right. Let us be like this. Let us just talk.

SOPHIE Okay.

*Silence.*

What should we talk about?

ORAN Do you like music?

SOPHIE No, I hate music.

ORAN Really?

SOPHIE Of course I like music, everyone likes music.

ORAN Not everyone— / oh, okay. I get it.

SOPHIE No, I'm sorry. Can I start over?

ORAN If you like.

SOPHIE I love music. I'm a musician.

ORAN Like me! This is wonderful! We should play together sometime.

SOPHIE Um . . . sure. Sometime.

ORAN When?

SOPHIE I don't know. I wasn't really expecting . . .

ORAN I was not expecting either.

SOPHIE Oh, come on. I mean, that's the thing about these trips, right. Everyone knows that. Come to Israel, sleep with a soldier, climb Masada, and you're done, right?

ORAN You're upset.

SOPHIE It's just. I know why you're doing this.

ORAN This?

SOPHIE I know you were told to—

ORAN Seduce you?

SOPHIE It's part of the job description.

ORAN It isn't forbidden, exactly.

SOPHIE Exactly.

ORAN But I would not have, if I did not like you.

SOPHIE This is crazy.

ORAN Look, we met. We were attracted. We had fun. This is normal, no?

SOPHIE I guess.

*Beat.*

I think—

ORAN Stop thinking. What are you feeling?

SOPHIE I feel . . . confused.

ORAN What else?

SOPHIE Happy. I guess.

ORAN I feel the same.

*Beat.*

SOPHIE I don't usually do things like this.

ORAN What? Sex?

SOPHIE So . . . quickly.

ORAN Me too.

SOPHIE Oh, come on.

ORAN Okay . . . okay. So I am not a virgin. I don't think you are, either.

SOPHIE No.

ORAN But I do not have sex with just anyone.

SOPHIE Really?

ORAN I am not, how you say . . . a slut?

SOPHIE Not that that's necessarily a bad, I mean I have been a—at certain times, and I think it's totally fine to express your sexuality—

ORAN I do not cheat.

SOPHIE Okay . . .

ORAN I am not a cheat. You should know this about me.

SOPHIE That's good.

ORAN I want to be good. I try . . . to be good.

SOPHIE I think we all do, don't we?

ORAN It is not always so easy.

*Beat.*

SOPHIE Have you—have you ever . . . Have you ever killed anyone?

*Beat.*

ORAN What do you think?

SOPHIE Have you ever killed anyone who was innocent?

ORAN Some times it is hard to tell the difference.

SOPHIE A child.

ORAN Sophiesophiesophie. It is good to ask questions. This is part of being Jewish, no? To ask questions. Ask me anything you like. I won't be offended.

*A long pause.*

SOPHIE What does it feel like?

ORAN What?

SOPHIE To kill someone. How does it feel?

## *JERUSALEM*

*The students get ready for the concert, tuning their instruments.* SOPHIE *talks to the audience.*

SOPHIE Hi, everybody! So, um, first of all, I'd like to thank you so much for having us. Today's performance is part of the Good Deeds Day. And as such, we are here to perform a good deed. But the deed isn't just the music. It's an offer. An offer to meet, to get to know each other. These young people are kind, they are generous, they have worked really hard to be here today . . . But I won't keep talking! I'll let the music speak for me! All the way from Palestine—

*There is a commotion in the audience.* SOPHIE *speaks louder.*

All the way from the West Bank, ladies and gentlemen— Excuse me, please! Don't get upset. Please. MAY I PLEASE HAVE YOUR ATTENTION!

*The audience settles down.*

Thank you. Ladies and gentlemen, we are the Horns of Freedom and we are playing for peace! One, two three, four . . .

*The students play the first chord, which turns into a soft sustained minor drone.*

RONEN *enters. He speaks over the music.*

RONEN *(to the audience)* Friends, we are losing our witnesses. It is necessary, vital, that we remember. But more than that. To remember is one thing, to refuse to let it happen again, that is another. People say, but how did this happen? We were many, they were few. How did we let this happen? At Masada we were warriors, why not then, too? Like lambs to the slaughter, we Jews did not fight back. Sometimes I don't understand it myself.

*Beat.*

But no more. We will fight to protect ourselves and we will kill if necessary. The world does not protect the peaceful, the timid. Jews have become warriors of necessity. To live in the middle of the Middle East, we must be eagles. We must be lions. We must show no mercy, for none was shown to us.

*The music stops.*

## INSIDE THE TAXIBUS

*SOPHIE, SAIF, HANEEN, and the students are on their way home. It is late evening.*

SOPHIE I can't believe that happened.

SAIF When they all stand up at the end!

SOPHIE When they all stood up at the end! Haneen, you were brilliant. Did you hear the silence during your solo? I've never felt a silence so powerful.

SAIF They said congratulations to me! I did nothing, I tell them. It is all Sophie.

SOPHIE I couldn't have done it / without you, Saif.

SAIF These little old women with blue hair and pink lips. They were scared at first. But then—

SOPHIE When I said Palestine, I thought there was going to be a riot!

SAIF I almost ran and hid behind the tuba!

SOPHIE Haneen? Are you okay?

*Beat.*

HANEEN They apologize to me. For the hardships. I never think they talk to me like this.

SOPHIE And that man at the end, the one that stood up and sang the song in Hebrew—

HANEEN He came after the concert and told me I look like his granddaughter. He told me about living in a hole for six months, eating dirt and leaves. He lost everyone. I feel . . . sorry for him. We are the same. We both suffer.

SOPHIE They shook my hand and said what a great job I did. What a huge step for peace. They told me they had never met anyone from the West Bank before.

HANEEN How old are you, they ask. Keep playing, they say. I feel so . . . so . . .

SAIF I cannot believe how good it went!

SOPHIE It couldn't have gone any better. The organizers were so happy. The newspapers came. I gave an interview!

SAIF My mother will be so happy!

HANEEN Maybe I will go study.

SOPHIE Maybe we can do another one . . .

*The taxibus comes to a stop.*

I wonder if I should contact the press back home?

*Beat.*

That's a lot of cars, why so much traffic all of a sudden?

SAIF It is a flying checkpoint.

SOPHIE What?

HANEEN It is when they put a checkpoint up where it is not normally there.

SAIF Anywhere there could be a checkpoint.

SOPHIE How long will it take?

HANEEN It could be long, we cannot tell. I know! If you go with your passport and say you are late for a very important meeting, they will let us through. Go. Go up.

SOPHIE Really?

SAIF This is true.

HANEEN We should not be late.

SOPHIE Okay, I guess. I'll just be a second.

*SOPHIE goes to talk to the soldiers that are guarding the checkpoint. She approaches two soldiers who have their backs turned. They carry automatic rifles.*

Excuse me? Hi. Sorry to bother you. I have a bunch of kids who need to get back home. I have a Canadian passport. I'm an international?

*One of the soldiers turns around. It is ORAN.*

ORAN Sophie?

*He grabs her in a large hug. They stay there for a while. Finally she pushes him away.*

I can't believe this.

SOPHIE What are you doing here?

ORAN I am doing my job.

SOPHIE Your job?

ORAN We are looking for someone. A terrorist.

*Back in the taxibus,* HANEEN *and* SAIF *notice what is happening.*

HANEEN Saif. Shoof. *[Look.]*

SAIF Mish ma'aool, bihdon fiha hal wisikh, hada elhaki mamnoo'a, lazim atla'a, wu a'amal ishi. *[This is impossible. She is embracing the donkey soldier! This is forbidden. I should go out. I should do something.]*

HANEEN Walah, ehda, tenheblish. *[Relax. Don't be an idiot.]*

*At the checkpoint,* SOPHIE *and* ORAN *continue.*

ORAN What are you doing here?

SOPHIE I'm here with my students. I need to get them home now.

ORAN In front of all these other people?

SOPHIE I need to get them home.

*Beat.*

ORAN Where are they?

SOPHIE The bus.

ORAN *walks slowly towards the taxibus. He shines his flashlight right into* SAIF *and* HANEEN*'s faces, resting on* SAIF*'s face for a few beats. He walks back to where* SOPHIE *is standing. She is frozen, watching him.*

ORAN Let me see your passport.

SOPHIE Very funny.

ORAN I mean it.

SOPHIE Fine.

ORAN *(looks at the passport and then shouts to the other sol-*

*diers)* Ten la la'avor, ani mekir ota, hee b'seder, ten la'em la'avor. *[Let her pass. I know her, she's harmless. Let them pass.]* Okay. Yallah.

*He reaches over and touches her face.*

We had fun, no?

SOPHIE I have to go.

ORAN Sure. Call me if you ever find your mind.

SOPHIE Right.

SOPHIE *walks back to the taxibus and gets in.*

It's okay. We can go.

SAIF You know this Israelian?

SOPHIE No.

HANEEN But, you look like—

SOPHIE Let's just get home.

*A sound brings us back to . . .*

## *SOPHIE'S HOTEL ROOM, TEL AVIV*

ORAN It is hot in the summer and sometimes my eyes lose focus, and everything, it starts to look the same. The light brown of the desert blends with my uniform, their faces. My enemy. One minute is all it can take.

He is walking towards me and he is smiling. I yell for him to stop. But he is still walking, walking and smiling. He could not be much older then ten, maybe eleven, twelve? But he is a fat one, all chub and flesh.

I shoot my rifle into the air. LA! But he doesn't stop, see? No, and he starts walking faster. I think he's laughing, see. Laughing at me. I shoot. Once for the legs, like I've been trained. Then again. People are screaming, but I do not hear them. Once more and then wait until the buzzing stops.

I walk forward, and there he is, on the ground. Ten, maybe eleven. I lift his shirt and see his fat little belly. And then I get it. He's . . . what do you call it? He's . . . retarded. Mentally retarded. And he's still smiling. That's the awful part. Three bullets and he's still smiling.

How does it feel? It feels like death grew inside me.

*A long silence.*

SOPHIE You were scared.

ORAN No, not scared. My brother, he joins the army next year. Paratrooper. Now I am scared.

SOPHIE People make mistakes in war.

ORAN This country is made of mistakes.

SOPHIE Then why do you do it? Why do you fight for—

ORAN What would you have me do?

SOPHIE You could say you've become religious, or that you have an anxiety disorder. There are ways. I read about it. Or you could refuse. People do that, too—

ORAN Only cowards let other people die for them.

*Beat.*

Besides. I have just finished my three years. I am free now.

SOPHIE What are you going to do?

ORAN I have no fucking idea.

*She kisses him.*

You know, when I start in the army, I want to make things better. I think it is easier to make change from within.

SOPHIE And is it?

ORAN Sophie, look at me. There are rockets that come down every night into the village where I was born. We have to protect our families.

SOPHIE But when does it stop? They send rockets, you send bombs. They blow up busses, you blow up schools—

ORAN They hide behind civilians—

SOPHIE So you kill the ones the get in the way? With weapons that keep people burning days after they were hurt. Bombing in dense cities. Houses gone. Children killed. It's inhuman.

ORAN This is true. We are not without blame. But what can we do?

SOPHIE Well, for starters, get out of the West Bank.

ORAN It's not that easy. I was one of the soldiers sent to rip settlements out of Gaza. Arresting our own men. Pulling women from their homes. And what did we get in return? More rockets.

SOPHIE But you're punishing Gaza. It's an open-air prison. It's a nightmare. How are people supposed to move on when they can't work, can't feed their families. When their families are dead.

ORAN I do not know. To be truth, I cannot see an end. Perhaps we get pushed into the sea, perhaps we kill them all. Perhaps we all keep living like this forever.

*Beat.*

Sometimes I would like to leave. Move far away.

*Beat.*

SOPHIE Where would you go?

ORAN Anywhere. Will you come?

SOPHIE We could move to Paris and write erotic poetry for a dollar a word.

ORAN We can go to India and learn to cook.

SOPHIE You don't know how to cook?

ORAN Cook, I wrote the book on cooking. But Indian food, this is something I would like to learn.

*Beat.*

You smell nice—

SOPHIE It's my shampoo.

ORAN —like lavender and sweat.

SOPHIE Hey!

ORAN I like this smell. I like you.

SOPHIE I—I like you too . . . I was thinking that after the trip, I would go there.

ORAN Where?

SOPHIE Palestine.

ORAN No, I will not allow—

SOPHIE Allow?

ORAN You don't know—

SOPHIE Don't tell anyone. Promise.

ORAN They are animals. If they know what you are—

SOPHIE Have you every actually met a Palestinian?

ORAN Sophiesophiesophie. I don't want to talk politics anymore. I am on vacation. Look where we are! Come here. Come back to bed.

*She does.*

*The scene shifts as* RONEN *appears.*

RONEN *(to the audience)* The Chinese have a country. The Italians have a country. The Arabs, they have many, many countries. Why should we, the Jewish people, not have a home? What will happen when next they want to slaughter us? And I say "when" and not "if." And you are fooling yourself if you think: "we are safe, we are assimilated . . ." What did the Jewish people think in Germany? What did the Jews of Russia think? We have *always* been persecuted. When, and not if, they next want to kill us, we will be ready. And you will be glad to have a refuge house. That is what we are: a refuge house, a sanctuary. We will not abandon you. Do not abandon us.

## WAEL'S OFFICE

SOPHIE, SAIF, *and* HANEEN *have just returned from the concert.*

WAEL Where were you?

SOPHIE I told you, we were at the concert. There was a flying checkpoint and—

HANEEN Yaba, it was amazing. We play for hundreds of people.

WAEL Where were you? And no more lies.

SOPHIE Lies? I—

WAEL Already there is an article online. "Canadian makes peace with music." Where. Were. You.

SOPHIE Okay, okay. Just—we went to Jerusalem, like I told you. But . . . it was just a bit different than I thought. You see, this organization that helped us get the permits, they have this, this mandate, for cross-cultural dialogue and—we played for a group of Holocaust survivors, old people with . . . with deep-set prejudice. They shifted. I could see them shift.

SAIF It truly was—

WAEL Sit down.

*They sit.*

You lied to me.

SOPHIE I didn't know it was going to be Israeli—

WAEL Do not lie to me again.

SOPHIE I . . . It was the only way it would happen.

*Beat.*

WAEL You took our children to play for Israelis. Without my permission.

SOPHIE Saif and I, we gave everyone forms to take home, and—

WAEL Shu mallak! Saif, how could you have been so—

SAIF Wael, it was Jerusalem.

WAEL I see now how you have abused, for your own—

SOPHIE Can we just calm / down—

SAIF She did not mean to—

WAEL Sneaking—

SOPHIE Not exactly—

WAEL Behind my back!

SOPHIE I just thought—

WAEL Did you mention my name?

SOPHIE I thought it would be good for the centre if—

WAEL Kharrabtu eddinya. *[You ruined everything.]* For the community to think I would allow their children to perform for Holocaust survivors.

SOPHIE I wanted to show them that both people have suffered—

WAEL Do you think this fight is equal? Between two equal victims? This is a struggle between the occupier and the occupied. This community has been invaded three times. It has been put under curfew for months at a time. The men and women have been arrested, beaten, and killed. They have watched their relatives in Gaza incinerated, all in the name of this Holocaust. Do you think there would be an Israel without the Holocaust? And now we are to be performing monkeys to weep with them?

HANEEN Yaba, it was not like that.

WAEL W enti wala— *[You keep your—]*

SOPHIE It was inspiring! If we built on this, we could really do something. I had so many requests for other performances.

HANEEN Yaba, if I learn to play so beautiful, they will listen. I can make them listen to me.

*Beat.*

WAEL You will pack your bags.

SOPHIE Now?

SAIF Wael, this—

WAEL This is for certain.

SOPHIE But my flight's not till—

WAEL Then you must go to Tel Aviv and lie on the beach and recuperate.

SOPHIE This isn't fair.

WAEL Fair?

SOPHIE I'm not ready to leave.

WAEL That is too bad.

*Beat.*

There are people in this community who do not feel gently for "normalization." I expect to see consequences for these actions, and soon.

SOPHIE I'll speak to everyone. I'll take responsibility.

WAEL It is much, much too late for that. I have lost their trust. I have let someone take our children. My child. What were you thinking?

SOPHIE I wanted to do something, to make up for, because I felt . . .

*Beat.*

WAEL Why did you come here?

*We hear campfire singing and a guitar strumming faintly in the background.* SOPHIE *is sucked back in time to remember . . .*

## *INSIDE A BEDOUIN TENT*

*RONEN is sitting on pillows. ORAN stands behind him.*

RONEN Come in, come in.

SOPHIE You wanted to see me?

RONEN A chat. You enjoyed the camel ride? Of course it was late and dark, and it was more like a camel sit, but still. A camel is a camel.

SOPHIE What are you doing here?

RONEN He is concerned about you.

SOPHIE What are you talking about?

RONEN He likes you.

SOPHIE *(to ORAN)* Why is he talking about you like you're not here?

RONEN What do you think of the army?

SOPHIE What?

RONEN What do you think of the Israeli Army?

SOPHIE I—I'm a pacifist.

RONEN But you feel for the terrorists, no? You support their right to violence, no?

SOPHIE I just want everyone to be safe.

RONEN What do you know about this conflict?

SOPHIE I've done my research.

RONEN You've taken a few classes in university, read some left-wing propaganda, and now you can give us all a lesson, is that how it is?

SOPHIE No, I just—

RONEN We are inhuman? No? We experiment on civilians? No?

SOPHIE Did you tell him what I said?

RONEN We are his family.

SOPHIE ORAN?

ORAN I want to thank you.

SOPHIE What?

ORAN For helping me clarify my position.

SOPHIE This isn't you, this isn't you talking.

RONEN Why did you come here?

SOPHIE You said . . . you know it's not right, you said . . . we talked about—

RONEN Why did you take our money? To spit in our face?

ORAN That does not mean I do not love my country.

SOPHIE A country that makes you kill?

ORAN My country.

SOPHIE But it isn't yours.

RONEN How beautiful, a Jewish love story. Filled with conflict and debate. Here this is possible. There the women cover their body, they do not leave their house. Here you are free to have whatever opinion you want. But. I don't want the other participants to feel uncomfortable. You will keep your mouth shut for the rest of the trip or you are on the first plane home.

SOPHIE You can't do that.

RONEN Watch me.

SOPHIE I won't go. I won't get on the plane.

*Beat.*

RONEN I'll leave you two alone. Oh . . . and if you're thinking of going there afterwards? I wouldn't mention you're Jewish if I were you. You might not like what you find.

*He leaves.*

SOPHIE You told him everything.

*Beat.*

I've found a place to stay. It's a music centre. I'll be working with kids, teaching music.

ORAN What do you think you are doing?

SOPHIE Something. It's better than nothing, right?

ORAN Not always.

*Beat.*

I will go back to the army. I have decided. Another five years.

SOPHIE This isn't you.

ORAN You do not know me very well.

*Beat.*

Don't tell them who you are. Trust me.

## *THE MUSIC CENTRE*

*SOPHIE's attention returns to HANEEN, WAEL, and SAIF.*

SOPHIE I'm Jewish.

*Beat.*

HANEEN So . . . ?

SOPHIE Jews killed your mother. I thought—

HANEEN Israelis kill my mother. Soldiers, they kill my mother. There is a difference.

WAEL So it is because of this? I should have known.

SOPHIE You knew?

WAEL Of course. I do my research.

SOPHIE And you let me—

WAEL There are many North American–Jewish people who come here to erase their guilt about Israeli racism, this is not new. That you come straight from spending time on a propaganda tour with soldiers, this gave me pause. But I did not imagine this.

SAIF You spend time with soldiers?

SOPHIE I went for a free trip. They give a free trip to anyone with Jewish heritage, so I . . . But now I—I'm on your side.

SAIF The soldier, at the checkpoint. Who is he?

SOPHIE He was on my trip.

SAIF Is he your boyfriend?

SOPHIE No, I . . . Saif. I met him on a trip. We—

SAIF You lie in a bed with a monster and you come here and infect us with your poison. Sharmouta!

WAEL Bas, bas!

HANEEN Saif!

*SAIF leaves.*

Yaba. We play for hundreds of people. I meet Israelis for the first time. Yaba, they were crying. They love me, Yaba. They listen to me. How is this bad?

*Beat.*

WAEL They love your mother very much, as well. She play many concert in Israel. You are not like other Palestinians, they say. This is a compliment? I am travelling abroad to raise money for the school. I take you with me. You miss your mother very much. When I hear about the invasion, I call her immediately. I am fine, just take care of our daughter, take care of Hayati. She tells me she is talking with her Israeli friends. They will not hurt me, she says. She is speaking to an Israeli news station, she calls them daily to report. She tells them a tank is approaching our house. Tell them we are civilians, she says. Tell them to go away. They attack the house while she slept. Her Israeli friends cannot help her. The Red Cross, stationed 100 metres away cannot help her. I cannot help her. For years, I tried to get justice. A mistake, they say. "Collateral damage." Now I do not believe to be on speaking terms with your enemy is the solution. We are not pigs to be slaughtered in our pen.

SOPHIE I . . . I . . . I—

WAEL This is why our people do not respond to collaborating with our enemy. We have watched our brothers and sisters burn in Gaza. How can we sing for our killers?

*We hear a loud banging, like a knock on a metal door or a prisoner hitting the bars of their cage.* SAIF *returns.*

SAIF The police are here. They want to speak with you, Wael. The parents, they call the police.

WAEL, SAIF, *and* HANEEN *leave.*

RONEN *appears.*

*While* RONEN *speaks, we see* SOPHIE *packing in her apartment.*

RONEN *(to the audience)* We are not here to convince to you move to Israel. No. We love our country, it is the best country in the world, and we would welcome you, of course. But we are not here to convince you of anything. We are here to show you another side. Not the side you see in the mainstream media. When you read in the newspapers about the evil Israel and its terrible soldiers, I want you to remember these soldiers. I want you to challenge those people who say: Israel, what a horrible, violent, no-good country. I want you to tell them, "I was there, and let me tell you, it's pretty nice!" This place is for you. For all of you. For Jews everywhere. Without you, why would we be doing this? Why would we be risking our lives and the lives of our children every day?

*Beat.*

I am a Jew. We are Jews. We are the same.

RONEN *leaves.*

## THE MUSIC CENTRE

SOPHIE *sits among her bags. The sound of a woman's voice singing in Arabic is heard.* HANEEN *enters.*

SOPHIE Haneen. I'm sorry. I'm so, so sorry. I just wanted to show them how beautiful you are.

HANEEN I have never felt so good.

SOPHIE But—

HANEEN When I was playing—I feel so . . . strong.

SOPHIE I shouldn't have brought you there.

HANEEN Maybe this is true. But you did. You bring us from Palestine to Jerusalem. This is a big thing.

SOPHIE A stupid thing.

HANEEN But a *big* stupid thing. And it is so big that it opens me, it cracks me open and now I feel big too, like I can make things change.

SOPHIE Well, I'm glad. I'm glad you feel like that—

HANEEN I want to come with you.

SOPHIE What?

HANEEN My father, he wants for me to go to America, to marry, but this is not what I want. I want to go with you.

SOPHIE I—Haneen.

HANEEN I know it is not easy, but maybe if we try hard, we apply for visa. Or, I go to America to marry, but instead, I run away. I will come and live with you. I can work, I will not just take from you. I will work hard.

SOPHIE Haneen, I can't do that.

HANEEN But you said I could be professional. You said I could be famous. But I need to train. You say this.

SOPHIE I can't take responsibility for you. I wrecked everything. The music centre's closed. Your father— He's already lost so much.

HANEEN But it is what I want that matters.

SOPHIE Don't you see? I fucked up! I made a huge, huge mistake. And I don't even know how I'm going to start making it right. But helping you run away . . . helping you disobey your father after I—I can't. I can't take responsibility—I'm not your mother.

HANEEN I am not wanting of you to be my mother.

SOPHIE Of course not. I—

HANEEN I am not wanting that because you are not even half as good as my mother. You are nothing compared to her. You are dirt.

SOPHIE Haneen, please—

HANEEN My mother was more beautiful than you can ever be, and smarter, and funnier.

SOPHIE Haneen—

HANEEN She play music better than you will ever play. She played so beautiful the air stood still and the birds stopped singing and the machines stopped working and I stopped breathing. I would stop breathing when she played. I wish the soldiers had killed you, instead of my mother, so she could be alive and you could be dead.

SOPHIE I . . . I—

HANEEN You make me big with your ideas and now I have nothing.

*SAIF comes in.*

SAIF Come, now. Haneen, Wael . . . he ask for you.

SOPHIE Goodbye. I'm sorry. I— Goodbye.

*HANEEN leaves.*

SAIF I will wait for you outside then we will go, yes?

SOPHIE I should have listened to you.

SAIF Yes.

SOPHIE I'm sorry.

SAIF You say that a lot, but what does it mean?

SOPHIE Right, I know. Canadians say sorry a lot, but really. I mean it.

SAIF My mother, she sends her regards.

SOPHIE Oh! I'm so . . . right. I see. Please, send her my regards.

SAIF And my regards to your family too.

SOPHIE Thank you for coming with me.

SAIF This is my job. Besides, I do not trust these drivers, they may ask you for five shekels instead of three.

*Beat.*

Why did you not tell me that you were Jewish?

SOPHIE Because I was scared.

SAIF And now? You are scared?

*SAIF leaves. SOPHIE is left alone. She goes to pack her guitar. She pauses. A sound brings her back to . . .*

## *CANADA*

*SOPHIE is alone onstage, holding a guitar. She looks out at the audience, as in the beginning. She opens her mouth and starts to sing "The Underneath City." She starts off quietly, almost hesitantly. As she sings, different instruments join her voice. Musical themes from throughout the play return. As the instruments join her, her voice grows in power and confidence.*

*The song finishes. SOPHIE looks out at the audience.*

*Blackout.*

# THE UNDERNEATH CITY

Lyrics by Natasha Greenblatt, music by Samuel Sholdice.
Sheet music can be obtained through the Gary Goddard Agency

*To the underneath city*
*To the people on the ground*
*To the hands that are burning*
*Screaming to be found*

*We all ache for freedom*
*But some of us have plenty*
*And it's written on our forearms*
*To prove that we are strong*

*I'm descended from suffering*
*That's made me tall and proud*
*We all fear the victim*
*'Cause he's angrier than God*

*It's an old revolution*
*And it's haunting us*
*Haunting like a hunger*
*When the hunger has no name*

*It's a younger sister's revolution*
*And we're hurting her*
*We're hurting and killing her*
*Making her feel shame*

*So it's time to weigh the losses and the gains*
*Against a future that is empty*
*'Cause there's no one left to trade*

*And it's time to shake the dust off these false idols*
*False idols we curse and foul and blame*
*Heavy shackles binding to a land we've claimed*

*To the underneath city*
*To the people on the ground*
*To the hands that are burning*
*Screaming out their song*

# REFLECTIONS ON *THE PEACE MAKER*

## INSPIRATION, CHALLENGES, AND EXPERIENCES IN WRITING AND PRODUCING THE PLAY

I am from Toronto, the child of theatre artists with a somewhat loose Jewish identity. When I was a kid, Israel seemed like the happy ending to the young adult Holocaust fiction I ravenously consumed. When I went to university in Montreal, at a school where students rioted when Benjamin Netanyahu came to speak, I realized there was a lot more I needed to learn. But the dates and facts never seemed to stick in my mind. I felt I had to go there to have an informed opinion.

In 2009, just after the horrifying attack on Gaza that left over thirteen hundred people dead, my friend Amy and I went to Israel on Birthright, a free trip available to young Jews in the Diaspora. Then, in an effort to spend time on both sides of the wall, we volunteered as drama teachers with Project Hope, an NGO based in Nablus, a city in the West Bank. During my time in Israel and Palestine I met many people who surprised me. I saw many things that devastated me. I laughed and cried and played a lot of theatre games.

On a bus back to Nablus from Jerusalem, I met a Palestinian-Canadian woman who told me about an Arab-Israeli music teacher who had recently taken a group of young Palestinian musicians from the West Bank to Israel to play a concert at an old folks' home. After the field trip, the music teacher was banned from the community and her school was shut down. The community had been outraged by what they considered an act of "normalization" of the occupation.

The story stuck with me. It rattled in my brain and wouldn't leave me alone. It seemed like such a clear example of how the best intentions can go awry. I decided to weave together the Arab-Israeli music teacher's story with my own experiences and create a new story: the story of a Jewish-Canadian woman who, in an act of hubris, brings together two worlds and finds herself doing more harm than good.

When I produced the play at the Next Stage Theatre Festival in 2013, we had just witnessed another harrowing attack on Gaza. Watching from a writer's residency on the Toronto Islands, I felt helpless. I thought about a Palestinian man who ran a community centre in Nablus, who had said "Go back and tell them what you saw." His words echoed our Birthright trip leader who said, "Go home and tell them that Israel isn't just guns and violence."

The response to the show was overwhelming. We consistently sold out a large theatre in downtown Toronto. People from all walks of life came to the play: theatre artists, Jews and Palestinians, people interested in the conflict, people who had heard it was a fun show. Some people had done volunteer work in countries outside the Middle East and said they identified strongly with the play. Others told me they learned a lot about the conflict. Many told me they loved the music.

Some said I was too pro-Palestinian; others that I wasn't strong enough in my criticism of Israel.

Some people have told me the play is "balanced" (a compliment), others have told me it is "unbalanced" (a criticism). I railed against both. I have tried to convey my experience, and my experience was not balanced. The situation isn't balanced. Life isn't balanced. And the more I thought about it, I wondered if plays *should* be balanced, and what balance in this context even means?

As I write this now, tensions in the West Bank are escalating and the tenuous calm that was held when I visited seems on the verge of collapse. There is still no sign of peace or justice. And so it remains very important to bring attention to the contradictions and confusions that lie at the heart of this terrible conflict.

When I began writing *The Peace Maker*, part of me wanted people to see what I had seen, so they would think like I thought. But then I realized that didn't make good theatre. So I decided to stick to the questions. And music. Everything is better with music.

# SABRA FALLING
BY ISMAIL KHALIDI

*To Mona and Rashid, who somehow managed to bring three kids safely into the unsafe world that was Beirut. And to the thousands who lost their lives in the summer of 1982.*

# ACKNOWLEDGEMENTS

This play, which long haunted me as an idea, would probably not have been completed without the generous and loving support of Pangea World Theater and Mizna. It was through a commission by the former, and a productive month-long residency provided by the latter, that the first drafts of this play came into being in 2013, during an especially snowy April in Minneapolis.

Sincere thanks are also due to the many theatres, directors, and actors that put together staged readings of this play as it developed. They include Noor Theatre in New York City, the Mosaic Rooms in London, and Golden Thread in San Francisco. Thanks also to the many readers who gave me valuable feedback and support at various stages of writing, including the editors of this volume, as well as Naomi Wallace, Peter Rachleff, Caitlin F. McLeod, Meena Natarajan, Dipankar Mukherjee, Torange Yeghiazarian, Octavio Solis, David Gothard, Noelle Ghoussaini, Lameece Issaq, Nancy Vitale, Rashid Khalidi, and Mona Khalidi. Much that is good in the play is due to their notes and observations, while any shortcomings or factual errors can be attributed to me and me alone.

The world premiere of *Sabra Falling* will be produced by Pangea World Theater in 2017.

*Here on the slopes of hills, facing the dusk and the cannon of time*
*Close to the gardens of broken shadows,*
*We do what prisoners do,*
*And what the jobless do:*
*We cultivate hope.*

. . .

*The siege is a waiting period*
*Waiting on the tilted ladder in the middle of the storm.*

—Mahmoud Darwish, from "Under Siege"

## CHARACTERS

| | |
|---|---|
| Sofyan | fifties, a refugee. The father of Hani and Eyad. |
| Leena | fifties, a refugee. The mother of Hani and Eyad. |
| Dalia | twenty. |
| Hani | early twenties, a PLO fighter. |
| The Pilot | midtwenties, an Israeli pilot. |
| The General | an ageless Israeli Army general. |
| Uli | twenties, the Pilot's girlfriend in Tel Aviv.* |
| Mira | fifties, the Pilot's mother.** |
| Eyad | a vision. *** |

*Uli is played by the same actor playing Dalia

** Mira is played by the same actor playing Leena

***Eyad is played by the same actor playing Hani

## SETTING

| | |
|---|---|
| Time | August and September of 1982. |
| Place | A home in the Sabra refugee camp in West Beirut. |
| The Set | A simple living room with doors leading off to two other rooms and one to the street. Minimal furniture. The roof has hole in it, which can be suggested by lighting if needed. |

# ACT ONE

## SCENE ONE

*The stage is dark. It is night. The thunder of bombing can be heard.*

*The sound of something falling to earth from a great distance. It gets closer, screeching, whistling, louder, closer, and then a* CRASH*!*

*Dust all around. Moonlight shines through a fresh hole in the ceiling, illuminating a large object in the middle of the floor.*

LEENA *enters with a gas lamp. She studies the object.* DALIA *and* HANI *enter behind her.*

DALIA *is in pyjamas.* HANI *wears nothing but his underpants. He holds a rifle.*

LEENA Hani, put that thing away. You remember what happened last time.

HANI It could be a shell.

LEENA It's not a bomb.

DALIA Don't get too close.

HANI Where's Babba?

LEENA That man sleeps through anything. He hasn't heard half of this fucking war. I envy him for that. Leave him.

*LEENA takes another step towards the object. She is about to poke it but HANI stops her.*

HANI Let me call the guys, they'll know what to do.

LEENA Dalia's in her nightgown.

HANI She can change!

LEENA I won't have a bunch of fighters obsessed with their guns and their cocks barging in my house to tell me what I already know.

*She reaches towards the object.*

HANI Don't touch it!

LEENA It's not a bomb.

DALIA How do you know?

LEENA Bombs don't breathe.

*She lifts the tattered remnants of a parachute to reveal a man in a pilot's jumpsuit and helmet.*

DALIA He's . . .

LEENA A soldier.

HANI An Israeli.

DALIA A pilot.

LEENA My god.

HANI Motherfucker.

DALIA He's alive.

HANI Not for long.

*HANI points his gun at the unconscious pilot but LEENA shoves it away.*

LEENA Dalia, help me lift him.

HANI He's the enemy, Mamma.

LEENA Yes, but he's a man, and none will be executed under my roof, or what's left of it. Not while I'm alive. Understand?

*They remove the man's helmet to reveal a bloodied face. HANI exits.*

*(to DALIA)* Get the bottle of whisky and the cloth and scissors.

*DALIA exits. LEENA is alone with THE PILOT.*

A human bomb. An enemy human.

*She unbuttons his shirt to reveal more blood.*

I swear, if you ruin up my carpet with all this blood, I'll let Hani kill you.

*DALIA re-enters with supplies. HANI re-enters behind her, dressed in mismatched fatigues.*

HANI We'd be shot as traitors if anyone in the camp saw this.

LEENA I suppose that's true. Dalia, lock the door. Hani, give me a hand.

HANI They hunt us from the skies and you tend to him as if he were a tiny bird fallen out of his nest.

LEENA He's fallen, so I tend his wounds. Yes.

HANI He's a vulture, not a dove, Mother. A killer.

LEENA Not a human?

HANI This piece of shit dropped the bombs that wiped out half the city.

DALIA He wasn't just passing over Beirut in a fighter jet.

HANI It was him and his friends. It's them that push the buttons.

LEENA Don't lecture me, boy.

HANI He can't stay here.

LEENA So take him. Drag him through the streets, treat him as an animal, the way the Israelis would treat you if they caught you.

HANI Exactly!

LEENA Exactly!

HANI Yes! Exactly!

LEENA Good!

HANI What?

LEENA It's settled. He stays.

HANI They'll come for him.

LEENA Who?

HANI Them. He has a tracking device on him.

*HANI starts stripping THE PILOT, searching him. LEENA tries to stop him but HANI tears off THE PILOT's uniform so that he is in his underwear.*

SOFYAN *(offstage)* What the hell is going on in there?

HANI Nothing, Babba.

SOFYAN Tick tack, tick tack, bang boom, like a goddamn silversmith in my own house!

LEENA Go back to sleep, Sofyan.

SOFYAN *(offstage)* I wouldn't have to go back to sleep if you hadn't woken me to begin with.

LEENA Either get up and help us or and go back to sleep!

DALIA Why do you shout at him like that?

SOFYAN *(offstage)* Because a hammer only knows how to do one thing, that's why.

LEENA Because I cook, and I sew, and I chase the roaches. Because I follow the news and watch the skies to stay one step ahead of this war.

DALIA We all do.

LEENA Except him. He sits and reads and writes and twiddles his balls.

SOFYAN *(offstage)* I would if you'd left me any, woman!

DALIA He's working.

SOFYAN *(offstage)* That's right! I'm working!

LEENA Of course! He prepares to direct his next play. With actors that have either been killed or fled; in a theatre that's been shelled, for an audience too terrified to leave their houses! *(beat)* Not to mention incapable of understanding Beckett.

SOFYAN *(offstage)* They understand Beckett! And when I do Molière or Shakespeare they'd understand that too!

LEENA What about when you made me play Pozzo! Half the audience took their cigarette break in the theatre and talked over me. Never again!

SOFYAN *(offstage)* Maybe you didn't understand Pozzo!

LEENA *(gesturing to* HANI *and* DALIA*)* Don't touch him!

*LEENA exits. THE PILOT moves groggily.*

DALIA He's starting to come to.

HANI What do we do?

DALIA He's a prisoner of war, no?

HANI Yeah, I suppose so?

DALIA So? *So*, if you'd listened in training instead of studying Zaynab al Kurdi's ass then maybe you'd remember.

HANI I do remember.

DALIA So let's hear it.

HANI Fine . . . When Zaynab's right leg crosses over the left, the back of her shirt slides up just enough to see that space where the small of her back transitions to the top of the peach-shaped entity that is her miraculous ass.

*Beat.*

DALIA I should slap the ass-shaped entity that is your face.

*DALIA takes a cigarette from HANI's sleeve.*

You know, the way you and your friends drool over her like a pack of hyenas, I'm not surprised Zaynab prefers women.

HANI You're full of shit.

DALIA I really don't blame her.

*DALIA smiles and exhales smoke in HANI's face then hands him the cigarette, which he smokes absently.* DALIA *then takes the gun from him and points it at* THE PILOT.

*(to* THE PILOT*)* You're now a prisoner of war in the custody of the Palestine Liberation Organization. Your wounds will be attended to and you will henceforth be treated according to the guidelines for combatants captured in war.

THE PILOT *does not respond.* HANI *takes back the gun as* LEENA *enters.*

LEENA I decide his fate. Now either help or get out.

HANI He's a prisoner now. You can treat his wounds, but then he's gone. We turn him in.

HANI *storms out.* DALIA *stays. The two women bandage* THE PILOT'S *head as lights fade.*

## SCENE TWO

THE PILOT, *with his head bandaged, sleeps.* HANI *tiptoes into the room, ties his hands together with rope, then exits, leaving* THE PILOT *asleep and bound. The light of dawn creeps through the hole in the roof.* SOFYAN *enters without noticing the sleeping man on his floor. He starts making coffee and puts a record on. It is Fairuz singing "Habaytak bel Sayf." As* SOFYAN *mixes his coffee over the small gas burner on the floor he sings along.*

DALIA *(offstage)* Babba, please, it's barely light out!

SOFYAN In Abu Shusha we'd wake up and sing as we tended the flocks in the dark.

DALIA *(offstage)* There aren't any flocks here. And there's no grass either.

SOFYAN *sings another refrain. The pilot wakes up, unbeknownst to* SOFYAN, *just as a neighbour's voice is heard from offstage.*

NEIGHBOR 1 *(offstage)* Godammit man, there's people trying to sleep in this camp!

SOFYAN (*shouting through the window*) Sleep is the last thing you need, Abu Ali. Get off your ass and do something instead of playing backgammon all day with that pipe stuck in your face!

NEIGHBOR 2 There's a war going on! No time for bloody love songs!

SOFYAN War is the best time for love songs! It's our best defence against that donkey fucker Begin and his friend the General!

*SOFYAN turns his attention back to his coffee and then freezes. He looks up and studies the hole in the roof, seeing it for the first time. He then looks directly down from the hole and sees THE PILOT, who is awake, sitting on the floor. They stare at each other. SOFYAN slowly and methodically circles THE PILOT several times. He inspects his hair, then grabs his chin and pulls THE PILOT's face up so he can see it better. He looks closely at his nose, his eyes, and then his hands. This goes on for several moments. Suddenly, SOFYAN mimes a cowboy walk, à la John Wayne, turns, and draws his finger as a gun on THE PILOT. THE PILOT is still. SOFYAN turns his back and again takes several cowboy paces away from THE PILOT before repeating the action. This time, THE PILOT has made his finger into a gun and pretends to shoot SOFYAN, winning the duel. The old man mimes an ornate death scene, eventually collapsing to the floor. THE PILOT lets out a laugh. SOFYAN looks him over.*

SOFYAN Eyad?

*THE PILOT smiles at SOFYAN. Darkness.*

## SCENE THREE

*Lights rise. Later that day.*

*LEENA, DALIA, and HANI speak to each other quickly and in hushed tones on one side of the stage. On the other side of the stage, just out of earshot, SOFYAN and THE PILOT sit together, SOFYAN changing the bandage on THE PILOT's head.*

HANI Is he fucking serious?

DALIA Be quiet.

HANI Why? Is it a secret that this is totally crazy? I *want* him to hear me.

LEENA He hasn't been like this for years, since . . .

DALIA Look how he's smiling.

HANI He's *lost* his mind!

LEENA Don't say that!

HANI You say it all the time.

LEENA I'm allowed to! Not you. And I don't mean it. Your father's not a madman.

HANI He's playing house with an Israeli soldier!

DALIA Look at him, Hani.

HANI I am!

DALIA Not Babba, the other one. Eya— . . . The pilot.

HANI You too?

DALIA No! But . . .

HANI But what?!

DALIA Nothing.

HANI Just say it!

DALIA Look at his eyes.

HANI He's got two of 'em. So what?

DALIA The nose.

HANI What about it?

DALIA The slope of it. How it's slightly bent to the right.

HANI So?

LEENA The scar on his chin.

HANI It's a wound, not a scar. Fresh.

DALIA He looks like him . . . Just like Eyad.

HANI My brother is gone.

LEENA You think we don't know that?

HANI The question is whether Babba knows.

DALIA It's not easy to say that . . . Even to think it, Hani. But—

HANI I'm taking the pilot to my commander. He'll decide how to handle this.

LEENA And what about your father?

HANI Tell him the truth. He's a grown man.

LEENA He thinks that's his boy. He thinks—

HANI He doesn't think. That's the problem.

LEENA He's thinks Eyad's come back to us. That he's escaped. From them. From some dungeon.

HANI And what about when that pilot realizes where he is and who he is? Or when their death squads come to rescue him and execute us? What then? Is that a better ending?

LEENA There are no happy endings. Not here. So what's the difference.

DALIA He must know.

LEENA He knows what he sees, and that boy—

HANI Soldier!

LEENA That *soldier* looks like my Eyad.

*In the other space,* SOFYAN *exits and re-enters with a pile of clothes. He hands it to* THE PILOT.

Hani, until now he talked about Eyad as if he was going to walk through that door any minute. For the past three years. So imagine how he felt when he saw. Him.

HANI The pilot goes.

HANI *takes out his pistol.*

LEENA *(calmly)* You're not going anywhere while they're hitting the camps, it's not safe. He'll harm no one in his condition.

*The thud of a bomb dropping. The lights flicker and then go out. There is darkness.*

Hani, go out and see if you can link us back to the generator at the clinic.

*After a moment* DALIA *has lit a gas lamp, illuminating the centre of the room.* THE PILOT *has appeared and now stands between them dressed in trousers and a button-down shirt . . .* SOFYAN *enters, then* HANI.

HANI No luck. The generator is—

*He sees* THE PILOT.

My god . . .

SOFYAN Can't work with this boom boom, doom and gloom.

HANI *(nodding towards* THE PILOT*)* Ask *him* when it will stop.

*For a moment all stare at* THE PILOT.

SOFYAN *(to* THE PILOT*)* Eyad, go rest your head. And you shouldn't be standing on that leg of yours either.

*THE PILOT starts to exit but HANI grabs his shoulder. HANI is about to say something but stares at him for a beat and then lets go. THE PILOT exits, unsteady on his injured leg.*

*(quietly)* Your brother escapes an Israeli prison and makes his way back through enemy lines, injured, confused—God knows what they did to him—and you treat him like a stranger?!

*A beat.*

HANI — So which play are we in now, old man? *Lear*? *Oedipus*? *Hamlet*? Just tell us so we can learn our lines and you can move us around your stage.

LEENA — Enough, Hani.

HANI — I want a part in my father's next play.

SOFYAN — I might have a non-speaking part for you.

HANI — I assume my brother Eyad has the lead?

SOFYAN — I'm going to ask him to write it.

HANI — Is that so?

SOFYAN — I've been searching for a play to shake the camps, to make this parched feeling peel away.

HANI — And what will it be about, this new play?

SOFYAN — The process of creation will reveal all, son.

DALIA — Maybe it's too soon for him. For Eyad.

LEENA — He can't write the play you are asking for.

SOFYAN — Why not?

LEENA — Because he's not . . .

*SOFYAN looks at LEENA.*

He's not . . . *well.*

DALIA He can barely talk. And his head.

SOFYAN I know. I can see his wounds. When he's better it will come back. And the words will flow again. But we have to help make him whole again; help him *remember* who he is. Then it will pour out of him. The poetry of revolution—revolution unlike any accomplished with third-hand rifles.

HANI Don't. Not again.

SOFYAN We've been taking up arms since I was a child. Against the British we tried. My father, God rest his soul, borrowed a rifle / from—

HANI & DALIA *(together)* From Abu Abbas.

HANI Yes we know. And he was torn in two.

SOFYAN And he was torn in two by British machine guns at Jaddin, in front of my brother's eyes.

HANI Not the first or the last.

SOFYAN Ten years later, we took up arms against the Zionists to defend our villages. With our decrepit rifles and Ottoman swords we were defeated and herded away, like so many sheep. Now look at us. Living and dying like animals.

HANI Which is why we fight. Perhaps you didn't fight well enough then. Just waited like fools, like sheep, for the Arab armies to save you.

SOFYAN Exactly. They never came! And they never will.

DALIA This time we've fought the Israelis to a standstill.

SOFYAN But not victory, dear. Where is your victory?

HANI All summer I've been in those trenches while you've

been perched in your room scouring those yellowed plays. We've held them off for two months, on our own.

SOFYAN — On your own. Against all odds?

HANI — Yes. We fight for ourselves now.

SOFYAN — And how long before their tanks and their planes overtake us? What happens in a day or a week or a month when you can resist no more?

*The dull thud of shelling in the distance.*

Hear that? That's the tick-tock of a clock and we're running out of time. Who will come to our aid? The Syrians? Their air force was wiped out. Those shits in Saudi? Bunch of backward hypocritical swine with oil pumping in their veins and cash the only cause they care about? Will they ride to our rescue? The Soviets? The French? The *Americans*?!

DALIA — They say the Americans will control the Israelis if we hold out long enough.

SOFYAN — Good luck, God be with you then if that's what you're relying on.

HANI — We rely on ourselves.

SOFYAN — No matter how many of the enemy you bring down we'll never be strong enough, boy, not even with the ghosts of Marx, Mao, and Che cheering you on from the great beyond.

HANI — But a play will save us, is that it? Lead us to victory? Lead us back home? Or will you crush their tanks with a sonnet?

SOFYAN — Perhaps, yes.

HANI — I'll let my commanders know to stock up on couplets and explosive soliloquies before the Israelis make their next push, then.

*HANI lights a cigarette.*

SOFYAN You make a joke out of it.

HANI You're the one making a joke out of it. People are dying. Out there. For you.

SOFYAN That's why I'm telling you we can win only when we show them that they can never win. We are liberated by laughing at their jets and their tanks. By creating beauty where they have left us none.

HANI Save them to save ourselves?

SOFYAN Perhaps.

HANI And how exactly do we do that?

SOFYAN With love . . . A certain kind of love. That's all I know.

HANI Will your love stop their bombs?

SOFYAN My village can't be bombed from my mind. It's safe there, along with our painters and our poets. They can't get them there.

DALIA They killed Ghassan and Kamal and . . .

SOFYAN No. Not really.

HANI Well, I won't sit here waiting for them to kill me.

*HANI begins to leave but stops as a jet breaks the sound barrier with a ferocious roar, shaking the house. They look up. HANI then futilely fires several shots through the hole above and exits, slamming the door.*

SOFYAN We should do something about that hole, Dalia.

*SOFYAN exits in the other direction. LEENA and DALIA stand alone, looking up through the roof.*

## SCENE FOUR

*Night falls on the house as the din of bombing occasionally breaks the silence.* THE PILOT *sleeps.* HANI *sits guard nearby but is asleep. The sound of jets overhead.* THE PILOT *tosses and turns. Voices are heard in Hebrew over a radio frequency.*

RADIO VOICE 1 You're in too close to your targets, Captain, watch the fire, pull out, pull out!

RADIO VOICE 2 Drop your load, pilot, and get the fuck out of there! Do you read? You're taking fire. Repeat. You are taking fire from below.

*Suddenly* THE PILOT *sits upright. He is wearing his pilot's helmet, its visor down. He struggles to breathe and tries to pull off the helmet as the sound of jets and the radio voices reach a deafening crescendo.*

RADIO VOICE 1 Eject, Captain! Your wing is fucked. Eject!

THE PILOT *punches the ground and with a thunderous sound is ejected upwards through the hole in the ceiling. He disappears.*

## SCENE FIVE

*With morning light* THE PILOT *floats down through the hole, featherlike, and lands in bed, asleep.* SOFYAN *stands over the two sleeping men.*

SOFYAN Coffee. Thick and bitter with a bite of cardamom to tame its punch.

THE PILOT *and* HANI *wake.*

HANI The water's only for cooking and washing. Mamma's orders.

SOFYAN Coffee *is* washing. Cleans away the night's sleep. Nightmares too. To her it's a luxury, to the artist it's fuel.

HANI She's gonna kill you.

SOFYAN But it will be a theatrical death, Hani, nothing more. I'll be alive again for the curtain call. Then we'll do it all over again tomorrow.

HANI It's not a game, you know. It's not theatre.

SOFYAN No. It's marriage. Which is a kind of theatre. *(beat)* Just like war.

*SOFYAN pours HANI a cup and then pours one for THE PILOT. They drink in silence, not making eye contact. After a moment HANI rises and prepares his gear.*

HANI There's more talk of a ceasefire. I'll let you know what I hear.

SOFYAN An end to all this would be a blessing. Break a leg, boy.

HANI I'll keep my leg if I can help it. Are Mamma and Dalia here?

SOFYAN In the other room. Don't worry. They'll keep an eye on us. If that's what you're worried about.

*HANI stares at THE PILOT, who sips his coffee quietly. SOFYAN too looks at THE PILOT, soaking in his every move.*

HANI Well. I guess I'll be exiting. Stage left.

*HANI starts exiting stage right.*

SOFYAN That's stage right. Remember, the audience would be there.

*SOFYAN points towards the audience and all three stare out for a moment. HANI exits.*

*(to THE PILOT)* Eyad, how do you feel today? Better?

THE PILOT My head.

*SOFYAN checks the bandage on his head.*

SOFYAN It will pass. I've brought your books.

*SOFYAN produces a small pile of books. THE PILOT looks through them.*

"Hungry man, reach for the book: It is a weapon."

*SOFYAN then produces a heavy object covered in a cloth.*

THE PILOT And that?

SOFYAN Another weapon. If used correctly.

*THE PILOT takes it carefully as if it is a bomb. He unwraps it to reveal a typewriter in a case.*

THE PILOT Is it mine?

SOFYAN I had Abu Ali's boy get it from your office downtown. Little shit made me pay through the nose. Mother Courage would have loved Beirut.

*THE PILOT opens the case to reveal the machine, its keys splattered with dried blood. The two men stare at it. SOFYAN carefully runs his fingers over the keys. A moment.*

THE PILOT Blood.

SOFYAN Yes.

THE PILOT Mine?

*DALIA enters behind them carrying medical supplies. She stands unnoticed for the moment.*

SOFYAN They must have wounded you and then taken you with them.

THE PILOT I don't remember.

*DALIA approaches THE PILOT.*

DALIA First, their commandos slipped through the city disguised as women.

*Standing over him, she checks the bandages on his head wounds.*

Then they made their way to your office downtown.

DALIA *prods his chin upwards to look at his cut. She uses the clamps to move his head, never touching him.*

They knocked. And when you opened it . . .

*She gently pries open his mouth, again with the clamps, and after a moment removes them, but* THE PILOT*'s mouth remains open wide, his eyes closed.*

. . . They made you disappear.

THE PILOT Why?

SOFYAN Because of those.

THE PILOT *opens his eyes.* SOFYAN *points to the pile of books.*

Do you remember?

THE PILOT *and* DALIA *look at each other for a moment.*

THE PILOT I remember writing. Yes. Typing.

DALIA Your wounds are healing fine. Don't pick at the cut on your chin or else it will scar.

DALIA *exits.*

SOFYAN What else?

*Beat.*

THE PILOT And Mamma. Standing behind me. Sometimes.

SOFYAN Your mother's always been too nosey for her own good.

THE PILOT — I remember a woman.

SOFYAN — You were engaged. To Dalia.

THE PILOT — I thought she was your daughter.

SOFYAN — She was orphaned. Lost her people. She was only seventeen. She joined the movement. That's where you met. In some meeting. She argued against you. And won. To your credit, you fell hard.

THE PILOT — A meeting.

SOFYAN — Later we took her in. As our own.

THE PILOT — And she stayed here all this time? Waiting?

SOFYAN — Surviving.

THE PILOT — Fighting?

SOFYAN — I suppose. She's not afraid to die. Not afraid of them. Out there. Up there. I know that much.

THE PILOT — She loved me.?

SOFYAN — But not because your books get published or because journalists from Europe came to talk to you. She could see you. From the beginning. And your writing imp roved too. With Dalia, something was growing in your words.

*SOFYAN removes a handkerchief from his pocket. He moistens it with his mouth and carefully wipes the keys clean of the blood. He then places the handkerchief back in his pocket and loads paper into the typewriter.*

Shall we? Begin?

*THE PILOT nods.*

I was thinking of one of their endless, immortal warlords. The fat general perhaps. Or the one-eyed war chief. Though he's a bit of a cliché, I think. Yes. The fat one is best.

THE PILOT I don't understand.

SOFYAN As a character. The general. We'd kidnap him. Imprison him within the walls of your play. It will drive them crazy, Eyad, I promise. Go on.

*THE PILOT moves his hands towards the keys but stops short of touching them.*

*(his eyes closed)* Lights up on the fat general, in the smouldering ruins of the city he has destroyed . . . Dancing.

THE PILOT Tango.

SOFYAN Good. That's good.

*THE PILOT still hasn't moved his hands to begin typing.*

I'm crowding you. I'll leave you to yourself.

*SOFYAN kisses him on the forehead and exits. THE PILOT, alone now, moves his hands towards the typewriter. As soon as his fingers touch the keys the lights shift abruptly, a flash, a crack.*

## SCENE SIX

*Lights rise on THE GENERAL, who enters to a distant tango. He dances with a skeleton in his arms. He notices THE PILOT but keeps dancing around him in circles.*

THE GENERAL Name and rank, soldier.

THE PILOT I'm not a soldier.

THE GENERAL Every Israeli's a soldier. And every Arab a terrorist. So what are you if not a soldier?

THE PILOT A writer, sir.

THE GENERAL You're a soldier. Air force I'd guess. Not a grunt. Name and rank?

THE PILOT Eyad Akawi.

*THE GENERAL drops the skeleton and stops his tango. He stares THE PILOT up and down then picks up a book and looks it over, circling THE PILOT.*

*He pokes him and sniffs THE PILOT and then the book before dropping it on the ground in disgust and exiting.*

*THE PILOT grabs a pen and starts writing.*

*Hebrew letters and words appear everywhere on the walls, glowing, illuminated, filling the space.*

*He looks at the sea of words around him, confused. SOFYAN enters and stares at the writing too.*

SOFYAN You must have learned their language in their prisons. Good. Use it to break their hearts. In their own tongue.

*SOFYAN notices the discarded skeleton and gently picks it up and cradles it in his arms as he exits. As soon as he leaves MIRA enters and starts tidying up around THE PILOT.*

MIRA Who was that?

THE PILOT My father.

*She stops what she is doing and feels his head and neck for a fever.*

MIRA That's not your father. Yours was a drunk who could barely rent us a flat in Tel Aviv, left when you were barely two. But I wouldn't go back to the slums where they kept all the Jews like me who came from Baghdad. Sprayed us with DDT when we arrived in '51.

THE PILOT Who are you?

MIRA Silly boy. But you're my silly boy. My Eyal.

THE PILOT Eyad. You mean Eyad.

MIRA *(overemphasizing the "L")* I mean Eyal.

THE PILOT Eyad.

*She takes his chin in her hand and turns it towards the writing on the wall.*

MIRA Eyal. You see those words you're creating? I can read them. *You* can read them. But they can't.

THE PILOT But I speak Arabic.

MIRA Because I would teach you every morning to read and write Arabic properly. The other kids made fun of you. Called you names.

*She speaks as she straightens his collar and closes the top button of his shirt.*

Do you remember the day when I dropped you at school, and you told me, "Never speak to me in that language around the others"? What could I do? Soon you were just like all the other Israeli boys and Hebrew took over your dreams. Arabic was our secret code. Our criminal tongue.

THE PILOT I learned Hebrew in prison.

MIRA No. You're a Sabra.

THE PILOT We're *in* Sabra. In Beirut.

MIRA I mean the other Sabra, the name of the cactus that grows by the side of the road, the name given to the new Jews, to make them tough and prickly on the outside. Make them feel they belong, that they can survive in this place.

*She looks around.*

Why would you want to stay in this shithole anyway?

THE PILOT I was born here. I'm from here. I—

MIRA Quiet! I washed Ashkenazi floors and stitched Ashkenazi clothes for twenty years so you wouldn't have to be from a place like this. That's why we moved out of the city to the settlements. The government paid us to move into a brand new house. I did that to escape from this.

THE PILOT I need to write.

*MIRA laughs.*

MIRA That's what I told you too. Before you went to the army. Your grandfather wrote books. In Baghdad. It's in your blood. But the sky called you.

THE PILOT The sky?

MIRA It's not your fault. It's the price we pay to become Israelis. Every one of us must have his war to make on the Arabs.

THE PILOT I want you to leave, please.

*MIRA runs her hand through his hair and over his cheeks.*

MIRA You always were a confused boy. So pretty and lost, in your own way. My little Sabra.

*She kisses him on the forehead and starts to leave but stops.*

Your Uli keeps coming by the house. Come back and save me from her insufferable crying.

*She exits. THE PILOT is motionless until there is a knock at the door. He opens it to reveal THE GENERAL in full drag holding a handbag.*

THE PILOT Can I help you, miss?

THE GENERAL Are you Eyad Akawi?

THE PILOT Yes.

*THE GENERAL whips a pistol out of his handbag and puts it to THE PILOT's mouth.*

THE GENERAL Bang!!

*A flash of light and then darkness.*

## SCENE SEVEN

*Lights rise as THE PILOT wakes in a terror, unable to breathe. LEENA stands over him and pours water on him.*

LEENA We don't have enough water for me to do that again. Now breathe. You slept all day.

*He breathes, calming down.*

THE PILOT Thank you.

LEENA You had a fever. It's gone down now.

*She presents to him a plate of food.*

Up. The battles will be fierce tonight. Up now, boy. You must be hungry. I made manaqeesh to send to the fighters. You should eat something.

*He rises unsteadily and slowly dresses himself. Once he is dressed LEENA is taken aback and stares at him for a long moment.*

*HANI enters from another room with his gear, preparing to leave. He too stops in his tracks and stares at THE PILOT.*

*LEENA notices HANI's presence and falls back into motion.*

*(to THE PILOT)* Take this and go to Sofyan. He must need help fixing the shelter. Go.

*She hands* THE PILOT *some of the bread as he exits.*

HANI — He's wearing Eyad's clothes?

LEENA — Yes.

HANI — Like a snake with a new skin.

LEENA — They fit him.

HANI — They fit me too.

LEENA — I made food.

HANI — I want to put a bullet through his head.

LEENA — I can't. Hate him.

HANI — It would be strange.

LEENA — I want to . . .

HANI — I would do it . . .

LEENA — But I can't . . .

HANI — I would.

*She hands him a package of food.*

LEENA — For the others.

HANI — There will be a ceasefire. Soon.

LEENA — You've been saying so for weeks.

HANI — We've been asking for one for weeks. The Israelis are stalling, buying time, to bleed us, to break through our lines, to hit the leadership.

LEENA — So they won't stop, then?

HANI — Our position is weaker every morning. The Israelis know it.

LEENA Trust in God.

HANI There is no God, Mamma. Only the Phantom and the Merkava; the F-15 and the howitzer. There's power and we don't have it. There is darkness and severed limbs for us. Bits of skull caked in blood, covering walls, mixed with dirt.

LEENA There's more than that. Not now, maybe. It's hard to remember, easy to forget.

HANI They're looking for him. They think his plane went down south of the camps.

*LEENA does not respond.*

I'm not asking for him to be executed. Just turned in, given back. In return for some small victory in this sea of death.

LEENA Would we get anything in return? Do we ever?

HANI Maybe.

LEENA I can't stop you.

HANI Tomorrow, then. When there is light.

*They are both silent for a moment. DALIA enters in fatigues.*

Where are you going?

DALIA A costume ball.

*DALIA picks up HANI's rifle and effortlessly checks the clip and reinserts it before resting it back on his chair.*

Where do you think?

HANI The front is dangerous right now, Dalia.

DALIA I know. And my job is to tend the wounded. If I need to fight I can do that too.

LEENA Stop pretending you can stop her, Hani.

HANI We'll turn him in. Tomorrow. For better terms.

*Beat. Everyone avoids eye contact.*

DALIA So be it.

*DALIA prepares her things.*

HANI *(to DALIA)* I don't like the way he looks at you.

*DALIA does not say anything. HANI exits. As he does, THE PILOT enters with the typewriter and sits on the floor. He begins typing. DALIA listens for a moment, then approaches to look at what is written on the typed page but THE PILOT covers it with his hand. She tries again and again he hides it, almost playfully. DALIA stops before it can continue and turns away, eventually exiting to the other room.*

LEENA Your appetite is coming back to you.

THE PILOT Yes. A bit.

LEENA Perhaps someone has some pigeons we can barter for. I'll go before the fighting gets thicker. Those poor birds, how they've suffered with all this metal and fire cutting through their skies and over the rooftops. After tonight, who knows how many will remain.

*She exits. THE PILOT begins to type. Lights shift.*

## SCENE EIGHT

*As THE PILOT types in a trance, THE GENERAL enters reading a file. He paces back and forth behind THE PILOT, who does not register his presence.*

THE GENERAL I'll dictate, you type . . . To the General Staff and the Cabinet: Request for more time to pound. No . . . *soften* West Beirut targets from the air, land, and sea. Stop. If we can delay ceasefire it is my belief, and that of my field commanders, that we can break the will of the terrorists and their left-wing Lebanese allies. Stop. Request urgently, repeat, urgently, that grass-fed cows from the Galilee be sent to the front lines for slaughter. Stop. Feast is in order to boost troop morale and iron levels. Full stop. End of message . . . Did you get all of that, soldier?

THE PILOT What?

THE GENERAL Get your head together! What's that nonsense you're typing?

*THE GENERAL rips the paper out of the typewriter and starts folding it as he talks.*

Now listen to me. Your comrades are in the air and positioned around this filthy snakepit of a city, risking their asses for you. And for Uli.

THE PILOT Uli?

THE GENERAL Yes, Uli. So the sooner we turn this city to rubble and drive out Arafat, the sooner you can get home to that tight little piece of ass waiting for you in Tel Aviv.

*THE PILOT turns back to his typewriter, trying to ignore THE GENERAL.*

*(hushed)* I see your angle. You're getting into the character, going deep undercover. Good. Smart. Fine. Keep playing along with these Bedouins and keep feeding us intelligence.

THE PILOT What do you mean?

THE GENERAL I mean I need you to tell me where this Hani character is going. Get me an address, get me coordinates so we can let your friends up above know where to hit once he's with his commanders. They must be taken out if we are to survive. It's that simple.

*THE GENERAL has folded the paper into an airplane. He tosses it in the air, making a whistling sound as it flies. As it lands, he gives an exuberant and childish imitation of the sound of a bomb exploding.*

THE PILOT I can't.

THE GENERAL You can. And you will. Then, look to the skies. You'll know it's time when the light of midday explodes the night. That is your signal to move.

THE PILOT Leave, sir. Now. I beg you. Please.

THE GENERAL, *hearing something, takes a step into the darkness as the lights flicker.* SOFYAN *enters from the other side of the stage carrying a leather bag.*

SOFYAN Take a break, son. I hear you pounding those keys like a madman. It does us good to hear the sound of our boy back in the house. Especially your mom. Come. Sit. The hour before dawn is the best time for a man to shave.

SOFYAN *sits him down, puts a towel around his neck, and lathers his face. With a razor he skilfully shaves* THE PILOT*'s face and neck as they talk.*

I used to be a barber, you know. In Abu Shusha. I apprenticed during the day, between tending to the flocks. I was young but I was good. I could give a man a moustache in the style of a British officer, thin and neat above the lip. Or in the Ottoman style for the old men, thick and full and twisted at the tips. Hold still.

THE PILOT What about the theatre?

SOFYAN Once I got to the camps . . . it was . . . I was different. We all were. I saw a poster one day for a play. *Othello.* I went. And I was hooked. After that, I would sneak into the city to be in the theatre whenever I could. Stay in the back and watch rehearsal. I volunteered to hang lights at first, cleaned costumes, swept the floors. They paid me a couple pounds from time to time, something to bring home. After enough time spent in that darkness your senses adjust. Things become clear and then people forget that you are just a nobody from the camps. So I acted, then I began directing. I was good. I even went to Prague once with a delegation. When you were younger. You wanted to come so badly. Do you remember?

*A moment of silence as* SOFYAN *cleans his blade.*

Working with actors is not so different from being a barber. In both cases you must take care of your space of work, keep your tools sharp. And the customer is much like the performer. You must be gentle yet firm with him. Let him relax, but always make sure you are in control so that he allows you to move him as you see fit.

SOFYAN *turns* THE PILOT*'s head with one hand.*

Both the actor and the customer must trust me, give in, and let me shape them, transform them. Because once they leave, once they cross the threshold from my space into the world and onto the stage, they're alone. As Antipholus of Syracuse said to Dromio, "There's many a man hath more hair than wit." He was right. And the same is true with talent.

So, in both cases, it's my job, while they are with me, to make them feel that they are intelligent and beautiful, that they are my favourite, the one I will always pay the most attention to. That way, they leave possessed of themselves. A new person. If only for a brief moment.

SOFYAN *has finished. He wipes* THE PILOT*'s face with a towel to reveal clean cheeks and chin, and a neat moustache on his face. He hands him a mirror.*

THE PILOT *is lost in the image of his new face.*

*A loud knock on the door.* THE PILOT *gets up and opens it to reveal, once again,* THE GENERAL *in drag, a red wig on his head.*

THE GENERAL You are Eyad Akawi?

*THE PILOT is frozen.*

To be or not to be, man, that is the question. Are you Eyad Akawi or not?

*THE GENERAL reaches his hand into his purse but THE PILOT slams the door in his face before he can draw the pistol again.*

SOFYAN Why the hell are you opening the door?

*THE PILOT looks at his face in the mirror again. After several moments there is another knock at the door. THE PILOT is paralyzed.*

Go on. Open it. It's probably your mother back from haggling with the neighbours all night like a madwoman.

*THE PILOT opens the door, flinching. LEENA enters with bags.*

LEENA *(to SOFYAN, matter-of-factly)* No pigeons. Sofyan, I traded one of your records for some meat.

SOFYAN Which one?

LEENA It doesn't matter.

SOFYAN Which one?!

LEENA The Bob Dylan one you love and I hate. Happy now?

SOFYAN Damn it, woman. I would've given you something else to trade. Ask me first!

LEENA He wanted *that* one. Anything else would have gotten us nothing but bone. Let it go. Get it back another time.

SOFYAN That's what you always say.

LEENA We haven't had meat for weeks now. And we can't eat Bob Dylan for dinner.

SOFYAN — And we can't make a pile of bones and gristle sing like Dylan either.

*HANI enters, rifle in hand, covered in grime. He is slightly injured. SOFYAN looks at him then exits.*

*HANI sits opposite THE PILOT as LEENA tends to his wounds.*

HANI — Ten dead just in my trench.

LEENA — And Dalia?

HANI — She's okay. Treating the wounded.

LEENA — You're bleeding.

*Beat.*

HANI — The tanks reached the other side of the sand barriers at nightfall. We could see right down their turrets. Every time we settled in, thinking the worst has passed, they'd hit us again.

LEENA — Be still. I have to sew up that shoulder.

HANI — I'm alive. Bassam and Salim are not. Dalia says Omar el-Issa won't make it through the day. Mamma, you know Shadia? From Shatila? The blonde one.

LEENA — Yes.

HANI — A shell.

LEENA — Is she?

HANI — Ripped her in half. That's what I heard.

LEENA — I'll visit her parents later.

*Beat.*

HANI — *(to THE PILOT)* Hey, Eyad. You remember Omar? Omar Safadi?

*THE PILOT shakes his head.*

Of course you don't. I'll help you recall. He was one of the fighters who protected the synagogue in Beirut. During the fighting in '76. Stood guard for nights on end to make sure it didn't come under fire. Hey! Don't you remember? You wrote a poem about it.

LEENA Hani.

HANI Recite it.

LEENA Stop.

HANI Come on. I heard you read it a thousand times.

LEENA Enough. Be still.

HANI Said you wanted it translated into Hebrew. So they could read it. So go ahead. Recite it.

*HANI moves towards THE PILOT. LEENA steps between them. THE PILOT speaks.*

THE PILOT There are armed men
Who stand outside the temple doors,
Vigilant, as death explodes from all sides.
Your books are safe with them.

Just as you too would have been
Had you not insisted on devouring
The wheat of our world
And crushing our stones;

Had you not insisted
On drinking our aquifers dry
And sacrificing our animals

At the altar of a God
Who chooses you
And only you.

Still, your prayers and candles will
Be safe; your star of six points too,
Which you fly upon your iron ramparts
And your engines of siege.

All will stay under the protection
Of those who were born lost in time
And without protection
Because of you.

One day you will thank them.
One day you will love them
As I do.

*SOFYAN enters as THE PILOT speaks the last lines. He is moved. After a moment of stillness, HANI calmly, quietly leaves the room.*

*Shelling rises in the distance. The electricity flickers and cuts to darkness.*

## SCENE NINE

*In the darkness there is rhythmic breathing. With the light of day we see HANI alone, doing push-ups, listening to the radio. LEENA enters.*

LEENA Are you going back out there?

HANI Yes.

LEENA Your arm?

HANI The stitches will hold.

*He finishes, jumps up, and switches off the radio.*

LEENA Will you speak to the others? About him?

HANI I don't know.

LEENA Your father . . .

HANI He is happy. With his Eyad. I know.

LEENA — Had it been you . . . He would have mourned you, Hani.

HANI — But he would have accepted it. That's the difference.

LEENA — He loves you.

HANI — I will not be the one to break his heart. But God help us if . . .

*HANI gathers his stuff, preparing to head to the front.*

LEENA — My little lion. Been a fighter since you were in my belly. Always trying to kick your way out. Just like you'd fight your way out of this camp.

HANI — This prison.

*Beat.*

Just because I'm not a poet like Eyad doesn't mean I don't understand love.

LEENA — I know that.

HANI — God knows, I wish I could do something every morning besides pick up this rifle. I do.

*He kisses his mother, picks up his gun, and exits. Lights fade.*

## SCENE TEN

*Lights rise. THE GENERAL enters as THE PILOT types.*

THE GENERAL — Since you are playing the part of the poet, I have a little something I jotted down for you.

*He takes out a folded piece of paper and reads it.*

A fiddle, a fiddle, an American fiddle
I play it soft, I play it hard,

Making music like a bard.

But I prefer the sounds of tanks,
The sounds of bullets,
The marching ranks.

So I play my fiddle
To the tune of war,
And the Americans dance
While my eagles soar.

*THE GENERAL crumples the paper into a ball and tosses it to the floor. It lands by THE PILOT.*

Peace is coming. Prepare for battle.

*THE GENERAL disappears into the darkness. It is quiet. There is no shelling, no jets, no gunfire in the distance. THE PILOT looks up from his typewriter. Lights fade.*

## SCENE ELEVEN

*Lights rise. DALIA and HANI alone. They speak quietly.*

DALIA We could have held out.

HANI Enough. It's done.

DALIA Hani, they would have been vulnerable. As soon as their tanks entered the city.

HANI Yes, but this is a Lebanese city, Dalia! We owe it to those who fought with us, who sacrificed their city and their families, we owe it to them to leave now, before it's too late.

DALIA We owe it to them to keep fighting!

HANI Beirut is not ours.

DALIA It's all we have.

HANI Not to turn into Stalingrad. The Israelis will not stop. Not until they have wiped this city off the face of the earth. You know that. We can all see that. They are mad.

DALIA We could have gotten better terms.

LEENA *enters the house with bags.*

LEENA The people are saying they've reached a deal. A ceasefire. Is it true?

DALIA We just heard.

LEENA *(calling offstage)* Sofyan!

HANI Under the terms, all the fighters will be evacuated.

*Beat.*

LEENA Evacuated?

HANI Some will leave by sea, others through Syria.

LEENA And once they've gone? What about us?

DALIA The Americans will come, to uphold the truce.

SOFYAN *and* THE PILOT *enter.*

LEENA Will you go? With the rest?

HANI If the fighters leave, I leave with them.

SOFYAN Where?

HANI Whichever countries will take us. Some will go to Yemen maybe.

DALIA Others to Iraq. Maybe even to Sudan.

HANI But the city and the camps will be spared more fighting. That is the price.

THE PILOT Dalia. Go. With Hani and the others.

*Silence. All look at* THE PILOT.

SOFYAN Eyad is right. You should leave with the fighters.

DALIA And who will take care of you?

SOFYAN We can manage. If they find you and say you are with the resistance, it will be dangerous.

DALIA It's been dangerous since I was born. And the last eight years of this shit, this whole war, the invasion. I'll stay. With you. Hani will be back.

THE PILOT They will kill you.

*Beat.*

DALIA Stay out of this.

LEENA Hani. Stay. With us.

HANI I can't. You know that.

LEENA Hide the gun. Throw it in the sea.

HANI I stay with the fedayeen. With my brothers. *(beat)* If that's okay with you, Father?

SOFYAN *doesn't answer.* HANI *starts to leave.*

SOFYAN I will be happy if my children get through this war alive. That is all I want.

HANI *exits.*

DALIA I'll go and help Hani get ready.

DALIA *exits.*

LEENA How can we let our little boy go?

SOFYAN The script is written, Leena. Trust it.

*SOFYAN exits.*

LEENA *(to THE PILOT)* Type. Don't say anything. Just write.

*THE PILOT sits and begins to type. Lights fade.*

## SCENE TWELVE

*Lights rise. HANI and DALIA sit alone as HANI packs. He places the last of his things in the bag and closes it. He removes a pistol and hands it to her.*

HANI Hide it well, but keep it near. The Americans guaranteed the safety of camps but I don't trust them or the Israelis. We're defenceless now and the Phalangist militias will want to have at us. Stay alert.

*She nods.*

And keep an eye on him. Keep an eye on the pilot.

DALIA I watch him sometimes, from across the house. I pretend he's him; imagine he was still here.

HANI Don't let it fuck with your head, Dalia. He's not Eyad. However much everyone wants him to be. However much you miss him.

DALIA I know.

HANI If anything happens, use him as you see fit. Use *that* as you see fit, too.

*He nods towards the gun.*

DALIA Yes.

HANI You sure?

DALIA I said yes.

HANI Trade him if you need to. If you can. And maybe you won't have to do anything . . . Hurt him, I mean.

DALIA I saw the way you look at him.

HANI How's that?

DALIA The same way you looked at Eyad. With a kind of love. And a kind of hate.

HANI I loved Eyad.

DALIA I know that. And I know it wasn't easy being his brother. But he thought the world of you, Hani. He told me that he wondered if he wouldn't be more use fighting than as a writer. Said he wasn't as brave as you. Used to tell me no one was as brave as his little brother. That he wanted to write a story about you.

HANI He never told me that.

DALIA Never got the chance, Hani. That's all.

*SOFYAN and LEENA enter. DALIA hides the pistol.*

SOFYAN Son.

HANI Father.

SOFYAN Today you're off to sea, like the sailors of old.

HANI I hadn't thought of it that way.

LEENA Food. For you and the others.

*She hands him a package of food.*

HANI Thank you, Mamma.

SOFYAN I'd like you to take this too.

*SOFYAN hands him his black beret.*

A "radiovka" they call it. Got it in Prague. I was keeping it. For when I could take your mother there. But there isn't much travelling left for us, I'm afraid. Let it get a good view from the top of your head. Just remember, it only understands Czech. And a bit of English.

*HANI wears it. The two men shake hands. SOFYAN pulls him in and kisses him. THE PILOT enters. HANI nods to him then turns to his mother and embraces her.*

*HANI leaves the house, stepping out towards the audience. DALIA follows behind. As they walk, we hear ululations, gunshots in the air, car horns. The two of them are at the port now with hundreds of others.*

*HANI turns to DALIA. She raises her hand into a victory sign. HANI does the same, then disappears through the audience.*

*Silence. All stare out towards the sea, into space. They speak to themselves.*

At the mercy of the same seas as Odysseus now.

LEENA I should have prepared more food.

*LEENA exits.*

DALIA They look so small on that boat.

SOFYAN "As flies to wanton boys are we to th' gods . . . "

DALIA Like little specks . . .

SOFYAN "They kill us for their sport."

DALIA Driven into the sea.

SOFYAN Again.

DALIA And again we are disappeared.

SOFYAN But there is another act yet to play out.

*DALIA exits. Only SOFYAN, THE PILOT, and the typewriter remain.*

I know it in my bones like rain coming over the mountains.

*SOFYAN exits as lights dim to black. The sound of a ship's foghorn gives way to the clacking of a typewriter in the darkness.*

# ACT TWO

## SCENE ONE

*It is night. THE PILOT sleeps next to the typewriter. THE GENERAL enters. He eats a piece of meat on the bone.*

THE GENERAL Up. Get up. Uli's waiting and here you are writing some faggot play. Up. You need to shoot your way out of this nest, soldier. Before it's too late.

*THE GENERAL sucks the marrow out of the bone and drops it on the ground. He sniffs the air.*

I can smell a weapon in here. The smell of steel is unmistakable, even through the stink of these Arabs.

THE PILOT What do you want?

THE GENERAL A napkin.

*THE GENERAL takes a sheet of paper from the typewriter and wipes his hands clean with it.*

And for you to act like a man. For the state. For Uli. You remember her, don't you? You can see her, can't you? Clear as day. In her apartment on Herzl Street, above the little pastry shop.

*ULI appears, her hair down, wearing a miniskirt. She sits across from*

*THE PILOT and smiles, her legs creeping open playfully.*

ULI — I'm here. Waiting, Eyal. Waiting.

THE GENERAL — Wondering when her man will return from the war and give her a good patriotic fuck. But she can't wait forever, soldier.

*ULI gets up, exits.*

And our country is full of men who are up for the job . . . if you aren't.

THE PILOT — What do you want me to do?

THE GENERAL — Find the gun. And be ready to use it. The time to move is near. We're getting closer. All you need to do is make your way to our lines and you're home. Wait for my signal. Look to the sky. When the light of midday explodes the night, the operation will have begun.

*THE GENERAL disappears. THE PILOT lies down. DALIA enters on tiptoes. She carefully removes the gun from its hiding place, then puts it back. THE PILOT sits up.*

THE PILOT — Uli?

DALIA — Go back to sleep. You're dreaming.

*DALIA exits. THE PILOT tosses and turns. A woman's voice can be heard offstage, singing a song in Hebrew. THE PILOT sits up again to see ULI re-enter. She sings and then dances above his head.*

ULI — Remember when we spent all night on the beach near Jaffa after training. The bonfire and the stars, up all night, dancing above us, and the empty stone houses framing the sky behind us? And then this song came on and you grabbed me by my hips and pulled off my fatigues . . .

*He grabs her and pulls her to the ground. They kiss and the passion builds. He starts to tear her clothes off and she does the same to his.*

*THE GENERAL reappears from the shadows.*

*He watches them as they become more and more intertwined.*

THE GENERAL Nothing hotter than a pair of horny Sabras if you ask me. Demographically speaking.

THE PILOT *(to THE GENERAL)* Not now, sir, please.

ULI You always talked about birds, about how you wanted to fly.

THE GENERAL And yet you couldn't keep from plummeting to the ground, could you?

ULI You could name the birds migrating over the sea from the way they moved their wings, the way they spoke to each other over the waves.

*THE GENERAL burps out the throaty call of a sea bird.*

THE PILOT Uli. I have to go. To Lebanon.

ULI No.

THE GENERAL Get up, soldier!

ULI Call me habibti, Eyal. Speak to me in Arabic. We're alone. No one will hear. I promise.

THE GENERAL I hear everything.

ULI Don't go. We'll leave. Travel. To Europe. We'll get away from here.

THE GENERAL Is that what you want, Sabra, to be a deserter?! A traitor?

THE PILOT No.

THE GENERAL You know where it is.

*ULI unbuckles THE PILOT's pants.*

THE PILOT Yes.

ULI Don't go. Don't fight.

THE GENERAL Get the weapon, soldier.

THE PILOT Uli.

THE GENERAL That's an order!

*THE PILOT, half-naked, jumps to his feet and goes to the pistol's hiding place. THE GENERAL slides over to ULI and begins to pet and undress her. THE PILOT takes the gun.*

Good.

*SOFYAN enters. He sees THE GENERAL and THE GENERAL sees him.*

SOFYAN *(to THE PILOT)* Eyad. What's he doing here?

THE GENERAL *(to THE PILOT)* Shoot him.

*THE PILOT points the gun at SOFYAN. THE GENERAL continues to undress ULI. She is down to her slip. She has become DALIA again. THE GENERAL restrains her from behind, petting her.*

DALIA Eyad. Help me.

SOFYAN Help Dalia!

THE GENERAL Help your country. She's a terrorist too, pilot. Armed! You have the proof right there in your hand. Let's take her, you and me, soldier.

SOFYAN *(to THE GENERAL)* "I know thee well—a serviceable villain."

THE GENERAL "I know thee not, old man." Leave us!

SOFYAN *(to THE PILOT)* Why is this beast in my house? Who let him in?

THE PILOT I don't know.

SOFYAN Eyad!

THE GENERAL Take the shot. He's a terrorist, and the father of a terrorist.

DALIA Give me the gun. Hani left it for me.

THE GENERAL *(to* DALIA*)* I'm going to destroy you, tear you up, make you cry.

SOFYAN *(roars)* Let her go!

*THE GENERAL releases her. DALIA turns around and slaps THE GENERAL. Hard.*

*(to* THE GENERAL*)* Now walk downstage, three paces.

*THE GENERAL follows all of SOFYAN's orders obediently and precisely now, almost marionette-like.*

Give me a pirouette . . . Good. Now cry, but gently. On your knees.

*THE GENERAL obeys.*

Now get down. On all fours. And bark like a dog. I want you to really feel your character . . . Nice . . . Now lick your crotch. Like a dog, lick your own balls.

*THE GENERAL tries but cannot reach and gets tangled, rolling onto his back.*

Get up. That's enough for today. Leave.

*THE GENERAL exits.*

Fucking actors.

*SOFYAN exits. DALIA stares down THE PILOT, then exits. THE PILOT is alone. He notices the gun, still in his hand. He sits on the bed and then sticks the pistol under his pillow. Lights fade.*

## SCENE TWO

*Lights rise.*

*MIRA sits by a sleeping PILOT.*

MIRA Your face has changed, Eyal. Maybe it's the Arabic that you speak with them, working the muscles of your jaw, around your mouth and neck and eyes. You look like my father with that moustache.

*She sings.*

Oh my boy, my boy
Who wanted to fly.
My boy, my boy
Who named the birds of the sky.

My boy who passed
Every one of their tests,
Who learned to fly hard
And was taught to look west.

Look away, look sharp,
Be ready to kill!
Be a master of war
Out for his fill.

Look west, not east
Though once that was home.
Look west, for your health,
It's every man for himself!

Look up, look up
Where the night sun shone.
Look alive, look alive,
It's each boy on his own.

*She leans over to kiss him as a jet overhead shakes the house. The electricity flickers off and then on. MIRA has disappeared, and SOFYAN now stands over a sleeping PILOT.*

SOFYAN Time to wake up.

*THE PILOT jolts awake.*

I have a surprise.

*SOFYAN brings out a small slide projector. As he sets it up THE PILOT checks under his pillow. The gun is still there. He hastily conceals it.*

You used to look at these pictures all the time. Made up stories with each one.

*SOFYAN starts the slides. A picture of a group of men in the 1950s.*

That's me at the university. I wasn't enrolled but I would attend classes anyway.

*A picture of an old village in the 1930s.*

Abu Shusha. Our house was right by the mosque. My mother always complained the muezzin's voice sounded like a tortured dog when he made the call to prayer.

*A picture of three women wearing dresses in the '50s, smiling.*

That's your mother, with Selwa and Thulafa.

THE PILOT Wait. Go back. Back.

*SOFYAN reverses to the picture of the village.*

THE PILOT I know that place. That's your village?

SOFYAN A long time ago. Yes.

THE PILOT I've seen that place. But it's different now. None of these buildings are left. Some stones in the valley. But I know it. It's full of new houses. And a parking lot. There's a supermarket. Right there, on the hill.

*THE GENERAL enters. THE PILOT is alarmed. SOFYAN cannot see THE GENERAL.*

I don't understand. But I remember it.

THE GENERAL Tell him.

THE PILOT I must be mistaken.

THE GENERAL Tell him.

SOFYAN Or remembering.

THE GENERAL Tell him you grew up on top of the ruins of his shitty little village, pilot.

THE PILOT No.

THE GENERAL That your mother would take you to that supermarket.

THE PILOT No.

SOFYAN What's the matter?

THE GENERAL Tell him how when you and your friends chased out the old Arab couple who tried to come back to their house. How you threw garbage at them and called them names. Dirty, dirty . . .

THE PILOT Arabs . . . Dogs. Roaches.

THE GENERAL That's it. While you're at it, tell him I remember his village too.

THE PILOT Your village.

THE GENERAL On our way back from Latrun in '48, some of us joined up with boys from the Giv'ati Brigade and paid a visit to Abu Shusha.

THE PILOT What happened?

SOFYAN One day they appeared. In Jeeps. They shot in the air. Then they shouted at us.

THE GENERAL Fucking *Araboosh*!

THE PILOT I don't want to know.

THE GENERAL Those were the good ol' days.

SOFYAN First they singled out the men who had fought against the British.

THE GENERAL You know what they say . . .

SOFYAN One by one.

THE GENERAL Once a terrorist . . . .

SOFYAN I saw it with my own eyes.

THE GENERAL Always a terrorist . . .

SOFYAN Then I saw two women. Taken aside.

THE GENERAL I heard they were asking for it.

SOFYAN They shouted and screamed. Kicked and pushed to get away but . . .

THE GENERAL They were used.

SOFYAN They came at dawn.

THE GENERAL And then they were disposed of, like filthy rags.

SOFYAN The men were shot on sight. I don't like to talk about it, boy.

THE GENERAL I don't talk about it much.

SOFYAN Not even after all these years.

THE GENERAL At the occasional dinner party, I suppose.

SOFYAN We fled. And we lost everything.

THE GENERAL I lost men at Latrun in the fighting. Took a shot to my groin. My foot too. So those shits in Abu Shusha deserved what they got.

SOFYAN No one deserves to die like that, Eyad. Nobody.

THE GENERAL I reckon we took out fifty of 'em that day. Give or take.

SOFYAN Some were axed to death. At least that's what some of the women said.

THE GENERAL No comment.

*THE GENERAL starts clearing his throat.*

SOFYAN We ran and at night, we slept in the groves, in the woods, in caves. After that day the sun didn't rise for a week it seemed. I couldn't sleep, couldn't even close my eyes. I can still hear the sound of my little cousin Selma rolling her green marble across the hard summer ground, over and over. No one could bear to tell her to stop.

*THE GENERAL hacks and then retches up a green marble, which rolls across the floor. THE PILOT and THE GENERAL watch it, but SOFYAN does not see it.*

Her family tried to return to their house afterwards. We walked north with the others. I was barely eighteen.

THE GENERAL Great birdwatching in that part of the country, you know. I went a couple years back with my wife. She's the real expert. She lured me with a picnic in the ruins.

SOFYAN I used to share a rifle with another boy named Rabea. An old gun. Ancient. One shot at a time. To scare off the jackals at night, to protect the herds. It wasn't a weapon meant for war.

THE GENERAL Saw a Eurasian hoopoe fall right out of the sky! Just like that. It was hot as hell. A drought year.

SOFYAN Rabea stayed and fought. He told me to go with the women and children that morning, so I did. I looked for him when we got to the border, and then the camps. But I never found any trace. I don't know what happened to him.

THE GENERAL It was quick. But unmemorable, really.

THE PILOT I didn't know.

THE GENERAL You never wanted to know.

THE PILOT I'm sorry.

THE GENERAL My god, you're fond of the old man, aren't you?

SOFYAN It's not your doing, boy.

*THE PILOT kisses SOFYAN on the top of his head. THE GENERAL stands over THE PILOT.*

THE GENERAL Just promise me that if you don't have the balls to use that gun on the trash in this camp, you'll be sure to use it on yourself.

*THE GENERAL exits. The two men sit in silence for several moments.*

*Time passes. Hours, days, with the two men sitting next to each other but alone.*

*DALIA enters. She sits and stares ahead. She is numb.*

DALIA The Americans are gone. They've left Beirut. We're alone.

SOFYAN It's not the first time.

DALIA I miss Hani.

SOFYAN And it won't be the last. *(beat)* You should have gone with them. I should have made you go.

DALIA They'll come back.

SOFYAN Too many departures for me to keep track of. Too many returns that never were, too many faces in and out of focus.

*SOFYAN rises. He looks older somehow.*

Stay with him. Perhaps it's time he remembers everything, too.

*SOFYAN exits, taking the projector with him. DALIA and THE PILOT are alone. She sits on the ground next to him. Between them on the floor is the marble. They both look at it. THE PILOT picks it up and hands it to DALIA. She turns it between her fingers. After a beat the electricity cuts out, giving way to darkness.*

THE PILOT Dalia.

DALIA Yes?

THE PILOT Help me . . .

DALIA Why should I?

THE PILOT It smells like death.

DALIA That's what life smells like here.

THE PILOT Eyad is dead. Isn't he?

DALIA Yes.

THE PILOT He was shot.

DALIA Yes.

THE PILOT I'm not like you. I'm not him.

DALIA No. And yes.

THE PILOT Tell me then. I want to know.

*THE GENERAL enters in the darkness.*

DALIA It starts with death, after the month of strawberries; the months when war comes to us, war and fruit and sticky red juice. They came in June, under the command of the fat general, crushing strawberries and villages underfoot.

THE GENERAL *(singing quietly)* War and fruit and sticky red juice
Dripping down arms
Dripping down chins
Dripping down walls into everything.

DALIA And with endless columns of armour, with their one hundred forty thousand feet and their seven hundred thousand toes on the ground they marched northward, supported from the skies by the best fire Washington could provide. To disappear us.

THE GENERAL It's in the west of the city and the camps that the cancer of self-determination has been allowed to grow unabated.

DALIA Because this is where our poets, our painters, and our warriors who wish to be free have assembled.

THE GENERAL So we planned our operation and executed it.

DALIA Then he arrived. In the August heat.

THE GENERAL My records say the eleventh.

DALIA When the skies and the sea rumbled with the science of an invasion meant to put the affliction of being Palestinian into remission.

THE GENERAL Bomb the affliction. Hunt the affliction. End the affliction.

DALIA And it was on one of those endless nights of endings that it began; that he fell to us from the sky; from where he flew pressing buttons to heal us from afar.

*She lights a match.*

His wings were on fire, so he jumped. And he fell.

THE PILOT — I'm afraid, Dalia. I'm shaking.

DALIA — He should have exploded too, like a ripe strawberry. From that height, he should have ended. But he didn't . . .

*THE GENERAL blows out the match, casting all into darkness.*

You should have ended. But you are right here, pilot. You are right here. Do you understand?

## SCENE THREE

*Lights rise.*

*THE PILOT stands over the typewriter. He wraps it carefully in the cloth it came in. THE GENERAL is behind him.*

THE GENERAL — Your mission is coming to a head.

THE PILOT — Yes, sir.

THE GENERAL — You seemed a bit turned around for a while. Mixed up. A touch of the Stockholm bug, perhaps. Normal for a soldier behind enemy lines. Especially one who fell from thirty thousand feet.

THE PILOT — A lot's still not there. Sir.

THE GENERAL — Well, you know what they say; a soldier with a short memory has a long career. You'll be taken care of back home.

THE PILOT — And these people?

THE GENERAL — Their time has come.

THE PILOT — Sir . . .

THE GENERAL — Focus on your mission. The camps must be cleansed.

You still have the gun?

*THE PILOT nods.*

Good. You'll neutralize all terrorist threats as you make your way south to our lines, five hundred metres from here. Understood, soldier?

THE PILOT — How will they know it is me?

THE GENERAL — Who?

THE PILOT — The soldiers.

THE GENERAL — A soldier of ours is easy to recognize. You just shout out in that Hebrew of yours, pilot.

THE PILOT — But I look like . . . one of them.

THE GENERAL — You do look like quite the camp dweller, don't you. Not to worry. They'll know. That said, you should consider joining one of the undercover units when you're back.

THE PILOT — Like the one that killed Eyad?

THE GENERAL — You mean the terrorist Akawi? Yes. And if you'd bothered to ask me, son, you'd know Akawi wasn't writing romance novels. He was writing seditious books, books that would rile up the Arabs living amongst us. Books and articles and poems that got those faggot leftists in Europe feeling guilty and righteous. And this *Eyad* was a spokesperson for a group that attacked us on our soil. He was eliminated to protect us, to protect democracy. The unit that put bullets through his tongue did a sacred duty.

THE PILOT — Yes, sir.

THE GENERAL — To your position, Captain. Look to the sky.

*THE PILOT salutes THE GENERAL. THE GENERAL exits. THE PILOT places the gun in its original hiding place and then sits on a stool directly below the hole in the ceiling and stares up. Lights shift.*

## SCENE FOUR

LEENA He's different. There's a darkness in his eyes.

DALIA I know.

LEENA He's starting to remember.

DALIA Yes.

LEENA Good.

DALIA I'm going to turn him over. For terms.

*Silence.*

LEENA Sofyan just sits and stares at the wall. Not a word. He would get like this after a show was finished.

DALIA He is ready. To see things. As they are.

*Beat.*

LEENA Always a bit of an odd one, that man. Either a happy man stuck in a world of sadness or a sad man floating through a happy room. But now . . . now it's only sadness.

*The sound of gunfire and tanks moving in the distance.* DALIA *goes off as* LEENA *grabs the radio. She turns it on but there is only static.*

DALIA *(offstage)* I can see the tanks above on the ridge. They've pushed past the ceasefire lines.

DALIA *reappears, takes the gun from its hiding place, removes the bullets, and counts them.*

They're surrounding the camps. We have to trade him.

LEENA And what if doesn't work?

DALIA What if it does? Maybe they'll pull back if we offer them a prisoner.

LEENA Let one of the men go, someone involved, someone official.

DALIA Who? There are no fighters left in the camp. And if a man approaches their lines, they won't hesitate to shoot. I can get closer. If it's me, there's a chance.

*DALIA reloads the bullets, inserts the clip, cocks the gun, and conceals it once again.*

Pack some things. I'll be back. Watch the pilot.

LEENA Dalia, wait!

*DALIA has already left.*

*(calling offstage)* Sofyan! It's time. Up!

*LEENA exits. After a moment THE PILOT enters, removes the gun, and tucks it into the back of his pants before exiting. Lights shift.*

## SCENE FIVE

*SOFYAN, in his pyjamas, looking dishevelled, enters from the other side of the stage just after THE PILOT has exited. The typewriter lies covered in its cloth on the ground. He carefully uncovers it as if trying not to damage a delicate creature. He runs his fingers over the keys. LEENA enters behind him with a bag.*

LEENA Sofyan . . .

SOFYAN *(gently)* "Cease; thou know'st. He dies to me again when talk'd of."

*A moment.*

LEENA There is no time.

SOFYAN He would tease me. My god, that kid was funny.

LEENA Yes. He was. Take these. Put them on.

*She hands him pants and shoes. As he speaks he dresses.* LEENA *helps him as they talk, though they do not make eye contact.*

SOFYAN Do you remember, Leena, how he would kiss me every time he saw me, just like when he was a little boy. He never stopped being tender the way most boys do when they become men.

LEENA I know.

SOFYAN You didn't want him to be like that with you, but I did, I cherished his attention.

LEENA I was always harder than you, Sofyan. But he had his ways of melting me, you know that.

SOFYAN How he would pound these keys when he was writing.

LEENA Like a piano player.

SOFYAN In a trance. Playing a hard jazz. My li'l Thelonious. When he wrote he was complete. Ecstatic.

LEENA And loud. The more he wrote the less we slept.

SOFYAN We shouldn't have let him rent the office in the city. They would never have been able to get to him if he had stayed here in the camps. With us.

LEENA Oh please, Sofyan. He was busy. Writing articles for the paper, meetings at all hours. He outgrew this camp, just like everyone does. He just had a ticket out.

SOFYAN But he was alone. He was alone when they came for him. Alone when those bullets tore through him.

LEENA No.

SOFYAN All I want is to feel him kiss my neck again, Leena. To call me Babba. To hear his laugh; that ridiculous laugh of his.

LEENA He wasn't alone. He was surrounded by his words. That I know.

*SOFYAN runs his hand over the typewriter again.*

You think Dalia and Hani don't miss him every day? He was stolen from them too. And me. For you I ate my grief. But he was my boy too. My baby.

*LEENA's body is overcome with a tremendous sadness, but she doesn't cry. The two look each other in the eyes for what seems like the first time in years.*

When he was little you would spend your nights at the theatre, and I'd be alone with him. I'd just listen to him speak, making up stories, the way children do. The endless details he would come up with. "This boy won't shut up," I would say to myself. "He just talks and talks and invents things as if he were an old man."

SOFYAN The cricket Sharif . . .

LEENA . . . and Rami the roach, who rode Mustafa the mouse to Beirut to meet the bird called Bilal. And he was only a little thing then. A little performer.

SOFYAN I thought he would be an actor. I tried. Maybe too hard. He never held it against me, though. I was grateful for that. But I never told him.

*The sound of tanks is again heard in the background.*

LEENA Sofyan.

SOFYAN I know. It is time.

*LEENA exits. SOFYAN is dressed by now. He takes out the bloodied handkerchief and puts it over the keys. He then rewraps the typewriter in its cloth. He exits.*

*Lights shift.*

## SCENE SIX

*DALIA stands facing out, towards the Israeli lines, towards the audience, waving her arms. She shouts to be heard.*

DALIA
: You! In the tanks. Yeah, you! I come on behalf of the people in the camps. To make a deal. There are no fighters left here. We are defenceless. But we have one of your pilots! You withdraw and you get him back, unharmed.

*A shot rings out. DALIA ducks and then stands again.*

I'm unarmed, man! I said we have your soldier! Fell from his plane on the eleventh. Look it up and let your commander hear my offer.

*Another shot over her head. DALIA flinches.*

We could have shot him on the spot, but we didn't. If you'd prefer we can try him for the crimes of your generals and end him right here in these alleys running with shit and blood. And I'll do it too, if I have to, I will!

*The sound of laughter in the distance*

I can see you laughing behind your tanks, assholes! Hey, you! Don't you want to go home? You drive us from our land and you're not even there! It wasn't enough to chase us out and build your parks over our villages? To erase the names and make them your own?!

*Another shot in the air. This time DALIA does not flinch.*

I've heard how you take off those uniforms and travel the world after the army: India, New York, Thailand. While we're stuck here. Your freedom to walk on the beach smoking hashish and strumming a guitar comes at my expense, soldier. So what more do you want from us?! You've hunted us into the sea, blown us into the sky, and driven us under the earth. Now there's nowhere for us to go! So take your pilot and leave us alone! Please!

Don't turn away from me! Hey! You can pretend not to see me but it won't be that way if I'm to die at your hands. You'll have no choice but to see me! All I ask for is a swap. Your man for our camp.

DALIA *paces back and forth as night descends on the world.*

So what's it gonna be?

*The darkness is broken all at once by the explosion of flares in the sky above her. The night is illuminated with the crude light of day.* DALIA *looks up and then all around her. The sound of shots and commotion rises in the distance. She runs offstage. Lights shift.*

## SCENE SEVEN

THE PILOT *sits on his stool looking through the hole in the roof. At his feet there is a stack of paper and the typewriter, back in its case.*

EYAD *enters. He sits across from* THE PILOT. *He looks up and the two are, for a moment, reflections of each other.* EYAD *then picks up the pages and flips through them. After a moment or two,* EYAD *takes a pen and begins to write on the last page. He does this for several moments and then returns the stack of pages to the floor. He looks at* THE PILOT *and then up through the hole in the roof before rising to his feet and exiting.*

*The light of the flares above suddenly illuminate the room through the hole.* THE PILOT *jumps to his feet.* SOFYAN *stands in the doorway.*

SOFYAN Hello, son.

THE PILOT Sir.

SOFYAN Sofyan. Sofyan will do.

THE PILOT I must leave.

SOFYAN You can stay. If you want. You're a good boy.

THE PILOT That's not possible.

SOFYAN And your writing?

*THE PILOT picks up the papers.*

THE PILOT It is not very good. I got stuck. My mind. It's messy.

*THE GENERAL appears and looks over THE PILOT's shoulder, reading what is written.*

THE GENERAL Oh, that's clever, soldier. I also love when you write "The End" . . . Very fitting. I like it!

THE PILOT *(to SOFYAN)* I wanted to be able to write. But I'm not who you think I am.

SOFYAN I know who you are. And who you aren't.

THE GENERAL I don't know who's more fucked up, you or the old man.

*LEENA enters with THE PILOT's ironed and folded uniform. She hands it to him.*

LEENA I almost lost my stomach washing and patching it for you.

THE GENERAL I want to throw up listening to these people, soldier.

LEENA No matter how much I scrubbed . . . It smells only of death to me, boy. But it's yours. If you want it.

THE GENERAL The moment has come. End this.

*DALIA enters, winded.*

DALIA They've lit the way for the militias and allowed them through. They're entering the camps.

*She goes to the gun's hiding place.*

THE GENERAL (*to* THE PILOT) Where's / the gun?

DALIA Where's my gun?

THE PILOT *pulls out the pistol, nervously, defensively.*

Give it to me, pilot. I won't hurt you. You can go. They won't shoot you.

*The sound of shooting outside, approaching.*

THE GENERAL Don't. They 'll kill you if you give it to them. You know your mission, soldier.

DALIA Let us defend ourselves. Or let us go.

THE GENERAL Tell them there's nowhere to run.

THE PILOT There's nowhere to run.

THE GENERAL Put them out of their misery.

DALIA You look like Eyad, pilot, but you are nothing like him. You're a coward.

THE PILOT No!

THE GENERAL, *standing behind* THE PILOT, *lifts his arm for him so that the gun is pointed at* DALIA, LEENA, *and* SOFYAN.

*The sound of screams outside, and more shooting.*

LEENA They're here.

SOFYAN I won't run. I refuse to die with a bullet in my back.

DALIA *turns and calmly barricades the door with whatever she can.* THE GENERAL *takes his hand away from* THE PILOT'*s arm.*

THE GENERAL I won't crowd you. See you in Tel Aviv, kid. Break a leg.

THE GENERAL *departs, singing quietly.*

*(sings)* War and fruit and sticky red juice
Dripping down arms
Dripping down chins
Dripping down walls into everything.

*Voices outside and more shooting, closer now.* SOFYAN *picks up the stack of papers.*

SOFYAN If this were your story, Eyad, how would it end?

SOFYAN *reads the last page then looks up at* THE PILOT *as a banging on the door is heard.* SOFYAN *lets out a kind of smile.*

*Lights cut to black.*

*All is silent. All is still.*

# HISTORICAL NOTE

Starting in about 1970, Beirut became a hub for Palestinian nationalism, culture, and resistance. Already home to tens of thousands of Palestinian refugees from the 1948 and 1967 wars, the Lebanese capital—long a centre of Arab culture—attracted Palestinian artists, poets, and intellectuals, as well as political and military cadres of the Palestine Liberation Organization (PLO). The PLO, after being expelled from Jordan by its Western-backed Hashemite rulers in 1970, made Beirut its base of operations. By the mid-70s Lebanon had become a sort of Palestinian parastate, a fact that perturbed Israel as well as many sectors of Lebanese society, especially the right-wing Maronite Christian population. As a consequence, during the bloody Lebanese Civil War, which started in 1975, the Palestinians were major players, along with the Syrians, the plethora of religious and political sects of Lebanon, and Israel. One of the main Lebanese Maronite militias, the pseudo-fascist Phalange, became sworn enemies of the Palestinians and their left-wing Lebanese allies. This, combined with their opposition to Pan-Arab nationalism, made the Phalangists and the other right-wing Lebanese parties natural allies of Israel. The animosity led to a series of massacres and instances of horrendous violence between Maronites and Palestinians during the Civil War, most notably the massacre of Palestinian refugees in the Tel-al-Zaatar camp in 1976.

During the period of Palestinian ascendancy in Lebanon (1970–1982), Israel increasingly interfered in Lebanese affairs both directly (Israel briefly invaded Southern Lebanon in 1978 before the massive invasion of 1982) and indirectly via their right-wing Lebanese allies, whom Israel hoped to prop up as a proxy or vassal state in Southern Lebanon.

During this same period many Palestinian artists, intellectuals, and political leaders were assassinated by Israel and her allies. Among those killed was the novelist, playwright, painter, and Palestinian spokesman Ghassan Kanafani and the poet/activist Kamal Nasser. Kanafani was killed by a car bomb along with his young niece in July of 1972 while Nasser was killed in his home in 1973.

In early June 1982, Israel launched a massive invasion of Lebanon. With well over seventy thousand men, the support of armoured divisions, and a powerful air force and navy, Israel pushed across its northern border and swept through Southern Lebanon in a matter of days, decimating the Syrian Air Force along the way. After roughly a week the Israeli army stood at the gates of Beirut. Once there, however, they met formidable resistance from an approximate fifteen thousand Palestinian fighters and their assorted left-wing and Muslim Lebanese allies. But the PLO and its supporters were pinned in their West Beirut stronghold, between the Israelis to the south and the Maronite militias to the north and east. For over two months Israel laid siege to West Beirut, subjecting the city to relentless bombing from air, land, and sea. Despite being desperately outgunned, the Palestinian irregulars and their Lebanese allies held the Israeli army at bay, staying in the field longer than any Arab regular army had managed to in over three decades of conflict with Israel.

On August 18, after some of the heaviest days of aerial bombardment (namely August 12), the PLO agreed to a ceasefire mediated by the US. Under the terms of the ceasefire, PLO forces would be evacuated from Lebanon and sent to different Arab countries in exchange for an Israeli withdrawal. US, French, and Italian soldiers would then enter the city as a peacekeeping force. One of the major tenets of the deal was the US guarantee of the safety of the tens of thousands of Palestinian civilians left in the city.

After the PLO withdrawal, however, the US Marines and their French and Italian counterparts quickly left Beirut, and after the September 14 assassination of Lebanese president and Israeli ally Bachir Gemayel, the Israeli army quickly reoccupied Beirut and surrounded the Palestinian refugee camps. On September 17, with the Israelis in control of West Beirut and with the help of Israeli flares, the Phalangist militias entered the Palestinian camps of Sabra and Shatila and over the course of forty-eight hours massacred over thirteen hundred men, women, and children.

This play, which takes place in the Sabra camp, begins in August of 1982, during the last days of heavy Israeli bombardment of Beirut.

# REFLECTIONS ON *SABRA FALLING*

### INSPIRATION, CHALLENGES, AND EXPERIENCES IN WRITING AND PRODUCING THE PLAY

I was born to politically active Palestinian parents in Beirut in 1982, a mere two months after the massacres at Sabra and Shatila. I do not have memories of Beirut then. Before my first birthday my immediate family was able to escape the city, and in 1983 we came to the United States. We were lucky.

My parents and many relatives lived through the Lebanese Civil War of the mid-70s and through the Israeli invasion of the summer of 1982, the latter taking the lives of nearly twenty thousand Palestinians and Lebanese. While my memories of those years are inherited, my two sisters' first memories are sprinkled with the trauma of war, from the constant shelling and machine guns to jets exploding the sound barrier, from chronic electricity cuts to other moments of terror. And yet we were lucky. Many Palestinian refugees living in the twisted, cramped alleys of the camps, in Tel-al-Zaatar, in Ain-al-Hilweh, in Sabra and Shatila, were not so lucky. Some died fighting valiantly; others were massacred in cold blood.

And yet despite the horror and tragedy and ultimate defeat that Beirut represented for Palestinians, there is also, for us, the pride in having stood up to the Israeli juggernaut as no regular Arab army had before, for months on end in the summer of 1982. I grew up with the stories and characters of those years constantly swirling about me; recounted at dinner tables or at bedtime; recalled in moments of sadness, in heated political discussions, in sober historical and political analyses, or in bursts of laughter at shared memories a relative or journalist from the Beirut days would share during a visit to our Chicago home. Beirut—like Jerusalem and Jaffa, Damascus, Cairo, Amman and Haifa—was and is an integral part of the Palestinian story, of my own story, of my family's story. As such, it filtered into my earliest writing.

And then one day, several years ago, an image came to me. The skies above raining fire on the camps in the city of my birth and then, BANG, a pilot falls to earth and into the lives of a family not so unlike my own. I knew there was a play there. And slowly, the web of the thing grew from that one image. There were from the beginning and still are to this day many challenges inherent in the writing and, perhaps more so, the staging of this play—from its shifting forms and tones to its "politics" and its physical and technical demands. But I believe that this is a play that challenges in good ways. I believe its theatricality is its strength, and its politics its soul.

It is my hope, therefore, that it will prove as rich and rewarding as it is challenging for those who stage it, and those who watch or read it, whether in Canada, the US, Europe, or any other place or language in which *Sabra Falling* comes to life.

# SPERM COUNT
BY STEPHEN ORLOV

*It is my honour to dedicate this publication of* Sperm Count *to the three amazing women in my life—my mother Vivian, my daughter Emily, and my wife Karen—for their love, their support, and their inspirational spirit.*

# ACKNOWLEDGEMENTS

I extend my deep gratitude to British dramatist Julia Pascal, the first woman to direct at England's National Theatre. Julia produced and directed the world premiere of *Sperm Count* in London during tense times of mass protests against the launching of the war in Afghanistan. I can't find words to express my appreciation and respect for Julia and her cast and crew, who collectively decided to bravely defy two anonymous bomb threats demanding the cancellation of the premiere production. I also thank Canada Council for the Arts for its travel grant to attend that premiere and the High Commission of Canada in London for promoting the production.

Special thanks to Playwrights' Workshop Montreal and its former artistic director, Peter Smith, for valued dramaturgical feedback on the first draft; Teesri Duniya Theatre's artistic director, Rahul Varma, for showcasing the play in its Fireworks Festival; former Segal Theatre artistic director, Bryna Wasserman, for hosting a scene reading at a conference that led to *Sperm Count*'s premiere; Brita Oeding for her German translation of the script commissioned by Whale Songs' Verlag in Hamburg; and numerous colleagues and friends who have kindly offered insightful commentary on various drafts of the script.

And much thanks to the Canada Council for the Arts and the Playwrights Guild of Canada for supporting stage readings of scenes from *Sperm Count* at various theatre events and especially to PGC for its invaluable work promoting our playwrights and ensuring that our rights and royalties are respected under contract.

The world premiere of *Sperm Count* was produced in November and December of 2001 by the Pascal Theatre Company at the Old Red Lion Theatre in London, England, with the following cast and creative team:

| | |
|---|---|
| David Stein | Mark Heenehan |
| Lena Cohen | Adi Lerer |
| Dr. Said Hamid | Abdala Keserwani |
| Jacob Stein | Jeffry Kaplow |
| The Sperm | Daniel Ben Zenou |

| | |
|---|---|
| Director | Julia Pascal |
| Set Designer | Paul McNulty |
| Lighting | Ian Watts |
| Costume Designer | Nadine Powell |
| Assistant Director | Emily Williams |
| Stage Manager | Saira Baker |
| Voice Coach | Jessica Higgs |

## NOTES ON CAST AND SET

Jacob speaks with a Yiddish accent and Said speaks with an Arabic accent. David, Lena, and the Sperm must all have brown hair for reasons of genetics. The stage is split between the Stein home and Said's fertility clinic, with action sometimes interweaving between the two, but some scenes are set elsewhere.

## CHARACTERS

| | |
|---|---|
| David Stein | A tall fit Jewish novelist in his early forties. A liberal in jeans, he tries to mask his insecurity behind a manly veneer and prove himself the antithesis of his father. |
| Lena Cohen | David's wife, thirty-nine, an independent, attractive Jewish sculptor attired with the flair of an artist. Career-driven, she is now determined to embrace marriage and motherhood. |
| Jacob Stein | David's father, seventy-five, a Holocaust survivor. Prone to anti-Arab prejudice and a quick tongue, he relies more on stubbornness than intimacy in grappling with family matters of the past, present, and future. |
| Dr. Said Hamid | A well-dressed Palestinian immigrant of medium build, fifty. Director of a Montreal fertility clinic, he strives to never allow the politics or personality of his patients compromise his professionalism or his identity. |
| Sperm | A figment of David's imagination. An adolescent with an attitude on a skateboard, he forces David to confront both his childhood scars and his fear of fatherhood. |

## SETTING

*Sperm Count* is set in Montreal shortly after the 1991 Persian Gulf War.

## ACT ONE

### SCENE ONE

*Stein home, bedroom. Early evening.*

DAVID *and* LENA *moan passionately in the dark.*

LENA Ohhh, David . . . you're so, so . . . so . . . so deep.

DAVID Oh, Lena . . . yeahhh . . . Mmmm . . .

LENA It feels sooo . . . Ohhh . . . It's so much better without . . . Mmmm . . .

DAVID Ohhh . . . without what? . . . yeahhh . . .

LENA It, ohhhh . . .

DAVID Mmmm . . . it? Mmmm . . .

LENA Ohhh, I, I didn't, ohhhhh—

DAVID Mmmm—

LENA I didn't put it in, ohhh yes . . .

DAVID It? . . . Oh.

LENA Oh what?

DAVID *(turns on the side lamp)* You should've told me.

LENA I just did.

DAVID After the fact.

LENA After what fact?

DAVID You didn't put it in.

LENA You didn't want it in.

DAVID Don't be so defensive.

LENA Defensive? I'm not defending anything here.

DAVID Precisely my point.

LENA You've been pushing me for months to make this move.

DAVID Yeah, but this could've been *the* moment. You should've told me it wasn't in, that's all.

LENA It's in.

DAVID Fine, thank you.

LENA You're welcome. *(beat)* I know how much you want this, David, and I do too, you know that. You're right, I should have told you. It's just that . . . well now that we've decided to go ahead, I don't even want to think about it, just let it happen.

DAVID Not so fast . . . I need some foreplay.

*DAVID tickles LENA into submission.*

LENA No! Stop!

DAVID You can't take it, eh?

LENA Stop! Help!

*LENA grabs DAVID's testicles under the covers.*

DAVID Don't you dare!

LENA One more tickle and I'll squeeze!

DAVID Okay! Cease fire!

LENA No more tickles?

DAVID *(raises his hands in surrender)* Truce?

LENA Truce. *(kisses him)*

DAVID Oh, Lena, you'll be a terrific mother.

LENA You think so?

DAVID Yeah, you'll be great with him.

*Spotlight on SPERM, wearing a T-shirt, sweatpants, unlaced basketball sneakers, and earphone buds, dangling. He holds a football and leans against the doorway.*

LENA Him?

DAVID Him, her, them. How about a dozen?

LENA Let's start with one and see how it goes.

*LENA shuts off the lamp. The spotlight dims on SPERM.*

DAVID Enough foreplay . . . Mmmm.

*The phone rings.*

Shit. Hold on. *(in the dark)* Hello . . . yes, David Stein . . . What?! Which hospital?!

*Lights fade.*

## SCENE TWO

*Hospital, an hour later.*

*The sound of a heartbeat amplifies into the beeping sound of a heart monitor, as lights rise on* JACOB *Stein on IV in a hospital bed with wheels.* JACOB, *eyes shut, plays possum, as* DAVID *enters.*

DAVID *(whispers)* Pop. *(louder)* Pop.

DAVID *bends over to check* JACOB*'s breathing.*

JACOB I'm not a pop.

DAVID How are you doing, Pop?

JACOB *(opens his eyes)* I'm nobody's pop, you hear me?

DAVID I heard you. I just want to know how you're—

JACOB I'm a father. Do you know what kind of father I am? I am a father without a son.

DAVID Jesus! You're just as . . . *(pause)* I didn't come here to fight with you.

JACOB You've come here to change my intravenous, I suppose.

DAVID I came because you're my father and you had a heart attack.

JACOB You didn't hear me? I am a father without a son.

DAVID You haven't lost your timing, not a beat. I don't know how Mom put up with all of your—

JACOB Don't bring your mother into this! It's between you and me.

DAVID Is that why you didn't let me speak at her funeral? Because it's between you and me?

JACOB Solly told you, a few words, you could say.

DAVID "As long as you don't bring your lady friend." Yeah, Uncle Sol told me.

JACOB At least your mother never had to meet any of your floozies, one *shiksa* after another.

DAVID Sure she did, plenty of times.

JACOB No. No, Rosie wouldn't do that, not behind my back. No, this is between you, me, and God, nobody else.

DAVID I thought it's just between you and me?

JACOB If you were lying here hooked up to this leaky baby bottle, you'd be praying yourself, Mr. Atheist.

DAVID Agnostic.

JACOB Excuse me. The truth is, Mr. Agnostic, I don't care about your radical philosophy, I never did. What I care about is what you said in that coffee shop when that Irish redhead of yours announced to me that no son of hers would ever wear a black beanie cap.

DAVID Or a cross. And she didn't put it that way.

JACOB Whatever way your feminist floozy put it, do you remember what you told her? *(pause)* That's exactly what you told her, nothing.

DAVID That was a long time ago. Can't we just—

JACOB One year and eleven months ago to be precise. The days, they pass very fast, especially in this fancy hotel.

DAVID I'm not going to play your games, not now. Look, I spoke with your doctor, he says you'll be out in a week. I want to bring you home.

JACOB Home? Since when is your house a home to me?

DAVID Just till you're back on your feet. If you want, I'll get a nurse to come in.

JACOB Don't waste your money or your breath. I swore I'd never step foot in your new house until—

DAVID Until when?

JACOB Go on, get out of here.

DAVID How about when your grandchild is born? Will you step foot in my house on that day?

JACOB Grandchild? She's pregnant?

DAVID Will you be there for your own grandchild?

JACOB Is she pregnant?

DAVID Will you be there for your grandchild? Yes or no? *(pause)* It's been nearly two years, Pop, if I walk out that door again, I won't be back. *(pause)* You stubborn old man.

*DAVID goes to leave.*

JACOB Yes.

DAVID What?

JACOB You heard me, Davie, I said what you wanted to hear.

DAVID *(touches JACOB's arm)* Pop—

JACOB *(swats away DAVID's hand and points his finger)* Will you raise the child a Jew?

DAVID Honey.

*LENA enters.*

Ask my wife.

LENA It's a pleasure to meet you, Mr. Stein.

DAVID *(pause)* Aren't you going to say hello?

JACOB Your wife?

LENA You didn't tell him?

DAVID Pop, this is—

JACOB She dyed her hair?

DAVID This is my wife, Lena.

LENA *(shakes JACOB's limp hand)* Cohen . . . Lena Cohen.

JACOB Cohen? What happened to what's-her-name?

DAVID Before you say a word, let's get this straight, it had nothing to do with you or your—

JACOB Of course not—

DAVID It just didn't work out, period.

LENA I think you two would feel a lot more comfortable discussing this alone.

JACOB Sure, sure. We got plenty of time for lectures later on. So let me take a look at you, Mrs. Stein.

LENA Cohen.

JACOB A hyphen at least?

LENA Mr. Stein—

JACOB Jacob. As far as I'm concerned, Lenie, these days ladies can call themselves whatever they like. Cohen, it's a fine name. Of course the children, that's another story. So when are you expecting? *(LENA glares at DAVID.)* You don't look very pregnant.

LENA *(smiles)* Neither do you.

JACOB Thank God, some things never change. Davie, a sense of humour, your wife's got. But you gotta start feeding her enough for two.

LENA David . . .

DAVID What, dear?

LENA Tell him.

DAVID Yes, of course. You see, Pop, Lena and I, we, uh . . . we were only married a week ago.

*LENA glares at DAVID.*

JACOB A week ago? Now you tell me?

DAVID We wanted a very small, intimate ceremony.

JACOB And you thought I wouldn't approve, because she's already . . . *(gestures a pregnant belly)*

DAVID I knew you'd approve, that's the problem.

LENA What problem?

JACOB His problem.

DAVID Whose problem?

JACOB Your problem.

DAVID My problem?

JACOB No problem? Then what's with that interrogation of yours? The big question you threw at me?

DAVID Some things are just between you and me, like you said. Before you met Lena, I . . . I guess I had to know—

JACOB What makes you so sure I didn't cross my fingers?

LENA I have no idea what you two are talking about.

JACOB Lenie, welcome to the family.

## SCENE THREE

*DAVID and LENA step into the hospital hallway.*

DAVID I didn't actually tell him you were pregnant. I just left things vague.

LENA That's how you start off your new relationship with him? Go back in and tell him.

DAVID I just want to get him home. Once he's settled in, I'll tell him. You'll probably be pregnant by then.

LENA *(holds DAVID's hand)* I'm thrilled you made up with your father, but three weeks?

DAVID We went over this in the car.

LENA *(lets go of his hand)* I'm not a nurse. I have a solo show in six months at one of the best galleries in Soho.

DAVID I told you, I'll handle it, including the cooking. I've got nothing else to do, I can't write a word with him around.

LENA I'm talking about space, not food.

DAVID Don't worry, you'll be left all alone, working in your studio.

LENA What a way to start a honeymoon, "all alone, working in my studio."

DAVID Look, once he's back on his feet we'll be on that island. And remember those marriage vows. (*DAVID raises her right hand*) "I, Lena Cohen, agree to be serenaded every night for three weeks by a seventy-five-year-old chaperon straight out of intensive care, who happens to be my father-in-law estranged from my husband for over a year, so help me God."

LENA I never dreamed it would be this good. Well, he's the only one left to spoil our child. If my parents were still alive . . .

DAVID *(embraces her)* Do you know that you have the most beautiful eyes?

LENA *(smiles)* Okay, you've got three weeks.

DAVID If I know Pop, he won't last an hour in our house before he packs his bags.

LENA An hour? *(checks her watch)* It might still be open. You're here, you might as well check.

DAVID Come on. Testing for Tay–Sachs, fine, but this?

LENA I don't want to try for seven or eight months and then find out we have a problem.

DAVID What happened to spontaneity? Isn't that what you want, spontaneity?

LENA Don't worry, my infertility tests were all negative.

DAVID I am not worried.

*DAVID kisses LENA goodbye and heads out.*

They're called fertility tests, not infertility.

## SCENE FOUR

*Fertility clinic, a moment later.*

*SAID, wearing slacks and a sports jacket without a tie, is engrossed in a report and barely acknowledges DAVID as he enters.*

DAVID Excuse me. Is Dr. Roth still here?

SAID Dr. Roth called in sick.

DAVID Oh. When do you expect him back?

SAID When he feels better.

DAVID Ah. And when is his next opening?

SAID The clinic is closed. And I do not book his appointments.

DAVID Uh-huh. Would you mind checking? I'd appreciate it.

SAID *(finally looks up and begrudgingly checks the appointment book)* Let's see . . . next week vacation . . . then conference . . . he is booked solid untilll . . . the thirteenth—

DAVID I'll take it—

SAID Of December.

DAVID Five months?! I'm not booking a wedding here, I just need three minutes with him to get my test result.

SAID *(re-checks the book)* Well, there is a cancellation next week, but not with Roth. And it is part of a research study. Do you mind if your statistics are published?

DAVID Why should I mind?

SAID Anonymously, of course. Your name?

DAVID Stein, David Stein. And it's with Doctor . . . ?

SAID Doctor Hamid. *(looks for DAVID's file)* S, s . . . Stein.

DAVID Hamid? What's his background?

SAID *(scans the file)* Co-founder of this clinic. Next Wednesday?

DAVID And before that?

SAID Wednesday is the earliest. Eight a.m.?

DAVID No, I mean, this Dr. Hamid, where is he from?

SAID *(abruptly shuts the file)* McGill's Faculty of Medicine. Look, Roth will see you in five months.

DAVID Next Wednesday at eight.

SAID *(hands* DAVID *a sealed cup)* I will need a sperm sample.

DAVID *(hands back the cup)* I just have to see the doctor.

SAID You are now seeing the doctor.

DAVID Oh. Oh, of course, I don't know why I . . . you're not wearing your . . . David. *(offers his hand)*

SAID *(shakes his hand)* Mr. Stein.

DAVID You see I've already turned in a sample to the lab.

SAID *(checks the file)* Yes, three weeks ago. It seems that . . . hmmm . . .

DAVID Hmmm?

SAID Hmmm, yes we will definitely need another sample.

DAVID Why?

SAID Two samples are better than one.

DAVID Is there a problem?

SAID Everyone has off days due to colds, medication, stress.

DAVID How far off are we talking about?

SAID It is best to make an analysis after the second test.

DAVID Look, can you just tell me what—

SAID Your sperm count is nine million.

DAVID Nine million! That's great!

SAID Eighty million is average.

DAVID *(pause)* Eighty million? *(SAID nods.)* Average?

SAID Minimum.

DAVID Minimum?

SAID The average ejaculation is between eighty and three hundred million.

DAVID Eighty million is normal? What's with this magic number? You're telling me seventy-nine million is abnormal? What the hell does that say about me?!

SAID You are not abnormal, you are below average. One out of five couples now experience infertility problems. But your sperm count is only—

DAVID I remember my count.

SAID It is your motility that I want to check again. If your sperm project straight and fast, conception is possible even with a below-average count.

DAVID And it only takes one good swimmer, right?

*SPERM, wearing goggles, a bathing suit, and cap, "swims" unnoticed across the stage.*

I mean we're not going for Olympic gold here.

SAID To use your analogy, most of your sperm are barely treading water.

*DAVID pauses and then grabs the sample cup.*

DAVID Your washroom?

SAID Wait one week. The tests should be done a month apart in different hormonal cycles.

DAVID Cycles? You're telling me men also have . . .

SAID Correct.

DAVID Even though we don't . . .

SAID Correct. Next time your count might be higher.

DAVID Or lower.

SAID Don't jump the gun. Let's wait for—

DAVID Don't jump the gun! Doc, I'm only shooting blanks! Just explain to me why? Why are my sperm so damaged?

SAID It could be any number of reasons—hereditary, viral infection, chemical exposure.

*SPERM, wearing army fatigues and a helmet, dodges bombs as he scampers unnoticed across the stage.*

The truth is we do not have many answers yet. But I do have a few questions, if you have the time? *(DAVID nods.)* Have you ever gotten anyone pregnant?

DAVID No.

SAID Any history of drugs?

DAVID No. Well, unless marijuana counts.

SAID It counts.

*SPERM, wearing a tie-dye T-shirt stamped with the peace symbol, tokes a joint of weed, flashes a peace sign, and staggers stoned across the stage.*

DAVID But it was years ago, once or twice . . . well, maybe

more than twice. Weed doesn't affect your sperm, does it?

SAID — Everything affects your sperm. Are you on any medication now?

DAVID — No, except a couple Aspirin. Just a headache.

SAID — Have you been feeling tense lately?

DAVID — No.

SAID — Are you seeing a therapist?

DAVID — Yes.

SAID — How long have you been in therapy?

DAVID — Two months, maybe three. Three, three months of marriage counselling.

SAID — How long have you been married?

DAVID — One week.

SAID — *(jots a note)* Are you under a lot of stress at work?

DAVID — No, I'm a writer. In fact, I'm working on a novel about Jewish-Palestinian families, immigrants over here . . . it's a comedy. *(SAID looks up from his notes.)* It has its serious moments. You wouldn't happen to be—

SAID — Yes, I would happen to be. Let's have a look.

DAVID — Great! I'll bring in a copy next week.

SAID — I need to look at your groin, not your manuscript. *(gestures for DAVID to pull down his pants)* Don't worry, no one is here.

DAVID — *(drops his jeans)* Maybe we could discuss it over a cup of coffee, if—

SAID I never drink coffee after breakfast.

DAVID I'm an early riser.

SAID They should be looser.

DAVID Looser?

SAID Your briefs. Buy some boxer shorts. The cooler your testicles, the higher your sperm count. Your underwear.

DAVID Yeah, boxers.

*SAID gestures for DAVID to pull down his briefs. SAID checks his testicles.*

SAID Cough. *(DAVID coughs.)* Again. *(DAVID coughs louder.)*

*DAVID quickly yanks up his briefs and SAID jots down a note.*

It is small.

DAVID *(long pause as DAVID glances down at his groin)* It does get bigger.

SAID Your left testicle is small.

DAVID I never noticed, I . . . very small?

SAID Yes, very small. *(pause)* Mr. Stein? *(DAVID pulls up his pants.)* I do need to test you for infection. Standard procedure.

*DAVID drops his pants again as SAID removes a long metal-tipped swab from its plastic wrapper.*

Stand up straight and inhale.

DAVID Hold on, where's that going? What is that?

SAID A swab.

DAVID A swab is cotton, that's metal!

SAID *(sticks it in* DAVID*'s face)* Just the tip is metal.

DAVID And you're going to stick that . . . how far?

SAID *(gestures for* DAVID *to pull down his briefs)* Not far.

DAVID How far?

SAID Just a couple of miles. Two millimetres.

DAVID How long will you keep it in there?

SAID (*holds* DAVID*'s penis*) I am not going to incubate it. Just a few milliseconds.

DAVID How long is a millisec-

*SAID pricks the swab into DAVID's penis.*

AHHH!

SAID That's how long. You can pull up your pants. Turn in your sperm sample the morning before our appointment.

DAVID No problem.

SAID Within an hour of ejaculation.

DAVID No problem.

SAID They'll do a sperm wash immediately.

*SPERM, wearing a towel around his waist, smells his armpit as he scampers across the stage.*

DAVID You wash my sperm?

SAID It siphons out the weak sperm in your semen, so that your sample is a concentration of the best.

DAVID — The best? And the brightest? Maybe we should test their IQ while we're at it?

SAID — If your washed count is higher, we'll freeze your sperm and then discuss your options.

*SPERM, with another towel across his shoulders, shivers his way across the stage.*

You should bring your wife along.

DAVID — My wife? Sure. *(turns to leave)* Thanks.

SAID — Mr. Stein?

DAVID — Of course, I'll bring her.

SAID — The cup. *(hands him the sample cup)* Don't be too discouraged.

DAVID — Yeah. Life is full of detours, Doc. At least this one's passing through my bedroom.

*Lights fade.*

## SCENE FIVE

*A week later. Stein home, bedroom. Morning.*

*Mae West's "Copulation Blues" plays as lights rise on LENA caressing DAVID on their bed. He holds the sample cup.*

LENA — Mmm . . . How's that?

DAVID — Yeah, that's good . . . uh, maybe you should hold the cup?

LENA — *(takes the cup)* Sure. *(strokes his scalp)* Now juuust . . . relax.

DAVID — Hold it still.

*SPERM peaks out from the edge of the stage and beams his flashlight on them.*

LENA Nice and easy . . .

DAVID Shhhh . . .

LENA Mmm . . . Now juuuuust—

DAVID *(rolls over)* I'm relaxed, okay?

LENA What's the matter?

DAVID Nothing.

*LENA turns on the lamp and SPERM exits.*

I'm not in the mood.

LENA David—

DAVID What?

LENA Sweetie, it's not your fault.

DAVID You're damn right it's not my fault!

LENA Hey.

DAVID I've got to come up with eighty million sperm in one hour. I think my watch is ticking a bit faster than your biological clock.

LENA You didn't even want to be tested, and now that you have a problem, you—

DAVID I have a problem?!

LENA Now that we have a problem—

DAVID You said you, not we.

LENA *(turns away)* Do it yourself.

DAVID That's the best offer I've had in days.

LENA Now that we have a potential problem, you shouldn't feel guilty, just—

DAVID What am I supposed to do, whip my sperm into shape?

LENA Will you let me finish one sentence without cutting me off? *(pause)* Don't worry, sperm have nothing to do with impotence.

DAVID *(yanks on his boxer shorts)* Impotence?! One single time I don't get it up for you when you want it, and—

LENA When I want it?

DAVID And I'm impotent? What do you expect, some robot with a switchblade between his legs?!

LENA You don't have to prove anything to me, David. Just admit that it's bothering you and you'll feel a lot better.

DAVID Okay, I'm upset. I just found out my dinky squirt gun is spraying nothing but hot air. Thanks, I feel so much better.

LENA At least you haven't lost your imagination.

DAVID Yeah, my brain count is right up there, and highly motile.

LENA And you are an incredible lover.

DAVID You don't have to say that.

LENA I know . . .

DAVID Incredible?

LENA The best. Don't worry, David, I'm not praying for miracles. Whatever happens . . . we're together.

DAVID Oh, Lena I . . . I guess I needed to hear that. This past week, first Pop, now this. (*grabs the cup*) I feel like I've been riding a bullet.

LENA This is all new to me, too. I need you to be here . . . right here with me.

*LENA kisses DAVID.*

The clay! I forgot to shut off the kiln!

DAVID Let it burn.

*DAVID shuts off the lamp as spotlight rises on SPERM in a track suit. He is poised at the starting line of a race. DAVID and LENA continue to kiss passionately.*

LENA Ohhh . . .

DAVID Mmmm . . .

LENA Oh, yessss . . . you're so . . . so . . .

DAVID Hard . . . Ohh. Ohh! Ohh!!

*Before DAVID can ejaculate into the cup in LENA's hand, JACOB, in a robe and slippers, enters the kitchen.*

JACOB What's for breakfast?!

*SPERM scampers off, as DAVID yanks on his boxer shorts and gestures apologetically to LENA.*

DAVID Oh shit!

LENA David!

DAVID Hold on, Pop. You're supposed to be resting in bed. (*to LENA*) I'll do it at the clinic.

*DAVID leaves the bedroom and enters the kitchen.*

JACOB Bed, shmed, I've been lying on my back for a week.

Whaddaya got to eat in this house of yours? Your bride, she knows how to cook?

LENA *(from the bedroom)* Jacob, I'll fix you up something.

DAVID No, you won't! That's my job. *(approaches* JACOB*)* I do the cooking in this family. Cereal's in the pantry, milk's in the fridge.

JACOB Oy, this marriage is doomed. I see who wears the pants in this family. Since when you wear boxers?

DAVID *(puts on his jeans)* I've got to run.

JACOB Where you running so fast, half-dressed?

DAVID Just out.

JACOB Listen, Davie, I've been thinking. I got this pension fund, I told you about it, remember? If you don't mind, I'd like to put it aside for university.

*Spotlight rises on* SPERM*, sitting on a stool, wearing eyeglasses, as he reads a textbook.*

DAVID University?

JACOB It's not much, but with interest, by the time the boy's ready . . . it'll help.

DAVID The boy?

JACOB Boy, girl, who knows? You gonna have Lenie take one of those amnios?

DAVID Eventually. Listen, Pop—

JACOB Good, that way we'll know what colour to paint the room. You don't want to start painting with smelly diapers all over the floor, you know what I mean?

DAVID You see, Lena is not actually—

*Lights out on* SPERM *as* LENA *enters. She hands* DAVID *his shirt and the hidden cup falls out.* JACOB *beats him to it.*

JACOB Just out? They want your piss or your shit?

LENA Neither.

DAVID It's for my sperm, okay? My sperm.

JACOB *(checks the cup in the light)* What sperm?

LENA That's the problem.

DAVID It's only a test . . . a fertility test.

JACOB Fertility test? Who in their right mind checks for fertility? *Infertility,* you test. Who's testing what? She's pregnant.

DAVID I never actually said that.

JACOB She's not pregnant?

LENA I'm not pregnant.

JACOB You're not pregnant?

DAVID She's not pregnant.

JACOB Who's talking to who here? What do you mean you're not pregnant? *(checks the cup upside down)* It's that bad?

DAVID *(gestures for the cup)* I'll do it there.

JACOB How'd you get this problem?

DAVID Get? Don't worry, it's not contagious.

JACOB I am not worried about catching your infertility, believe me.

DAVID It's probably bad genes.

JACOB Oh? So you're just a figment of my imagination?

LENA Hey, calm down, both of you. Maybe this sperm wash will help. It can't get any worse.

DAVID Thanks.

JACOB So who's your bad sperm doctor?

DAVID I've got a good doctor.

JACOB Not good, the best, that's who you need, the best. What's his name? We gotta check him out.

DAVID *(checks his watch)* I checked him out. The cup?

JACOB Doctor who?

DAVID *(turns to leave)* I gotta go.

LENA You're leaving me here to answer his questions?

DAVID *(halts)* Hamid.

JACOB Hamid?

DAVID Dr. Hamid.

LENA He heads the fertility clinic at General. He's published in the top journals, an excellent surgeon.

JACOB He's good with a knife? That's reassuring.

DAVID He's the best in the city. You wouldn't believe how long it took me to get an appointment with him.

JACOB Since when do you trust my grandchild with an Arab butcher?!

DAVID You see, Lena, you hear that!

LENA David—

JACOB You ain't heard nothing yet.

DAVID As a matter of fact, Hamid is a Palestinian butcher!

JACOB Palestinian?! You out of your mind?! You do what you want with your own life, but not my grandchild!

DAVID Your grandchild?! What grandchild?! Don't you get it? There might not be any grandchild!

JACOB Good! A child needs a *mensch* for a father!

DAVID Go to hell!

*DAVID dashes off.*

*Lights fade.*

## SCENE SIX

*Hospital clinic, later that morning.*

*A toilet flushes in the dark.*

DAVID Impotent, eh?

*Spotlight rises on a closed toilet stall. DAVID, his pants dropped to his shoes, shuffles his feet as he turns and sits on the seat. His pants and shoes are exposed below the door.*

What does she expect under these conditions? We'll just ask Miss Bunny-of-the-Month what she thinks about my impotence.

*DAVID removes a Playboy magazine from a bag and flattens the centrefold on the floor.*

Wow, are those real? How do you do? Do you come here often?

*DAVID drops the cup.*

Shit.

*DAVID, on his bare knees, reaches blindly for the cup. He peeks out from under the stall door and retrieves the cup. He settles back onto the toilet seat, pulls down his boxers, and grunts to ejaculation.*

Mmmm . . . mmm . . . mmm . . . Ahhh!!!!!!! Thank you, ma'am.

*DAVID puts the magazine in the bag and pulls up his pants.*

Nice meeting you. A little tender loving care, that's all a guy needs. Christ, what does she expect, a sex maniac on steroids?

*DAVID steps out of the stall and gazes at his semen in the cup.*

Impotent, my ass! Not bad. Anyone home?

*Spotlight rises on SPERM, wearing an earring, a heavy metal T-shirt, jeans torn at the knees, untied running shoes, and a baseball cap on backwards. He spins his skateboard wheels. DAVID flinches.*

Come on, fellas, it's show time. Dash for that end zone, boys, score that winning touchdown for your old man.

*SPERM can finally speak now that DAVID has ejaculated.*

SPERM Football? You gotta be kiddin'.

DAVID So when you lay your head on the pillow tonight and things are festering inside, deep inside, you just replay that run over and over, every feint, every move, going for glory. You wake up a hero and your old man's beaming a grin at breakfast. Dream on, boys, dream on.

SPERM Sorry, pal, I got my own dreams.

DAVID *(flinches)* Millions, eh? How many million? I just need one, one little Davie, Jr.

SPERM Don't look at *me*.

DAVID Hey, did I tell you fellas about my dream last night?

SPERM I don't give a damn about your dreams!

DAVID So you don't want to hear that one now? Well, it can wait.

*DAVID finally faces SPERM for the first time. They eye each other.*

And when that moment finally arrives, when I hold you in my arms that first time and hear your cries . . . from that day on, I'll stand by your side. I'll never leave you. Do you hear me? Never . . .

## SCENE SEVEN

*Same moment, Stein kitchen.*

*Lights crossfade onto JACOB and LENA at the kitchen table. She drinks from a cup of coffee. He cracks open a soft-boiled egg and scoops it on toast.*

JACOB Two cups of coffee? You call that breakfast? You sculptors, you don't eat in the morning?

LENA Eating is not the problem, digestion is. Never before noon.

JACOB You don't know what you're missing. *(tastes the eggs)* Mmm, delicious. You want my recipe for Davie?

LENA Boiled eggs are boiled eggs.

JACOB I hate to be contrary, but on the contrary, these aren't just boiled eggs, they're soft-boiled eggs. And timing is key with soft-boiled eggs. A second lost here or there and you got hard-boiled eggs on your plate. White eggs, brown eggs, all the same, but there's a world of difference between soft- and hard-boiled eggs, no matter how much salt and pepper you shake. Then the toast has to pop up in time so it's still hot when you scoop on the egg. And you can't even see what's going on inside the toaster or the egg. Along with that, a warm cup of coffee you need to sip down each bite. So it's not so simple a procedure.

LENA Jacob, I would like your recipe.

JACOB I knew you'd see things my way. Tell me, Lenie, why'd you marry my Davie?

LENA Love is a bit more complicated to explain than a good recipe for soft-boiled eggs.

JACOB But a good recipe for marriage, that's a lot more complicated than falling in love. Then you throw in a baby, you really got your hands full. Not that I'm complaining about his choice, believe me.

LENA You asked about my choice, not his . . . so you could learn something about who I really am.

JACOB Talmudic logic. It works. Five minutes and I've already learned you're a smart lady, and you put your cards smack on the table. That's good. So why'd you marry him?

LENA You are persistent.

JACOB At my age, persistency becomes a virtue of necessity, not a vice of curiosity.

LENA I first met David at an opening, a group show at a decent gallery on the Main. It was pouring out. I had just finished my last sculpture. My hair was soaked, my fingernails half-baked in soapstone.

*Spotlight rises on* DAVID. LENA *stands.*

Out of the corner of my eye, I see this man staring at me across the room. He walks straight toward me and—

DAVID *enters and* LENA *turns to face him.*

DAVID It's nasty out there. Hi, my name is David.

JACOB He tries to pick you up with a line about the weather? My son, the writer?

LENA *(to* JACOB*)* From the moment we started talking, I felt this immediate connection with David.

DAVID Your sculptures?

LENA *(to* DAVID*)* Which one do you like the best?

DAVID The best? Well . . . there's an extraordinary piece over there across the room, a bust of an old peasant woman. You'd swear it was the hands and heart of Rodin. Do you know the sculptor? *(*LENA *nods.)*

JACOB So you married him because he insulted you? You have a problem with self-esteem?

LENA *(to* JACOB*)* No, he spoke his mind . . . and I was able to be myself. By the time he drove me home, we were talking about everything. At one point, I actually heard myself say . . . *(to* DAVID*)* Yes, I believe a great romantic love is possible in marriage. But that kind of romance is sustained by intimacy . . . and trust is the breath of intimacy.

DAVID So you're a poet as well?

LENA Someone wrote that to me a long time ago. She told me to never accept anything less.

DAVID Do you think your great romantic love is possible with kids? *(*LENA *laughs.)* You don't have to answer that.

LENA I'm not sure.

DAVID That will change.

LENA Really?

LENA *turns to* JACOB. *Lights fade on* DAVID.

JACOB He's got some smarts, my Davie, and lots of *chutzpah*. You're right, Lenie, he's honest . . . stubborn, but honest. So tell me, this, uh, this great romance idea of yours, how do you know it works? Two weeks you've been married. Of course, your mother, I'm sure she trusted your father.

LENA I don't know.

JACOB Now my Rosie and me, talk about trust, we—

LENA I said I don't know. My mother died when I was twelve.

*Lights fade.*

## SCENE EIGHT

*Stein kitchen and the hospital clinic, the next day.*

*The action interweaves between SAID, LENA, and DAVID in the clinic, and JACOB on the phone in the kitchen with a business card in his hand.*

*Lights rise on DAVID, LENA, and SAID.*

DAVID It doubled!

LENA Sixty-two million below normal?

SAID Your motility also improved, enough that we froze your samples.

*Spotlight rises on JACOB, talking on the phone.*

JACOB You don't have that kind of information or you won't reveal it?

SAID How many times a week do you have intercourse?

DAVID Four or five.

LENA One or two, sometimes three.

DAVID *(looks at* LENA*)* Three or four.

JACOB I know that's not your job over here, but this is not a police matter—

SAID Every other day is best—

JACOB This is a Jewish matter.

SAID And you should climax before she does.

DAVID I should?

LENA You don't.

DAVID I could.

JACOB You won't?

LENA Every time?

SAID That doubles your chances of pregnancy.

JACOB You can't help me? Well, Mr. Peretz, maybe I can help you. Maybe I can help you remember that fifty years ago your grandfather and I, we shared a bunk bed together, no pillows, no mattress.

SAID Have you considered adoption?

DAVID Adoption?

LENA We're not here to adopt.

JACOB You got my word. If anybody asks me, your name is Deep Throat.

SAID The safest clinical option is donor sperm.

JACOB *(checks the card)* Hamid, Doctor S. Hamid.

SAID It is also the quickest, easiest, and cheapest.

JACOB Thank you, Mr. Peretz.

DAVID We're not interested in donor sperm.

LENA *(to* DAVID*)* Just give me a second.

JACOB And your grandfather, he was a fine man.

*Lights out on* JACOB *as he hangs up the phone.*

LENA Who are your donors?

*Spotlight rises on* SPERM *with a stethoscope around his neck.*

SAID Most are medical students. All are screened anonymously for disease, lineage profiles, even DNA. You have some choice: physical features, personality traits. But we do not sell "designer sperm." For that you must go to a private clinic. Prices there range from very expensive to exorbitant.

DAVID Look, you froze my sperm, let's use it.

SAID Artificial insemination works best in cases with low sperm count but high motility. Take a look.

LENA *and then* DAVID *look into a microscope as* SPERM *dashes across the stage to "Camptown Races."* SAID *changes the microscope slide.*

But considering your low motility . . .

*The music slows down as* LENA *looks into the microscope and* SPERM *tries to pirouette.*

LENA David.

SPERM *faints from dizziness as the music scratches to a halt.* DAVID *looks into the microscope.*

DAVID My sperm are like those?

SAID Those are your sperm. That is why your chances are far better with IVF.

DAVID Test tubes?

LENA Petri dishes.

DAVID But that's a lot more complicated.

LENA And more invasive.

SAID *(to LENA)* Correct. Nightly hormone shots maximize your production of mature eggs. We remove them surgically, fertilize some in the lab with *(to DAVID)* your sperm, reinsert them, and then wait.

LENA Until the next try.

SAID More often than not.

LENA What about side effects from the hormones?

SAID Mood swings, hot flashes, abdominal swelling. But we monitor you daily with blood tests and ultrasounds.

LENA Every day?

DAVID What about the surgery? What are the risks?

SAID Minimal, slight chance of infection, but we can treat it. There is no major incision, we simply—

LENA You suck out my eggs and stick them back in.

SAID Correct.

DAVID Hold on, Doc, is there's anything I can do to increase my count or motility before she considers surgery?

SAID You might consider surgery.

LENA *(pause)* Oh . . .

SAID — When I examined you, I noticed that you have a large varicose vein in your penis. It creates excessive heat and that limits sperm production. Removing the vein might increase your count and motility slightly.

LENA — What kind of surgical procedure would this entail?

DAVID — He wants to cut my prick!

SAID — I don't want to do anything. But I do not cut the penis. The procedure is done internally from your nasal passage down.

DAVID — My nose is connected to my prick?

LENA — What are the side effects?

DAVID — Side effects? What's the main effect?!

SAID — None, the vein is unnecessary. Recovery within a week.

DAVID — How much for those designer sperm?

LENA — *(to* DAVID*)* We don't have to decide anything right now.

SAID — Ms. Cohen, I should mention that our clinic does not attempt IVF with a woman older than forty.

LENA — And I am thirty-nine.

SAID — Yes. It is all a numbers game and time is never on your side . . . and you should know that giving up is traumatic for many. I can provide the medical statistics, but only you can measure the psychological risk.

DAVID — Through my nose . . . ?

*Lights fade.*

## SCENE NINE

*Stein house. Evening.*

*Lights rise on* DAVID, LENA, *and* JACOB.

JACOB Through your nose?! He wants to cut your *shmuck* through your *schnozz*?!

DAVID It's not a cut—

JACOB You let this Arab go fishing down your nose, he'll catch a lot more than your swollen worm.

DAVID Look, I haven't decided anything yet.

LENA That's enough! You men are totally fixated. Ranting and raving about your precious family jewels! Don't you have anything to say to me?

DAVID You don't need any hormone shots.

LENA Screw you!

DAVID No, I mean it, Lena, forget the shots, forget the whole damn thing.

JACOB Forget it?

DAVID It's not worth it.

LENA Really? So what's it going to be? Another woman's baby or another man's sperm? *(*DAVID *turns from her.)* Don't walk away.

DAVID I'm not going anywhere.

JACOB That's obvious.

DAVID *(to* JACOB*)* And I suppose you've already made up my mind!

JACOB You're asking my opinion?

LENA Jacob, David and I need some space right now. Please?

JACOB *(steps to the side)* Sure. *(pause)* How much space you need?

LENA Thank you.

JACOB You're welcome. If only he knew what *I* went through.

*JACOB exits.*

DAVID What did he mean by that?

LENA *(LENA starts to leave)* He's your father, go ask him.

DAVID Where are you going?

LENA To my studio. You're not ready to decide anything.

DAVID *I'm* not ready?

LENA Okay. Here's the deal.

*Lights fade.*

## SCENE TEN

*Stein home. A week later.*

JACOB *(offstage)* You called that a good deal? Your *shmuck* for her *tochas*?

*Lights rise as JACOB enters with two mugs of coffee and a bag of bagels dangling from his mouth. DAVID sits at the table, reading a medical journal. LENA, alone in her studio, works on an abstract sculpture the shape of a large egg. JACOB grunts.*

DAVID Just drop it, eh?

*JACOB spits the bag on DAVID's lap.*

*(puts a hand protectively over his groin)* Hey!

JACOB A week already and your pipe's still frozen. I warned you. So what was he doing over there?

DAVID You don't judge a man's professional competence by his political opinions.

JACOB Which you happen to agree with!

DAVID Agree with what? I don't know his politics. You don't even know my politics anymore. Now are you going to tell me what you meant by that comment?

JACOB A half-dozen Jewish fertility specialists in the city and you choose a Palestinian to fix your *shmuck*. That's your politics. What comment?

DAVID *(mimics JACOB)* "If only he knew what *I* went through!"

*LENA loads a needle from the hormone vial.*

JACOB Don't change the subject.

DAVID You went through what?

JACOB No, you tell me what your doctor friend was doing in Kuwait during the Gulf War?

DAVID How do you know Hamid was there?

JACOB I got my sources.

*LENA begins to enter but stops to listen.*

DAVID Since when is it a crime to be trapped in a country that's been invaded?

JACOB Wrong. Hamid arrives in Kuwait *after* Iraq invades there, he leaves Kuwait *before* Saddam gives up.

DAVID So?

JACOB — So? So what was he doing there?

DAVID — I don't know and I don't care. Maybe he was treating civilian casualties injured by our bombs.

JACOB — Sure, maybe he volunteered free of charge, so Saddam can buy more Scuds to hit Israel. And now you're paying this Arab witch doctor to find out if you got what it takes?

DAVID — Back off.

JACOB — What's he gotta do to make a man of you?

DAVID — You son of a bitch.

*LENA enters.*

LENA — David—

DAVID — What?! *(LENA glares.)* What?

LENA — I'll do it myself.

DAVID — No, where is it? I'm sorry. *(to JACOB)* Are you going to stand there and watch the strip show?!

*LENA stomps off to her studio. DAVID follows.*

That had nothing to do with you. You got caught in the crossfire.

LENA — Really? At least Jacob finally seems fit enough to go home.

DAVID — It won't happen again. *(eyes her sculpture)* I like your, uh . . . egg?

*LENA rolls her eyes and puts on her work apron.*

I know it's not really an egg, it's more symbolic. At least you've been able to work through all of this. Christ, I haven't been able to write a word since . . .

LENA Since that poem you wrote me on our wedding night?

DAVID Since I saw Pop in that hospital bed. Lena, we have to talk. *(hands her the journal)* This article, it says these fertility hormones might cause ovarian cancer.

LENA Those hormones were pulled off the shelf three years ago.

*LENA drops the magazine on the floor and SPERM dashes in and picks it up.*

DAVID Oh. But Hamid still should have told us.

LENA I phoned him about it.

*SPERM tries to warn LENA by waving the magazine in her face, but she can't see or hear him.*

SPERM What about lag time?

DAVID Years down the line your shots might prove to be even more dangerous.

LENA Or a lot safer.

SPERM It's your ovaries and my ass!

DAVID Then at least wait on the surgery. Let's try artificial insemination, one cycle.

LENA Either way, I shoot up. You saw your sperm floating on that microscope. Denial won't get us anywhere.

SPERM *(to LENA)* Don't I have any say in this?!

DAVID *(to SPERM)* No! *(to LENA)* You said it yourself, artificial insemination is less invasive. Give it a chance.

LENA Give what a chance? My body or your sperm? *(pause)* I'm sorry, David, I shouldn't have said that. I don't want to argue, not over this.

DAVID Just one try. If it doesn't work, we go with IVF.

LENA No, David, I have one year, that's it.

*LENA hands DAVID another needle. He pauses and then preps it with a squirt, as LENA pulls up her skirt and bends forward. DAVID injects the medicine and LENA grunts in pain.*

*Lights fade.*

## SCENE ELEVEN

*Later that night. Bedroom.*

*Lights rise on DAVID at his desk, as he taps on a football and stares at an open laptop screen as SPERM appears.*

SPERM What tune you tappin'?

DAVID I'm working.

SPERM I don't see a word on that screen.

DAVID Stop bugging me.

SPERM This ain't my idea.

DAVID I'm trying to write about this bad dream. It's always the same. My old man takes me fishing, he hands me a broken pole. He takes off to get some tape, the dock starts to float away. Before I know it—

SPERM I told you, man, I don't give a fuck about your dreams!

DAVID Well you'll damn well hear this one! Because sooner or later you'll be in it!

*LENA awakens.*

LENA David!

*The spotlight dims out on* SPERM. DAVID *rushes to her bedside.*

DAVID Honey, what's wrong? Are you okay?

LENA *(rubs her backside)* God, I'm sore. It's so late. Were you shouting at Jacob again? Do you two have to argue about everything?

DAVID Honey, I know having him around has been hard on you. I'm sorry. Christ, he's even got me talking to myself. Do you know how he paid for my bar mitzvah?

*Spotlight on* JACOB *placing a tallis—the Jewish prayer shawl—on a young* DAVID, *played by* SPERM.

JACOB Davie, you know what this day means for me?

SPERM I know, Pop, this cost you a lot. This big hall, Bobby Marcus and his band, I never expected you to—

JACOB Forget the cost, your cheques will cover the bills.

SPERM Pop, those cheques are my gifts! I'm supposed to save the money for university. Mom said—

JACOB Don't worry, you work hard, you'll go to college. No, Davie, your bar mitzvah, it means you're no longer my little boy. From this day on, you're a *mensch*!

*Lights crossfade to* DAVID *and* LENA *as* JACOB *exits.*

DAVID . . . every single cheque.

LENA Talk to him about it.

DAVID About that? You just said you're fed up with us arguing. Look, I know we've been going at it, but for some reason, he's sticking around . . . and I guess I'm not ready for him to leave yet.

LENA Well, I've just about had it. It's hard enough trying to get through this on our own. With Jacob here—

DAVID He never took me fishing.

LENA What?

DAVID He never played with me.

LENA He must have played some games with you.

DAVID I had this buddy, Charlie Jackson. He spent a couple of summers on the lake with his mom and sister in a cottage next to ours. His dad would drive up on weekends. As soon as he'd arrive, Charlie would grab his football and they'd throw it around in our yard. One day, I'm watching them, just peeking through the blinds. His dad must've spotted me, the next thing I know Charlie's running in, he slaps the ball in my gut. I got all embarrassed, but when I went out and started throwing that ball around with them . . . It doesn't sound like much, does it?

LENA Enough that you remember.

DAVID And my dad? He worked, that's all I remember about him back then. Even when he wasn't at work, he was still working.

LENA That must have hurt . . . a lot. I can't imagine the baggage he's been carrying around all of these years.

DAVID You sound like my mother. *(Yiddish accent)* "Not a day goes by, Davie, I don't wake up and thank God you'll never follow your father's footsteps into that camp, not a day." No details, no stories, just "thank God." But there was only one thing I wanted to hear.

JACOB *(offstage)* Davie! Go get your ball! Let's throw it around!

DAVID The closest he ever came to playing with me was when he came to my high school games. He didn't know a thing about football, but suddenly all the neighbours were talking about his boy.

LENA He went to watch his son.

*Spotlight rises on* SPERM *holding a miniature football.*

DAVID Yeah, to watch me score my touchdowns. But after a while, I started running away from him. Honey, I'm tired of running. *(*DAVID *glances over at* SPERM.*)* I can be a better father than he was to me.

*Spotlight fades on* SPERM *as* DAVID *gazes into* LENA*'s eyes.*

I can, Lena . . . I know I can.

*Lights fade.*

## SCENE TWELVE

*The bedroom and the clinic, several hours later.*

*A red spotlight rises on* LENA *and* DAVID *in bed, as* DAVID *dreams to the sound of eerie music.* SAID, *wearing medical scrubs with a basket of eggs in hand, enters dragging a canister vacuum cleaner.* SAID *wakes* LENA *and places the basket of eggs under the blanket. He sticks the nozzle between her legs and turns on the vacuum to suck out eggs varying in size, shape, and colour from bird to dinosaur eggs.* SPERM *does sit-ups at the side.* LENA *carefully hands one egg at a time from under the blanket to* SAID, *who chucks the small eggs into a garbage bin and places the large ones on a sheet.*

SAID A beauty! . . . Too small *(smash)* . . . That's great! . . . Nope *(smash)* . . . Not quite, wellll maybe. *(calls out)* Mr. Steiiiin . . . That's onnnne dozen.

LENA *(louder)* David! We're ready.

SAID *(louder)* Twoooo dozen—

LENA Where's your sperm!

SAID Threeeee— Woops! No more. Now get some rest. I'll call you with the results.

*LENA falls asleep. SAID pulls out a skillet and spatula from the canister, puts on a chef's hat, and cracks some eggs from the carton into the skillet. He fries them on a hot plate, shaking in DAVID's sperm from two medical collection cups, like salt and pepper. SPERM does one last sit-up and wipes his sweaty brow and underarms. SAID tastes the eggs and spits them out. SAID exits with the sheet full of eggs slung over his shoulder. Lights dim.*

*The telephone rings louder and louder, as DAVID awakens from a nightmare. LENA answers the phone as JACOB, in a bathrobe, listens in on a phone in the kitchen.*

LENA Hello . . . No, Dr. Hamid, it's not too early. *(pause)* Thank you.

*LENA hangs up the phone and shakes her head. She stands limp as DAVID tries to comfort her with a hug. JACOB enters.*

JACOB He's the best?

DAVID Not now!

*LENA shakes her head in disgust and heads into her studio.*

JACOB What did you expect from—

DAVID I said I don't want to talk about it now!

JACOB You never listen!

*JACOB waves his hands in frustration and exits. LENA smashes the sculpture on the floor.*

DAVID Lena? Christ!

*DAVID rushes into the studio.*

What happened? You dropped your—

LENA My what? You call that art? That wasn't art. It was a contrived piece of . . . of everything I hate. Jacob has to leave.

DAVID (*takes her hand*) Honey—

LENA (*yanks back her hand*) Tell him to go.

DAVID Why don't we try to—

LENA If you don't, I will.

DAVID Okay, I'll tell him. But we switch doctors.

LENA You think he's responsible for your adolescent tantrums with Jacob?

DAVID Look, I know I've been acting like a jerk, like a five-year-old, but—

LENA No, you've been acting like a seventy-five-year-old. Why do you want to drop Hamid? Do you think his father ever played football with him when he was a boy?!

DAVID This has nothing to do with my father! Hamid didn't do his job, period.

LENA And what did you do, David?! What did you do the moment I put down that phone?!

DAVID I hugged you and you just stood there.

LENA What do you expect?! When I see you acting that way with Jacob!! Will you be that way with my child?! Jacob has to go!

DAVID Is that what's going on now? Is that why you smashed your sculpture? It's not just me and Pop!

LENA Don't blame Hamid for your problems!

DAVID Lena!

LENA He's trying to help you with your damn . . . !

DAVID Lena! (*grabs her*) I love you!

*LENA drops to her knees in tears.*

LENA How can I create anything? *(clutches her stomach)* I can't even . . .

DAVID *(stoops down and embraces her)* I love you.

LENA Oh, David . . . I, I just want . . .

DAVID We will, Lena . . . Lena, honey, we will . . .

*Lights fade.*

## ACT TWO

### SCENE ONE

*Stein home. The next day.*

*Lights rise on DAVID and JACOB at the kitchen table. Their repartee is fast and cutting.*

DAVID Only if you feel up to it.

JACOB I feel fine.

DAVID You're welcome to stay.

JACOB I want to go home.

DAVID You're sure?

JACOB Sure, I'm sure . . . next month.

DAVID Another month?

JACOB Or two. When you find a different doctor.

DAVID Don't get me going, Pop.

JACOB Get you going! You get yourself going wherever you want to go! You always have and you always will.

DAVID I think you should leave.

JACOB She wants me to leave?

DAVID I want you to leave.

JACOB I don't want to leave.

DAVID You don't want to leave?

JACOB *She* doesn't want me to leave.

DAVID She *doesn't* want you to leave?

JACOB You want me to leave.

DAVID *We* want you to leave. You and I can't talk for more than a minute without arguing. It's driving her crazy.

JACOB *She* said that?

DAVID She *said* that.

JACOB You want to talk, let's talk.

DAVID I don't have anything to say.

JACOB Well I got something to say.

DAVID I've heard it all before.

JACOB You asked me what I did.

DAVID I don't care what you did.

JACOB When I said to Lenie, "If only he knew what *I* went through."

DAVID I know what you went through.

JACOB You don't know.

DAVID I do know! I want you to leave!

JACOB I killed someone for you!!

*Lights crossfade to the clinic.*

SAID Another clinic or another doctor?

LENA Another opinion. I can't take another failure.

SAID I could refer you to a private clinic but your husband might not be accepted.

LENA Why?

SAID This is a research hospital, publicly funded. Private clinics are out to make a profit. They do not want to take high-risk cases that might damage their reputation.

LENA There must be an alternative somewhere?

*Lights crossfade to the kitchen.*

JACOB I thought she would be safer hiding there. We had been married one month, only one month.

DAVID I always thought you and Mom were together in the village when they came.

JACOB We all heard rumours about their "voluntary labour camps." Another roundup of deportations from the ghetto, we knew it would come. When? No one knows. Night after night we all debate. Finally, the underground decides, this time we resist. Your mother and I, we talk and talk, do this, do that. I tell her, "Go with your sister to her village, Rachel has good neighbours, it's safe. I'll stay." Your mother, like talking to a wall. Finally she says, "Okay, Jacob, I'll go with Rachel to her *shtetl* if you do one thing. You come with us and stay one night in the village, just one night with me." Sneaking out of the ghetto, it's not so easy. But an hour later, the garbage truck drives away. The stench . . . We bathed in the river for a half-hour before I slept with your mother that night. My Rosie, she was happy that night. The next morning I head back for Warsaw. By the time I arrive, the ghetto is in flames, completely surrounded by soldiers. They even gassed the sewers. I wait on a hill, the street fighting, all night I hear it. By dawn, no more shots. So I go back to Rachel's *shtetl*. I walk into the house, your mother, she's sitting there on a chair. Five soldiers interrogating her. The next day we're on the train for Treblinka.

DAVID You said that you did this for me?

JACOB Don't you see? I went to the village for you.

DAVID But I wasn't even born yet, not for another ten years. How could . . . ? Pop, did I have a brother or a sister?

JACOB No . . . you did not have a brother or a sister.

DAVID You killed someone for me? What are you talking about? Those soldiers, did they rape Mom? Who did you kill? Who was it?

JACOB I . . . I killed my own child. I conceived a child who never had a chance to be born. Not a chance.

DAVID You went to that village with Mom to conceive a child?

JACOB Rachel knew the garbage man who loaded the truck, it was leaving the ghetto in an hour, we had no time. If anything happened to me during the next uprising, at least your mother might have our child. That's what Rosie said.

DAVID And then she lost the baby in Treblinka? *(pause)* Mom must have been so weak. How many months pregnant?

JACOB Does it matter? Two, three months? Does it really

matter? Answer me, Davie, does it matter?

DAVID No, it doesn't matter. Pop, you didn't kill your child. Don't blame yourself for a miscarriage.

JACOB A miscarriage?

DAVID Mom aborted the baby?

JACOB The wire was not hard to find, it surrounded the camp. But the antiseptic, I bribed a guard with a gold crown from my tooth. When I passed the bottle to her through the fence, she didn't say a word . . . not a word.

DAVID Oh, Pop . . . I'm sorry. But you and Mom, you did what you had to do. They killed pregnant women. There's no reason to feel ashamed about what happened. Pop, this . . . this might be hard for you to hear right now but . . . I've spent most of my life trying not to be like you. Maybe all I really needed was for you to talk with me the way you just did.

JACOB Davie . . . please . . . get me my suitcase.

*Lights crossfade to the clinic.*

LENA Subzonal drilling?

SAID It is a new procedure. The sperm are injected directly into the wall of the egg. The initial results are encouraging for men with poor sperm motility. So far it has only been done in England, as a last resort.

LENA But it is on your agenda?

SAID With the right patient.

LENA If I go ahead with this, this drilling procedure, what assurances can you give me?

SAID Assurances?

LENA It's a last resort, I need it to be right.

SAID I have never performed this procedure and I am reluctant to start with a woman of your age.

LENA With all due respect, Doctor, I'm the one who's taking the risk, not you.

SAID You are thirty-nine, by the time—

LENA You're my doctor! You're not some car mechanic. You are my doctor! Just do it! It's going to work. Tell me you'll do it . . . tell me it will be all right . . . Please . . .

SAID Yes, I am your doctor, I am not a prophet. Do not put me on any pedestal.

LENA You won't do it . . .

SAID Under the circumstances, I am sorry.

LENA Sorry? Why did you become a doctor?

SAID I do not discuss my personal life with my patients.

LENA Don't worry, your politics won't offend me.

SAID Whether they are Jews, Muslims, Christians, Hindus, Buddhists, or atheists. That is a matter of principle, not politics.

LENA Yes, yes, I know. I don't mean to pry into your private life, it's just that . . . I need to trust someone.

SAID Shouldn't that person be your husband?

LENA My husband is not my doctor.

SAID Then trust yourself, Ms. Cohen, trust yourself.

LENA Who do you serve, Dr. Hamid, your patients or yourself?

*LENA eyes SAID and then turns to leave.*

SAID Jabalia. *(LENA stops in her tracks.)* Jabalia was a one-night stopover that lasted seventeen years. A UN refugee camp.

LENA You became a doctor to help your people in the camps?

SAID No . . . to help them in our country. I have worked in the camps, but the answer is more complex. I was seven years old when we fled our village. Many generations of my family tilled our land, the spirits of my ancestors remain buried in its soil.

LENA You've never returned?

SAID For a visit? We did not choose to leave, we were driven out. None of us have ever been allowed back. A displaced refugee is forced to carry his home in his heart for many years but we never relinquish our will to return. In Jabalia life was hard . . . hard enough that a young child grew old very fast. We lined up for food, for water, our clothes never seemed to fit. And we buried too many too young. Despite the poverty, we found our own playgrounds and we laughed like children everywhere. But we grew up with a hatred in our hearts. There was only one thing I hated more than Israelis—

LENA It was in the middle of a war, a war that Jews didn't—

SAID Do you want me to debate your political opinions or answer your personal question? *(pause)* Resilience was our childhood mantra. As a child, I listened to the stories of my elders, I chanted the slogans, I sang the songs, and I waited . . . for something or someone to finally arrive and bring us home. But I had no idea who or what or when that would be. At times that endless waiting to prevail provoked a sense of desperation. But too often it felt passive, almost deadly. By the time relatives in Beirut got us out of Jabalia I was determined never to wait for my death.

LENA But why did you choose to become a doctor?

SAID A poem and a friend.

*Lights crossfade to the study.* DAVID *sits motionless in front of his laptop as* SPERM, *a cigarette tucked behind his ear, gulps from a beer can.*

SPERM It's about time you got to work, Davie boy.

DAVID Where the hell have you been?

SPERM Hangin' out.

DAVID It's past your curfew.

SPERM Curfew? Aren't you a bit premature? I mean what makes you so sure I want in on this?

DAVID You keep coming back, don't you?

SPERM I go through the motions.

DAVID The motions, eh? I see how you are around Lena.

SPERM She can't even hear me.

DAVID Just own up to your feelings and she'll hear you soon enough.

SPERM I don't own a thing, pal, especially my own feelings. And I wouldn't talk, if I were you.

*Lights crossfade to the clinic.*

SAID He was more than a friend. We all called him Uncle Waheed. He had a smile as wide as the valley and a donkey almost as stubborn as himself. One night his donkey was spooked and Uncle Waheed went chasing after it right out of the camp. We found him just across the border, barely alive. The UN doctor was away working in another camp, and we could not save him. Your people stole our land and shot an old man chasing his donkey. Uncle Waheed was my friend, he hated no one, and no one hated him. All I wanted then was to kill a Jew, any Jew I could find, even though I knew none would dare enter our camp. At the funeral, my father handed me a poem. I walked to the coffin and looked up at the angry crowd. Then I read it, a poem of revenge.

LENA A hate poem inspired you to become a doctor?

SAID When I turned to place the poem on Uncle Waheed's heart, finally I could see his face. I just stood there and stared at his face. I wanted so much to see him smile again, but his eyes remained shut. At that moment, rage flooded my veins and all I wanted was a rifle. As the years passed by, I asked myself many times, what would Uncle Waheed want me to do? I could not see him holding a gun, and all I could do was pick up a stone. When it came time to choose my courses at university in Beirut, I already knew . . . I chose a scalpel, not the sword. And I still see Uncle Waheed's face in my dreams.

LENA *(pause)* One last question?

*Lights rise on the study.*

DAVID What do you got against me, anyway? What have I ever done to you.

SPERM Nothin'. Absolutely nothin'.

SAID Kuwait?

DAVID Well, that'll change, you'll see.

SPERM Oh yeah? All of a sudden we're gonna have a lovey-dovey relationship, just because you finally experienced this one moment of paternal bonding with Gramps?

DAVID There's more to it than that. Besides, he still won't

listen to me, he's in there packing his bags.

*DAVID finally starts to type on his computer.*

Sorry, I've got work to do.

*SPERM gives DAVID the finger and exits.*

LENA If that's what you were doing in Kuwait, why won't you try this drilling procedure on me?

SAID I already told you—

LENA Your uncle Waheed, what would he say to me now? "No, you're too old. Sorry, no child for you." Would he say that to me? Look, the results are impressive, you said that yourself, and you're ready to try it. Dr. Hamid, how long must *I* wait for my husband's child? The rest of my life? Just one try, that's all I'm asking.

*SAID eyes LENA.*

*Lights fade.*

## SCENE TWO

*An hour later, early evening.*

*Lights rise on DAVID, typing rapidly at his desk as LENA bursts in and kisses him hello.*

DAVID Hi, honey.

LENA You're writing, that's great!

*LENA sits on DAVID's lap and scans his computer screen.*

What is this? "The air I breathed in that garbage truck smelled fresher than the stench of death we inhaled in the boxcar." Jacob's story?

DAVID Now I know why he wants to stay. He's worried about you.

LENA *(reads on)* He never told you any of this before? *(DAVID shakes his head.)* Where is he?

DAVID Packing his bags. Tell him you want him to stay. Please?

LENA Hey, good news from Hamid.

*Lights crossfade, as LENA heads toward JACOB.*

DAVID What news?

JACOB *(packing a suitcase)* It's better for everyone if I just go home.

LENA *(sits on a chair)* I want you to stay.

JACOB Excuse me.

LENA I said—

JACOB You're sitting on one of my *ghatkes. (yanks his red boxer shorts from underneath her)* Reduced, 60 per cent off. He told you?

LENA I read it.

JACOB He's writing it down? *(LENA nods.)* You know what people went through. I was lucky, Rosie was lucky. That was then, now is now.

LENA That's not why I want you to stay.

JACOB I thought I could make things better for me and my son, and for you. But I just get in the way, I can't help myself. That's how I am, I'm too old to change.

LENA I started to think that David couldn't change, but—

JACOB In spite of me, not because of me.

LENA He's in there typing away, that's a good sign. *(pause)* Jacob, when I was fourteen, Al Rosen, my first puppy love, invited me to a New Year's Eve party. I was in my bedroom, all dressed up, putting on lipstick, I was so excited. And then the doorbell rang. I froze. I changed into my pyjamas and got into my bed. My father walked in and he just looked at me lying there. He didn't say a word. He went downstairs and told Al I wasn't feeling well.

JACOB He told him the truth, no?

LENA For weeks after that night, I would stand in front of my mirror and I'd ask my mother, "Why? Why couldn't I get out of that bed?" But she wasn't there. Jacob, I never had a chance to face my mother and say, I hate you. For so many years, I hated her for abandoning me. All I have now are photos and fantasies, and I miss her so much. Can't you give your son a chance to show how much he loves you? If you don't give him that chance, he will be less of a father for my child. I need you to stay.

JACOB So . . . you know how to get what you want.

LENA Then you'll stay?

JACOB What choice do I have? *(They embrace.)* Lenie, darling, about the child . . . don't give up hope.

LENA What choice do I have?

JACOB That's good. That's very good.

LENA Now, you've got some unpacking to do.

JACOB But maybe you should give up on this doctor.

LENA There's something you should know about Hamid.

JACOB I know all I need to know about this man.

LENA He was doing research in Kuwait.

JACOB Research? The man travels into a war zone to do infertility research?

LENA Genetic research. His DNA tests had nothing to do with the war.

JACOB Genetic research? Ah, that's different. Half the world is dropping bombs, and he's out there collecting DNA samples.

LENA You've never even met him—

JACOB And I know what he represents.

LENA He's my doctor, that's what he represents to me.

JACOB And you trust this, this—

LENA Yes, I do.

JACOB This doctor of yours?

*Lights fade.*

## SCENE THREE

*Stein home and the clinic. Several weeks later.*

*The stage is dark as we hear the sound of a jackhammer breaking up asphalt. The drilling fades out as lights rise on* JACOB, DAVID, *and* LENA *at the kitchen table. Silence reveals their tension as they pass around food, utensils, and then eat. The phone rings.* JACOB *answers. A spotlight rises on* SAID *at the clinic.*

JACOB Cohen Stein residence, no hyphen.

SAID Good afternoon, this is Doctor Hamid speaking.

JACOB Good afternoon? I hope you are a man of your word. And who do you wish to speak to on this good afternoon?

SAID Either Ms. Cohen or Mr. Stein, please.

JACOB I am Mr. Stein, Doctor.

DAVID *jumps for the phone.*

LENA Jacob!

JACOB But I think you are referring to my son. I'll see if he's around. Davie! It's for you. *(hands* DAVID *the phone)*

DAVID I'm sorry about that, Doctor Hamid, my father retains his sense of humor in the strangest moments.

SAID A gift that one acquires with maturity, I am sure. Well, as you know, this morning I tried to fertilize your wife's eggs through subzonal drilling.

DAVID Yes.

SAID Excellent results . . . six fertilized eggs.

DAVID Yes!

SAID I am sure you are pleased, but don't celebrate yet.

DAVID No.

SAID Tomorrow morning at eight, we will reinsert five of her six eggs. And hopefully she will leave here pregnant.

DAVID Yes!

SAID *(checks his appointment book)* So I will see you tomorrow at . . . oh, wait. No—

DAVID No?

SAID I have another appointment at eight. Can we make it forrr . . . ten?

DAVID Yes.

SAID See you then.

*Spotlight dims on* SAID. DAVID *hangs up the phone and* LENA *gestures impatiently for an answer.*

JACOB Yes or no?

DAVID *sticks up five fingers and smiles.* LENA *sticks up five fingers in reply and embraces* DAVID. JACOB *steps into* LENA*'s studio, checks a business card, and dials the phone.*

Mr. Peretz, please . . .

*Lights fade.*

## SCENE FOUR

*Stein home. Later that night.*

*Lights rise as* JACOB, *in bathrobe, follows* DAVID.

JACOB A regular Frankenstein, that's what he is! I knew it!

DAVID Who the hell are your spies?

JACOB I already told you, Deep Throat. Turns out your good doctor, he's into gene mapping, gene manipulation. These are his terms in his articles, published articles. And not just in Kuwait, here in his lab, right under your nose. And he's doing it with your sperm! Next thing you know, he'll be turning Jews into Arabs.

DAVID Yeah, human cloning, that's what genetic research is about these days. That's the future, Pop, whether you like it or not.

JACOB The future?! That's the past! What do you think those scientists, those Nazi madmen, what do you think they were doing in their labs? And we were their rats! It's the same thing.

DAVID For different reasons, with different results. And Hamid's guinea pigs in Kuwait are Arabs, not Jews.

JACOB Wake up, Davie, and look into the mirror. With those Arab birth rates, what's that mean for Israel?

DAVID All I care about is whether Hamid can help Lena get pregnant. If he delivers us a child, will you finally get off my back?

JACOB I have nothing more to say.

DAVID How about good night?

*JACOB stomps out.*

*Lights fade.*

## SCENE FIVE

*The bedroom. Later that night.*

*Lights rise as DAVID softly kisses LENA, now fast asleep, and then types away on his computer. He yawns and falls asleep at the table as a red spotlight rises on him. DAVID moans to eerie music and the chiming strokes of a clock. SAID enters wearing a traditional Arab robe with a swastika arm band and a keffiyeh draped under a football helmet. He waves goodbye to his last patient with a Nazi salute and carries the pouch full of eggs over his shoulder.*

SAID Next! Cohen! Get in here! Now!

*Red light remains on DAVID as he dreams. LENA gets out of bed like a zombie and sits on a swivel chair.*

Spread those legs!

*SAID plucks five variously sized eggs as a marching band rendition of the Notre Dame Victory March ("Cheer, cheer for old Notre Dame . . .") overdubs the eerie music. LENA rolls her swivel chair around the room and ducks in fear as SAID winds up like a quarterback and throws one egg after another into the pouch that LENA holds on her lap.*

One touchdown . . . Two . . .

LENA David!

SAID Three touchdowns . . . Four. How old did you say?

LENA Almost forty!

SAID And a fifth one for good luck. Happy birthday!

*Spotlight rises on* DAVID *as he awakens suddenly from his nightmare.*

DAVID Lena!

*Lights fade.*

## SCENE SIX

*Stein home. The next day, a few hours after the procedure.*

*Lights rise on* JACOB, DAVID, *and* LENA *at the kitchen table.*

JACOB So your procedure, it hurt? *(*LENA *shrugs.)* You got cramps? *(*LENA *shakes her head.)* Nauseous? *(*LENA *shakes her head.)* How about—

DAVID It's only been five hours. We don't even know if she's pregnant and you're asking about morning sickness?

JACOB Pardon me for inquiring about your wife's health. She's not eating if you hadn't noticed. You okay, Lenie?

LENA I'm fine, thank you.

*The phone rings.* DAVID *beats* JACOB *to it.*

David.

DAVID *hands the phone to* LENA *as lights rise on* SAID, *who speaks in a reserved tone.*

LENA Hello.

SAID Ms. Cohen—

LENA Yes.

SAID This is—

LENA Yes.

SAID You are—

LENA Yes?

SAID Yes, but—

LENA YES!!!!!

*LENA screams for joy, drops the phone, and leaps into DAVID's arms.*

Yes! Yes! Yes! David, I'm pregnant!

DAVID We're pregnant?!

LENA Yes, we're pregnant!

DAVID We're pregnant! I don't believe it! Lena! Did you hear that, Pop! We're pregnant!

*DAVID embraces JACOB.*

JACOB Yes! Yes, I heard, Davie, I heard!

DAVID You're going to be a grandfather!

SAID Hello! Hello!

*DAVID embraces LENA as JACOB picks up the phone from the floor.*

JACOB Hello.

SAID Mr. Stein?

JACOB Senior.

DAVID I'm so happy! I'm so sorry!

LENA What?

DAVID I've been impossible to live with!

SAID I need to see them tomorrow.

LENA I'm pregnant!

DAVID We're pregnant!

JACOB They seem to be preoccupied at the moment. Tell me the time, they will be there.

SAID The clinic opens at eight.

JACOB They will be there.

SAID It's important. Be sure to tell—

JACOB Dr. Hamid.

SAID Yes?

JACOB *(begrudgingly)* Thank you. And, uh . . . good afternoon.

*Lights fade.*

## SCENE SEVEN

*Stein home. Later that evening.*

*Lights rise on* LENA *in the studio as she works cheerfully on a new abstract sculpture. She rubs her stomach, as lights crossfade to* DAVID, *typing on his computer at the table.* DAVID *hears a knock, looks around, then resumes his typing. Spotlight rises on* SPERM *in a white bathing suit, breathing through a snorkel.* SPERM *knocks from behind a closed window.*

DAVID What are you doing in there?

*SPERM garbles through the snorkel.*

What?

*SPERM gestures for DAVID to open the window. DAVID opens it and SPERM removes his snorkel and gasps for air. They talk through the open window.*

SPERM It's about time!

DAVID *(gestures for a bear hug)* Come here!

SPERM Whoa! Not yet!

DAVID What's going on?

SPERM I ain't goin' nowhere, Pops. I'm grounded for nine months, thanks to you.

DAVID Well, at least we can talk.

SPERM You and me talk? For nine months?!

*SPERM puts on the snorkel and goes for the window.*

DAVID Wait!

SPERM You don't have a clue what I'm goin' through right now.

DAVID You're right, tell me how you feel. You think this will be easy for me? You wouldn't believe the pranks I pulled on my old man. Get this, I'm fifteen, no licence. I take the old Chevy out one night to—

SPERM You don't know shit! You ask me how I feel and before I can open my mouth, you're ramblin' on about somethin' you did twenty-five years ago. If it wasn't for her, I'd walk right now.

DAVID You're right—

SPERM Stop tellin' me I'm right and just listen. *(pause)* You want to know what's goin' on inside here? The thing is . . . I don't know what I'm goin' through any more than you do. How do I feel? I can't even feel my pulse yet. I don't know what colour hair? How tall? What size nose?

DAVID Do you realize that nose of yours is connected to your . . . sorry.

SPERM Will I look like you? Or her? How will I feel when I ride my first bike? Kiss my first girl? Maybe I'm gay. I might even be a girl. All I know is that you've dealt me this hand from a stacked deck, and I haven't even played my first card yet. *(pause)* I'm finished. *(pause)* You ain't got nothin' to say?

DAVID I know how lonely you must feel in there right now.

SPERM Lonely? I'm not lonely, believe me. Look, if you don't mind, it's been a really long day.

*SPERM puts on the snorkel and slams the window shut.*

DAVID Hey, how do I get in touch with you if . . .

*Lights crossfade to the studio as JACOB knocks on the studio door. LENA works on her new abstract sculpture as JACOB steps in.*

LENA Jacob. Hi.

JACOB Am I interrupting?

LENA No, not at all.

JACOB *(spots her sculpture)* Your new sculpture?

LENA It's not quite done, but it's close. What do you think?

JACOB Who am I to judge? I was an electrician all my life, most of my life. Now it seems I have a new occupation on the horizon . . . grandfather. I don't suppose you can study that at night school? Lenie, I, uh . . . I want to be a good grandfather.

LENA And you will be. You'll be a great grandfather.

JACOB I'm not that old. Grandfather will do for now. Well, you have to get up early tomorrow . . . that appointment.

*JACOB kisses LENA goodnight.*

LENA Sleep well. *(pause)* Is there something you want to discuss?

JACOB No, no. *(eyes her sculpture)* I like it. Good night.

*JACOB turns to leave then halts.*

Lenie, I was thinking, if you and Davie want, maybe I would—

*Lights fade.*

## SCENE EIGHT

*Clinic. The next morning.*

*Lights crossfade to DAVID, JACOB, LENA, and SAID.*

SAID I was hoping to talk with the two of you alone.

JACOB Don't worry, Doctor, I don't take it personally.

*JACOB plunks himself down in a chair.*

SAID It is a rather complex issue.

DAVID *(pulls out a chair for LENA and then sits down)* My father is a rather complex man.

SAID *(sits)* All right, but we will take this one step at a time. Part of the complexity, Ms. Cohen, is that you are pregnant with triplets.

DAVID *(pleased)* Triplets! Wow!

LENA Triplets?

JACOB *(raises three fingers)* Three?

DAVID You said there was a chance of twins, but triplets?

SAID I said that triplets are uncommon, not rare.

LENA I don't know about triplets.

SAID This does raise issues of lifestyle and career—

JACOB And bills.

SAID And health. For various reasons, many couples choose not to risk a multiple pregnancy beyond twins.

DAVID You're not suggesting—

SAID I am not suggesting anything. I am presenting the options and there is another factor to consider.

LENA Let's be clear, you're saying I should consider aborting one embryo.

SAID Premature birth is certain. And at your age, some complications might arise, especially from stress, but you are healthy and we can closely monitor the pregnancy. In your case, selective reduction is an option, not a necessity.

JACOB Selective reduction? Where do you people come up with this terminology? It sounds like something straight out of the Aryan manuals of the 1930s.

SAID I did not coin the term, Mr. Stein, and I do not make those decisions.

DAVID And you call this a fertility clinic?

SAID Nothing is simple about reproductive technology. Listen, we do need to discuss another—

LENA How do you do it with triplets?

DAVID You're not actually considering an abortion?

JACOB Consider what? She asked a question.

SAID It is the same procedure we use for a single embryo.

LENA Yes, I know, but how do you choose which embryo to abort?

DAVID Lena, I think I've heard enough for today.

SAID No one chooses based on gender or any other factor except health. For us, it is a matter of professional ethics. For the couple, it is best for their emotional stability. We would abort whichever embryo is closest.

DAVID *(sarcastically)* That seems fair enough. First come, first served.

SAID The only exception, of course, is when an embryo has a medical abnormality.

DAVID *(stands up)* You have your answer, Doctor, can we go now?

LENA *(to DAVID)* No.

DAVID No?

JACOB She said no, open your ears.

SAID We need to discuss another factor. *(DAVID sits.)* This might not turn out as bad as it sounds, and you may even choose to ignore it. But others are involved so—

JACOB Enough with the preface already.

SAID Ms. Cohen, yesterday afternoon, my nurse discovered two remaining Petri dishes in your compartment . . . two more fertilized eggs.

JACOB With triplets coming, we need another two?

DAVID I thought you said you fertilized six of her eggs?

LENA And you inserted five into me?

SAID Correct. But two are still in your compartment.

JACOB Hold your horses. You took out six of her eggs, you put back in five, she's got two left? But six minus five is . . . *Oy vey iz mir!*

DAVID Look, maybe you've miscounted? Maybe you only put in four instead of five.

SAID Possible but unlikely. The patient before you also started with six eggs, the nurse handed me five, I inserted five. But the woman has no eggs left in her compartment. *(beat)* Her last egg is missing.

LENA Maybe it's one of the two eggs in my compartment?

SAID No.

DAVID You've checked all the other compartments? *(SAID nods)* Every patient?

JACOB Check? How do you check? You brand their names on the eggs?

SAID My nurse noticed the error last night when she sterilized the used Petri dishes. She always stacks separate piles for each patient and removes them before the next procedure. One of the woman's empty Petri dishes, marked with her name, was stacked in your pile.

*LENA rises, eyes SAID, and turns to leave. DAVID gently leads her back.*

DAVID Honey.

SAID Do not assume that you are pregnant with her embryo. Everything is circumstantial.

JACOB Lenie, it was only one out of five eggs. Five to one, I'll take those odds any day.

DAVID No, three to one.

SAID Actually you are both right. It started at five to one and it is now three to one. That's assuming—

LENA Enough! That's my body you're talking about! I have been violated . . . 100 per cent violated! Do you hear me, Doctor?!

SAID Yes, you have every reason to be upset. And this has been just as traumatic for Mrs. Hassan and her husband.

DAVID Mrs. Hassan?

JACOB *(to DAVID)* Hassan! The woman who lost her egg! A Palestinian, no doubt.

SAID Correct. This was her last cycle and she did not conceive. Normally I would never raise this with you for obvious reasons, but she insisted that I ask whether you would take a DNA test, and if it proves positive, whether you would consider—

LENA A surrogate mother? She wants me to carry her child?

DAVID How can you ask such a question?

JACOB *(paces about)* I told you, Davie, I told you!

SAID It is her question, not mine. Mrs. Hassan turns forty next month. It's over. If the roles were reversed, I would have posed your question to her.

DAVID Who do you think you're talking to here?

JACOB And what's next? She owns the egg?

SAID That legal question has not yet been tested in court.

DAVID In court?! It's my fucking sperm!!

SAID Maybe, maybe not. If there was a mix-up, we are not sure when it occurred, before or after lab fertilization.

DAVID I don't believe this . . .

LENA Doctor Hamid, this Mrs. . . .

JACOB Hassan!

LENA I'm supposed to carry these three babies, my babies, for nine months, and then hand one over to her?

DAVID *(rises)* You have our answer.

SAID Thank you for considering her request. I will pass on your regrets. Do you have any questions about anything we've discussed?

LENA David, would you mind leaving for a moment. I'm fine, really.

JACOB *(pause)* Me, too?

*DAVID and JACOB step into the hallway.*

SAID *(long pause)* I know how you must feel and I—

LENA No. No, no you don't. You don't know how I feel. I have been raped.

SAID Ms. Cohen—

LENA What now, Doctor?

SAID This has never happened before in our clinic, I—

LENA Then I am really setting a precedent. Are they my babies? Can you tell? Is there some kind of test?

SAID Yes, in a month or so we can test their embryonic fluid.

LENA — But you won't do that test for an abortion?

SAID — Correct. That is our policy. Ms. Cohen, I will not make any excuses for this error. It had nothing to do with the drilling procedure. I am responsible, and I sincerely apologize.

LENA — I have so many questions, but none that you can answer. You were right, I do have to trust myself. This time, I'll call you. And it will be very soon.

*LENA enters the hallway and stands ice-cold as DAVID embraces her.*

DAVID — *(calmly)* Pop, stay with Lena.

LENA — Don't go in there.

DAVID — I'll just be a minute, honey.

*DAVID kisses her gently on the cheek and then barges into the clinic.*

You goddamn son of a bitch!!

SAID — Obviously I have not answered all of your questions.

DAVID — Who the hell do you think you are? Never in my wildest dreams could I have ever thought up the script you just delivered. One minute you tell my wife to get an abortion and the next minute she's supposed to be a surrogate mother for some friend of yours. And you call yourself a doctor? Professional ethics? Bullshit!

SAID — Are you finished?

DAVID — Yes, I am finished with you and your clinic.

SAID — Well, that is your prerogative.

DAVID — No, that's my right! Every man has the right to a child! It's people like you who profit from calling it a privilege.

SAID No man or woman has ever had the right to a child.

DAVID And so we sit here in awe, watching you in your white gown wave that magic wand, reading those stats like . . . like some emperor passing judgment on who should live and who should die. You, Doctor, you control the ultimate power trip, all in the name of humanity.

SAID My job is to—

DAVID What is your job? Who the hell gave you the right to play God here, in Kuwait, or anywhere else?

SAID *(rises)* Kuwait?!

DAVID I cannot believe the degree of incompetence you've displayed from the moment I stepped into this office.

SAID Why are you changing the insult?

DAVID I don't care what the hell you were doing in Kuwait.

SAID Well, I am going to tell you what the hell I was doing in Kuwait! You talk of rights? I have a right and a responsibility to serve my people, and I am not talking about Saddam Hussein or any of those feudal oil barons. Ten Palestinian children, all of them carriers of a genetic disorder you've never even heard of, made their way to Kuwait for my DNA tests. They had been booked months ahead. You have the right to a child? Those children have the right to a healthy life! You tell me that I should have cancelled on them because Kuwait was occupied? That is like telling me I have no right to visit Palestine—*my* homeland, not yours. *My* birthplace, not yours. You think Saddam Hussein was fighting for Palestine? No matter which side won that war in the Gulf, my people had nothing to gain either way. Do not preach to me about rights.

DAVID *(pause)* That was quite a sermon, Doc. I only wish my wife could have heard your words of comfort.

You know what? You and God do have one thing in common. Neither of you can apologize for anything.

*DAVID stomps into the hallway.*

Let's go.

JACOB Sit down! It's my turn.

*JACOB enters the clinic.*

SAID And what can I do for you, Mr. Stein?

JACOB Doctor Hamid. Doctor Hamid said this, Doctor Hamid said that. Week after week, that's all I've been hearing. You have a first name, or aren't you the kind that tells?

SAID My name is Said Hamid, and I am not the kind that tells. I have patients waiting for me.

JACOB I bet you do. There are many things I could say to you, Doctor. Many things I would never regret saying. But right now only one thing is important. Answer me one question, and I will leave you to your patients.

SAID And what might that question be?

JACOB My Lenie . . . how would you feel if she was your wife right now?

SAID Impregnated by a Jew? That's what you want to know?

JACOB I do not need to know how you would feel about that, believe me. No, let me rephrase the question. If my Lenie was your wife, would you tell her to abort one of the three embryos or not?

SAID I already addressed that issue a few minutes ago.

JACOB I remember very well what you said—it's Lenie's decision, not yours, Hassan's question, not yours. But you, Doctor, you set the limits of choice.

SAID The health of my patients sets the limits of choice.

JACOB That's only half the answer. If she was your wife, would you tell her to abort?

SAID I cannot answer that question.

JACOB You cannot or you will not? I am not just asking for your medical opinion now. Put away your charts and just tell me, what would you tell your—

SAID I said I cannot answer that!

JACOB Mr. Said! *(beat)* I am asking you a question from here. *(taps his own chest, over his heart)* I need an answer.

SAID *(beat)* I am not avoiding your question. It would be easy for me to respond with some ambiguous answer, depending on this or that factor. You want the truth, Mr. Stein? *(pause)* I do not know what I would tell my wife to do . . . I do not know.

*Lights fade.*

## SCENE NINE

*Stein home. Soon after.*

*Lights rise as* JACOB, LENA, *and* DAVID *enter with their coats on.* LENA *retreats directly into her studio to work and* DAVID *turns on his computer.* JACOB *is left standing alone. He turns toward the study but then heads into the studio.*

JACOB Lenie . . .

*The phone rings and* LENA *answers.*

LENA Hello.

JACOB It can wait.

LENA *(visibly upset)* Yes . . . no, we haven't started dinner yet . . . you're not bothering me . . . Yes, Mrs. Hassan . . .

*Lights crossfade to the study.* DAVID *shuts his laptop and taps his football to the sound of oxygen bubbles rising from a scuba tank. Lights rise on* SPERM *in a clean white towel pinned like a diaper and a snorkel in his mouth.* SPERM *taps on the window.* DAVID *tries to ignore him but eventually responds.*

DAVID I'm busy. *(tap)* I'm busy! *(louder tap)* I said . . .

DAVID *yanks open the window and* SPERM *removes the snorkel and gasps for air.*

I'm busy.

SPERM Where the hell have you been?

DAVID Not now.

SPERM *pulls the window halfway down and tries on a tallis (a prayer shawl) as if looking in a mirror.*

SPERM Oh, so now you're the boss, eh?

DAVID Forget it. You're on your own.

SPERM Now you tell me! Too late, Pops, this deal was struck months ago.

DAVID What deal? We had no deal.

SPERM I seem to remember you sayin' a while back somethin' about never leavin' my side? Does that ring a bell?

SPERM *removes the tallis and tries on a keffiyeh.*

DAVID I said it to myself.

SPERM The hell you did! You held up that cup and looked me straight in the eye. Still playin' games, eh? How about the old shell game? Hungry? Have a peanut.

*SPERM flips DAVID a peanut, then cracks one open and gulps it down.*

Hits the spot. Try it.

*SPERM cracks open another peanut, covers a nut under one of three shells he lines up on the windowsill, and then shuffles them around.*

Go ahead. If you guess right, you can eat the little bugger.

DAVID I don't play games!

SPERM Come on, lighten up. It's just a peanut.

*DAVID checks out the shells as if he's about to choose one, and then swats them away.*

DAVID What do you want from me?!

*SPERM yanks off the keffiyeh.*

SPERM You know damn well what I want.

*Spotlight rises on LENA still talking on the phone.*

LENA Yes, of course, I understand how you feel, all too well.

DAVID What the hell do you want?

SPERM I want a life!

DAVID Maybe I don't have one to give.

*DAVID goes to shut the window but steps back as SPERM pulls a gun on him.*

SPERM Or take?

LENA No please, Mrs. Hassan, there's no need for that . . . What are you going to do?

SPERM Don't worry, it ain't loaded . . . yet. Two bullets in a six-shooter, same odds.

*SPERM loads two bullets into the chamber and spins the cylinder.*

Seems to me you've been wheelin' and dealin' behind my back for quite a while now. It's about time you ante up or throw in your hand.

*SPERM slaps the gun into DAVID's hand as a heart beats loudly.*

DAVID Just like my old man, eh? Why not? If he could do it, so can I.

*DAVID spins the cylinder, and points the gun at SPERM.*

SPERM Who are you kiddin'? You can't blame this one on Gramps.

DAVID Maybe you'd rather have me play this game?

*DAVID aims the gun at himself.*

SPERM Go ahead, you don't have the balls. Pardon the pun about your tiny testacle. I didn't mean to hurt your feelings, I just don't give a shit. Too violent for your tastes? Nothin's too violent for me, not yet. You see, I can't die, I've never been born. Unless, of course, you believe the pope. Enough bravado, Pops. That bullet you've been ridin' all these months? The target's right here.

*SPERM adjusts DAVID's aim at SPERM's own head.*

Now are you gonna cock it and squeeze or do I have to swallow that sucker and pull the trigger myself?

*DAVID cocks the hammer, pauses, then throws the gun on the floor and heads into the studio.*

LENA Goodbye, Mrs. Hassan.

*LENA hangs up the phone.*

DAVID Mrs. Hassan?

JACOB The woman who lost her egg!

DAVID The nerve of her to call here!

LENA She called to apologize.

DAVID Oh.

LENA She begged Hamid to approach us. Now she's considering adopting, maybe an orphan.

JACOB And you, Lenie? What are you going to do?

LENA What do you think, David?

DAVID I think I'm playing Russian roulette with my own kid. Let Hamid do the genetic screening.

JACOB Then what? Cloning?!

DAVID *(nods him away)* Pop.

JACOB *(JACOB goes to leave.)* You need a lot more than space right now.

LENA Why don't you stay, Jacob?

JACOB She wants me to stay.

DAVID Okay, but first me and Lena. *(to LENA)* What about the screening? (*pause*) Honey?

LENA And what if it shows that I'm bearing her embryo?

DAVID If it comes to that . . . we'll have twins.

LENA Twins?

DAVID But not just any random abortion. If Hamid won't make the choice we want, we'll pay someone who will.

LENA At a private clinic?

DAVID There are a few here, more in the States.

LENA Why did you change your mind? Back in the clinic you were dead set against an abortion.

DAVID Lena, do you think I wouldn't love that baby? Even if it was half Palestinian?

LENA What if it's pure Palestinian?

DAVID Don't play games with me now.

LENA You call this a game? *(taps her stomach)* That's real.

DAVID Are you saying that you don't want an abortion?

LENA I want to know why you changed your mind.

DAVID Because I don't want to kill our own child. I won't take that risk.

LENA Then you'd still consider triplets? We wouldn't terminate any embryo no matter who it came from.

DAVID Honey, if we do nothing we risk all three babies and you as well. I'm not willing to bet your life on anything.

LENA And what are the risks?

DAVID You heard Hamid.

LENA I heard plenty of betting odds thrown out, but none about my health. I know the odds for healthy triplets at my age. Do you?

DAVID I don't care what the odds are. They're not good enough for me when it comes to your health.

LENA Really? My health or your lineage? Somehow we keep coming back to that same question.

DAVID You didn't want donor sperm either.

LENA They hadn't impregnated me at the time. Admit it, David, you want purebreds and nothing else.

DAVID Purebreds?! We're not going to a dog pound to choose some bastard mutt.

LENA Not without your genes.

DAVID We're talking about our family!

LENA Just admit it, you don't want a Palestinian child.

DAVID What's wrong with twins?!

LENA What's wrong with all three?!

DAVID Because I want my own kids! Okay? Is that a crime? To want your own kids? Maybe that doesn't sound right to you, but that's how I feel and there's nothing I can do about it. I want my own kids. Our children.

LENA *(pause)* I see. And what do you think, Jacob?

JACOB Are you through, Davie?

DAVID Go ahead, maybe you can drive some sense into her.

JACOB Lenie, for us Jews, this abortion issue—

DAVID Pop, just—

JACOB You were first, now I'm second. This abortion question, it's not so clear. But according to our tradition, when any moral choice comes down to the health of a mother, she takes priority.

DAVID Forget the goddamn tradition, just tell her what you think is right.

JACOB In this case, it happens to be the same. Lenie, it's your health that counts, whatever you decide.

DAVID I don't believe this!

LENA Thank you, Jacob.

DAVID After everything you've been through in your life, how can you possibly—

JACOB And you know everything?

DAVID Never once have you passed up a chance to tell me what to do. This is a life or death issue, and you pass the buck all in the name of our goddamn tradition!

JACOB Who are you to lecture me about life or death?!!

DAVID *(turns to leave)* I don't need to hear this now.

JACOB Don't you dare run away from me again!!

LENA David.

DAVID Don't push me away again!!

LENA Stop it!! Both of you!

JACOB I shouldn't have, Lenie, I—

LENA I will not be forced into making any decision I might regret for the rest of my life. After everything I've gone through to become pregnant, I—

DAVID Everything *you've* gone through? Lena, you are pregnant with my babies. You're not some teenager trapped in a ghetto. You are thirty-nine years old and—

LENA Almost forty, and I am pregnant! Not you, me. *(grabs her belly)* I am carrying them here . . . right here. How could you possibly know what that feels like?

DAVID I don't know, but—

LENA But what?

DAVID But I have a right to my own feelings. Honey, I know the thought of an abortion makes you feel sick. I respect your feelings, but I—

LENA It's not just feelings I'm carrying inside of me, David.

DAVID You've already decided, haven't you?

JACOB Decided what? I didn't hear any decision.

DAVID Lena, this will affect my life as much as yours. Can't you see that? You are my wife. You're not in this alone.

*DAVID stares into LENA's eyes.*

Or maybe you are.

LENA You want an abortion? Here!

*LENA slams her sculpture into DAVID's abdomen.*

Smash it! Go ahead.

JACOB *(gently)* Davie . . . give it to me, Davie.

*JACOB carefully takes the sculpture and tries to hand it to LENA, but she stomps into the bedroom and crawls into bed.*

Davie . . .

*DAVID rejects JACOB's gesture of comfort. Crossfade to the bedroom as he approaches LENA, who is cradled in bed with her back turned.*

DAVID Lena . . . Lena, honey. Can we talk? *(pause, as DAVID tries to hold back tears)* I'm trying to be there for you, Lena, I am. But nothing is the way it's supposed to be, not one damn thing. I can't even pass a baby in a stroller without turning my head away. My gut's so twisted and tight, I don't even know where I'm going half the time. And just now, when we were arguing back there, I looked into your eyes and for the first time . . . I couldn't see you. You're so far away. *(pause)* Can't you even look at me?

LENA *looks up at* DAVID *and then turns her back to him.* DAVID *stomps out the door. Another door slams in the distance. A car starts and drives off.*

LENA David . . .

LENA *buries her tears in her hands. Lights dim to black.*

## SCENE TEN

*Stein bedroom. Moments later. Darkness.*

LENA Ahhhh!!!

*Lights rise on* LENA *as* JACOB *rushes in to find her standing motionless, her back turned.*

JACOB Lenie! Lenie, what's wrong? Are you all right?

LENA *turns to reveal her blood-stained dress.*

LENA Jacob, I'm spotting.

JACOB *drops the sculpture and it breaks.*

JACOB Oh my God, the babies!

LENA Where's David? Where is he?

JACOB I don't know, I heard the car.

LENA Call the clinic.

JACOB *(dials the clinic)* Sure, sure, Lenie.

LENA — Tell them to get Hamid. Please, hurry.

*JACOB scribbles a note as he talks on the phone.*

JACOB — Hold on, Lenie, I'm going to get you there. *(on the phone)* Hello, get Dr. Hamid! It's an emergency! . . . Not there? Then page him! Tell him that Mrs. Stein—

LENA — Cohen! Lena Cohen!

JACOB — Cohen, Lena Cohen, she's having a miscarriage!

LENA — Thanks!

JACOB — Yes, that's the address! Tell the ambulance to hurry!

*JACOB knocks the phone off the hook as he tries to hang up.*

Come, Lenie, come.

*LENA and JACOB rush out as a spotlight rises momentarily on DAVID listening to a busy signal in a phone booth. JACOB dashes back quickly to leave the note for DAVID.*

LENA — *(offstage)* Jacob!

JACOB — I'm coming, Lenie, I'm coming!

*JACOB dashes off. Ambulance sirens and honking horns in the dark transition into the sound of a dial tone. Lights crossfade to the Stein home, as DAVID enters and looks for LENA.*

DAVID — Lena! Lena? Pop?

*DAVID spots the phone on the floor and hangs it up. Lights crossfade to the clinic as JACOB stands next to LENA lying on a hospital bed. SAID rushes in, whips off his tuxedo jacket and checks her pulse.*

SAID — Mr. Stein, please wait outside.

JACOB — I stay right here with my daughter.

SAID Leave now!

LENA Jacob.

JACOB She wants me to stay.

LENA Jacob!

JACOB You take care of her, Doctor, you hear me?

SAID I hear you.

*JACOB kisses LENA's hand and exits. SAID, his back to the audience, spreads LENA's legs apart and examines her.*

What happened? Did you fall?

LENA No, nothing happened, just an argument. I started spotting.

SAID I'm afraid it's more than spotting.

*SAID turns around to face the audience with his hands dripping in blood.*

Nurse!

*Lights crossfade to the Stein home. DAVID spots the broken sculpture on the floor and picks up a piece in each hand.*

DAVID What's happened to us? What the hell happened?

*Lights crossfade to the hospital hallway. JACOB paces as SAID enters wearing a blood-stained frock.*

JACOB How is she?!

SAID She is very weak, but she is going to make it.

JACOB Good, that's very good. And the babies, what about the babies?

SAID I should discuss that with your daughter-in-law first. As soon as the sedative wears—

JACOB What's wrong?

*Lights crossfade to the kitchen.* DAVID *spots* JACOB*'s note and reads it as the spotlight rises on* SPERM*, in a blood-stained diaper, holding himself up, his bloody face plastered to the window.* SPERM *taps his snorkel on the window too softly to catch* DAVID*'s attention.* SPERM *takes a step back and is about to ram his head through the window.*

DAVID *(finishes reading the note)* Oh my God!!

*Blackout.*

*The sound of a shattering window.*

*Lights rise on* SAID *standing next to* LENA *lying in bed on intravenous medication.*

LENA I was bleeding so much. How many died?

SAID It could have been worse. If you had not arrived here when you did, you might not have pulled through yourself. I am sorry but—

LENA All three?

*Lights crossfade as* DAVID *bursts into the hospital hallway.*

DAVID Pop! How is she?

JACOB Davie! She's fine. Lenie's fine.

DAVID Where is she?

JACOB Hamid, he told me she's okay.

DAVID The babies? What about the babies?

*Lights crossfade to the hospital room.*

SAID You need to rest now.

LENA After what you just told me, how can I possibly rest?

DAVID *and* JACOB *rush into the hospital room.*

DAVID *(rushes to* LENA*'s side)* Lena!

LENA David.

DAVID Oh, Lena, honey. Are you all right?

JACOB Lenie . . .

DAVID I was so worried.

LENA David . . . two of the babies . . .

DAVID Two died?

*LENA covers her tears. DAVID embraces her.*

JACOB But the other one, it's fine? *(*SAID *nods.)* Oh, thank God. And Lenie, she's fine. That means you and Davie, you'll have a child. Sure Lenie, just like you wanted.

LENA He only heard one heartbeat, only one.

*DAVID rises, eyes SAID menacingly, and approaches him slowly.*

JACOB The nurse, she told me she paged the doctor at a wedding, a family wedding. He was here, Davie, when we arrived. Thank God, he was here.

LENA David, I was bleeding so much I could have lost all three.

SAID My condolences, Mr. Stein. We did everything we could.

DAVID *(pause)* Thank you.

SAID You should thank your wife for her strength. Some women would have given up. I have seen it happen before.

DAVID The two babies that died . . . can you tell whether they were—

LENA I don't care which ones died! I don't care . . .

*DAVID turns back to comfort LENA.*

SAID If you are asking about a DNA match, I cannot answer that until—

LENA No more tests, I've had it with tests.

DAVID I know, honey. *(to SAID)* But the one who survived, do you know if it's a boy?

SAID You could find that out later, with an amnio.

LENA I don't want to know anything about that baby until I hold it in my arms.

JACOB The odds are good, Davie, 50-50 it's a *boychick*.

LENA *(to DAVID)* All you can think about now is having a son?

JACOB You know, Davie, sons, they can be difficult at times, believe me.

DAVID Pop, would you mind? Dr. Hamid?

*JACOB kisses LENA's hand and exits with SAID.*

## SCENE ELEVEN

DAVID Lena, when I got home and you were gone, I thought . . . I thought you had left me.

JACOB *(offstage)* So tell me, Doctor, you have a son?

DAVID And then I saw Pop's note. Lena . . . I love you so much?

LENA Yes, yes I know.

DAVID *(holds LENA's hand)* Honey . . . the babies . . . I'm sorry

. . . for everything I've put you through. I'm so sorry. *(pause)* I talked to him.

LENA Who? Who did you talk to?

*A dim silhouette of* SPERM *lies motionless, bent over the window frame with the snorkel in his mouth and shattered glass on the floor.*

DAVID A boy. I don't know his name, but . . .

LENA David, what are you talking about?

DAVID I know this sounds weird, Lena, but I talked with him . . . this, this imaginary boy. I know he wasn't real, but he was real enough that I could hear him . . . deep inside of me, I could hear him. We talked to each other . . . about my past, about the future, our future, things I was afraid to talk about with Pop and . . .

LENA And with me? *(gently releases his hand)* What do you want me to say? Congratulations? You have a baby boy?

DAVID No. No, that doesn't matter anymore. No more tests, Lena, no more. It's over.

LENA *(touches her belly)* No, David, it's not over.

DAVID Don't worry, everything will be okay.

LENA I just lost two of my babies and you tell me "don't worry." David, I'm sorry but . . . I need to be alone.

DAVID Okay . . . I'll, uh, I'll be in the hallway, just out there. I'll sleep out there tonight, I'll just pull up a chair. I'll be here for you, Lena.

LENA I need to be alone.

DAVID *(pause)* For how long?

*. . . but* LENA *doesn't move.* DAVID *turns to look at* SPERM *as a heart beats and a spotlight rises on him in a clean, white bathing suit. He is no longer sucking on a snorkel.* SPERM *stands up weakly and scoops off the window frame a tallis around one wrist and a keffiyeh around the other. He spreads his arms far apart, gazes first at the tallis, then at the keffiyeh, and finally looks up with a pondering gaze at the audience.* DAVID *turns to* LENA.

LENA *holds her gaze on* DAVID, *momentarily touches his hand, then turns and curls up in the fetal position.*

DAVID *waits for a response but* LENA *doesn't move.* DAVID *starts to walk out, looks at* SPERM, *and then turns to* LENA.

I just want a kid . . .

DAVID *looks off into nowhere.*

A normal, healthy child.

*"It's a Wonderful World" by Louis Armstrong plays as lights on* DAVID *and* LENA *dim slowly.*

*Final spotlight on* SPERM *dims slowly to black.*

# REFLECTIONS ON *SPERM COUNT*

### INSPIRATION, CHALLENGES, AND EXPERIENCES IN WRITING AND PRODUCING THE PLAY

I was born in Boston and raised in an immigrant working-class family that had few qualms about my quitting Hebrew school after my bar mitzvah. I didn't learn much Hebrew but those biblical and historical stories of how our ancestors had fought oppression, reinforced by childhood nightmares about the Holocaust, left its mark on my psyche. Support for Israel was a given, a birthmark of the tribe, though we rarely discussed politics around the dinner table.

As a student activist, I began to question conventional wisdom on many social issues at home and abroad. The more I studied, the more I asked why Jews, who had founded a state to end their oppression, were now depriving Palestinians that same right? It's no surprise that I later tackled in my second and third plays (and now another in development) a major theatrical taboo that challenges to the core my identity as a progressive Jew—the Israeli-Palestinian conflict.

I've chosen to set my Jewish and Palestinian characters in the Diasporas of North America because that's the world I know best. And the more serious the theme, the more I rely on dark comedy to deliver it. So in *Sperm Count,* I draw on male infertility as a multi-layered metaphor that pinballs gender, generations, and cultures, mainly for comic and dramatic value, partly because I faced the problem myself. I opted for adoption, but a close childhood buddy and his wife experienced some of the same invasive procedures, inherent within the bizarre world of reproductive technology, that are dramatized in this play. A sperm on a mission for lineage—a fitting allegory for birthright and statehood.

Understanding the politics of the Israeli-Palestinian conflict is complicated, but creating authentic characters to dramatize it realistically for stage is complex, and far more challenging for me. Overt didacticism destroys drama because it overshadows what makes us human. It's not enough for my "other" characters to express believable dialogue defending their religious beliefs and political convictions. The real challenge is to create authentic characters of both sides, free of stereotypical depiction, that are well-rounded with all the complexity, good and bad, of human nature, characters that are true to their culture, to their world, and to their times.

My greatest test dramaturgically in all three of my Diaspora plays is trying to capture the emotional subtext of my Palestinian characters, to give voice to their narrative and their memory, to portray the nuances of confluence between tradition and displacement on family relations from one generation to the next, all with anecdotal accuracy, not rhetoric. Reading Palestinian prose and poetry and listening to their stories in person have helped me scale, however briefly, those ghetto walls of language and identity. And attention must be paid to the rhythm and syntax of dialogue—how Jewish and Palestinian (not merely Arab) immigrants speak English.

As for the production challenges, I flew to London to polish the script soon after 9/11. And the play opened shortly after the War in Afghanistan began, when London was rocked by mass demonstration, one of which I joined. Despite the progressive theme of my play, the theatre received two anonymous bomb threats demanding its cancellation, perhaps because it was identified with England's major festival of Jewish arts and culture, on at that time. The cast and crew met alone and collectively decided to bravely defy the threats, and fortunately the play opened without any problems.

Not many in London or New York were venturing out for a night of theatre during those tense weeks, as war raged on abroad in the aftermath of 9/11. So many theatres on both sides of the pond recorded record-low attendance and some shows closed. The audiences at the *Sperm Count* premiere were spirited in their applause, and I was heartened to hear their compliments and expressions of thanks in the lobby after the show. Considering the cultural challenges of writing such a play, I was particularly encouraged by compliments on Said's character from Palestinians and other Arabs who had attended the production and earlier stage readings or had read the script; I heard comments, such as "I hear Said's voice" and "We know many like him."

I was moved by the enthusiastic reaction of my fellow playwrights familiar with the script and actors who had performed in its production and stage readings. Most of the reviews offered praise, including those from London's Jewish press. Julie Reichman wrote in *Jewish Renaissance*: "The play was attraction from start to finish . . .

A highly intelligent script with unexpected twists and interesting observations, it holds the audience's attention throughout." And John Nathan's review in England's *Jewish Chronicle* was equally positive: "Well conceived! Orlov has spun into his play a web of political and emotional anxieties . . . The fascinating core of his play [is] the trust between Palestinian doctor and Jewish patient. But the author gets a lot of comic mileage out of the emasculating effect of a low sperm count and where he scores particularly well is in his sensitive handling of man's brooding need for a child."

Artistically, I feel I did my job. But premiering the play in the aftermath of 9/11, in the midst of a controversial war in Afghanistan, followed soon after by an even more unpopular war in Iraq, proved disastrous for second productions. The political climate in North America was so toxic toward Arabs and Muslims that few theatres dared to consider staging plays that portrayed them in a positive light. Many theatres rejected my pitch and most that had agreed to give the script a read didn't reply. And some on the Left felt the play was not violent or tragic enough, which ignores the fact that it's a Diaspora story set in North America, not on the battlefields of the Middle East. During the premiere run in London, I was invited to discuss *Sperm Count* at an international Jewish theatre conference in Tel Aviv during the Second Intifada, and a few days after my arrival, Ariel Sharon bombed Yasser Arafat's compound in Ramallah. A number of artistic directors, including Israelis, asked to read the script but none returned my correspondences.

After a year of rejections, I filed the play and went on to my next project. A decade later, the brutal Israeli bombardment of Gaza in 2014 prompted me to pull out *Sperm Count* from my files and the idea of editing this anthology was conceived.

# TALES OF A CITY BY THE SEA

BY SAMAH SABAWI

*To my father, Abdul Karim Sabawi, and his beloved city by the sea.*

# ACKNOWLEDGEMENTS

No words can adequately describe my sincere gratitude to Liz Jones and the La Mama staff for believing in the value of this work and for giving me unquantifiable support, starting with providing the space for our first public reading in 2012, through to co-producing our premiere in 2014 and our remount in 2016.

My deep appreciation to Daniel Clarke and Rand Hazou, who guided me and mentored me every step of the way, and to Petra Kalive for her dramaturgical interventions. My love and gratitude to Steve Payne for his encouragement, guidance, and friendship.

I would like to acknowledge the amazing *Tales of a City by the Sea* cast and crew in Australia and in Palestine, with special thanks to Abdelfattah AbuSrour and the Alrowwad Cultural and Theatre Society team in the Aida refugee camp in the West Bank. Their efforts to stage the play, despite the shortage of funds and in defiance of Israeli military curfews, was nothing less than inspirational.

I am indebted to the A.M. Qattan Foundation Child Centre in Gaza for hosting the public reading in 2013, and to Haidar Eid, Ayah Bashir, Eman Hilles, Sameeha Elwan, Mohammad Ghalayini, Manar Zommo, Alia Abu Oriban, Ayman Qwaider, Alaa Shublaq, Najwan Anbar, Khaled Harara, Mahmoud Hammad, Lubna Al Rayyes, and Salah Sabawi for their dedication to the work, their support, and their valuable feedback.

My appreciation and heartfelt regrets to Ali Abu Yassin and Aya El-Zinati in Gaza, whose efforts to stage the show were thwarted by the brutal war on Gaza in 2014. Those long Skype calls we shared as the bombs fell will remain etched in my memory forever.

Lots of appreciation to my sister Khulud, who is always the first to read every script I write, and to Siham, Hamed, Nahedh, and Faris for putting up with me when I'm in the writing zone.

Most of all, thank you to my life partner and best friend, Monir; your love nourishes my creativity and feeds my soul.

*Tales of a City by the Sea* premiered simultaneously in Australia and in Palestine in November 2014.

## IN AUSTRALIA

Staged in its original English language, the play was co-produced by La Mama Theatre in Melbourne and directed by award-winning director Lech Mackiewicz, who brought together a range of theatrical styles, including epic theatre, with the actors visible at all times. The play was set on a minimal stage with a non-realistic set characterized by its makeshift sensibility. The set was operated by the actors giving the audience a full view of set transformations. Before the start of the play, the actors mingled with the audience and introduced themselves as actors who were there to share a story. There was no effort to create the illusion that they were their characters. Instead, they ensured the audience understood that they were being shown something. This type of Brechtian alienation is an element of epic theatre that separates the audience from the story they are being told. While this technique created a sense of alienation, there was also a live singer performing traditional songs a capella in Arabic who acted as a kind of emotional narrator throughout the play: existing outside the action while connecting to the audience. The performance at La Mama Theatre showcased the following cast and creative team:

| | |
|---|---|
| Jomana | Nicole Chamoun |
| Rami | Osamah Sami |
| Lama | Emily Coupe |
| Ali | Reece Vella |
| Abu Ahmed | Majid Shokor |
| Samira | Wahibe Moussa |
| Mohanad, Homeland Security, father in hospital | Ubaldino Mantelli |
| Um Ahmed, Homeland Security, mother in hospital, nurse | Cara Whitehouse |
| Singer | Aseel Tayah |

| | |
|---|---|
| Director | Lech Mackiewicz |
| Assistant Director | Izabella Mackiewicz |
| Set Designer | Lara Week |
| Lighting Designer | Shane Grant |
| Photographer and Graphic Designer | Ahmad Sabra |
| Sound Designer | Khaled Sabsabi |
| Sound Mixer | Max Schollar-Root |
| Assistant Stage Manager | Nada Mustafa |
| Stage Manager | James O'Donoghue |
| Dramaturge | Petra Kalive |

| | |

## IN PALESTINE

In the West Bank, the play was translated into Arabic, staged by the Alrowwad Cultural and Theatre Society in the Aida refugee camp and directed by Abdelfattah AbuSrour. During the rehearsals and the performances, the cast and crew were subjected to various challenges ranging from travel restrictions to curfews and Israeli incursions into the camp. But with determination and much beautiful resistance, the play was finally premiered almost one week past its initial scheduled opening night. The performance at the Alrowwad Cultural and Theatre Society showcased the following cast and creative team:

| | |
|---|---|
| Jomana | Amira Abusrour |
| Rami | Ribal AlKurdi |
| Lama | Hala Alyamany |
| Ali | Issa Mustapha |
| Abu Ahmed | Mohamad Shalan |
| Samira | Marwa Romi |
| Assorted roles | Issa Nour |
| Lighting and Sound | Ahmed Ajarmah |
| Set Design | Issa Ismael, Mahmoud Dyab, and Issa Nour |

Though this play is best performed by a full cast of eight actors and a live singer, it can be performed with a minimum of six actors who can double in other roles. The singer can be substituted for an audio recording of the traditional songs named in the text.

## CHARACTERS

| | |
|---|---|
| Jomana | A Palestinian journalist in her late twenties, born and raised in the Al-Shati refugee camp in Gaza. |
| Rami | An American doctor of Palestinian origin in his midthirties, born and raised in the US. Arrives in Gaza as part of the first Gaza Freedom Flotilla in 2008. |
| Lama | Jomana's cousin, a woman in her early twenties looking for love and adventure. |
| Ali | Lama's fiancé. He is in his late twenties and owns one of Gaza's notorious tunnels. |
| Samira | Rami's mother, a stylish wealthy Palestinian-American woman in her late fifties. She lives in the US. |
| Abu Ahmed | Jomana's father. A struggling fisherman in his late fifties. He lives in the Al-Shati refugee camp. |
| Singer (optional): | A woman dressed in traditional Palestinian clothing. |
| Um Ahmed | Jomana's mother. |
| Mohanad | An Egyptian doctor coming through the tunnels. |

Mother in hospital
Father in hospital
Homeland Security Officer 1
Homeland Security Officer 2

*Tales of a City by the Sea* is inspired by events the author and her family have personally experienced during the past several years. Most of the poetry in the play was written during the three-week bombardment of Gaza in 2008/2009.

## SCENE ONE

*Gaza beach. The singer sings the opening song, "Nialak ma ahda bal-ak: lucky you have peace of mind," as the audience enters the theatre. The sound of waves heard in the background throughout the scene.*

*Onstage, JOMANA sits on the beach with a diary in her hand. She is wearing a long-sleeved shirt and jeans. Her hijab is wrapped loosely around her shoulders. She is completely absorbed in writing. LAMA is standing nearby, looking into the sea. LAMA is also dressed in conservative, casual clothes but her hair is totally covered under her hijab. Once the audience is settled in their seats, the singer stops her song and JOMANA begins to read aloud from her diary.*

JOMANA *Gaza, August 2008*
The landscape constantly changes
Only the sea remains
Salty
Fluid
Mysterious
Moody
A consistent presence amid the chaos

*The sound of an Israeli drone interrupts JOMANA. She looks up at the sky and follows the drone with her eyes until the sound fades out. She returns to her diary.*

Its whooshing waves whisper tales
Of occupiers that have come and gone
Crusaders, tyrants, and warlords

Riding on their horses
Riding on their tanks
Riding on their F-16 fighter jets
Always riding through
Leaving their footprints
And part of their history
Leaving their artifacts and ruins
Leaving fire and debris
Always leaving . . .
Only the sea remains

LAMA I love coming here.

JOMANA I know.

LAMA If you stand with your back to Gaza facing the sea, you can easily imagine you are someplace else: Beirut . . . Alexandria . . . Tripoli . . . Santorini . . .

JOMANA Countries . . . continents . . . the whole world is out there.

*LAMA sits next to JOMANA. They stare into the sea.*

LAMA If only we could ride the sea.

JOMANA If only our bodies were bulletproof.

LAMA If only our boats were made of steel.

JOMANA If only our dreams were real. *(beat)* Look! You can see the Free Gaza boats from here.

LAMA They must be ready to leave. You know, I stayed up all night fantasizing about sneaking on board these boats. Imagine me . . . an adventurous stowaway sailing off to see the world.

JOMANA Sure . . . on what passport?

LAMA I said stowaway . . . Must you ruin every fantasy?

JOMANA Fantasies get stuck at the border; they never make it passed the checkpoints.

LAMA Well a few fantasies must have snuck on board these boats because I'm having them.

*Faint sound of music in the distance.*

JOMANA Really?

LAMA Music!

JOMANA What more will they do for these activists?

LAMA How exciting! This is the most entertainment we've had here in years.

*JOMANA's phone beeps; she reads a text message, smiles, and texts back*

Who are you texting?

JOMANA One of my many admirers, of course! Listen, why don't you go to the pier and take a closer look at the action. I know you're dying to.

LAMA Only if you come with me!

JOMANA I want to finish writing this poem and you are distracting me.

LAMA You can write this poem some other time! Come on! Maybe we'll be lucky and make it on the news tonight.

JOMANA I wouldn't want to steal the show from the activists.

LAMA You won't have to . . . The politicians have stolen the show a long time ago, with all the speeches and photo ops. Come on! We are the people . . . we too deserve our share of the spotlight.

JOMANA Fascinating! Girls your age dream of being discovered by film producers or modelling agencies and you dream of being discovered by news networks.

LAMA This is Gaza; we make do with whatever we have.

JOMANA I guess. Our entire life seems to be one long news story!

LAMA Oh, lighten up! Yallah, come with me. I want to watch the dancing.

*JOMANA's phone beeps again; she checks the text message and smiles. LAMA looks at her with suspicion.*

Oh my God! This smile . . .

JOMANA What?

LAMA I haven't seen this smile before. This is new. Jomana, who are you texting?

*LAMA reaches for the phone but JOMANA quickly sticks it in her pocket.*

JOMANA This is none of your business. But you know what is your business? Your fiancé, Ali! Why don't you go and find him. After all, you're supposed to be with him, not with me.

LAMA You want me to find Ali? Let me tell you, Ali is inevitability. He is like death. It doesn't matter where I hide from him, he will find me.

JOMANA You are terrible!

*ALI arrives holding two cups of juice. He is wearing dress pants and a shirt and has a cigarette tucked behind his ear.*

ALI There you are!

LAMA Told you!

*ALI hands LAMA and JOMANA the juice. He kneels next to LAMA and pretends to whisper.*

ALI Okay, let me try to explain how this is supposed to work . . . you and I are supposed to ditch the chaperone. Yet, every time I've taken you out, you and your chaperone end up ditching me.

LAMA Oh, Ali, a little effort is not going to kill you! You're supposed to chase after me, so do your job and stop whining.

ALI I don't mind chasing, but today with all the international media, I thought it would make good PR for Gaza to have a gorgeous couple like us walking around . . . holding hands . . .

*ALI leans closer to LAMA, flirtatiously. She pushes him away and he falls. JOMANA laughs.*

JOMANA Yes, Lama, you should totally do it for Gaza.

ALI Damn right she should! How else can we humanize the men in this place?

LAMA Fine! I will be a martyr for the cause. I will come with you, hold your hand, and look at you with adoring eyes, but this act will cost you much more than a juice cup, Romeo.

ALI Name your price.

LAMA Dinner at The Lighthouse.

ALI Done.

JOMANA Great! Off you go. This chaperone would love nothing more than to be ditched by both of you. Yallah, leave before I change my mind.

*ALI stands up, offers LAMA a hand, and pulls her up.*

ALI Let's hurry! I promised Rami we'd meet him at the pier.

*JOMANA hides a smile. ALI and LAMA don't notice.*

LAMA Hang on. Let me fix my hijab. *(She tightens her scarf around her head.)* Jomana, are you sure you don't want to come?

JOMANA Positive! I'll catch up with you later.

LAMA Fine. But please cover your hair if you plan to stay here by yourself. You are not in Europe, you know.

JOMANA But you said I could imagine I am someplace else.

LAMA Ha ha . . .

*LAMA yells as ALI pulls her away.*

Seriously, you can't sit alone looking like this! Cover your hair. You know how strict they've become about these things.

*JOMANA stands up and reaches for her scarf reluctantly as she watches them leave, then in a deliberate move, she lets go of it and begins to fix her hair, mumbling to herself.*

JOMANA Oh, they won't be strict today. They want to show the world how progressive they are . . .

*RAMI enters but JOMANA doesn't see him. He stands right behind her wearing rolled-up, worn-out jeans, a keffiyeh, sandals with socks, and a backpack covered with Palestine solidarity badges and stickers. JOMANA continues.*

. . . After all, the guests they are bidding farewell to are a bunch of non-hijab wearing feminists, lefties, and gays . . .

RAMI And which category do I fall into?

JOMANA *(startled)* Rami!

RAMI Well?

JOMANA Let me see . . . I think you are the tormented diaspora Palestinian who wears Palestine as if it were a fashion statement . . . but there is hope for you.

*RAMI walks closer to her and stares in total adoration.*

RAMI And hope is what sustains me. I'm so glad you came!

JOMANA I'm on chaperone duty so I had to come.

*RAMI gently strokes her face with his fingers. Shyly she steps away from his reach. He looks down at her diary.*

RAMI What are you writing?

JOMANA A new poem.

RAMI I look forward to reading it.

*RAMI steps closer but JOMANA backs away, nervous.*

JOMANA Do you see the port? The circus is over *there*.

RAMI I only see you.

JOMANA Music, balloons, and dabke.

RAMI Time went by quickly. I can't believe I've only been here for six days. I don't know how I will leave this place.

JOMANA Then don't. Don't leave! It was a miracle that you even made it in in the first place.

RAMI I know. We made history! We broke the siege for the first time!

JOMANA And did it on two small wooden boats . . .

RAMI Impressive, right?

JOMANA Is this the part where I'm supposed to melt?

*They share a smile, but JOMANA's smile doesn't last long. She turns her back to RAMI, looking increasingly sad.*

I heard one guy from Italy decided to stay.

RAMI Yes. Vittorio. He is lucky he can do that.

JOMANA He is? So why not you? This is your homeland. You

should be the one staying here. You shouldn't have to run back to America.

RAMI So you want me to stay?

JOMANA I don't care what you do, I'm only pointing out what your duty is to your country . . . you know . . . from purely a nationalistic point of view. Gaza needs you. That's all!

RAMI Believe me, Jomana, I need her too. I think I've fallen in love . . . with her.

JOMANA Really? . . . But you hardly know her.

*RAMI holds JOMANA's hand.*

RAMI I have known her all my life. *(He kisses her hand; she blushes and quickly pulls away. RAMI looks around.)* You know, I think this is it. This is the exact spot where my grandparents took that photo of their first outing together. It was back in 1954. My grandfather was dressed in his best suit and tarboosh, and my grandmother looked like a Hollywood movie star. My grandfather stood behind her like this . . . *(RAMI stands behind JOMANA.)* . . . and he had one hand on her waist, like this *(RAMI tries to put his hand on JOMANA's waist. Nervous, she looks around and quickly removes it.)* I never thought I'd come here and stand in this spot . . . with a love of my own . . . I love you, Jomana!

JOMANA Then don't leave! Please don't leave!

RAMI My patients . . . my clinic . . . my interns . . . my mother . . . I have things I must do in the US. Too many people are waiting for me. But I promise you I will sort things out and will come back.

JOMANA Please just don't! Don't make promises you can't keep. How and why would you come back? There is nothing here for you.

RAMI Not even from a nationalistic point of view? *(JOMANA is not amused.)* There is plenty for me here. My heart is here. My everything is right here.

JOMANA Don't call me your "everything" and in the same breath tell me you have to go.

RAMI I will return.

JOMANA How? We're under siege.

RAMI Look over there at these two wooden boats. They sailed rough seas, stood up to one of the world's most powerful armies, and made it here. They . . . we . . . broke the siege. The boats will come back and I will come back.

JOMANA Beautiful words, but all I hear is you saying goodbye . . . I'm so stupid! I'm so stupid. *(She begins to wrap her hijab around her head covering her hair.)* I really thought I could convince you to stay.

RAMI I wish I could . . . I really do . . . but I just can't drop my entire life . . . Jomana, what has gotten into you?

JOMANA Don't you get it? Over here every time we say goodbye to someone, we say it like it is the last time, and most often this turns out to be the case. No one can get in . . . WE CAN'T GET OUT.

RAMI Don't be so dramatic.

JOMANA *Dramatic*? Ya allah! What was I thinking . . . ?

*She tries to leave but he pulls her back.*

RAMI Jomana, wait . . . I don't understand . . .

JOMANA But I do! I've seen your type many times before.

RAMI What is that supposed to mean?

JOMANA You know . . . your type. Palestinians with international passports . . . They come here on a feel-good adventure to see the poor people of Gaza. They take photos, make promises, and then they run back home to their comfortable lives where once in a while, they talk about the plight of their people over polite dinner conversations with other sophisticated, privileged people . . .

RAMI You can't be serious . . .

JOMANA Perhaps your friends will be entertained to know that on top of our poverty and terrible living conditions we also seem to suffer from irrational and *dramatic* separation anxiety.

RAMI What the fuck is the matter with you . . .

JOMANA Don't use that disgusting American language here.

RAMI Don't tell me what language I can or cannot use. You think this is a hobby? You think I'm on a search for entertaining topics for dinner conversations? You really think that the Free Gaza boats are some kind of adventure tourism? Is this what you think of me? Is this what you think of the activists who risked their lives for you, for us, for our people?

JOMANA Oh, please . . . our people? Look at us! Look at where I live. Then think of your life. Rami, there is no "our people." There is *my* people and then there is *your* people!

RAMI So you get to decide if I am Palestinian or not? Jomana, I came here to make a difference, to stand up for what I believe in and to reconnect with my roots and you know what, I admit it. YES! I FEEL GOOD ABOUT IT! I don't have to apologize for that and in fact, I don't have to apologize for being born in the US or for having a decent and secure life there.

JOMANA Well I've lived here all my life and I am trapped and insecure and tired of being abandoned by those who leave and never return.

RAMI — It is tearing me up to have to leave but you must understand that I am not running away. *(He pulls her in and holds her hands.)* I am not running away. I couldn't do that even if I tried.

JOMANA — I just . . . feel as though I've waited for you all my life . . . and now that you're here I'm supposed to watch you leave . . .

RAMI — I've waited for you too. For so many years, I've read your blogs, your poems, every letter you've written . . . every word . . . every sentence drew me in deeper and deeper. I have fallen in love with you even before I set foot in Gaza. I cannot imagine a life without you.

JOMANA — I too have kept every email you've sent . . . memorized every word . . . tried to imagine what it would be like if you came here . . . God! I was so naive to think that you'd take one breath here and feel so at home that you would never want to leave.

RAMI — Habibti, I love you! . . . Let's not fight anymore. I don't want the last of our time together to be like this. Have faith in me when I say I will return. I promise! I promise!

*The singer sings "El Asmar al loon," the heartache song, as the couple walks away from each other. The singer continues as lights fade.*

## SCENE TWO

*Split stage. On one side JOMANA and LAMA are sitting in JOMANA's living room in the Shati camp on a modest sofa with Palestinian embroidered cushions and a simple coffee table. There is an open laptop on the coffee table. The two women are laughing. On the other side RAMI is sitting on a lush leather sofa in his upscale southern US home looking at his laptop screen. Throughout the scene JOMANA's mother's voice is heard offstage from the kitchen.*

UM AHMED — *(offstage)* What are you two giggling about? Enough nonsense and come to the kitchen.

LAMA Khalto, I'm telling Jomana a very juicy story. Just give us a few minutes.

JOMANA Well? Don't leave me hanging. What did Salim say?

LAMA My poor brother *(laughing)* . . . when her father opened the door, he had no choice but to pretend he was actually visiting him and not coming to see Dalya.

JOMANA That's hilarious!

LAMA Her father looked a little suspicious, so Salim had to pretend he was a fan of his poetry.

JOMANA *(laughing uncontrollably)* Oh no . . . not the poetry . . .

LAMA *(between bouts of laughter)* Yes . . . the poetry . . . so . . . Salim spent the night with Dalya's father listening to really bad poetry and pretending to enjoy it.

JOMANA Tell me at least Dalya was there.

LAMA That's the best part. She wasn't. She was at our house . . . looking for Salim. When she saw me she pretended she came to see me. Thinking Salim would be back soon, I tried to hold on to her for as long as I could. We watched a movie then we played cards . . . When she finally gave up and headed for the door, Salim came home. By then it was too late and she didn't want to make it obvious so she left.

JOMANA That's just too funny . . . Don't they know it already *is* obvious . . .

LAMA I know . . . Aren't they the sorriest lovebirds in Gaza . . .

*A Skype call comes in, ringing.* JOMANA *looks at* LAMA, *pleading.*

JOMANA Please!

LAMA *gives her a stern look.*

LAMA Why is he calling you? Jomana, this relationship will never work. Don't answer.

JOMANA I wish it were that easy. I'm in love with him.

*Skype continues to ring, punctuated by* UM AHMED*'s voice calling from the kitchen.*

UM AHMED *(offstage)* Jomana . . . Lama . . .

RAMI Jomana . . . please pick up.

JOMANA Please, Lama, cover for me. Think of all the times I covered for you. Am I not always the best chaperone you can ever dream of? Please . . .

UM AHMED *(offstage)* What is this ringing?

LAMA Nothing, Khalto, I'm coming to help now.

LAMA *gives* JOMANA *one last look of disapproval, then leaves.* JOMANA *quickly fixes her hair and pinches her cheeks, then answers the Skype call.*

RAMI Finally! I worried you wouldn't answer.

JOMANA I had to convince Lama to leave us alone.

RAMI And we both know how much she likes me.

JOMANA She can be a little overprotective.

RAMI Well she needs to get off my case and dedicate her time to doing what she does best: tormenting Ali.

JOMANA Are you really going to waste this call complaining about Lama?

RAMI No! I would much rather tell you how beautiful you look and that I love you. I love you. I love you. I can't wait to hold you again.

JOMANA I miss you.

RAMI I heard a suitor is coming your way in the next couple of weeks.

JOMANA Where did you hear that?

RAMI I know him very well. He is an amazing catch.

JOMANA Rami, how could you say that?

RAMI He is good for you. He is a handsome doctor from a good family. That is like the top of the suitor ladder for Palestinians worldwide.

JOMANA I see . . . what if I still refuse him.

RAMI Nonsense! He is the best.

JOMANA Really?

RAMI Ask my mother. She'll tell you how great he is.

JOMANA Really? You're coming in a few weeks?

RAMI Yes.

JOMANA But the Rafah Crossing is shut? How will you get in?

RAMI My mother has some impressive connections she will put to good use.

JOMANA I don't know what to say. I can't believe you are coming back. You will stay this time won't you?

RAMI *(hesitating slightly)* . . . Yes.

JOMANA I have to tell my parents. They don't know about you yet. There is so much to do. I am so happy. Oh my God . . . You're coming back!

RAMI And word has it we are going to be the hottest couple in Gaza.

JOMANA I'm sure the cameras will follow us around for days.

RAMI Yes . . . they will call us "Ramana."

JOMANA "Ramana"? What does that mean?

RAMI You know . . . Rami and Jomana . . . like Brangelina.

JOMANA What is a Brangelina?

RAMI Never mind. It is an American thing.

JOMANA I don't understand, but speaking of American, you need to make sure you dress less American and more Palestinian when you come this time.

RAMI Now I'm the one that can't understand.

JOMANA It's just that no one here believes you are a real doctor. Torn jeans . . . really, Rami? You looked like a pauper. This stuff just doesn't work here. You have to make some major adjustments, get a haircut, and wear a nice cardigan. Oh yeah . . . and never ever wear socks with sandals. That's just forbidden.

RAMI Do I need to adjust my medical skills too?

JOMANA Yes, of course. They need to be more suited to the conditions at the Gaza hospitals.

RAMI So . . . learn how to operate without anaesthetic?

JOMANA And treat cancer patients while smoking cigarettes.

RAMI And lecture diabetics while offering them sweet pastry.

JOMANA And perform surgeries without electricity.

*A knock on the door.* JOMANA *panics.*

Baba is home.

*JOMANA's father enters just as she shuts off her laptop and stands up. RAMI remains seated with a big smile on his face. JOMANA walks over and kisses her father's hand. He holds her hand in his and kisses her on her forehead.*

How was your day, Baba? Any luck fishing?

ABU AHMED The army shot at our boat, this time they damaged the engine. We didn't get too far.

*JOMANA helps her father out of his coat. Meanwhile, on the other side of the stage, RAMI's mother enters with shopping bags. She is dressed elegantly in a knee-length sleeveless dress and meticulous short hair. RAMI looks up and smiles as she walks over and kisses him on the head.*

SAMIRA I thought if I went to the farmers' market early I would avoid the crowd, but it was packed! Still, I managed to buy everything we need for Thanksgiving.

RAMI Wonderful! You always cook an amazing feast.

*RAMI carries the shopping bags into the kitchen. SAMIRA throws herself on the sofa, kicks off her shoes, puts her feet up, and shuts her eyes. JOMANA brings her father his house slippers.*

JOMANA What about the human rights boat with the Italian guy that sailed with you?

ABU AHMED They shot at his boat too.

JOMANA Is he all right?

ABU AHMED Yes, habibti, he is. He picked up some really good Arabic swear words and put them to good use.

JOMANA *(laughing)* Vittorio is truly amazing!

ABU AHMED Every time I start to lose sight of what is good in this world, I think of him and others like him who have given up comfortable lives to come here and to stand by our side.

*The lights go out in* JOMANA*'s living room.*

It seems every day we get less electricity than the day before.

ABU AHMED *takes out a lighter from his pocket and lights it so he can find his way to the sofa in the dark.* JOMANA *walks into the kitchen.*

RAMI *(from the kitchen)* How many people are we expecting?

SAMIRA Not many . . . ya albi . . . maybe fifteen!

RAMI *(from the kitchen)* Coffee?

SAMIRA Yes, please!

LAMA *comes in with a lantern; she places it on the table and gives* ABU AHMED *a hug.*

LAMA Merhaba, Ammu.

ABU AHMED Ahlan, my favorite niece. As much as I love seeing you here, I have the feeling you should be at home right now. Isn't Ali invited there for dinner?

JOMANA *comes from offstage carrying a shisha and places it in front of her father. She begins to massage his shoulders.*

JOMANA That explains why she's here.

ABU AHMED Lama, you can't treat the man this way. No one is forcing you to marry him, so you either break up with him or you set the date for the wedding. You can't string him along forever.

LAMA I know . . . I know . . . I know . . . but a bird in one hand . . . a geeky bird with no sense of style, but still . . .

ABU AHMED Lama, shame on you!

LAMA I'm kidding . . . I will go once I'm done helping Khalto in the kitchen.

*LAMA walks back into the kitchen. ABU AHMED begins smoking his sheesha, thoroughly enjoying it.*

ABU AHMED It's a shame no one has come up with a way for us to use our water pipes to generate electricity. With all the sheesha smokers in Gaza we could light up the entire Middle East.

*RAMI enters with two coffee mugs. He puts one on the table and hands his mother the other one. SAMIRA sits up.*

SAMIRA Can you turn down the air con, ya albi, it is freezing here?

*RAMI grabs the AC remote control and adjusts the temperature.*

RAMI What are you planning to make for dessert?

SAMIRA Not sure yet . . . let me see, kanafah, baklava . . .

RAMI Mom, this is Thanksgiving, not Eid.

SAMIRA I was only pulling your leg. Of course you'll get your pumpkin pie . . . You always get your pumpkin pie. You know there is no Thanksgiving in Gaza, don't you? No pumpkin pie . . . no cranberry sauce . . . no stuffing . . . no gravy . . . no basics . . . hell . . . no water . . . no . . . electricity . . .

ABU AHMED Only four hours of electricity a day! I think the Israelis want to push us back into the dark ages.

LAMA *(from the kitchen)* Speaking of the dark ages, Ammu, the water has run out.

ABU AHMED I'll call the water truck to refill.

SAMIRA I just remembered, make sure you tell Piedro to clean the pool and turn the heater on. Your sister's kids will want to swim. This will probably be their last swim for the season.

ABU AHMED Um Ahmed, take it easy with the water, you have to make it last longer.

UM AHMED (*offstage*) It's not like I'm bathing in it. Why don't you bring me some stones and I can just rub them against the pots like they did thousands of years ago.

ABU AHMED They didn't use pots thousands of years ago.

UM AHMED (*offstage*) That's not a bad idea. Maybe I shouldn't use pots either. You can live on salad from now on.

ABU AHMED (*whispers to* JOMANA) Sometimes, your mother's tyranny exceeds that of the Israeli army.

UM AHMED (*offstage*) I heard that.

*JOMANA and ABU AHMED laugh.*

SAMIRA I got a call from Abu Emad today. He said we have a good chance of getting into Gaza. But it is not 100 per cent guaranteed.

RAMI How much do we need to pay him?

SAMIRA Two thousand dollars for the both of us.

RAMI Bloody thieves!

JOMANA Baba, what will you do with the boat?

ABU AHMED I have to borrow some money again to fix it.

SAMIRA The money is the easy part.

ABU AHMED But there is something else that's on my mind?

SAMIRA I'm worried about you.

ABU AHMED Why did my daughter greet me at the door, bring me my slippers, make me a shisha, and even offer a massage? (*JOMANA shifts nervously.*) Is there something we need to talk about?

SAMIRA We need to talk about this.

JOMANA (*taking a deep breath*) Remember in August.

SAMIRA When you went on the boats.

JOMANA When the boats came in.

SAMIRA I was so proud of you, ya albi, for doing something that is good for our people.

ABU AHMED That was a proud day. How can I forget it? No one in Gaza can forget that day.

JOMANA Do you remember the Palestinian doctor that came on one of the boats?

ABU AHMED What doctor?

SAMIRA That was my son, born and raised his whole life in Texas, living a life of comfort, having achieved the highest levels of education.

ABU AHMED The only Palestinian I remember was an American hippie in torn jeans and sandals with socks.

SAMIRA That was Doctor Rami . . . giving back to his people and taking on a brave journey. If your dad were alive he would have been so proud of you.

JOMANA Baba, in America, doctors don't really care how they look.

RAMI Strange to hear you say this now, Mom, seeing you didn't approve of me going on the Free Gaza boats.

ABU AHMED Hum . . . . And you, my child, do you care how he looks?

SAMIRA I worried about you. You were running back into what we ran away from.

JOMANA Baba! He is coming with his mother in two weeks. He would like to drink a cup of coffee with you.

SAMIRA — Now I'm even more worried. I mean you're not going this time on a short humanitarian mission . . .

ABU AHMED — He's coming all the way from America with his mother, and once again wants to break through the siege to drink coffee with me? I am flattered!

RAMI — Mom, I know this is difficult.

JOMANA — Baba, stop teasing me. You know what I mean.

ABU AHMED — I do. Habibti, I have to be honest with you . . .

SAMIRA — It is beyond difficult. It is hard for me to accept.

ABU AHMED — I'm not sure I like this.

JOMANA — Baba, he is a good man . . . a doctor.

RAMI — Mom, she is an incredible, educated woman.

ABU AHMED — He has American citizenship.

SAMIRA — She is a stateless refugee.

ABU AHMED — His feet aren't rooted in this soil.

SAMIRA — She is trapped in Gaza.

ABU AHMED — He has wings and the freedom to leave when things get tough here.

SAMIRA — You will lose your freedom and be trapped if you stay with her.

ABU AHMED — What if he takes you with him to America? I would never see you again.

SAMIRA — I would never see you again.

ABU AHMED — Your sister lives in the West Bank, a stone's throw away, but she may as well be living on the moon.

SAMIRA Look at how hard it is for us to go there now.

ABU AHMED We have tried for years to get permission from Israel to allow us to visit each other and you know what that's like.

SAMIRA Impossible . . . it would be impossible to visit you . . . or see your children.

ABU AHMED She has three children who only know me as a virtual grandfather that speaks to them from inside a computer screen.

RAMI Don't worry, Mom. I may be able to convince her to leave Gaza eventually and to come to live here with us.

JOMANA Don't worry, Baba, I told him I would never leave you. He promised me he would stay in Gaza.

SAMIRA You weren't honest with her?

ABU AHMED And you believe him?

SAMIRA You need to tell her you may not stay there.

RAMI Then she will refuse to marry me.

JOMANA I want to believe him.

RAMI I wasn't being dishonest. I just don't know. Maybe there is a place for me in Gaza. Maybe that is God's plan for me and I just don't know it.

JOMANA He asked me to have faith in him.

ABU AHMED How will he get in? Israel is turning back the boats now and all the crossings into Egypt are shut.

RAMI I don't have all the answers, but I know I have to be with her.

JOMANA Connections! He said he knows some people high up in the Palestinian Authority.

RAMI Can't we just take it one step at a time?

SAMIRA One step at a time?

ABU AHMED He is counting on the Palestinian Authority?

SAMIRA We don't even know we can make it in.

ABU AHMED Even the president of the Palestinian Authority needs permission from Israel first and at times it can be denied.

*JOMANA looks very sad. RAMI is agitated by his mother's words. Both parents feel bad and try to console their children.*

SAMIRA I am sorry, ya albi, if I upset you.

ABU AHMED Don't worry, habibti. Inshallah, God will bring what is best.

SAMIRA I'll try to be positive. What is meant to be will be.

ABU AHMED If you're meant to marry him, you will. Let's put our faith in God's hands.

RAMI Mom, can I have your blessing?

JOMANA Baba, do we have your blessing?

ABU AHMED You always have my blessing.

SAMIRA Always!

*The singer sings "Ya khayee qool laommy we la tqool laboya," the parents' song. The singer's voice continues as lights fade.*

## SCENE THREE

*Split stage. One side is dark, while on the other side* RAMI *is in a furnished apartment in Cairo. He stands with his eyes glued on* SAMIRA *who is pacing back and forth while holding a phone to her ear.*

SAMIRA — But . . . wait . . . okay. Yes, I know . . . we tried that already. What else . . . sure . . . tayeb . . . tayeb . . . khalas . . . shukran.

SAMIRA *puts her phone down and turns to* RAMI. *She shakes her head.* RAMI*'s anger explodes. He slams his fist against the desk.*

RAMI — NO.

SAMIRA — I am sorry, ya albi, this was God's will. There is nothing we can do about it.

RAMI — Let's leave God out of this one.

SAMIRA — We did everything we could.

RAMI — I am so sick of this. Fuck! I am so sick of this . . . I'd try the boats again but there is no use . . . Israel is now turning those away. I want to see her. I have to get back in. I promised her I'd return . . .

SAMIRA — Perhaps this is one promise you shouldn't have made. You can't promise something that is not in your hands to give. You have to understand that you both live in separate worlds.

RAMI — This is not helping right now. I should have stayed! . . . She was right, I should have stayed . . . She knew this was going to happen . . . I called her *dramatic,* can you believe what a fucking moron I was? . . . She was right all along. I should have stayed.

SAMIRA — Just like that? Dropped everything you've worked your entire life for? Then what? I have to tell you my heart ached when I thought you would be living—even if for a short period of time—behind those walls. It is not a place I want to see my grandchildren being raised. I probably wouldn't be allowed to see them at all.

RAMI Mom, please . . . just stop.

*SAMIRA shakes her head, exasperated, but decides to say nothing more and walks away. RAMI buries his face in his hands.*

*The lights rise on the other side. JOMANA sits in her living room. She is wearing a beautiful dress and her hair is done up with small flowers in it. She wipes a tear off her face, grabs her diary, and begins to write.*

JOMANA *Gaza, December 2008*
Are your loved ones trapped behind the wall
Do they need the army's permission
For their prayers to reach the sky
For their love to cross the ocean
And to touch your thirsty heart
Are your loved ones trapped

*RAMI turns on his laptop and calls JOMANA on Skype. She drops her diary and quickly grabs her laptop.*

RAMI Jomana, please pick up . . .

JOMANA Hey, you! At last!

RAMI You look beautiful.

JOMANA I got all dressed up for you. I even had my hair done up.

RAMI They wouldn't let us in.

JOMANA When I heard the Egyptians turned you back, I didn't have the heart to take off the dress or to let my hair down! I thought at least you could see me on Skype . . . I mean after all of this effort.

RAMI You look incredible! Just, wow!

JOMANA I'm sure it's not every day that a woman spends hours beautifying herself for you.

RAMI Definitely not every day. Only once or twice a week usually!

JOMANA Lucky you!

RAMI You have no idea what seeing you look like this is doing to me! I would die just to touch you. I want to fly through their damned borders, sit beside you, and pull those flowers out of your hair, one little flower at a time. I want to watch you move. I hold my breath every time your shawl slides down your arms . . . My heart stops at the thought of holding your hand in mine. You take my breath away, Jomana . . . You really shouldn't have shown me how amazing you look tonight . . . You have no mercy!

JOMANA I could turn off the camera.

RAMI NO . . . better yet, how about you stand up. Let me have a look at your dress.

*JOMANA stands and takes a few steps away from the computer. She twirls so he can see the back and front of her dress. RAMI watches her with a sad smile, his countenance filled with desire.*

I want to hold you.

JOMANA I want to hide in your arms.

RAMI Don't give up on me.

JOMANA Promise me you'll never stop trying.

*They both share a silent moment staring into their screens.*

How is your mom?

RAMI The drive to Rafah was hard and the waiting even harder . . .

JOMANA I can imagine.

RAMI But she is a strong woman.

JOMANA And you?

RAMI I'm broken.

*Faint sounds of shelling commence in the distance and remain throughout the rest of this scene.*

JOMANA And so begins our nightly lullaby . . .

RAMI They seem to be a bit louder tonight.

JOMANA I know. Rami, I can't wait anymore. I want to tell you now . . . I love you! There, I've said it.

RAMI Finally! I thought I'd never hear you utter those words.

JOMANA I wanted to say it to your face. But it seems we are condemned to a Skype love affair.

RAMI I am starting to worry we might end up getting married and having babies on Skype.

JOMANA That's a scary thought. I'd better sign off then before I find myself pregnant.

RAMI Noooo, don't go!

JOMANA I'm sorry, habibi. It is really late. Yallah, good night!

RAMI Goodnight, habibti, I love you.

*The lights go out on both sides. The sound of shelling becomes gradually louder. This goes on for a couple of minutes. When the lights come back on,* JOMANA *is sitting on her sofa wearing casual clothes. She looks frightened. She is writing into her diary.*

JOMANA *Gaza, December 27, 2008*
I search . . . desperately . . . for words . . .
I have no words . . .
I have no words . . .

*Sound of a loud explosion close by.* JOMANA *jumps in fear, dropping her diary. She shouts angrily.*

I NEED NEW WORDS!

*Determined, she picks up her diary.*

Siege . . . hunger . . . collective misery
Familiar words in my head they linger
Bombs fall from the sky every day
Powerless words . . .
Powerless words . . .
I can't use any longer
I need new words

*A loud explosion erupts, this time with sounds of glass shattering.* ABU AHMED *enters, alarmed.* JOMANA *runs to him.*

Baba!

ABU AHMED Everyone is fine, but we must leave now. Just grab your things and let's go fast.

JOMANA But . . . our home . . . Baba. Where do we go?

ABU AHMED I don't know but it is definitely not safe here.

JOMANA *packs a few items quickly . . . the diary . . . the pen . . . her scarf. She grabs her coat as lights rise on the other side of the stage.* RAMI *looks at his computer, horrified. He calls* JOMANA *on Skype. She is about to pack her laptop when the call comes in. She looks at her father, pleading. He nods.*

ABU AHMED Make it fast. I'll take these things to the car.

*The sound of shelling continues to grow louder.*

JOMANA Rami, we've been through many bombings, but this is the worst. There are people, bodies . . . children . . . death everywhere, Rami . . . I can't speak. I can't put it in words. I have no words. I have no words. We have to leave the house. The shelling is very heavy at the camp. I don't know where our families will go. We'll be out of touch for a while. Pray for us. Pray for us.

*Loud noise like missiles falling. The light on* JOMANA'S *side of the stage goes out.*

RAMI Jomana . . . Jomana . . . Jomana . . . Damn . . . Connection lost.

RAMI *grabs his mobile phone.*

Ali, I've decided to join you. Please make the necessary arrangements.

SAMIRA *enters, alarmed.*

SAMIRA What was that about?

RAMI Mom, I have to go.

SAMIRA No . . . no . . . no . . .

RAMI I'm not going alone.

SAMIRA No . . . ya allah . . . no!

RAMI There is a group of Egyptian doctors who are going. My friend Dr. Mustafa tells me the hospitals are overwhelmed with the injured. They need our help. Israel and Egypt won't allow people through the normal channels. No one is allowed in or out of Gaza . . . you know that. So we have to do what we can to get there.

SAMIRA *collapses on the chair, sobbing.* RAMI *lowers to his knees.*

The hospitals were already short of everything because of the siege. Mom, I was trained to save lives. I can't sit and watch. We will be taking critical medical supplies with us. The tunnel we're using is one of the best and safest. *(He kisses her hand.)* Mom, please . . . I need your blessing.

*SAMIRA stares at her son with tears streaming down her face, then tries to get up.*

SAMIRA Let me make you something to eat before you go.

RAMI It is not a good idea. There are no toilets in the tunnel and we'll need to crawl for hours underground. We were advised to keep our stomachs and bladders light.

SAMIRA Ah, ya albi! The places you go!

*RAMI smiles tenderly.*

RAMI I have brains in my head.
I have feet in my shoes.

SAMIRA You still remember . . .

RAMI Dr. Suess!

*Samira and Rami recite a small section of* Oh, the Places You'll Go! *by Dr. Suess.*

SAMIRA You were such a typical American boy! And now this?

*They embrace, SAMIRA sobbing.*

Ah, ya albi! When will I see you again?

*The singer begins to sing "Ala tareeq ghaza ya ommy," the farewell to mother song. RAMI kisses his mother's hands and her face and starts to walk away. The singer continues as lights fade.*

## SCENE FOUR

*Gaza Tunnel City. The stage is bare with a white tent at the centre. ALI stands outside the tent facing the audience, smoking a cigarette. Throughout this scene sounds of shelling and explosions are heard in the distance.*

ALI Welcome to Gaza. It is now 11:50 p.m. local occupation time. The temperature today is simmering with white phosphorus showers expected. An umbrella will not help . . . nothing will.

*MOHANAD and RAMI crawl out of the tent.*

Thank you for choosing to travel with Ali's Tunnels. We hope you enjoyed our in-tunnel entertainment and hospitality.

*The men look exhausted. They shake hands with ALI and stand stretching their arms and legs.*

RAMI My entertainment was in 3D: sight, sound, and odour. I was crawling directly behind Mohanad.

MOHANAD I told my wife that beans might not have been the best food to eat.

RAMI Oh, is that what it was? I thought we were carrying biological weapons of mass destruction.

ALI Yallah shabab. You should be grateful you no longer have to look at each other's butts.

RAMI It's no use. After seven hours crawling behind Mohanad I can tell you his butt is now engraved in my mind.

ALI I'll take you to my house first to get some rest, shower, and have a meal, and tomorrow morning we'll go to Al-Shifa Hospital.

RAMI No, Ali, I want to go straight to the hospital.

MOHANAD We are anxious to roll up our sleeves and get to work. What are the numbers now?

ALI Thousands in critical condition. Hundreds dead, including many children. The doctors are puzzled by a strange kind of burning of the skin. They think it is caused by the white phosphorus bombs. It burns people from the inside out. Oh, and they blew up the mosque next to the hospital, so part of the hospital sustained damage and there is no glass in any of the windows.

RAMI Let's go.

ALI I have to warn you, our trip will be difficult. The shelling is random and merciless. *(They start walking, looking around them in absolute horror.* ALI *looks at his watch.)* Hey, pretty boy, give me a kiss. It is almost midnight.

RAMI I'd rather you remain a frog . . . Here comes 2009 with the most destructive fireworks ever. What a beautiful new year!

## SCENE FIVE

*Shifa Hospital, Gaza City. Lots of injured people. Some on beds, others on blankets on the floor. The place is buzzing with doctors and nurses. There are periodic sounds of gunfire and missiles in the distance. A couple is standing outside the operating room. The woman is crying.* RAMI *enters, his hands and hospital uniform stained with blood. He takes off his bloodied gloves and looks at them apologetically.*

RAMI I am sorry. We lost him.

*The woman screams and falls to her knees. The man tries to help her but his knees give in too. They are on the floor, sobbing.*

What is a life worth? This was the fifth child I lost today.
Damn it.
What is a life worth?
A grain of earth
A drop of oil
A flag on a hill of holy soil
A cross . . . a star . . . a crescent moon . . .
Is it worth ending a life too soon

What sacred verses can explain
Sniper fire . . .
And white phosphorus rain
What holy scripture gave the command
"Thou shall wipe out their villages
And scorch their land"
And after the massacre
Will they lament
Will they seek forgiveness
Will they repent
Will they try to sanctify their burdened souls
For besieging a people behind their walls
No rest for the less sacred, no safety, no light
No benediction no prayer no end in sight
No bread, no medicine, no shelter, no salvation
No angels can survive this holy Occupation
TELL ME THIS
What is a life worth
On this God-forsaken earth

*RAMI exits. JOMANA enters carrying her phone. She sees the bereaved couple sobbing on the floor. She takes photos of them with her phone's camera. They struggle back to their feet and walk away as LAMA comes into the foyer.*

LAMA Jomana!

*They run into each other's arms.*

JOMANA Lama! Habibti, you're a sight for sore eyes!

LAMA I knew I'd find you here of all places.

JOMANA Yes! Of all places! Here I am taking photos and doing interviews. Hoping that somehow I can compel the world to help us. Yes, we can be saved any minute now, my dear Lama . . . one more posting . . . one more status . . . one more Tweet . . . wait and see . . . just one more photo is all it's going to take . . . one more dead baby and the world will rise. Don't worry; I know how delusional I really am. How is the camp?

LAMA You are lucky your family left . . . it is like absolute hell being there. I literally had to step over blood and human bits in the street on my way here.

JOMANA How is your family?

LAMA We've all gone insane. Last night, while everyone in the house was hiding under beds and tables, something in me snapped. I found myself crawling out from under the kitchen table and without even thinking, I started making a za'atar sandwich. As the bombs fell around us my za'atar obsession got worst . . . and I was making more and more sandwiches. By the time the morning came, I found myself standing over the kitchen table along with my mother and my aunties and we were staring at a huge pile of za'atar sandwiches . . . it seems at some point during the night that I can't even recall the women in the family joined me. Can you imagine all four of us making sandwiches to the sound of bombs and sirens? I swear we are losing our minds.

JOMANA Crazy is the in thing now.

LAMA So crazy we used up all the bread we had, which was supposed to last our family till the end of the week.

JOMANA So what will you do now? You can't buy bread anymore.

LAMA Does it matter? Does the rest of the week matter? Jomana, we can't even plan the next hour.

JOMANA And what did you do with the sandwiches?

LAMA I came here and gave them out to the families who wait . . . the ones waiting on the floor . . . the ones waiting on the stairs . . . the ones under the staircase . . . Many refused them, some accepted with weary smiles . . . No one really has an appetite.

*ALI enters looking sombre.*

ALI — Lama . . . *(He holds* LAMA*'s hand. She starts to tremble.)* May God give you strength and patience.

LAMA — No . . . no . . . no . . . no . . .

JOMANA — Who? Ali? Speak. Who?

ALI — To Allah we belong and to him we return . . . your house was destroyed . . . your parents and brothers have been martyred.

*LAMA screams and her knees give way. JOMANA and ALI stop her from falling. The singer sings "Rahoo," the song of mourning. Lights fade out for a few moments. Only the voice of the singer continues. When the lights rise, JOMANA is alone, frantically going from bed to bed looking at the faces of those injured. She sees a nurse.*

JOMANA — Excuse me! Nurse, I heard the ambulance just brought in a family from Toffah. Can you tell me who they were?

NURSE — It was terrible. They're still bringing them in.

JOMANA — Who were they . . . which family?

NURSE — I think they are from the Saleh family.

*JOMANA breathes a sigh of relief.*

JOMANA — Thank God . . . Oh thank God! I mean I'm sorry for the Saleh family but I'm so glad . . . I thought my parents . . . thank God . . .

*The woman leaves. The spotlight rests on JOMANA as everything around her fades into darkness.*

I have a confession to make
I stand between shame and relief
I breathe . . .
The missiles missed this time
Truth is they didn't really miss
Someone's house is destroyed
But not the house I know so well

Someone's family is grieving
But not the one whose name I carry
I linger . . .
I linger between shame and relief
I breathe . . .
I . . . breathe . . .
I tell myself
This flesh, torn and scattered
Is not flesh I have ever embraced
I soothe myself
Nor are these small lifeless hands
The ones with a crayon I've traced
I . . . breathe . . .
This time . . .
The missiles missed those
Whose names are engraved on my lips
This time they didn't stop those hearts
Beating in my chest
They live . . .
And I breathe . . .
But I must confess
Every time the bombs fall
I want answers
Where did they strike?
Which street did they blow up?
Which neighbourhood did they destroy?
Which lives did they steal?
Aware of my guilt I whisper a prayer
Dear God,
Please don't let it be the ones I know
Dear God,
Please don't let it be the ones I love
Dear God . . . .
Ya allah . . .
Ya allah . . .
Ya allah . . .
And when it's over
And while a less fortunate family weeps
I stand between shame and relief
I breathe . . .
I breathe . . .

Thank God my loved ones were spared . . .
This time!

*RAMI enters and sees JOMANA.*

RAMI Jomana!

JOMANA Rami?

*The two run into each other's arms, JOMANA sobbing.*

You're here . . . you're here . . . you're here . . .

*The singer sings "Yamma moweel alhawa," the song of lament. She continues to sing as lights fade.*

## SCENE SIX

*JOMANA's living room. LAMA and JOMANA are wearing black and sitting on the sofa. LAMA has her head resting in JOMANA's lap. JOMANA is stroking LAMA's hair.*

LAMA I feel so empty. It is all gone. Mama . . . Baba . . . Salim . . . Mahmoud . . .

JOMANA Your family is in Paradise.

LAMA And I am in hell. I have nothing. No one.

JOMANA Don't say that. You have us.

*Sounds of a passing funeral procession outside their home.*

LAMA I wonder whose funeral this is.

JOMANA Either the Jaro or the Abu Shaban family. They both have funerals today.

LAMA I am so sick of death.

*A knock on the door. ALI enters carrying two takeout boxes.*

ALI Ya sater.

*LAMA sits up quickly and pulls her hijab over her hair.*

LAMA You shouldn't have!

ALI It's nothing. I wish there was something more I could do to make you smile again. But seeing I can't, at least let me ensure you don't waste away.

*He hands her one box and gives the other to JOMANA.*

Please promise me you will try to eat. Please, Lama . . . I can't stand the thought of anything happening to you.

JOMANA Ali, why don't you join us?

ALI I can't. We are trying to make the streets in the camp safe for passage. There is so much rubble and lots of dangerous explosives scattered all over the place . . . We have so much work to do.

LAMA I heard you went to our house . . . what remains of our house . . . and you salvaged some of my family photos. I am grateful!

ALI No need to be. I'm keeping them all in a box for you, you can go through them when you're feeling better. Yallah, I'll be back tonight. I don't want to see any food left then.

LAMA Ali, please be careful. Promise me you'll be careful.

*ALI's is visibly touched by LAMA's tenderness. He holds her hand and kisses it, then leaves. JOMANA opens LAMA's box and hands her a piece of pita bread.*

JOMANA Yallah, you heard the man. Eat!

LAMA Whenever I see bread, I remember my last night with my family obsessing over za'atar sandwiches. It's as if we knew we had to use up all the bread before the house was blown up. It's strange when you think of your last moment with someone . . . standing across the kitchen table from my mom stuffing all the za'atar sandwiches into plastic bags . . . I could have said so much to her if only I knew that was our last time together.

JOMANA Lama . . . habibti . . .

LAMA I miss her. I miss them all. I keep thinking at least my parents lived a full life. But my brothers, they were killed before they even had a life. They were handsome young men with so much left to do.

JOMANA Yum! You should try these. They are the best falafels you can get in this city.

LAMA They never got married or had children. Remember Salim's crush on Dalya.

JOMANA The things he used to do just to catch a glimpse of her.

LAMA I know. He was quite the Romeo. I wonder if he was still alive how his life would have been? Would he have married her? How many children would they have had?

JOMANA Lama, there is no point in trying to imagine . . . habibti, he is in heaven now!

LAMA He never even kissed her. Can you believe he had the chance a few times, but he never kissed her. Now he's dead. Jomana, I don't want this to happen to me. I don't want to die before I really know what life feels like.

JOMANA Well you will die if you don't eat. Come on, Lama, just try to take one bite. You need to start eating again.

LAMA Do you know what I mean? Jomana, I am sick of death. I want to live, I want to love. I want to kiss someone . . .

*JOMANA looks at LAMA in shock. LAMA ignores JOMANA's glare. She wills herself to bite into the sandwich, chews with deliberate motion, and then forces herself to swallow. She looks at JOMANA with determination.*

Jomana. The mourning period of forty days is almost over. Soon there will be weddings in every neighbourhood in Gaza. I want my wedding to be one of them.

JOMANA WHAT?

LAMA I want to get married. I want to feel life growing inside of me. It is the only way I can defeat death . . . by making life . . . I want to have babies . . . lots of babies . . . I want to fill the house with their cries and laughter.

JOMANA But, Lama, you weren't so sure about Ali . . .

LAMA Things have become so much clearer now. Ali is a good man. He loves me. He stood by me through the worst days of my life. He would move mountains to see me smile. Besides, I can't wait for a romantic love story that may never be. A missile could fall from the sky tomorrow and we could all be dead. I simply will not postpone living anymore. Ali is a good provider and his tunnel business means we will never be hungry and we will never have to suffer the shortages.

JOMANA But now? Are you sure you're ready now?

LAMA I am sure this will save me.

*A wedding drumbeat begins. The two girls leave the room as ALI and RAMI enter dressed in suits and carrying three photo frames, one of LAMA's parents and two of LAMA's brothers. All three frames have a black ribbon tied around them. ALI and RAMI are joyful in spirit. They are both laughing.*

RAMI You finally did it!

ALI Was it necessary for you and the thugs I call my cousins to manhandle me in the shower and to shave my . . . ?

RAMI We wanted to make sure the goods we deliver are not grotesque. Lord knows it took forever to convince the poor girl to marry you.

ALI Hey, don't believe these lies. She has chased after me for a long time. She is lucky I will let her have her way with me.

RAMI So, what are we doing with these frames?

ALI We will put them up at the wedding reception. We'll be hanging all the photos of those killed in both my family and in Lama's.

RAMI I don't know how you do it?

ALI If I were to define Gaza in two words, it would be funerals and weddings. You know, soon it will be your turn to have a wedding.

RAMI Inshallah.

ALI What is that about? Do I sense some doubt?

RAMI I don't doubt my love for Jomana. But the more time I spend here the more I'm convinced that I can't raise a family in this place.

ALI Rami, here there is no room for grey comfort zones where we can have the luxury of indecision. When it comes to matters of the heart, in this place, you have to know what you want and hold on to it for dear life.

RAMI I want Jomana, but I want to take her away.

ALI You want to uproot her? Sever her links with her family because you're too scared to live here.

RAMI That's not fair. I am not scared for myself.

ALI — Brother, you have to be honest with yourself and with Jomana. It seems to me you are keeping one foot in this soil, and the other in some foreign land. Don't spend your whole life lost in-between.

*ABU AHMED enters, dressed in a suit.*

ABU AHMED — Ali, are you ready?

ALI — Yes, Uncle.

ABU AHMED — I don't have to tell you this, but I will. Lama is my daughter now after my brother has been killed. So consider me your father-in-law and know that until the last day of my life, I will see to it that you are treating her with the love and respect she deserves.

ALI — I will. She is the love of my life. I will honour her forever.

*ABU AHMED shakes hands with ALI and kisses him three times on both cheeks. He then turns to RAMI.*

ABU AHMED — Inshallah, your turn will be next, Doctor!

RAMI — Inshallah! I've been waiting for the right time to talk to you.

*ABU AHMED and RAMI shake hands, and kiss in the same way.*

ABU AHMED — I know. May God bring what is good for you and my daughter Jomana.

*Sounds of zaghareet as LAMA and JOMANA enter. LAMA is wearing a white wedding dress and holding a flower bouquet. JOMANA enters behind her in a beautiful evening gown. They both look stunning. JOMANA offers another zaghroot. The singer sings "Qolo la immoh tifra we tit-hana," the wedding song, and continues to sing, lowering her voice when there is dialogue throughout this scene and into the next.*

JOMANA — Ayeee, The groom is very lucky
Ayeee, Married into a great family

Ayeee, Lama is a beautiful bride
Ayeee, she is meant for Ali
Lolololololoyeeeee

*Everyone laughs with delight. The lights go out suddenly and everything is pitch black for a few seconds.* ALI *lights up the room with his cellphone until* JOMANA *lights up the lantern. She takes the flowers out of* LAMA*'s hand and puts them on the table then gives her the lantern to hold instead.*

This is more useful now.

*Holding the lantern,* LAMA *takes a deep breath, looks at* ALI *and smiles.* ALI *walks over to her and lifts her veil.*

ALI — I am the luckiest man in the world. I will devote my life to making you happy. *(*ALI *kisses* LAMA *on her forehead, then holds her hand and looks at her, smiling.)* Are you ready?

LAMA — I am! I've never been more ready in my life. You are a good man, Ali, and I am lucky to have you.

*The procession begins to move with* ALI *and* LAMA *in the front holding the lantern The lights fade while the singer continues her song.*

## SCENE SEVEN

*Gaza beach.* JOMANA *and* RAMI *enter holding hands.*

JOMANA — Here we are . . . We keep finding ourselves in the same place.

RAMI — I can't believe a year has passed since we first met.

JOMANA — Don't tell me a year has passed. You can't measure our lives by a calendar. Time stands still here.

RAMI — Frozen on the shores of this old, battered city.

JOMANA — One calendar year can never contain our lives, our sorrows, desires . . .

RAMI — Then let us be lost in the absence of time and linger in this moment forever. *(He holds her and gently kisses her on the lips. She pulls away slowly.)*

JOMANA — You are fully taking advantage of our engagement.

RAMI — Not fully! Not yet!

*He pulls her closer one more time. They have one long kiss.* JOMANA *pushes him away slowly and looks around, worried.*

JOMANA — You know we can get arrested for this.

RAMI — Arrested for kissing? *(*JOMANA *steps away.)* This place keeps growing on me every day.

JOMANA — What was that?

RAMI — I'm just so sick of this . . . the waiting. Remind me why are we not married yet?

JOMANA — Because you still need to go back to Texas and close your clinic and move your things.

RAMI — No, I mean why are we waiting? Let's just have the wedding and then you can come with me to Texas— It's a great place. You would love it there. You know kissing is actually celebrated and not criminalized in that part of the world.

JOMANA — Well then let's go!

RAMI — I am serious. I want us to get married now and leave . . . both of us . . . together.

JOMANA — Leave? We've talked about this. You promised me we would stay here. I can't leave, if I leave I may never see my family again.

RAMI — Well, what about my family? My mother can't come here. What about her right to be with her grandchildren? What about my sisters, my friends . . . my practice . . . what about our future children . . . Don't they have the right to the best education, the best environment, and the best life?

JOMANA What exactly is this about? You promised me we would stay here. I thought . . . I thought we had a plan.

RAMI Plans don't work in this environment of uncertainty.

JOMANA I would have never allowed myself to get so close to you if I knew you planned to uproot me. You promised . . .

RAMI I did. But that was before I knew what it was like to live here. Now I know.

JOMANA Now you know? They tried to warn me, but I didn't want to listen. My father told me your roots were not dug deep in this soil, I told him I had faith in you . . .

*JOMANA turns around and tries to leave, but RAMI pulls her back.*

RAMI Stop. Jomana, stop. I need you to hear me. *(Angry, she pulls her hand away and tries to leave again, but he yells.)* Jomana, you must hear me! *(She stops.)* You know I would go to the moon for you. I love you. But you have to understand we are talking about marriage and raising a family . . . here. This complicates things. Since I've come here, I've treated hundreds of children with bullet wounds, shrapnel, white phosphorus burns, explosives . . . I keep wondering what if I have children here? What if one day, my own child is brought to me on a stretcher? How do I protect my family here from this sky that rains death? What if the woman I love . . . ?

JOMANA Don't "what if . . . ?" Rami, my life is here. My family is here. I was raised here. This place is my home.

RAMI This place is a prison. You are trapped behind a big wall. Do you really want to condemn our children to this fate? I want a better life for us, for our children.

JOMANA Yes, we are trapped behind a wall, but Rami, look around you. Open your eyes. See all the stories of how we survive; the trees we've replanted, the homes we've rebuilt. Inside these walls, Rami, old men still fiddle with their prayer beads. Mothers still bake ma'amoul on Eid. Families still gather under canopies with loaded bunches of grapes dangling above their heads, they nibble on watermelon seeds and drink maramia tea. Women still perfect the art of matchmaking. Men still dream of freedom and democracy. Children climb on the almond trees. Lovers woo in secrecy. And no matter how adverse the conditions are, over here we have learned to defy the universe! Every day inside these walls, Rami, we defy the universe!

RAMI I don't know how you do that. I can't . . . I'm not used to this . . .

JOMANA I know it is not easy for you. You have a life out there that I can't even imagine. But my life is right here. My life is right here.

RAMI This has been a very difficult year.

JOMANA I know! Rami, we've been through hell this year. I know that neither one of us is the same person we were that day on the beach a year ago. I'm not the same woman that begged you to stay. I really do understand . . . so if you have doubts . . .

RAMI I don't doubt my love for you.

JOMANA You are free to leave.

RAMI I can't live without you. *(He wraps his arms around her.)* I can't live without you.

JOMANA So what now?

RAMI I will come back. I'll finish my work in the US as fast as I can and I will come back. I promise.

*The singer sings "Ma'a alsalameh ween rayeh," the farewell song. The singer continues her as lights fade.*

## SCENE EIGHT

*An airport lounge, somewhere in the US.* RAMI *is on the phone talking to his mom. Two Homeland Security officers stand a few steps away from him, watching.*

RAMI Hi, Mom, just one last plane and I'll be home. You won't believe how many random checks I was subjected to. They've just made a final boarding announcement. I'm going in. Just remember, don't prepare any Arabic food for me . . . I've had way too much of it this past year . . . what I really miss is your hearty chili con carne. Spice it up, Mom! Yallah, I'll see you soon. I love you.

RAMI *stands with his ticket in his hand. He takes a look around him and smiles.*

Finally! Home sweet home!

*The two Homeland Security officers approach him.*

OFFICER 1 I'm sorry, sir, you've been selected for an extra random security check.

RAMI No kidding! Again? I am curious, how random can a random check be when it is consistently applied?

OFFICER 2 Please remain calm. This won't take long.

SAMIRA *appears on the side, watching* RAMI *with a gentle, beautiful smile. She is not visible to the officers.* RAMI *smiles back at her. She remains throughout this scene.*

RAMI *recites the refrain from Dr Seuss's* Green Eggs and Ham.

OFFICER 1 Sir?

RAMI *(to the officers)* I have brown skin and I don't eat ham
Whenever I fly . . . random I am

OFFICER 2 Sir, we need you so step aside.

OFFICER 1 We must search you.

RAMI I have nothing to hide
I have brown skin and I don't eat ham
Whenever I travel . . . random I am

OFFICER 1 Would you spread your legs?

OFFICER 2 Roll up your shirt.

OFFICER 1 Stretch out your arms.

OFFICER 2 This won't hurt.

RAMI I would spread my legs,
Roll up my shirt
Stretch out my arms
AND THIS DOES HURT
I have brown skin and I don't eat ham
So once again . . . random I am

OFFICER 1 Would you, could you say why you're here?

OFFICER 2 Would you, could you calm our fear?

RAMI I would and have at every gate
Please let me go, I don't want to be late
I'm constantly selected to step aside
Photographed, fingerprinted, I've nothing to hide
I've spread my legs, rolled up my shirt
I've stretched my arms, in spite of the hurt
I have brown skin and I don't eat ham
I am an Arab . . . so random I am

OFFICER 1 Why are you here?

RAMI I am an American citizen on my way home.

OFFICER 2 Why would an American visit a place like Gaza?

RAMI To marry the woman I love . . .

OFFICER 1 And where is she?

RAMI Still in Gaza. Look, officer, is there a reason for this interrogation? I'm going to miss my flight.

OFFICER 2 How did you get into Gaza?

RAMI I . . .

OFFICER 1 Your passport has no entry stamp into Gaza, only an exit one. So . . . we're curious . . . How did you get in?

RAMI Where is this going?

OFFICER 2 You know Hamas is a listed terrorist organization in the US.

RAMI Of course I know.

OFFICER 1 Yet you used illegal underground tunnels to get into Hamas territory? You are under arrest for having links with a terrorist organization.

RAMI I demand a lawyer.

OFFICER 2 You need one. This is a matter of great national security.

*The singer sings "Ya thalam alsijin khayem," the prison song. The singer continues her song as lights fade.*

## SCENE NINE

*Gaza beach.* JOMANA *sits, holding her diary. Sounds of waves in the background.* ALI *and* LAMA *enter holding hands.* LAMA *is visibly pregnant, wearing a maternity dress. They sit next to* JOMANA *and all three stare into the horizon.*

ALI Still no news from Rami?

JOMANA His mother has assigned him good lawyers, but I think it will take a long time. It is not clear who will be freed first, him or this old city.

LAMA Why don't you come and spend the day with us. We miss our chaperone!

ALI No offence, but I don't miss the chaperone so much.

JOMANA Come on, Ali, you had it easy.

ALI I did. Thank you.

LAMA We are going to the zoo to see the zebra.

JOMANA You mean the donkey that was spray painted to look like a zebra?

ALI Shhh! Don't ruin it.

JOMANA It is nice to see you, Lama, so glowing and so happy.

ALI There is more to this place than broken hearts and tragic tales.

LAMA *(touching her belly)* There is life here!

*JOMANA looks at ALI holding LAMA's hand.*

JOMANA There is so much love here.

LAMA I only wish you could have that.

JOMANA But I do! My heart is so filled with love . . . and an infinite amount of patience!

*JOMANA stands up. She takes a few steps away from the couple, reading from her diary. The spotlight follows her.*

The landscape constantly changes
Only the sea remains

A cure for the trail of broken lives left behind
A landmark untouched by human greed and destruction
Oblivious to war, occupation, and aggression
Defiant to the rules of man
There is no end to the sea's audacity
It breaks the siege every day
One defiant wave at a time
The landscape will change
Only the sea will remain
Its whooshing waves will whisper new tales
Of occupiers that have come
And gone

*The singer sings "Haddy ya baher haddy," the sea song. Lights gently fade to black.*

# REFLECTIONS ON *TALES OF A CITY BY THE SEA*

### INSPIRATION, CHALLENGES, AND EXPERIENCES IN WRITING AND PRODUCING THE PLAY

My source of inspiration for the play is the strength and defiance of ordinary people in Palestine, who despite the horrific war, siege, and brutality of the Israeli Occupation still insist that life is worth living and love is worth celebrating. I am inspired by those who believe that having babies and raising families is a human right that must not be held to the whims and dictates of the most sophisticated military power in modern-day history. The stories I have weaved into this play are drawn from real-life stories my family and my loved ones in Gaza have experienced over the years.

During the writing phase, the challenge for me was to ensure the authenticity of the Gaza City settings and characters. I wrote with ease the characters of Samira and Rami, the two Palestinian Americans who live in Texas, but I was nervous as to how close to reality my Gaza characters would be. I have visited Gaza many times throughout my life, and was familiar with its sights and sounds, its streets and its alleys. My parents never stopped talking about their memories of Gaza and we always remained tightly connected to our family back home. Still, I wanted to be sure that the people in Gaza would find that the characters and the world I created mirrored their own. I wanted to make sure especially that women in Gaza could see themselves and their experiences in Jomana and Lama, my two lead characters. So in 2013, after seven hours of waiting at the Rafah Border Crossing, I was miraculously allowed into my home city, Gaza, also known as the world's largest open-air prison. I organized a public reading for the play at the A.M. Qattan Foundation Child Centre. I was thrilled by the audience feedback, with so many people thanking me for accurately depicting their lives. So I was happy that this first challenge was overcome.

During the production phase, there were many challenges. At least one was insurmountable. The play was set to premiere in 2014 in three cities on the same night: Melbourne, Gaza, and the West Bank. This was our way as Palestinian artists in Gaza, in the West Bank, and in the Diaspora of defying the borders that separate us. Never did we imagine that a far more brutal assault on Gaza than the one in 2008–2009, which was the backdrop to our play, would take place during our pre-production phase. Israel's war on Gaza in 2014 reduced almost two-thirds of the Gaza Strip into piles of rubble and left thousands of people dead or injured.

Our Gaza team, who were set to begin rehearsals in October 2014, suffered the loss of loved ones, the total destruction of their neighbourhoods, and endured absolute terror for fifty days of constant and indiscriminate bombardment. The situation in Gaza in the aftermath of that war was far worse than it had ever been before. Given the widespread devastation of the city's infrastructure, the psychological trauma of the people in Gaza, including our production team, and the absolute lack of resources, the staging of the play in Gaza was indefinitely postponed.

This had a significant impact on the Melbourne and the West Bank production teams. The production of the play at La Mama Theatre in Melbourne and at the Alrowwad Cultural and Theatre Society in the Aida refugee camp in the West Bank became more important than ever. We wanted to bring the tales of the people of Gaza to life by using theatre as a means of raising awareness and encouraging "beautiful resistance," an expression coined by the Alrowwad's director, Abdelfattah AbuSrour.

The second challenge we faced was raising funds for the West Bank production, which became impossible since most donors preferred to send their money to Gaza to address the desperate and urgent needs there. Giving money to theatre seemed frivolous at a time when almost half a million of Gaza's population were displaced from the war. We understood that priorities change and accepted that we would fall far short of raising enough money for the Alrowwad's production to continue. However, Abdelfattah AbuSrour and his team in the Aida refugee camp insisted on carrying on with their production, even without sufficient funding. To them, this was an act of beautiful resistance that needed to be staged.

As we got closer to the opening night, a third challenge arose. The Aida refugee camp was subjected to various curfews by the Israeli army, which interfered with the actors' ability to meet at the theatre and rehearse in time for opening night. This resulted in various delays, pushing the West Bank opening night behind that of Melbourne's by a whole week.

In Melbourne, the production ran smoothly, albeit on a shoestring budget. But as we watched the devastation in Gaza, and as we witnessed the delays and the harassment our colleagues in the West Bank faced from the Israeli occupying forces, our cast and crew in Melbourne came to appreciate how privileged our lives were. We came to understand how difficult, if not impossible at times, it is for Palestinians under occupation to do something as simple as putting on a theatrical show.

The audience response to the show in Melbourne was overwhelmingly positive. We had a standing ovation almost every night during the run with so many audience members raving about the show on social media and inviting their friends to see it. The entire season was sold out, and in response to audience demands, La Mama Theatre added an additional performance that sold out within hours.

Having said that, perhaps the most important feedback for me was not that following the Melbourne premiere, but rather a comment I received while in Gaza after the public reading in 2013, when a member of the audience in Gaza posted on my Facebook Timeline this message: "You did a good thing. You broke the Gaza culture siege."

So overall, do I feel I have succeeded in reaching the goals I set out to achieve when writing this play? I think I did, but only in part. I have fulfilled my dream of bringing the stories that needed to be told to Australian mainstream theatre audiences. I am proud to say that in May of 2016, *Tales of a City by the Sea* was remounted at La Mama Theatre for a longer sold out run and has been staged in Adelaide and in Sydney to full houses and standing ovations. It was also selected for the Victorian Certificate of Education drama list, so hundreds of high school drama students studied the script and came to see the show. For that I am grateful. But, sadly, I have not been able to fulfil the dream of staging this love story in its home city, Gaza. I still hold the hope that one day . . . this dream will be possible.

# TWENTY-ONE POSITIONS:
## A CARTOGRAPHIC DREAM OF THE MIDDLE EAST

BY ABDELFATTAH ABUSROUR,
LISA SCHLESINGER, AND NAOMI WALLACE

*Twenty-One Positions* was commissioned by the Guthrie Theater. In 2008, the Fordham University Theatre Program in association with The Public Theater first produced the play with the following cast and creative team:

| | |
|---|---|
| Fawaz Al Haj | Ian Quinlan |
| Rashid Al Haj | Chris Larkin |
| Rund | Marjuan Canady |
| Hala | Jessica Farr |
| Danny T. | Ronan Babbitt |
| Murad Salih Daniel | Jacob Wallach |
| Maryam | Jillian Goins |
| Soldier 1 | Chris Masullo |
| Soldier 2 | Julia Zangrilli |
| Soldier 3 | Tom Pecinka |

| | |
|---|---|
| Director | Lisa Peterson |
| Scenic Designer | Rachel Hauck |
| Costume Designer | Michelle Phillips |
| Lighting Designer | Chad McArver |
| Sound Designer | Lindsay Jones |
| Composer | Gina Leishman |
| Musician | Zafir Tawil |
| Properties Designer | Teralyn Bruketta |
| Stage Manager | Donald Fried |
| Production Manager | Kai Brothers |
| Dramaturge | Mandy Hackett |

*"And so I think you should stay here with your sword drawn if you're set on it and your anger is big enough. You have good cause, I admit. But if your anger is a short one, you'd better go."*

—Bertolt Brecht, *Mother Courage*

| | |

*"When was the last time we slept without dreaming we died."*

—Nathalie Handal, *The Lives Of Rain*

## A NOTE ON THE TEXT

A slash (/) indicates the point at which speech is overlapped.

## CHARACTERS

| | |
|---|---|
| Fawaz Al Haj | Late twenties, American. |
| Rashid Al Haj | Fawaz's younger brother, American. |
| Hala | Bride-to-be of Rashid, Palestinian. |
| Rund Barghouti | Eleven-year-old girl, Palestinian. |
| Danny Tirza | A master builder and architect of the wall, Israeli. |
| Murad Salih Daniel | An elderly archaeologist from Baghdad, Israeli. |
| Maryam | Hala's aunt, Palestinian. |
| Chorus | Three soldiers, Israeli. |

## SETTING

| | |
|---|---|
| Time | Now, and the past. |
| Place | Bethlehem, West Bank, as it might remember itself, in reverie. The Israeli West Bank wall is staggering, always there, but neither obvious nor concrete. |

## PROLOGUE

*Lights rise.*

*FAWAZ walks out onto a stage which is bare but for a single toy-size model hang-glider that is suspended from above. He is not yet fully dressed, a jacket and tie hang over his arm, and he carries a simple, old-fashioned square suitcase. He puts the suitcase down. FAWAZ sets the glider gently spinning, and keeps his eye on it as he buttons up his shirt. Then he begins to put on his tie. After some moments, RASHID appears, from another time and space. He carries a simple chair and places it down. RASHID helps FAWAZ with his tie: they are now teenagers again.*

RASHID Your hands are sweating.

*FAWAZ tries to wrestle his tie from RASHID but RASHID wins out.*

Let me do it. Girls don't like sweaty hands.

FAWAZ How would you know? You've never had a girl.

RASHID Yeah, but at night I have them one by one and damn are they sweet.

FAWAZ Shhh. Mom'll hear you. *(beat)* Make sure Dad takes his meds before he goes to sleep. If he doesn't, he'll feel it in his hip all week. And make sure Mom gets—

FAWAZ/RASHID *(together)* Her hot milk and piece of toast.

FAWAZ I'll be home before eleven.

RASHID It's a drag having old parents. I can't remember them without grey hair. I'm sixteen years old and my father looks like the pope.

FAWAZ Don't fuck up again. Last time I went out you forgot to let the cat out so it pissed on the Persian. You fed the canary a whole peanut, not halved like I told you, and it choked.

RASHID To death, yeah. Mom is still pissed. *(He has finished* FAWAZ*'s tie. He gets* FAWAZ*'s jacket ready, picks off some lint, smooths it.)* But she's still gonna lend me the eighty bucks to get the motor on my glider rejigged!

FAWAZ I'll rejig your ass if I come home and anything is out of place.

RASHID You know, when you turn eighteen you're supposed to be cool. You are definitely not cool, Fawaz. And this jacket proves it. Yuck. Looks like Granddad's.

FAWAZ Yeah? Well at least I've got a working plan. For both of us—

RASHID *(mocking)* —for the rest of our lives?

FAWAZ Damn right. First we go to university—

RASHID *(interrupting)* Not "we," bro. I told you I've got other—

FAWAZ *(interrupting)* Yes, "we." Both of us together. Now shut up about it.

*RASHID helps FAWAZ into his jacket. They are silent some moments.*

RASHID When I'm up in that glider, there's no plan and all of it's just wide open space. Up in that thing, I'm God's right-hand man.

FAWAZ Up in that thing you're an idiot as much as you are down here. Open your books for a change. You're gonna fail chemistry. I'm warning you.

RASHID I got to tell you something. Something private.

FAWAZ If this is about your erections I don't want to hear it.

RASHID No. No. That time we were at the State Fair and I saw my first hang-glider?

*FAWAZ just looks at RASHID, resisting this conversation.*

The Mosquito! Yeah. By Swedish Aerosport. Commonly known as Mozzie. Thereafter known to me as the Mozz. I didn't realize it at the time but we were looking at the new NRG model, with streamlined front entry harness—

*FAWAZ relents and joins the excitement with RASHID.*

FAWAZ Electric start—

RASHID Radne Raket—

FAWAZ One hundred cc two-stroke engine—

RASHID With 10 horsepower at 88 hundred rpm.

FAWAZ Fan-cooled, clutch-equipped—

RASHID With decompressor for easy pull starts. The largest pilot to fly with that system was 1.98 metres tall and weighed—

FAWAZ A hundred and ten kilograms. Naked weight.

*RASHID taps the model glider and they both watch it turn.*

That glider moved above us like an eraser 'cross the sky. *(He makes the buzzing sound of a motor as they watch the glider spin.)*

RASHID And I, Rashid Al Haj, was one of those notions it wiped clean: an eleven-year-old Arab, an American citizen, a non-practising Muslim at Ranger Grade School for Catholic Boys, just standing there, looking up, with one hard, surprisingly painful erection.

*FAWAZ stops the buzzing sound.*

FAWAZ I knew it. It's always about your dick!

RASHID But the Mozz wasn't only my first sexual experience: it was my first love. After a rush like that, I was enlisted as a lover for life of that impossible, contraptual vision:

FAWAZ/RASHID *(together)* The Motorized Hang-glider.

*Suddenly FAWAZ and RASHID just stare at each other. Neither moves. FAWAZ is now his adult self once more.*

FAWAZ Where the hell are you, Rashid?

RASHID *(shrugs)* I don't know. But I know where you are.

FAWAZ Oh yeah?

*RASHID spins FAWAZ around and sits him down in the chair.*

RASHID You've got no date tonight. Matter of fact, I'd guess you haven't had a date in a while.

*RASHID slips off his belt and uses it as a seat belt across FAWAZ's lap and around the chair. He pulls the belt tight. Now we begin to hear the distant sound of a motor, slowly getting louder.*

And you're on a 747 KLM night flight from Cincinnati through Amsterdam to Tel Aviv, bro. And you ate too many pretzels. Took you to pretzel land.

FAWAZ Where are you?

*RASHID won't answer.*

I'd like to hit you, you irresponsible son of a bitch. For leaving us.

RASHID That was years ago.

FAWAZ Fucking feels like right now. Not a word from you in years. Nothing. Until now.

RASHID 'Cause I'm getting married!

FAWAZ I don't believe it.

RASHID Neither do I! And you, my brother, are going to be my best man.

FAWAZ No, I'm not.

RASHID Yes, you are. You're already on your way. *(He exits.)*

FAWAZ *(yelling after him)* But I will come and find you 'cause Mom told me not to come back without you. And after I kick your ass for all the damage you did by leaving us, I'm going to stuff a rag in your mouth, fold you into my fucking suitcase and ship you home!

*FAWAZ is alone again. The motor sound of the jet grows enormous, then dead silent some moments before an explosion. He is startled, and wakes, having landed. We hear over the intercom a smooth voice: "Welcome to Ben Gurion International Airport." Blackout.*

# ACT ONE

## SCENE ONE

*FAWAZ, carrying his suitcase, has arrived at the airport in Tel Aviv. He holds his passport tightly against his chest. The Chorus, three Israeli soldiers, are seated in wheeled office chairs. Two of the SOLDIERS are pushing the third back and forth, across the length of the stage. As though the chairs are a part of their bodies, they move with grace and rapidity. At one point the soldiers, seated in their flying chairs, circle FAWAZ. FAWAZ hardly moves throughout the scene, only if he must get out of the way. What we witness here is the confidence, even grace, of a well-managed bureaucracy.*

*Song of the Welcome to Ben Gurion Airport:*

SOLDIERS
We can read you, we can see you, like a shiny pane of glass.
We can hear you, we can taste you, we can even pinch your ass.
We are kindly and intelligent, we are members of the club.
But we have got a job to do so we do it, there's no rub.
We've got enemies beyond the gate and evil that will creep.
We've got bang, bang in our front yards and bang, bang in our sleep.

SOLDIER 1
What holidays do you desecrate?

FAWAZ
Bethlehem.

SOLDIER 2
What language do you celebrate?

FAWAZ
I need to get to Bethlehem.

*The SOLDIERS sing various lines, sometimes together, sometimes apart. FAWAZ speaks his lines.*

FAWAZ I'm a US citizen.

SOLDIERS He's an American guy, from the sweet Ohio State.
Owns his little store, a good worker, never late.

FAWAZ I have my own line of products.

SOLDIERS Has his own line of products. He knows who he be.
Got a store that sells nutrition—

FAWAZ —and homemade vitamin E.

SOLDIERS You are what we know you are, red-blooded through and through.
But we know your little secret and we know you know we do.

FAWAZ Could you please hurry it up—

SOLDIERS Be a good boy, brush your teeth. Say thank you if you please.
You'll have a pleasant journey if you mind your Qs and Ps.

FAWAZ I need to get to my brother's wedding.

SOLDIERS Oh, look at that, a downcast face, he doesn't like protection!
This is for you we do this dance, so please don't feel rejection.
But my God this is a banquet, said the termite to the house.
I'm going to call my embassy, said the cheese to the mouse.
No need to call your embassy, of course we'll let you pass.
But one thing 'fore you do, one small thing we have to ask:

Is he innocent? Is he innocent? Is he innocent as can be?
Fawaz Al Haj. Is he an innocent to a T?

FAWAZ Of course I'm innocent!

*The* SOLDIERS *sing the following in quick succession.*

SOLDIER 1 Said the rectum to the hose.

SOLDIER 2 Said the finger to the nose.

SOLDIER 3 Said the dance to the pose.

SOLDIER 2 Put on your clothes.

SOLDIERS Welcome to Israel.

FAWAZ *leaves Immigration. The* SOLDIERS *signal to other visitors, and the public, to enter Israel. They wave tiny Israeli flags.*

Welcome. Welcome. Welcome home.
Welcome to Israel. Welcome home.

## SCENE TWO

*Bethlehem.* RUND *is wearing her school backpack. She does a backward hopscotch.*

RUND *(chanting, first in Arabic, then in English)*
Jaras
Elmadrassah run
Wel ostath inj jun
Welkutub ibtekra lahalha
Wel aklam bitnam
I can hear the school bell.
The teacher's getting mad.
The books are reading by themselves,
The pencils acting bad.

*Suddenly* FAWAZ*'s suitcase comes crashing across the stage. It is followed by* FAWAZ*, who stumbles and trips, hitting the ground, having been shoved hard from behind.* FAWAZ *dusts himself off, enraged at this treatment. He shouts back at the checkpoint.*

FAWAZ I'm gonna report your big ass to my embassy! You can count on that! *(to himself)* Stupid son of a bitch . . . *(to checkpoint)* Sissy! *(to himself)* Two damn hours to get through. *(to checkpoint)* Ass-bone . . .

*FAWAZ sits on his suitcase to look at his map. Then he notices RUND, standing near him, silently observing his outburst.*

RUND I take it that was your first checkpoint? You have a dirty mouth.

FAWAZ And you have a dirty face, kid. You know where the Saraya Hall is?

RUND You're from the other side of the Wall.

FAWAZ Yep.

RUND Israeli side.

FAWAZ The Whatever Side.

RUND That side used to be this side.

FAWAZ The Saraya Hall. You know it or not?

RUND Maybe I do.

FAWAZ I'm looking for a wedding. The Al Haj wedding?

RUND Maybe I don't.

FAWAZ Could you show me on this map?

*RUND snatches his map.*

RUND I know maps.

FAWAZ Hey, give it back!

RUND I can fix your map. *(She tears off a small piece of the map.)*

FAWAZ I just bought that!

RUND The Saraya Hall? Try Tulkarm first.

*RUND tears off another small piece and lets it fall to the ground. With each village or town she tears a small piece and lets it fall. As she walks and tears, FAWAZ follows behind, trying to pick up the pieces of map.*

Then try Qalqilya. Or Salfit. Or Nablus.

FAWAZ Stop that, you brat!

RUND Then Bil'in and up to Tubas. Down again to Ramallah, across to Jericho, zip zip back to Abu Dis—

FAWAZ You're gonna buy me a new one!

RUND —through Beit Sahour, then Bethlehem, skip skip over to Hebron. Oh, Hebron. Or slip through Al-Quds, Jerusalem. And then the little places.

*FAWAZ gives up.*

FAWAZ Damn it.

*RUND tears even smaller pieces.*

RUND Qalandiya. Dahiet Al Bareed. Beit Hanina. Shuafat. At-Tur. Beit Safafa. Sur Bahir. Rashid Al-Haj. Um Tuba.

FAWAZ Wait. Rashid Al-Haj?

RUND Beit Safafa. Checkpoint number 303.

FAWAZ That's my brother. You know my brother? He was supposed to meet me at the airport and he didn't show. The bastard. Just like him to leave me stranded.

RUND Have you seen my cousin Hala?

FAWAZ Hala?

RUND She's the bride. Looks like morning even when it's night, that's what they say.

FAWAZ Take me to her.

RUND What will you give me?

FAWAZ I don't know. What do you want?

RUND One of your socks.

FAWAZ Huh?

RUND One of your socks or no deal.

FAWAZ I need my socks.

RUND So do I. Lost one of mine at a checkpoint.

FAWAZ How'd you do that?

RUND It didn't hold up to interrogation.

*RUND holds out her hand. FAWAZ finally takes off his shoe and his sock and drapes it in her hand. She sniffs it.*

This sock has travelled. Yuck.

FAWAZ Didn't have time to change.

*RUND puts on his sock. She now wears a long adult sock on one foot and her little one on the other.*

RUND How do I look?

FAWAZ Take me to my brother's fiancée. *(He looks down at her socks.)*

RUND They do not match.

FAWAZ Of course they don't. I'm twice your size.

RUND They'll tease me on the playground. If I can find the playground . . .

FAWAZ Look, kid. Get going. Take me to Hala or I take back the sock.

*FAWAZ pushes RUND forward.*

RUND Do you always push kids around?

FAWAZ If they need it.

RUND I'm not sure I like you.

FAWAZ Ditto. Now do as I say.

*RUND shakes FAWAZ off her arm and leads the way.*

## SCENE THREE

*HALA and MARYAM are arguing. HALA stands on a small stool in her wedding dress.*

MARYAM Hala, Ishlahi elfoustan. Take it off!

HALA No. I won't take it off. I'm going to wear it.

MARYAM Don't be so stubborn!

HALA I'm going to sleep in it!

*RUND has led FAWAZ to HALA.*

MARYAM Then you will sleep as a fool!

FAWAZ Hala? Are you Hala?

*HALA and MARYAM are startled by FAWAZ's sudden appearance.*

HALA Who are you?

RUND Says he's your brother, Hala.

HALA What?

FAWAZ To be. I'm your brother-to-be.

*FAWAZ holds out his hand. HALA does not take it.*

Fawaz Al Haj. Rashid's brother. Older brother.

RUND *(to HALA)* It's true. Too bad, cousin.

*RUND runs to HALA and swishes hard at HALA's dress.*

MARYAM *(to FAWAZ)* Rashid doesn't have a brother.

HALA *(to RUND)* Stop that, Rund!

MARYAM Living. Rashid's brother died.

FAWAZ What? He said I died? No!

MARYAM He said you were trampled at a demonstration.

FAWAZ Trampled at a demonstration? When?

MARYAM Years ago. Where did Rashid say his brother died, Hala? In DC, I think he said.

FAWAZ I can't believe it.

MARYAM The police attacked, the crowd ran, and Rashid's brother was crushed under their feet. Tragic. Tragic, but courageous.

FAWAZ I've never been to a demonstration.

HALA Then you're not Fawaz.

RUND I want to see your legs, cousin. Are you wearing socks?

*HALA and RUND struggle a moment as RUND tries to pull up HALA's dress and HALA tries to hold it down, uncomfortable in front of FAWAZ.*

I need another sock!

FAWAZ The lying little punk.

HALA Stop it!

MARYAM Leave your cousin alone, Rund.

FAWAZ Why would he say I was dead?

HALA Stop it, you rascal!

MARYAM *(to RUND)* This is not Hala's day.

*MARYAM takes RUND by the arm and leads her away from HALA. They ignore FAWAZ.*

Rund, my sweet. Go on now.

FAWAZ Why would he lie?

RUND No, Auntie!

MARYAM Get on home!

*RUND stomps one foot, then runs off.*

*(to FAWAZ)* Whoever you are, you should get home too.

*FAWAZ gets his passport out and flashes it at MARYAM. She glances at the passport, clocks the information, and nods to HALA, as if to say "Yeah. It's his brother."*

FAWAZ Look here, I'm sorry to disappoint you but I'm Rashid's brother. How do you think I knew about the wedding? Because Rashid wrote to me about it. He asked me to come. I didn't want to come. I don't want to be here at all. But my mother begged me because she hasn't seen her son or had a call from him in years. So I'm here for her, to bring him home. With or without the bride, if that's how it has to be.

MARYAM The wedding's off.

FAWAZ What?

MARYAM Off. Over. Kaput. Kapowed.

HALA Be quiet, Aunt. *(to FAWAZ)* There has been a *(beat)* postponement.

*MARYAM snorts.*

FAWAZ A postponement?

MARYAM Now take off that dress!

FAWAZ Where's my brother?

*HALA and MARYAM ignore FAWAZ.*

Hey, where is Rashid? We need to talk.

*HALA stares at FAWAZ a moment, then decides to tell him the truth.*

HALA We don't know.

*MARYAM chortles.*

We don't know and we don't need to know. He'll be back. No problem. More importantly, why did your brother deny you all these years? What did you do to him?

FAWAZ I tried to save him from himself. He didn't like that. More importantly, why did he lie to you about me? Not a good way to start a marriage, lying about family.

*HALA looks away.*

Cuts both ways, doesn't it? So where is he?

HALA Go away. I said we don't know.

FAWAZ I don't believe you. My brother was a liar. Makes sense he'd marry one.

HALA You are nothing like Rashid. Now leave us. Maryam, there's a button loose. Can you fix it?

MARYAM Why should I fix it? The wedding is off.

HALA Today. I'm not getting married today. But tomorrow Rashid will be back and then I'll need this dress. Please. Fix it.

MARYAM Affirming: when I find the needle.

FAWAZ You're the bride and you don't know where he is?

*MARYAM finds a needle and begins to sew on the button.*

MARYAM Call in the UN. They're always ineffective.

FAWAZ Oh. I get it. I get it.

MARYAM You can hail them like a cab. They drive like cabbies, too.

FAWAZ Rashid did a runner on you.

MARYAM Reaffirming: you are not getting married.

FAWAZ I knew it. I knew it!

HALA Ya allah. Leave us alone.

FAWAZ He used to do this to me all the time.

HALA Do what all the time?

FAWAZ Mess. Things. Up.

HALA You don't know Rashid.

FAWAZ Oh yeah I do. And he's a selfish, thoughtless, disappearing little bastard. *(sees something on Hala's dress)*

You've got a spot on your dress. Listen, if you and Rashid had problems, maybe I can help. I can tie things up, take you both back home with me. My brother can work in my store.

*HALA bursts out laughing.*

HALA — Rashid work in your store?

FAWAZ — I can get you a green card.

*HALA finds the spot on her dress.*

HALA — Mister. I'm not interested in your green card. I have a degree in engineering from Imperial College London. I intend to use it here. *(to MARYAM)* Have you got something for a spot?

FAWAZ — I do. Where I come from, travel can be a dirty affair.

*FAWAZ takes out a pack of stain-removal tissues. HALA opens and smells it.*

HALA — Is this what you sell in your store?

FAWAZ — Yep. Environmentally friendly. Use it on cotton, rayon, and—what happened between you and my brother?

HALA — Keep your nose where it belongs, Fawaz, and not in my business.

RASHID — Well, it's obvious you had a bust up.

HALA — *(to herself)* Brother? Huh. My enemy, my brother . . .

*HALA starts to clean the spot on her dress but MARYAM stops her.*

MARYAM — Wait! Article 1. Welcoming the solution: I hereby state my concerns about the integrity—of the fabric. It's silk. While endorsing the British with credibility—disregarding everything they ever promised historically, of course—I cannot agree. Use salt.

Sometimes plain old-world peasantries are more effective. Old wives tale, two hundred thirty-two. *(She rummages in her pockets for salt.)*

FAWAZ That dress is . . . a good fit.

HALA It's not for your eyes.

FAWAZ Rashid's a lucky man.

HALA Luckiest man in Bethlehem.

*MARYAM finds the salt and rubs it on the spot as she speaks.*

MARYAM Article 2. Concerning the dress. I never liked it. It's too tight.

Article 3. Do you know what your problem is? A. You can't even walk in this dress. B. It's not paid for, and C. Your groom has adiosed because D. He lacks disciplinary imperative.

Article 4. Start over, Hala. But you can't have new ideas while wearing an old-fashioned dress.

*MARYAM now gets out scissors and begins cutting HALA's dress until it is a manageable, ordinary garment. HALA gasps in shock, but keeps silent. FAWAZ watches in fascination.*

Article 5. Confirming. You were always uncertain about him. That's a fact.

Article 6. Reaffirming. What spins your bolts is gravity and hydraulics.

Article 7. So forget the loser who didn't show, and stick with aerodynamics!

See, you feel better already!

*HALA looks somewhat dejected, but when she jumps off the stool she looks lighter, fashionable. She spins in a circle, momentarily joyful.*

HALA Rashid's going to love this dress!

FAWAZ Whoa . . .

*HALA throws FAWAZ an angry look.*

As we say back home.

MARYAM *(to HALA)* Article 8. If it's true that Fawaz is his brother, then may Allah help Rashid because that man is not family I would choose. *(She starts to leave but then turns back and looks intently at FAWAZ.)* When I reread the Universal Declaration of Human Rights the document came through as the UN-DECLARATION. Then I understood absolutely everything.

*MARYAM exits. HALA gathers up the cut pieces of her dress.*

FAWAZ What's up with your aunt?

HALA She has a UN stick up her ass. She worked for them for twenty years.

*HALA puts the pieces of fabric in FAWAZ's arms.*

The weather was clear this morning.

FAWAZ Okay. The weather was clear. But he's an idiot, my brother. To leave you with half a dress.

HALA Yes. Rashid's an idiot. But a smart one.

FAWAZ He sure turned your head.

*HALA studies FAWAZ's face.*

HALA Your brother is more handsome than you.

FAWAZ That's not what most cheerleaders thought back in high school.

HALA Were you always jealous of him?

FAWAZ *(laughs)* Is that what he told you? That I was jealous?

HALA No. But I guessed it.

FAWAZ He couldn't put two and two together unless I helped him.

HALA You haven't seen him in years.

FAWAZ Seven years. I keep count. I missed an important convention to come here: my first invitation to speak at the Association of Family-Owned American Health Food Stores. Fully paid. Weekend at the Holiday Inn. The little shit.

HALA *(without sentiment)* He says he loved you when you were kids.

FAWAZ Yeah, well the real issue is: does he love you? And if he does, why did he leave you standing?

*HALA stares hard at FAWAZ. He throws the scraps of dress at her feet, then exits.*

## SCENE FOUR

*FAWAZ, tired, has been walking for some time with his suitcase. RUND enters.*

FAWAZ So the wedding's off. Hell. What am I supposed to do now? How am I supposed to find Rashid?

RUND *(shrugs)* Travel? Yep. You got to travel to find him. Look how easy it is. *(She takes a handful of the map pieces from her pocket.)* It's all here. I can take a handful, see? And travel that fast. Just seconds or minutes. Otherwise, it's hours to get there. And sometimes not at all. Sometimes never again. But the best way to get around quick, quick is like this.

FAWAZ Where'd you learn your English?

RUND Map eating. *(She takes a small piece and eats it.)* Al Khadar. Mint. Yum. Try Beit Jala.

*RUND holds out a piece to FAWAZ. He steps back. She looks through the pieces, looking for a tasty morsel. Finds a piece.*

Ah. Shit. Here it is again. I ate it yesterday, but each time I eat it, it reappears: Washington, DC. A very Palestinian village. You try. Eat it.

FAWAZ Stop it, kid. Things are tough all over. Wipe your eyes. Buck up.

RUND Buck up. I like that.

FAWAZ If you know where my brother's run off to, tell me.

RUND Buck up.

FAWAZ You're wasting my time.

*RUND holds out the paper again.*

RUND Eat it. Eat it or I will never tell.

FAWAZ All right. Give me Washington.

*RUND holds out the piece to him. FAWAZ eats it.*

There. Done. Where's my brother?

*RUND does one of the twenty-one shoot-to-kill movements she's learned from watching the Israeli Army. But she's modified it to be her own. It's strange and grotesque. FAWAZ watches some moments, then grabs her roughly by her collar.*

If you've got news for me, give it now and give it fast.

RUND Wow. Say that again. But meaner this time.

FAWAZ Tell me what you know right now or I'll, I swear I'll—

RUND *(says it for him)* Ram my fist down your scrawny, pitiful throat! Okay, okay, cowboy. I heard. And it's only what I heard. But I heard . . . And what I heard may not be what I hear tomorrow. I heard . . .

FAWAZ Damn it, just spit it out.

RUND That your brother is involved . . .

FAWAZ Yeah?

RUND If Washington is back again tomorrow I'll consider myself cheated by you.

FAWAZ Agreed.

RUND Rashid Al Haj is involved in an *(whispers)* operation.

FAWAZ No. No way.

RUND I have been eating maps since I was five. My shit is made of paper.

FAWAZ That's ridiculous. I don't believe you.

RUND Come after dinner. Usually I poop at that time. I'll show you.

FAWAZ No. My brother may be a fuck-up but he's not a criminal. And he doesn't have the brains to put together any kind of operation. Your info is crap, kid, so don't spread it.

RUND Look. You need to find your brother. I need to find my school.

FAWAZ Where's your school?

RUND It was just about *(looks around her)* here. But now it's gone. The wall came through and round and snatched it. Now it's on the other side. But I know a crack we could squeeze through.

FAWAZ I'm not doing anything illegal.

RUND But you won't get through the checkpoint. They'll stop you.

FAWAZ Not me, kid.

RUND Oh yes, they will.

*Song of the Necessary Permit:*

Before you face the M16
From Hebron to Bethlehem,
To pass all checkpoints in between
You gotta have a permit.
From Bethlehem to the city of Ramallah
If that is where you want to go,
You need to say a prayer to Allah
And get a permit.
If you want to pass through the wall,
Go to the hospital or swim the sea,
If you want to die, and be buried at all!
You gotta have a permit.

FAWAZ They didn't stop me coming in.

RUND It's a one-way system. You can come in but usually you can't get out. But we could break your hand and say you need a doctor.

FAWAZ This works?

RUND Sometimes. Probably not. But there's a man at Sawahreh who has a crane. For a hundred dollars, he can lift you up, up thirty feet and you can step right onto the wall. A diving board!

FAWAZ How do you get off the wall on the other side?

RUND *(shrugs)* Never tried it. Give me your other sock and I'll get you where you want to go.

FAWAZ You know, your kind give Arabs a bad name. Ever

since I landed all I hear is you people whine. Can't get here. Can't get there. Can't work here. Can't work there. And Bethlehem? There's trash everywhere. Don't you have pick-up?

*RUND just stares at FAWAZ until he takes off his remaining sock and gives it to her. She takes off her small sock and puts on his. Then she throws her little one at FAWAZ. He catches it and holds it up, gingerly. She looks at her two matching socks.*

RUND Now I'm fully dressed and ready for class. But where's my school?

FAWAZ No idea, kid.

RUND Let's go. If we find my school, we might find your brother. Your brother always liked school. He had a pile of books by his bedside that touched the ceiling. And his favourite was Hemingway.

FAWAZ Yep. *The Old Man and the Sea*. But he always fucked things up for me.

*RUND walks away, then looks back to see if FAWAZ is following.*

## SCENE FIVE

*Somewhere in between. RASHID sits playing checkers with himself. Each time he moves a checker piece, he speaks a line. If he makes a mistake in his calculations, he moves the piece back to its place. He is wearing a light harness with ropes that drag on the ground.*

RASHID It was five thirty-five in the morning. I slipped in through the window. Hala was asleep. I kissed her cheek. Once. No. Twice. I kissed her on the left cheek twice. She didn't wake. I went down to the basement. We'd built it together. Sort of. Really, she built it but I would do the first test. *(beat)* The weather was clear that morning so it was all sky. Slick, raw. Seventeen minutes and I landed. No. I didn't land. Yes. Yes. I landed. A good land. A fucking good land. And then. And then. I can't remember.

Was it with the takeoff? Think. Think. What went wrong? Retrace. Restart. Was it a problem with the glider's landing? Typical landing approach.

*In another time and place,* HALA *is teaching* RASHID, *speaking partly in Arabic, partly in English.*

HALA Long steps. Long steps. Resist the temptation to push out the control bar. *(She takes the steps herself, demonstrating.)* Let the wing get its own best trim, best glide. Look for the lift, Rashid!

RASHID *hears his name. He leaves his checkers game.*

RASHID Baby, how much lean?

HALA *and* RASHID *are now back in the past. She demonstrates with her body. He mirrors her instructions with his body, arms outstretched like a flyer.*

HALA That depends on the wind. But don't shift your feet, just lean forward. Now lean again.

RASHID *(leaning)* How much lean. This much?

HALA *laughs at his awkward lean.*

HALA Habibi, you idiot, no way you're taking my glider on a virgin flight!

RASHID *shifts.*

RASHID This much?

HALA Better. *(leaning, showing him)* Now, further.

RASHID This? Come on, Hala. Let me fly it.

HALA A little more.

RASHID You can't build a glider and never fly it.

HALA Concentrate.

RASHID If I prove to you that this thing can fly, will you marry me?

HALA I don't know. Shit, I don't know.

RASHID Why won't you say yes?

HALA Now push against the headwind.

RASHID Well I'm gonna fly the damn thing without your permission and I'll bring you back a gift. Something rare, something wild, as you are.

HALA Shut up, sweet mouth.

RASHID I know you want me.

HALA Let's try takeoff. *(beat)* Push the bar. *(She demonstrates.)*

RASHID Say you want me.

HALA Push harder.

RASHID I can smell you, Hala.

HALA Don't.

RASHID Touch me, Hala. I'm stiff as a rock.

HALA Pay attention. Push.

RASHID I want you.

HALA Harder, damn you!

RASHID Please.

HALA/RASHID Stop. *(They quit pushing.)*

HALA This isn't an amusement.

RASHID Neither is love.

HALA This is not about love. This is about instruction. You could fall out of the sky— *(snaps her fingers)* —just like that. Your bones for kindling.

RASHID I won't ask you to quit teaching or to leave the university. I just want, at the end of each day, to lie down beside you for the rest of my life.

*HALA starts to laugh, but then checks herself.*

HALA Damn it, Rashid. I can fuse the engine of a motorcycle to a vacuum cleaner.

RASHID Yeah, and make a vehicle that sucks hard tarmac as it burns down the road.

HALA If the glider's not in perfect working order. If I make a mistake. If I make a miscalculation . . .

RASHID Not afraid to die, Hala. I'm afraid to live without you.

HALA Stop it. *(beat)* But I'll make you a deal: you practise to fly it right, practise to fly it like a professional and I'll . . .

RASHID Marry you.

HALA Yes. *(beat)* But don't ever fly it without me.

RASHID Done.

HALA I want a tight dress for the wedding.

RASHID So tight you can't breathe.

*HALA smiles, but wonders about this. RASHID exits. Only when he's gone does HALA suddenly turn as though someone were there, watching her.*

## SCENE SIX

*Bethlehem checkpoint. FAWAZ is angrily kicking his suitcase across the stage, back and forth. RUND appears and watches him awhile.*

RUND Give me that suitcase. You don't deserve it.

FAWAZ What? No! I already gave you my socks. *(He continues to kick the suitcase.)*

RUND I lost my book bag. I need your suitcase for my books.

FAWAZ There's not much in it. Change of shorts. Toothbrush. I wasn't planning a long trip.

*RUND holds out her hand for the suitcase but FAWAZ ignores her and continues to kick it, more like a game now, coming closer to her, and shooting it past her, just missing her.*

Those bastards still wouldn't let me pass through.

RUND Told you so.

FAWAZ How am I supposed to find Rashid if I can't travel?

*FAWAZ kicks the suitcase past RUND's feet but she stops it, impressively, with her foot.*

RUND Practise. And be a soldier. Be a soldier at my checkpoint.

FAWAZ I don't do games, little girl.

RUND Kick-the-Suitcase isn't a game?

FAWAZ No. It's a physical manifestation of Fuck-Travel-in-This-Country.

RUND Do you miss Rashid?

FAWAZ No.

RUND He says he missed you. After you died.

FAWAZ The liar. I was a damn good brother to him in Cincy. I laid the road and led him by the hand. He never had to worry about a thing. He never even had to think 'cause I did that for him. I schemed for both of us. And it came to nothing.

RUND Please. Be a soldier.

*FAWAZ shakes his head "no."*

If you play my game I'll take you to the man who built the Wall: Danny T. The man who invented the wall. They say he knows your brother.

FAWAZ Bullshit.

RUND That's what they say.

FAWAZ They?

RUND I swear.

*FAWAZ considers, then plays the soldier, barking, with relish.*

FAWAZ Identification card. Identification card. Identifica—

RUND Hello, soldier. Here's my ID for one schoolgirl, Rund Barghouti, two shoes, two big socks, a ruler, skirt, blouse, *(whispers)* underpants, *(loudly)* geography book, gum—

FAWAZ Gun? Gun? She's got a gun!

RUND No. Gum. Gum. As in chew, chew. But saving it. Tucked away behind my left molar, see?

*She shows FAWAZ with an open mouth.*

FAWAZ I could make you spit it out, you know?

RUND It's Doublemint.

FAWAZ Oh. All right then.

RUND Three hair barrettes.

FAWAZ I only see two.

RUND Third one is in my bag in case of emergency.

FAWAZ There is always emergency. Have some respect.

RUND And three pencils . . . And this is when the pencils burst the bag and bust out. It's a jailbreak! It's astonishing. I hear a rumbling, then a tearing. The soldier hears it too.

FAWAZ What the hell is that rumbling and tearing?

RUND I don't hear anything. *(She makes impressive sounds of rumbling and tearing.)* But the soldier will not be fooled!

FAWAZ I won't be fooled!

RUND And he calls his buddies.

FAWAZ Buddies! Buddies!

RUND And he's rude too!

FAWAZ Get your asses over here, quick!

RUND Oh my.

FAWAZ Two, maybe three pencils. They skedaddled—

RUND Imagine it. He actually uses the word "skedaddled"!

FAWAZ They skedaddled when she opened her bag. But they can't have gone far. Search everyone. Send the women home.

RUND And tell the men to strip!

FAWAZ Tell the men to strip! Those pencils, they wouldn't run if they didn't have something to hide.

RUND "They wouldn't run if they didn't have something to hide." A cliché. We learned that last week in English. And then the soldier says:

FAWAZ And you, little girlie, plop down right here. You're not going anywhere until we find those pencils and disable them.

RUND And we know what disabling a pencil means. *(She plops down on his suitcase.)* So I sit down. Three hours later I'm still here. Extra late for school. And that's the whole truth.

*FAWAZ speaks as himself again.*

FAWAZ So kid, where's this builder who knows about my brother?

RUND You're a pretty good soldier, Fawaz.

FAWAZ Thanks.

*RUND picks up FAWAZ's suitcase and begins to leave. RUND motions with her head for him to follow.*

RUND But next time use another word. A checkpoint soldier would never say "skedaddled."

## SCENE SEVEN

*RASHID is moving along the wall, as though reading it with his body, arms outstretched.*

RASHID *(sings, partly in Arabic, partly in English)*
Sticky summers, itchy and slow.
And the glides that didn't end.
Why did I leave Cincinnati, oh,
My straight roads and the river bend.

*MURAD, an elderly Jewish immigrant to Israel and an archaeologist, enters pushing a single-wheeled measuring contraption ahead of him. He seems to be looking for something in the ground and at first does not acknowledge RASHID.*

*(sings)* I took a jumbo jet across the world
And when it landed here, oh yes,
Lemon trees and a pile of shit,
And always garbage burning.
On top of it all, on this mountain of grit,
Was Hala, and I was yearning.

*MURAD runs into RASHID with his wheeled contraption.*

MURAD Ben zonah!

RASHID Shalom.

MURAD Next time announce yourself. You could get shot popping up like that.

RASHID Shit. Wein Ana? What side of the wall am I on?

MURAD My side. Our side.

RASHID Which side?

MURAD Jewish side.

*RASHID studies MURAD's contraption.*

RASHID What've you got there?

*MURAD wheels away.*

MURAD I'm an archaeologist. Though I'm self-employed. I'm looking for our origins.

RASHID "Our" origins?

MURAD The accumulation of time in order to profit. If I find the right site, I'll get a job teaching at Hebrew University! Though Hebrew University doesn't want a man. Like me.

RASHID Yep. No matter what you find. Hey, can I use that?

MURAD Certainly not! *(He begins to push his contraption again.)* The measurements must be off.

RASHID No. You're in the right spot. There are thousands of years of trash on top. It's just deeper than you think.

MURAD What is "it"?

RASHID Can I borrow your hammer? *(He lifts the hammer from* MURAD*'s belt.)* "It" is the beginnings.

MURAD The First Temple?

RASHID Before that. *(He kneels and begins to gently tap the ground.)*

MURAD There is no before that.

RASHID Before David and the Israelites: Us. Canaanites.

MURAD Oh, them. We conquered them.

RASHID There! There! You hear that?

MURAD *falls to his knees next to* RASHID *and begins to listen.*

MURAD There's definitely a hollow down there. What do you think?

RASHID It's a tunnel that runs this way. *(He indicates the route.)* You could dig here. Under the wall.

MURAD All right. But if the site's late Bronze Age or Canaanite, well then we'll—

RASHID Bulldoze it?

MURAD The university will only accept the beginnings. Nothing before that. Everything else . . . We'll dig it up and throw it out.

RASHID If you destroy it, the whole thing will collapse. Like a house of cards.

MURAD The Davidic Empire, the United Monarchy, Solomon's Temple. That is where it all begins. The rest is prehistory.

*RASHID manages to snatch the measuring contraption from MURAD. He begins to circle MURAD while he speaks.*

RASHID I've been there. There is no such thing as prehistory.

MURAD The university says otherwise. This is my calling.

RASHID So a person can really find something with this, huh? You think it might work for me?

MURAD Most definitely not.

RASHID Where you from, old man?

MURAD My wet nurse was a Muslim. Breastfed me alongside her own son. I called her Umi bi'l-riddaa. Mother by nursing.

*RASHID stops circling and studies MURAD.*

Baghdad. The oldest Jewish community in the Arab and Islamic world. There were one hundred thousand of us in Iraq.

*RASHID runs the contraption into MURAD's feet.*

RASHID Do you know what happened to me? What did I do that morning? I can't remember.

MURAD All right. That's enough now. I order you to leave.

RASHID But I did something. What did I do?

MURAD You are corrupting my site!

RASHID What the fuck happened to me?

MURAD Silence! *(beat)* That's none of my concern. I am an archaeologist.

## SCENE EIGHT

*RUND has led FAWAZ to the wall. DANNY T. is walking backwards, measuring his steps.*

DANNY T. It's not a matter of location or geography.

FAWAZ *(to RUND)* Where are we?

RUND Shhhhh.

DANNY T. It's a matter of heels and toes.

*RUND exits.*

DANNY T. Heels and toes.

FAWAZ Wait!

DANNY T. Seven, eight, nine. Here. Also a bit of there. And "there" is actually more important than "here" because "there" is always in dispute. "There" is out of sight but all we need is . . . thirteen, fourteen, fifteen. *(He does some fast footwork steps and bumps into FAWAZ.)* A little fancy footwork and there and there, and in any event way over there becomes an indisputable here. Where I'm standing. Mine. And you. You shouldn't be standing here or there at all. One phone call and you are "poof." Into air.

FAWAZ I was told you'd be able to help me: I'm looking for my brother—

DANNY T. *(interrupting)* Oh, aren't we all. Aren't we all? Because it's lonely out here, charting the route, away from the drills and the dozers. I call them my bulldogs, the dozers. They get nasty now and then, and sometimes throw a fit, but they mean well. Scratch them behind their treads and they're yours for life.

*For the first time,* FAWAZ *takes in the enormity and the height of the wall.* DANNY T. *watches him some moments.*

What do you think of my dream?

FAWAZ *(astonished)* Wow. Fucking hell . . .

DANNY T. Exactly. A few hundred kilometres at present. When she's finished, eight hundred and thirty-two kilometres of hard, hot, can-go-all-night wire and concrete.

FAWAZ Impressive, yeah. Of course there are those who say it's—

DANNY T. Don't say it. Don't say it. "Illegal"? I'm an architect. I am outside the law. Like flowers and flying creatures. Do you know why? Because I, Colonel Danny Tirza, say so. And don't talk to me about the Green Line. It's not on our map. We call the line the Seam Zone and this seam zone is very flexible while laws are not. As to the health of your people, the wall will encourage every man, woman, and child to walk three, four, five times as far, all to the same exit point. Imagine the exercise! The increased strength in the calf muscles. The decrease in heart attacks. The lowering of blood pressure. My friend, what you are looking at right now is a work of monumental proportions, an impossible sculpture, a statement etched upon the land. *(beat)* I enjoy a bit of poetical language, don't you?

*Song of the Dream of Zion:*

*(sings)* Oh, ho, what an incredible, wonderful dream:
To re-begin thousands of years of history,
To restart our ancestor's great work, that's the thing,
It's enough to turn the driest eye all teary.

Bathsheba, Bathsheba,
Like the land, like the dream,
She's everything, everything.
Oh, ho, what an incredible, wonderful dream:
The miraculous rebirth, the light unto nations,
A land without a people, a people with nothing:
Has there ever been, sir, such vital recreations?
Bathsheba, Bathsheba,
You just go have her!
It's biblical, archaeological, and really it's . . . right;
You'd be absurd or worse to oppose such a feat,
And like King David and Uriah the Hittite
We'd have to engineer your unhappy defeat.
Bathsheba, Bathsheba,
Like the land, like the dream.
You just go have her!

FAWAZ Mister Tirza. If you've got no info, then let me pass through this wall.

DANNY T. But Mister . . . ?

FAWAZ Fawaz Al Haj.

*DANNY T. registers FAWAZ's name.*

DANNY T. You can't pass through a wall.

FAWAZ We can be reasonable. We do that in Ohio.

DANNY T. Ohio, huh? I've got an uncle there. Is it all it's cracked up to be?

FAWAZ At the movie theatres, you can get an extra extra large popcorn. You can get a popcorn so large that you can strap it into the seat right next you and climb inside it, if you don't mind the butter on your shirt.

DANNY T. How entertaining!

*FAWAZ looks at the wall again.*

FAWAZ You really think a people can thrive, trapped behind walls?

DANNY T. Such violent language you people use. Such negativity. "Trapped." They won't be "trapped." They will be cradled within the monument. Have you given a thought to the fact that they'll have wind protection within these walls?

FAWAZ Hey, it's pretty obvious that you're swallowing the land, uprooting the olive tr—

DANNY T. Oh please. Not the olive-tree snivel. You people of the olives. The olive-tree people. Every time you open your mouth it's about those pits. Talk about oranges for a change. Try some originality.

FAWAZ History's not always original.

DANNY T. History is a donkey. Beat it with a stick and it will pull the load. *(He begins his walk again, back to work.)* As does the Holocaust: an evil so far-reaching there's not a piece of history forged on this earth since that hasn't been, in some way, corrupted by this evil. Add to this an appalling history of anti-Semitism endured and our wound was forged. And this wound has, over time, become the scar. My allegiance is to this scar, not its original wound. Because that wound, that very Jewish wound, would not always co-operate. Was not properly ruthless. And truth be told had too much prattle about socialism, brotherhood, and anti-Zionism for my taste. I am a servant of expansion and consolidation. A servant of pre-emption. In short, I am a servant of the scar.

FAWAZ Look, Mister Tirza, my apologies. But I don't give a damn about your scar or your wall. I need to find Rashid and get on home.

*DANNY T. regards FAWAZ a moment in silence.*

DANNY T. I see. *(beat)* Well, I believe he just up and left the country.

FAWAZ Which country would that be?

FAWAZ Palestine? DANNY T. Israel!

*They are both silent a moment.* DANNY T. *goes back to work.*

DANNY T. As a matter of fact, I think he did more than just up and leave. I've heard it said that he "skedaddled."

## SCENE NINE

*It is night. Streets of Bethlehem. There is curfew.* RUND, *carrying the suitcase, springs out in front of* MARYAM, *who is walking briskly.*

RUND Give me ten shekels, Auntie! I need to buy a notebook.

MARYAM Inti majnounah ya binit! We're under curfew, Rund. The IDF are looking for someone. Get off the street!

RUND *blocks* MARYAM'*s way.*

RUND Who are they looking for? What has he done?

MARYAM There's been an *(whispers)* operation.

RUND So they say.

MARYAM So they say.

RUND Did they find him? The one who did the operation?

MARYAM Not yet. So they say.

RUND So they say.

MARYAM Now get, little girl.

RUND Oh it's terrible to be a woman alone. So many choices! Hijab. No hijab. Good thing you're not pregnant. You could go BANG!

MARYAM I mean it: get home.

RUND First, play my game: give me five shekels.

MARYAM You don't have time for games. By the time you try on your first bra the world might be over.

RUND You shouldn't scare little children.

MARYAM We don't have time for children. Grow up.

RUND You're threatening me with apocalypse and Armageddon.

MARYAM I'm threatening you with restrictive undergarments. Now get out of my way.

RUND No.

MARYAM You could be shot.

RUND Yep.

MARYAM You could vanish. Pop. Into air.

RUND Liar.

MARYAM No. It's true. And you must learn to hold two truths at once, child, and learn that it is crucial to document X in order to declare Y, therefore—reaffirming that each declaration should follow its necessary precedent—

*RUND puts her hand over MARYAM's mouth to shut her up.*

RUND Did you ever lose your school?

*RUND takes her hand away. MARYAM speaks more calmly now.*

MARYAM Yes. When I was young, I quit the university. Couldn't get to my exams because of the checkpoints and curfews. So I went to work for the UN.

RUND — Did they fire you?

MARYAM — No. But when I tried to get young people like you out of jail, they wouldn't help. They sent some flour instead. With mealworms. So finally I quit. But I still believe in articles.

RUND — Of clothing?

MARYAM — No, child. In articles of law. And one day I'm going to make those articles believe in us. *(sharply)* But that's enough. Now get off the streets. Or you will disappear too!

*MARYAM stomps her foot. RUND turns to run off but turns back.*

RUND — But who are they looking for, Auntie?

MARYAM — I don't know.

RUND — Is someone dead? Is someone killed?

MARYAM — I don't know.

RUND — Is someone missing?

MARYAM — Someone is always missing. Now go!

## SCENE TEN

*HALA is untangling a roll of wire, rewinding some of it, cutting other bits off, making something mechanical with the wire. FAWAZ is watching her work.*

FAWAZ — I'm going in circles, Hala. Two checkpoints and I'm out of Bethlehem, but three more and I still can't get past the wall. Another two and I'm back here with you.

HALA — Rashid always says, "My brother was ace."

FAWAZ — *Is* ace. "My brother *is* ace."

HALA Are you ace, Fawaz? Or just another pack of cards?

FAWAZ I don't know where to go. No one will tell me anything.

HALA We don't trust you.

FAWAZ What are you doing?

HALA I'm making a model. I need to figure out what went wrong. But it's all such a mess.

FAWAZ What do you mean "what went wrong"?

HALA Please. You're distracting me.

FAWAZ Here, I can help you with that.

*FAWAZ begins to untangle the wire, but as he does so, he binds HALA's hands, so quickly that she is caught off guard.*

HALA Let me go.

FAWAZ Not until I get some answers.

HALA Who do you think you are?

*FAWAZ tightens the wire around her hands and arms.*

FAWAZ I'm the good guy, okay? I said no to everything I wanted so that kid would turn out right. And what did he do for me in return? He just. Walked away.

*HALA just looks at FAWAZ.*

HALA You've longed for your brother all these years.

FAWAZ Nope. But my mother has. She's sick with longing. My father died from it.

HALA Rashid is all you think about.

FAWAZ I don't give a shit about him. I just need to take him home.

HALA Maybe you can't find him because you don't know him anymore.

FAWAZ I know my brother. Time doesn't change that.

HALA What's his favourite colour?

FAWAZ Blue.

HALA He mostly wears black. His coffee?

FAWAZ Milk and lots of sugar.

HALA No sugar. Doesn't like sweet.

HALA Favourite season?

FAWAZ Spring.

HALA Autumn. Likes the leaves. Favourite pet?

FAWAZ Dog.

HALA Canary. What does he sing in the shower?

FAWAZ I have no idea.

HALA Neither do I, Ace. Why don't you speak Arabic?

FAWAZ Because I don't need it.

HALA Your brother is fluent. He taught himself.

FAWAZ If you know him so well then where is he? Just tell me and I'll leave you alone.

*HALA holds out her bound hands for FAWAZ to untie her. After a moment, he does, slowly unwinding the wire, getting too close for her comfort.*

Well?

HALA I don't know.

FAWAZ You don't know? Sure. Right.

HALA It's the truth.

FAWAZ Excuse me, Hala, but fuck this place. *(He throws down the wire and starts to exit.)*

HALA Fawaz Al Haj. There is a lack of respect in your communications with your people.

FAWAZ Don't start that "your people" stuff with me. My mother was always after me. My father was, too.

HALA May he rest in peace.

FAWAZ I wasn't born here.

HALA But your father was. That's what Rashid says. *(with emphasis)* Mustafa Al Haj.

FAWAZ Well, at least Rashid didn't deny their existence.

HALA Your grandfather was born in the village of Beit Nattif, the district of Hebron, in 1929. In 1948, his village was—

FAWAZ/HALA —attacked by the Zionists and destroyed.

FAWAZ I know this blather by heart, Hala.

HALA For two months your family slept in the fields, waiting to return, but every time they did the soldiers shot at them and forced them back.

FAWAZ La-di-da. Blah blah blah.

HALA Your family went to the refugee camp in Bethlehem.

FAWAZ La-di-da.

HALA Your grandfather sold—

FAWAZ/HALA —tomatoes—

FAWAZ Blah blah blah.

HALA But your father could never accept being—

FAWAZ/HALA *(together)* —a refugee.

HALA That's why he took your mother to the—

FAWAZ States. Right. My brother the idiot—

HALA —returned and became a West Banker. Why not you?

FAWAZ Because I'm a resident of the state of Ohio.

HALA You're a Palestinian, Fawaz.

FAWAZ Christ. *(mocking)* "You're a Palestinian, Fawaz." What does that mean? That I've put my life on hold since 1948? Haven't changed my shoes in fifty years cause the dirt from my village still clings to them? "You're a Palestinian, Fawaz." Yeah. Right. Waiting for the day the sun rises on my ass and sets me alight? My father did that. He died a homesick, nostalgic, frightened old man, and not in his hometown of Beit Nattif that he never stopped dreaming about. Know how he died? Buying graham crackers in the fourteenth aisle of a Kroger shopping mart. Heart attack.

HALA *(matter-of-factly)* I'd like to visit your zoo in Cincinnati. They say it's one of the best in the world. We had a zoo in Rafah. The Israeli Army bulldozed it.

FAWAZ Look. I quit crying over spilt milk when I got old enough to wipe my chin. Why don't you try it?

*FAWAZ and HALA just stare at one another.*

Or better yet, take off that scarf.

HALA No.

FAWAZ Let me see your hair.

HALA Never.

FAWAZ You know it's no big deal where I come from. It's just hair.

*HALA looks at FAWAZ.*

HALA Why don't you take something off?

FAWAZ I'm not wearing a scarf.

HALA Your shirt, then. Go on. Take it off.

*FAWAZ glances about him, uncertain.*

FAWAZ You sure? *(beat)* Would you like that, Hala?

*FAWAZ starts to unbutton his shirt. HALA smiles. He undoes another button. Then she slaps him in the face.*

HALA Button your shirt, Yankee. When an abandoned bride asks the brother of her beloved to take off his clothes he's supposed to take pity on her. He's supposed to say no. Say it, "no."

FAWAZ No.

HALA Thank you. *(beat)* Now go find Rashid. Bring him back to me. And then leave us alone.

## SCENE ELEVEN

*MURAD and RASHID at night, in a garden in the Israeli settlement of Gilo. MURAD sits on a chair. As he speaks, RASHID is looking for a particular piece of ground.*

MURAD *(to himself)* Miss Baghdad had a mole on the side of her neck. No. Somewhere strange. In her armpit. In the shape of a fish. *(sees RASHID)* Oh. It's you again. Sit down. Would you like a cup of tea?

RASHID No, thanks.

MURAD Do you have friends? I am looking for friends. But what are you doing on this side of the fence again?

RASHID Wall.

MURAD *(shrugs)* Whatever.

RASHID Where am I?

MURAD The Gilo settlement. You're meshtahim, from the West Bank. A West Banker!

RASHID I'm lost.

MURAD So am I. Though I know where I am. *(beat)* You're breaking the law just to stand here.

*RASHID seems to have found what he's looking for.*

RASHID Buddy, it's been a long day. You've no idea. Now get up.

MURAD How did you pass through the barrier? Hmm. You're not the first, you know. This morning, I saw another one like you. He was in the air. Flying. A flying man. I said "Good morning, Flying Man." And he said— *(calls as though from high up)* "Good morning, brother." He called me brother. Even when I live on this side. I appreciate that. I said, "What's your name?" But he was disappearing into the sky by then. I think he said . . .

RASHID Rashid.

MURAD Yes. Rashid. Would you like a biscuit?

RASHID Move your chair. Just to there.

MURAD Why?

RASHID That's mine. Was. My mom and pops grew up here.

Under your chair. Long ago. I never was able to make it over here before. Just want to step on it a few times. For old times' sake.

MURAD Please. Don't be sentimental. Me, I've always lived on both sides of the coin: lucky and unlucky, hero and traitor, dreamer and destroyer. Yet I do believe in fairy tales. Why else would I stay here? We dreamed of a binational state, Jew and Arab living side by side. It was possible. See? Both sides of the coin. But here is the rub: I labour against any messianic bullshit and end up living in a messianic nation. Do you think Miss Baghdad could have loved a skinny runt of a peasant's son?

RASHID I doubt it.

MURAD Get out of here. You give me the shivers!

RASHID Just let me look at that piece under your chair. I just want to look, old man. Please. Just move.

*MURAD finally gets up and moves the chair. MURAD and RASHID look at the spot of earth. RASHID steps on the spot triumphantly.*

MURAD Hey.

RASHID Now I'm home again.

MURAD Excuse me?

RASHID Home on the range. Right on this spot.

MURAD Move, please. I must put my chair back.

RASHID This was our palace, old man. This is it. And I need to feel the dirt on my soles.

MURAD This is unacceptable.

RASHID You're damn right it is.

*RASHID begins to take off his shoes. MURAD watches him. RASHID enjoys his bare feet on the ground while MURAD speaks.*

MURAD This is your palace, hmm? Mine was in Baghdad. We wanted to stay in Iraq. It was our home. But we would be saved even though many of us did not want to be saved. The politicians made secret deals to evacuate the entire community of Baghdadi Jews by air and bring us here. But they didn't talk to us. The French and British were the bastards, really. They did all they could to widen the gap between Arab and Jew. A bitter wind. But a wind that began in Europe, not in Iraq.

*RASHID lets out a howl of glee, ignoring MURAD, happy to be home.*

Don't laugh at me. I listen to Farid al-Atrash.

RASHID And Umm Kulthum?

MURAD Yes. And Mohammed Abdel Wahab. But at a checkpoint, I could shoot you dead. Then go home to my family at night.

RASHID You know, there comes a time when a guy needs to take a serious road trip.

MURAD I am lonely. I need a friend.

RASHID Lift off, leapfrog over the obstacles—

MURAD My name is Murad Salih Daniel. I am an Arab Jew.

RASHID —glide out of the turbulence, and dig in deep. Take a stand.

MURAD I cannot go back because this is now my country. But I'm still a stranger here after so many years.

RASHID Damn, it's good to be back in the 'hood.

MURAD I am a nigger in the land of the Jews.

## SCENE TWELVE

*FAWAZ, this time from the other side of the stage, is thrown through the air and lands hard, sprawling. He is dishevelled and rants with all the energy he's got left. The quotes are IDF soldiers speaking, which he imitates/mocks.*

FAWAZ That's the last time you shove me, buddy! I'm an American citizen. You hear me? You don't shove Americans! You don't search Americans! "Why are you here?" I don't want to fucking be here! If I could, I'd flush this noxious, putrid, dirty, crumbling beast of a country—countries!—down the compactor. Yeah! Yeah! *(mocking)* "We are looking for someone." Well I hope you never find him. I don't know you people. I don't care about you people. "But you're not only an American, are you?" *(He lets out a long howl of rage.)* Mister Asshole. I have to find my brother. Then I'll get out and I'll never come back. "His name? His name?" I won't tell you. I won't tell you his fucking name. *(calls out)* Where are you? You little shit. You double-crossing, backstabbing, piece of . . . Palestinian shit! Ha. Yeah. Ha. You eat that one, Rashid!

*RASHID enters, from the past, carrying FAWAZ's suitcase, as though it were his own. He sets it down between them. After a moment FAWAZ is also back in the past.*

RASHID These are the facts: I love the air.

FAWAZ No, you're obsessed with it.

RASHID Yep. 'Cause it's better up there than down here. So I'm flying across the ocean, bro. I'm going home to Bethlehem.

FAWAZ Yeah. Mom told me. I told her not to worry 'cause I won't let you.

RASHID I'm eighteen now.

FAWAZ You're going to join me at university next fall. Everything is on track.

RASHID Fawaz. I'm already packed.

FAWAZ Then I'll help you unpack.

RASHID You want to drive me to the bus station?

FAWAZ Rashid. Don't you dare.

RASHID We're Palestinians.

FAWAZ We're Americans.

RASHID We're Arab-Americans. That in itself is un-American.

FAWAZ Stop it. You're hurting them. Mother's walking at night. Father just stares.

RASHID They're just afraid.

FAWAZ Of course they're afraid. They think you'll never come back.

RASHID I'll just go and check things out. Find the place where Mom and Dad grew up. I won't stay.

FAWAZ You're not going anywhere. I won't let you ruin our plans.

RASHID But there's not enough space for me here. I'm falling even when I walk.

FAWAZ It's called being a teenager. Get over it.

RASHID I'm going.

FAWAZ You won't have any rights over there. None. Only as a tourist. You think it will feel like home?

*RASHID doesn't answer.*

Answer me. You think Bethlehem will feel like home? You've never been there. How could it feel like home? Answer me.

*Silence.*

Answer the goddamn question, Rashid. Will it feel like home? *(beat)* No. It won't. Not ever. This is your home. Right here, with me.

RASHID *(changing tactics, relishing)* Brother. They say the women there make a sound when you touch them. A kind of hum and it makes you so hard you weep. I'm going to find me one of those women. *(He makes a humming sound.)*

FAWAZ Stop it.

RASHID Why don't you come with me?

FAWAZ *laughs in exasperation.*

Don't make me go alone.

FAWAZ If you leave, I won't come after you.

RASHID We could go together—

FAWAZ *(interrupting)* Don't start.

RASHID I don't want a steady job. I don't want to pay my taxes, put up an above-ground swimming pool in my backyard. I don't want a barbecue—

FAWAZ What the fuck is wrong with a barbecue?

RASHID I just want to find some . . .

FAWAZ Fucking common sense?

RASHID Yeah. Something like that. So when I wake up in the morning and step out of bed, it matters. When I walk outside, it matters. When I speak to another person, it matters—

FAWAZ *(interrupting)* Hold it right there, bud. I'm gonna call the talk shows right now 'cause that's the kind of cold, hard intelligent thinking that everyone needs to hear. *(beat)* Nothing you can do over there is going to make a difference because without me, you're too small, Rashid. Without me, you're just a fucking kid.

RASHID I'm your brother.

*FAWAZ suddenly turns on RASHID, furious and afraid.*

FAWAZ Then don't leave me!

RASHID I have to.

*RASHID tries to get past FAWAZ to leave but FAWAZ blocks him. RASHID tries again and FAWAZ blocks him. Then FAWAZ loses control and knocks RASHID down, pummelling him, hard. RASHID doesn't fight back. As FAWAZ repeatedly hits and kicks RASHID, he shouts the following:*

FAWAZ You're not going anywhere! You're not going anywhere! You're not going anywhere!

*FAWAZ suddenly quits beating RASHID and gets off him. RASHID lies still a moment, stunned and battered. Then he painfully, slowly, gets up, picks up the suitcase, and leaves. Only after RASHID is gone does FAWAZ call to him. His call echoes all around him.*

Rashid! Wait. Come back!

*The SOLDIERS appears, having heard RASHID's name.*

*(calling)* You come back here, you bastard! Don't leave us alone. Rashid! Rashid Al Haj! Come back.

*FAWAZ, collapsed in grief, doesn't see the SOLDIERS. They begin to dance and their dance is both muscular and graceful. The song begins as heartfelt but becomes increasingly ironic.*

*Song of the Yearning Youths:*

SOLDIERS When we were little tots,
We licked our lollipops.
When we hit puberty,
We hankered for our liberty.
Then the black letter came.
We had to leave our game.
We put down the soccer ball.
We left our shoes in the hall.
We missed the kiss in the dark.
We missed the girl in the park.
Slippers for army boots.
Slingshot for a gun that shoots.
Snug bed for the all-night watch.
Sweet dreams for the lonely crotch.
We say we are not afraid
That soon we will meet our grave.
Mother, can you bring me home?
Daddy, don't leave me alone.

*The* SOLDIERS *circle* FAWAZ, *who is crouched on the ground.*

We missed the kiss in the dark.
We missed the girl in the park.

*The* SOLDIERS *perform, one at a time, six shoot-to-kill positions. These positions are accurate and frightening.* FAWAZ *slowly wakes into their reality and raises his arms, frozen.* RASHID *appears, from another time and place, and watches.*

Fawaz Al Haj.
Fawaz Al Haj.
Fawaz Al Haj.
Brother to the Terrorist Rashid Al Haj.
Brother to Terrorist Rashid Al Haj.
We got you. We got you. We got you.

FAWAZ *is arrested and handcuffed. Suddenly* RASHID *understands.*

RASHID So that's what happened. *(beat)* I'm dead.

*FAWAZ hears RASHID's voice and at the same moment the brothers lock eyes. There is the loud bang and the echo of a cell door closing, followed by many more.*

*Blackout.*

# ACT TWO

## SCENE ONE

*Lights rise.*

*RUND enters with the suitcase, opens it, and takes out a handful of flower bulbs. She stands on the suitcase as though it were a box. She juggles the bulbs as she chants.*

RUND — Wildflowers. Wildflowers. Where are my friends?
I hear them on the playground, but I can't see them.
Wildflowers. Wildflowers. Can you hear that quick bell?
Time to study for geography, new maths, or old hell.

*DANNY T. appears. He snatches the bulbs from RUND.*

DANNY T. — Where did you get these?

RUND — They have an underground storage system, these geophytes.

DANNY T. — Yes. Wildflowers. Begin. Begin! *(He now acts as her teacher.)*

RUND — The organ, the bulb, allows them to survive through difficult times of heat and dryness. As the wall is built, Israel will move eight thousand five hundred bulbs to a temporary home until it is time to replant them safely.

DANNY T. Quite right. With the help of Israflora, we will invest 1.25 million shekels in locating, marking, digging up, and replanting thousands of rare bulbs. Stand up straight when you speak to the class.

RUND You have counted each orchid and tulip.

DANNY T. And?

RUND *can't remember.*

Chin up. Shoulders back. Enunciate. And?

RUND Iris. Each orchid, tulip, and iris.

DANNY T. The rarer blooms are marked individually.

RUND Bulbs in larger groups are marked as clusters.

DANNY T. It would've been cheaper to buy a few thousand new bulbs from a nursery and plant them, but?

RUND But we are strict—

DANNY T. Wrong pronoun. Eyes straight ahead. Wide, wide. Surprised almost. As though you had spotted, well, myself in your classroom!

RUND But you are—

DANNY T. Yes.

RUND But you are strict about returning the original flowers to their natural habitat. You are so strict you will be returning the original soil to replant the bulbs.

DANNY T. Yes, we will be returning the original soil to replant the bulbs. Correct. Correct. This way, no foreign genetic material is introduced. Five stars for the girl on the box.

RUND You're not my teacher. Where is Fawaz?

DANNY T. Exactly where he should be.

RUND What have you done to him? Where is my school?

DANNY T. Ah, now there are some things even Danny T. cannot answer.

*RUND jumps off the suitcase.*

RUND Give it back! Give me back my school!

DANNY T. Perhaps your school didn't like you and just up and left.

RUND No. Wrong answer. Get on the box. Get on the box!

*DANNY T. gets on the suitcase.*

Ears back. Eyes straight. Leg in the air!

*DANNY T. attempts to follow RUND's instructions.*

Now. Who are you?

DANNY T. I'm your new classmate.

RUND No. Arms out. Hair up. Who are you?

DANNY T. I am . . . I am . . . an architect who drew such lines on history that it didn't have a chance to mark me.

RUND I am a bulb.

DANNY T. A bulb?

RUND Yes. I am a bulb.

DANNY T. You are a girl.

RUND No. I have an underground storage system that allows me to survive under difficult circumstances.

*DANNY T. quits his posing.*

DANNY T. Kid, you are confusing yourself with a geophyte.

RUND Wrong. Sit at the back of the class.

DANNY T. Geophytes live in the ground.

RUND No star for you! Now write one hundred times: "You are a bulb."

DANNY T. No.

RUND And you relocated me.

DANNY T. Actually, we plucked you out. We needed the room.

RUND Say it: *you are a bulb.* Say it or my storage system will explode.

DANNY T. My, my. All right. You are a bulb.

RUND Yes. I am a bulb. And I will return to my original soil.

*RUND disappears. DANNY T. examines the bulb, thinking.*

## SCENE TWO

*FAWAZ is in jail in Jerusalem. The SOLDIERS are interrogating a shape on the ground as large as a man. They slowly circle the shape, making distorted movements with their bodies. FAWAZ watches them, mesmerized.*

SOLDIER 1 That was a kiss. Just a little kiss. *(beat)* You want another one? Another smakeroo?

FAWAZ Hey. What are you doing?

SOLDIER 2 Oh, oh, oh. Are you crying, sweetheart?

FAWAZ Stop it! Leave that man alone!

SOLDIER 3 Let me see those tears.

*SOLDIER 1 kicks the shape on the ground.*

FAWAZ Shit. Look at his face. You kicked him in the face.

SOLDIER 2 We have a paper for you to sign. Are you willing to sign? Mister Al Haj?

*FAWAZ moves in closer to have a look.*

FAWAZ Fuck. That's me.

SOLDIER 3 Just sign the paper to admit you were involved with your brother's operation. And we'll be nice to you.

SOLDIER 1 No? No? Okay. Then I'm going to kick your ass and every time you have to count.

SOLDIER 2 When the number is high enough, let me know, and he'll stop.

SOLDIER 1 *(gives the shape a kick)* Count. *(another kick)* Count, you motherfucker, or I'll call in my buddies and we'll do it with the band.

*He goes to crush FAWAZ's head with his boot but FAWAZ starts counting, steadily. SOLDIER 1 doesn't acknowledge FAWAZ but hears the counts.*

FAWAZ One.

SOLDIER 3 That's right.

*He kicks the shape.*

FAWAZ Two. I won't sign.

SOLDIER 2 Again.

FAWAZ Three. What did my brother do?

SOLDIER 1 Four.

FAWAZ I had nothing to do with it! Five.

*FAWAZ stops counting and sings. The SOLDIERS continue the interrogation throughout the song, but they move in slow motion.*

*When Torture is Good for Your Health:*

*(sings)* I've been sleeping all my life, it took you to wake me.
I'll do anything you want, only make sure you make me.
Take away all sight and sound 'til I all I do is weep.
I can feel it growing big, yeah the love is growing deep.
Torture makes you heat up, makes your blood run clean.
Torture takes you places where you've never even been.
Torture makes you flexible, torture makes you real.
Torture teaches you to open, teaches you to feel.
Kick me in the gut again, you can make me dance.
Shock me in the groin and I'll shit in my pants.
Hang me from my wrists and I'll surely be your friend.
Choke me with cold water and I'll love you 'til the end.
I will love you . . .

*He stops singing and then calls out in despair.*

RASHID!

*FAWAZ's voice echos through the cell, then the prison, as he collapses onto the shape on the ground.*

## SCENE THREE

*MURAD appears and finds RASHID in his garden. RASHID's eyes are closed and he's listening to something. We can still faintly hear FAWAZ call his brother's name. MURAD pushes RASHID but RASHID holds his ground.*

MURAD I thought I kicked you out? You ingrate.

*RASHID shoves MURAD back. The shoving begins to mirror the back and forth of the argument.*

RASHID Nah. I bounced back. You trespasser. Weather's been great.

*MURAD shoves RASHID again, harder. RASHID holds his ground.*

MURAD What is it you want? God's pig.

RASHID Right now I want . . . a space. Ass-bone! *(He shoves MURAD back, harder.)* A space to piss.

MURAD How dare you?! You will not piss in my garden!

RASHID Now that I've settled in, I think I'll put in some tomatoes. Never seen so much water.

MURAD Ha! Diverted from the West Bank. Operation Oasis. For our settlements. Looks like vacation houses in Switzerland.

RASHID So I could plant oranges?

MURAD Oranges.

RASHID Grapes?

MURAD Grapes.

RASHID Lemons?

MURAD Lemons!

RASHID My brother's somewhere out there, I can feel it. Know where he is?

MURAD Only rumours: that he never left his store in Ohio. That he took a detour and he's drunk in the Louvre. That he jumped off the Hilton in Amsterdam.

RASHID Well. I'm going to bring him to this spot. My father walked here. Ate here. My mother too. Sex even. Maybe right on this spot.

MURAD — No! No! There is no sex on this ground.

RASHID — Their moans are in the grass. Hear them.

*RASHID makes mournful, masculine moans.*

MURAD — Well, if that was the sound your father made, young man, then it doesn't sound like your mother was getting much action.

RASHID — I don't like you.

MURAD — And I don't like you.

*MURAD and RASHID are silent a moment together.*

But this is not about liking. This is about—

RASHID — Yeah. This is about . . .

*MURAD and RASHID both sing a lonely song, apart and together.*

*The Wandering Song Club:*

MURAD — *(sings)* There's no place in the world for us,
Once we've left, we are gone,
There's no one to go back to.
We just move on, we move on.
I'm from the wandering song club,
I'm from the wandering song club.

RASHID — *(sings)* Nowhere is a sandpit,
A river full of spit.
We are thirsty, we are hungry.
We have no place to shit.

MURAD/RASHID — *(together)* I'm from the wandering song club,
I'm from the wandering song club.

*RASHID takes out a dirty old flask.*

RASHID — I've been saving this. Was my great uncle's.

MURAD Yuck. It is rusted. When was the last time he drank from it?

RASHID 1948. Come.

*RASHID shares his water, dripping it into MURAD's mouth.*

MURAD Are you living alone?

*RASHID casts a glance around his tiny space.*

RASHID Not sure. Yeah, maybe. At present. I was going to get married but I died.

MURAD Yes. I heard that rumour, too. *(beat)* Is it possible . . . could it be possible . . . might you need a roommate? Only to cut expenses, of course. Two is cheaper than one.

*RASHID does not move. MURAD waits. Then RASHID slowly and carefully moves just a couple of inches over. MURAD squeezes in next to him, into his space.*

Yes. You are right. It's actually quite spacious.

*MURAD and RASHID stand tightly together in the space, side by side, in silence for some moments.*

In Baghdad they used to say that if you lose someone, talk to your feet and they will lead you. The foot is a compass.

RASHID Yeah? Well there's not a compass in this godforsaken land that isn't broke. But thanks. I'll give it a try. And now I gotta piss. Turn around, please.

*MURAD manages to turn around, staying within their shared space. RASHID pisses into MURAD's watering can then hands it to MURAD. When MURAD turns back around, RASHID is gone.*

## SCENE FOUR

*FAWAZ is still in jail, collapsed on the floor. He begins to hallucinate. HALA enters humming happily. She has a white bridal veil over her face and is completely covered. FAWAZ is frightened.*

FAWAZ Who are you?

HALA Shhh . . . *(She hums.)*

FAWAZ I know who you are. You're my brother's woman.

HALA Your brother has no woman. He's a sweet, dead man. And I'm not really here.

FAWAZ You are—

HALA *(secretive)* Yoni.

FAWAZ Hala.

HALA Shhh. It's a secret. You're not supposed to know.

FAWAZ You shouldn't be here.

HALA You shouldn't be here. This is the women's side.

FAWAZ I mean I shouldn't be here. Either.

*MARYAM enters. She ignores FAWAZ.*

I can't. Leave.

*MARYAM takes off HALA's veil.*

HALA He won't leave.

MARYAM Never mind. Maybe he'll learn something!

*HALA and MARYAM giggle together.*

There are limited methods, manoeuvres, and mechanics, but there are endless techniques. Let's begin with the twenty-one positions of love. Essentially there are five positions, and the other sixteen are built upon them: 1) he is on his back and you are on top, 2) you are on your back and he is on top, 3) you are facing each other, 4) you have your back to him, or 5) you are seated facing each other. What's your pleasure?

HALA All of the above.

*HALA rolls up her sleeves to get ready. HALA and MARYAM are enjoying themselves.*

MARYAM One. A goblet-shaped six-petalled bloom. Two. Double cypress. Three. Curving outward.

*HALA demonstrates some of the positions by herself. She ignores FAWAZ, who watches her, fascinated.*

Four to seven blooms per branch. Five sometimes parrot.

HALA Parrot?

MARYAM That's what the book says.

HALA What does that mean?

MARYAM Squawkers?

HALA Imitators?

MARYAM Talkers.

HALA Oh, I like the talkers.

MARYAM Really? I like quiet. A little breath. That's all.

HALA No, I like when he says—

*From a good distance, HALA whispers, in Arabic, the things she likes to hear.*

FAWAZ No.

HALA No? Yes.

*Now,* HALA *repeats the postures. This time* FAWAZ *mirrors her movements. He is tortured by the involuntary positions his body is making.* HALA *never touches him.* FAWAZ *is in an extreme pain that longs to be pleasure.*

FAWAZ No. Stop it. You're burning him.

MARYAM Eyes—

FAWAZ Me.

HALA Nose—

MARYAM Ears, fingers—

FAWAZ Stop.

MARYAM Throat.

FAWAZ Please.

HALA I love when he says please.

FAWAZ Me.

MARYAM The mouth.

HALA You've told me nothing about the mouth. *(She moves so close to* FAWAZ *she could kiss him.)*

FAWAZ *(coming to)* No. No. I can't. Please.

HALA *and* MARYAM *begin to perform the positions together as the* SOLDIERS *enter and join the women in these more aggressive, yet still beautiful, positions.*

MARYAM There are limited methods, manoeuvres, and weapons, but there are endless techniques.

FAWAZ You don't belong here.

MARYAM There are limited methods, manoeuvres, and blood but there are endless techniques.

FAWAZ I don't belong here.

SOLDIERS There are endless techniques.

*The* SOLDIERS *all surround* FAWAZ *and take him in their arms.*

FAWAZ Damn you. Give me back my fingernail.

FAWAZ *is suddenly alone again. He passes out.*

## SCENE FIVE

FAWAZ *is still asleep in his cell.* RASHID *is standing over him.*

RASHID Hey, big brother. You're looking kinda small since I saw you last?

RASHID *nudges* FAWAZ *with his foot.* FAWAZ *startles awake.*

FAWAZ Shit, Rashid. You're dead.

RASHID Haven't seen him in years. First thing he says, "Shit, Rashid. You're dead." You sure know how to do reunion, don't you? Did you see my Hala? Not a woman so fine. Ice and water. Vinegar and salt. She's a mechanical engineer. Knows where things fit.

FAWAZ What did you do?

RASHID I went for a ride in Hala's flying machine.

FAWAZ You killed someone.

RASHID No.

FAWAZ Yes, you fucking did or I wouldn't be in here taking your beating.

RASHID Maybe you threw a stone?

FAWAZ Where am I?

RASHID An Israeli jail, called Mascubiya a.k.a the Russian Compound. In West Jerusalem. I didn't kill anyone.

FAWAZ But you tried.

RASHID I did what needed to be done. I took action, brother.

FAWAZ You sound like a fanatic.

RASHID Don't sign. They'll release you in a few days. How bad are you hurting?

FAWAZ I didn't know the human body could withstand that kind of impact.

RASHID I love Hala. I want you to know that.

FAWAZ Then why did you fuck things up?

RASHID Did you miss me?

FAWAZ We didn't hear from you for years so we got used to it. Why'd you tell people I was dead?

RASHID *(shrugs)* The last time I saw you, you hit me twenty-seven times.

FAWAZ You deserved twenty-eight.

RASHID That's why. That's exactly why, Fawaz. You haven't changed.

FAWAZ Fucking neither have you.

*RASHID laughs.*

RASHID Ah, but I fell in love. I was so happy that last morning. The years that lie ahead of me and all made up of her. Of Hala. She laughed when she was sad.

It was like a bell in my chest. You know what was the best part? I could turn my head to the left or to the right and see her standing there, like a miracle, right beside me.

FAWAZ You don't deserve her. *(beat)* She's beautiful.

RASHID If Hala will have you, you can have her. I mean that.

FAWAZ But she's yours.

RASHID Not anymore. I won't say I'm happy about it but rather you than anyone else.

FAWAZ Hala doesn't like me.

RASHID Hala wouldn't look you in the eye when she met you. That means she likes you. And you better appreciate that. Hala doesn't like a lot of people. *(beat)* Fawaz. I need you to find out how I died. And why. I can't rest. I can't even be dead like I'm supposed to be. I need a picture in my mind.

FAWAZ You're dead. Aren't you all-knowing?

RASHID Now that's the kind of crap you Breathers make up. Look, not knowing what I did, not knowing what happened to me because of it, I've never felt that kind of pain.

FAWAZ I'm in jail. I can't do anything. But soon as I get out of here I'm going back. Home.

RASHID Home. Always liked that word. Kind of like a horn. Home. *(says the word "hooooooome" like the sound of a horn)* Home.

FAWAZ You know this will finish Mom off, don't you? *(beat)* Why did you leave us?

RASHID I never could sleep when we were kids. This country kept me awake. First time I ever slept right was the night I landed here. Without sleep we die. I didn't want to die.

FAWAZ Yeah well, Father died.

RASHID I know.

FAWAZ But you couldn't bother to come home, not even for his funeral. Mom stopped speaking. Even to me. So I did it alone. I did it all alone. Everything. You fuckin' sand nigger. Raghead.

RASHID Injun Joe. Salami Sam.

FAWAZ Camel fucker!

RASHID Yeah. Those were the good old days at Ranger Grade School. Sometimes I miss those endearments.

FAWAZ It's not so bad once you get older.

RASHID Sure. *(He spits on* FAWAZ.*)* How about that one? I bet you still get that one?

FAWAZ I'm still alive. You're dead. So who's the smartass?

RASHID Ouch. Goal. *(beat)* I'm sorry about Dad's funeral.

FAWAZ Easy to say now.

RASHID If I'd left here they wouldn't have let me back in. I couldn't risk it.

FAWAZ Fuck you.

RASHID So what do you think of this country?

FAWAZ Dirty—

RASHID Poor—

FAWAZ Crowded—

RASHID Pissed off—

FAWAZ Hungry—

RASHID *(celebrating)* And fully occupied. Yeah! Have we got the edge on paradise or what?!

FAWAZ You're not better looking than I am.

RASHID Maybe not. But I'm younger.

FAWAZ Not anymore.

*FAWAZ and RASHID eye each other some moments.*

RASHID This is the centre of the earth, Fawaz. What goes down here will go down in Cincinnati, will go down everywhere. You know that.

FAWAZ Rashid. Don't start.

RASHID 'Cause we're a people who never quit. We're a people—

FAWAZ Bullshit. You know what we are, brother? You know what we are? We're a people who fight for a homeland for fifty years and at the pinnacle of negotiations for a state of our own we show up without a map. Without our own fucking map. It's shameful. The corruption of our leaders. Our shabby compromises. Our ignorance of Israel. Our—

RASHID *(takes over for him)* —cult of personality. Our general lack of seriousness. Our corrosive divisions.

FAWAZ Exactly. There's no point.

RASHID We've got to keep working. Readjusting our sightlines.

FAWAZ Even after sixty fucking years? Just words, Rashid. Just words.

RASHID Yeah. But choosing the right ones. Keeping the pace against all that diminishes us, diminishes everyone around us. That's what it's about. Being alive, Fawaz. It's about being alive.

FAWAZ There are other ways to be alive.

RASHID Yeah. But they kill the libido. Resistance is good for your erections.

FAWAZ Whatever you've done here is. Meaningless. Nothing has changed and you're dead. So I'll always be. Without you.

*After some moments—*

RASHID Find out what happened.

FAWAZ I can't.

RASHID We need you. Here.

FAWAZ Sure. Maybe I could tear the wall down with my own bare hands, huh?

RASHID Now doesn't that get you hard just thinking about it? *(beat)* Promise me you'll stay here.

FAWAZ *(with finality)* I'm going back to the States.

RASHID Okay. Okay, sure. Well, say goodbye, bro.

FAWAZ *just stares at him.*

Say goodbye. But answer me one question: does it feel like home? Your sweet Ohio city, does it feel like home? Hey. *(He pushes* FAWAZ.*)* Hey. Answer the question. Does it feel like home? *(He pushes* FAWAZ *harder, until he answers him.)* It's not a difficult question. Answer me, Fawaz. Answer the goddamn question? Does Cincinnati feel like home?

FAWAZ Yes.

RASHID Still the liar you've always been.

FAWAZ — *(shouts)* It feels like home.

*RASHID just stares at FAWAZ. Then he disappears.*

Right here, Rashid. With you.

## SCENE SIX

*Jail compound. Three SOLDIERS as jail clerks, fully loaded. MARYAM enters, disguised in big sunglasses.*

SOLDIER 3 — We don't speak Arabic.

MARYAM — You understand English: I'm here to obtain the release of Fawaz Al Haj.

SOLDIER 1 — All we know in English is "hello"!

SOLDIERS — Hello!

MARYAM — What are the charges against him?

SOLDIER 2 — And "how are you?"

SOLDIER 1 — Soldiers—

SOLDIERS — Yes, please!

MARYAM — Boys. Article 1) whereas disregard and contempt for human rights have resulted in barbarous acts—

SOLDIER 3 — English, please!

SOLDIER 2 — *(to SOLDIER 3)* What's barbarous?

SOLDIER 1 — You cook on it!

SOLDIER 2 — That's a barbecue.

MARYAM — Article 2) whereas he is allergic to dust and, Article 3) peanuts. Therefore he could asphyxiate. Article 4) and furthermore you will be held responsible.

SOLDIER 3 *(to* SOLDIER 2*)* What is "asphyxiate"?

SOLDIER 1 This is a war! Are you kidding?

MARYAM Article 5) his clean underwear and socks. Article 6) concerning democracy.

SOLDIER 3 Oh, democracy!

MARYAM Article 7) "Be a light unto nations."

SOLDIER 2/3 *(together)* No, thank you!

MARYAM Article 8) reaffirming their determination to live in peace—

SOLDIERS Aagh! The P word!

MARYAM Article 9) recognizing that peace requires the transition—

SOLDIERS Aagh! The P word—

SOLDIER 3 You want to take away our jobs?

SOLDIER 2 You think we want to sit on the beach all day?

SOLDIER 3 And look at girls?

SOLDIERS Huh?

MARYAM Article 10) "Objective: to attack the village of Qibya. 11) occupy it and cause maximal damage 12) to life and property" Officer Ariel Sharon.

SOLDIER 2 Why you pickin' on Sharon?

MARYAM Article 13) affirming that this agreement marks the recognition of the right of the Palestinian—

SOLDIER 2/3 *(together)* The P word!

MARYAM Article 14) the equal rights of respected citizens.

SOLDIER 3 Now just who are you calling citizens?

MARYAM Fawaz Al Haj. He's a disagreeable man.

SOLDIERS Never heard of him.

MARYAM Arrogant, and stubborn as a mule.

SOLDIERS Never heard of him.

MARYAM But he's family. Article 15) "All existing things are really one." Chuang Tzu. I thought it might be. Possible.

SOLDIER 1 Lady. One more P word and you're done.

*The P Song:*

SOLDIERS *(singing)* Let's call someone. You know, we don't want visitors here.
You woke us from our naps, when you leave we'll crack a beer.
No (permits), No (peace), No (possibilities).
Don't give me that, don't give me that.
No words that start with P.

MARYAM Article 16) raise your black flags, boys: refuse to obey manifestly illegal orders.

SOLDIER 3 How does she know about the black flag?

SOLDIERS This is out of hand. We're just here to protect our borders.
This is how we do this. Don't be messing with our orders.
No (permits), No (peace), No (possibilities).
Don't give me that, don't give me that.
No words that start with P.

MARYAM Article 17) refuse to serve in the territories. Article 18) whereas this situation is not heavenly ordained. 19) this is collective punishment.

SOLDIERS *(singing)* No permits, No peace, No possibilities.
Don't give me that, don't give me that.
No words that start with P.

MARYAM Article 20) in the name of all declarations, release Fawaz Al Haj.

SOLDIER 2 That's twenty.

SOLDIER 3 Twenty?

SOLDIER 1 What's twenty-one?

MARYAM That I will never tell you.

SOLDIERS Huh?

MARYAM I'll stay right here until you get him.

## SCENE SEVEN

*FAWAZ has been released from jail. He is sitting huddled on the street, bruised, dishevelled, dirty, and disorientated. After some moments RUND appears. She studies FAWAZ. FAWAZ doesn't respond to her.*

RUND I need to buy new pencils. Give me five shekels. *(beat)* All right. Then give me four.

*FAWAZ doesn't respond at all, just stares into space. RUND cocks her head.*

They were looking for someone. I guess they found *you*.

*FAWAZ still doesn't respond. RUND shrugs, then searches his shirt pocket. She finds one of her socks. She searches another pocket. Finds the other sock. She holds the two socks up and examines them.*

My other sock! I knew it had been arrested. You must have found it in Mascubiya. Thank you, thank you. Now they're together again. *(She looks down at the big socks she's wearing.)* But I've got new socks for school. *(She looks at* FAWAZ*'s bare ankles.)* You don't have any socks. You can keep my old ones.

*RUND rests the socks, one each, on top of FAWAZ's shoes. FAWAZ is still in a daze. Then RUND kisses FAWAZ on the cheek.*

Wake up. *(beat)* Please. Wake up.

*FAWAZ comes out of his daze. He looks at RUND and really takes her in. She takes a handful of map pieces from her pocket.*

Do you want your map back?

*After a long moment, FAWAZ holds out his hand. RUND lets the pieces of map sprinkle and fall into his hand. Some of the pieces fall onto the floor. DANNY. T appears at the other end of the stage, carrying FAWAZ's suitcase. He and RUND eye each other. She runs away. FAWAZ ignores DANNY T. FAWAZ begins to pick up the tiny map pieces, carefully noting each piece and putting them into his pocket.*

DANNY T. I heard they let you out. *(beat)* Thought you'd need this, for your return journey.

*DANNY T. shoves the suitcase with his foot and it slides across the stage. It comes to rest beside FAWAZ.*

Did you know that your Arafat, God rest his soul, named me Abu Kharita? Father of the map.

*FAWAZ continues to pick up the map pieces as he speaks until he's gathered them all into his pocket.*

FAWAZ *(quietly)* What if the people miss the wind?

DANNY T. What?

FAWAZ What if the people behind your wall miss the wind? No reason to open the windows anymore because there is no breeze. Might get angry. Might get very pissed off. *(He has finished gathering the pieces.)*

DANNY T. Are you threatening me?

FAWAZ Yes.

DANNY T. Are you going to get extreme?

FAWAZ Send you a rocket? Or strap on a belt, step on a bus, blow as many Israelis to pieces as possible? Nah.

DANNY T. Don't be too hard on yourself. We kill your civilians as well. At a nineteen to one ratio.

FAWAZ I think you mean ninety to one.

DANNY T. *(shrugs)* I am not in denial. But what bothers me is your particular way of killing. We use Apaches, missiles. Or bullets. Quite often to the head. But we keep our distance. You, on the other hand, you kill yourselves inside our buses—

*FAWAZ moves to face DANNY T.*

FAWAZ Inside your cafés, inside your restaurants? We murder you so close up we can smell your fear and you can see ours. We kill ourselves inside you.

DANNY T. That kind of intimacy is unforgivable.

FAWAZ How did my brother die?

DANNY T. I'm under no obligation to tell you anything.

FAWAZ He needs to know.

DANNY T. Your brother is dead. Are you feeling all right? Perhaps they went a little hard during questioning?

FAWAZ I need to know.

DANNY T. *(holding out the suitcase)* What you need to know is the time your flight leaves. Go home, Fawaz. *(beat)* Go home.

*FAWAZ slowly takes the suitcase as though to leave but then walks right up to DANNY T. until their noses are touching.*

And what the hell is this?

FAWAZ This. Is. Me. And I think I'm going to stay right here forever.

DANNY T. Even forever gets tired and goes away.

FAWAZ Not my kind of forever.

*DANNY T. and FAWAZ stare each other down some moments.*

I've only been here a few days and already I can't breathe. The maps have more to do with cloud formations than the facts on the ground. Every day you take a little more. Your wall is the skyline. Today I read that you opened your first butterfly festival. I can hear your laughter on the other side.

DANNY T. You complain about our laughter?

FAWAZ When you're finished most of the settlers will live outside the wall. Eighty-nine per cent of Palestinians will be trapped inside it.

DANNY T. *(sharply)* This wall is a necessity!

*FAWAZ speaks into DANNY T.'s ear. He begins his response as a whisper, then builds. The "no" seems to echo around them.*

FAWAZ No.

DANNY T. To protect us.

FAWAZ No.

DANNY T. From your voices.

FAWAZ No.

DANNY T. From your hunger.

FAWAZ No.

DANNY T. From your intimacy.

FAWAZ No.

DANNY T. From your blood lust.

FAWAZ No.

DANNY T. From your murder.

FAWAZ Say it once. Just this once: your wall. Your dream. It's about acquisition. It's about real estate.

*DANNY T turns around.*

DANNY T. *(exploding)* Yes. Real estate! *(calmly)* With papers from God.

*DANNY T. and FAWAZ eye each other, neither budging. RASHID appears. FAWAZ and RASHID are aware of each other but DANNY T. does not see RASHID, nor does RASHID look at DANNY T. DANNY T. speaks to FAWAZ, though at times he seems to hear RASHID.*

FAWAZ My brother will haunt you.

*DANNY T. considers this.*

DANNY T. I'm going to be upfront: I don't believe in ghosts.

RASHID Let me be equally straightforward: I don't believe in Zionists.

DANNY T. You want to know how he died? That's what they all want to know. Can't you people be a little more alert in your last moments of life?

FAWAZ What did my brother do?

DANNY T. *(suddenly angry)* Your brother attempted to disrupt our . . . operation.

FAWAZ What operation?

DANNY T. Operation Geophyte, we call it. The Battle of the Bulbs.

RASHID I woke at five thirty-five in the morning. Still dark. I slipped in through the window. Hala was asleep.

DANNY T. In actuality, an operation of compassion: we save the bulbs as we build the wall. Then we replant them.

RASHID It was our wedding day. I kissed her cheek. Twice. I zipped up my jacket and wanted to shout 'cause I felt so damn good.

DANNY T. Your brother stole one of our bulbs.

FAWAZ My brother is dead because of a bulb?

RASHID *(remembering)* The bulb! Shit . . .

DANNY T. Not just any bulb. We discovered it two metres west of marker 186: the rare single bee orchid.

FAWAZ My idiot brother wasted his life to steal a bulb?

DANNY T. Your brother was, in actuality . . . brilliant. He found a way to hurt us that did not kill us. That kind of strategy, I envy.

FAWAZ The single bee orchid, huh?

RASHID It's pretty cool, bro.

DANNY T. To have seen it in bloom. You would have wept.

FAWAZ Yes. I think I would have.

RASHID Not some flowers from the corner store but something rare as Hala: the single bee orchid.

*HALA and RUND appear. DANNY T., FAWAZ, and RASHID do not see them, nor do HALA and RUND see the three men.*

FAWAZ So how did he die?

DANNY T. I'll tell you—

RUND I'll tell you, Hala.

HALA *(to* RUND*)* But how could you know that?

DANNY T. —if you promise to leave me in peace.

RUND I was looking for my school.

FAWAZ/RASHID *(together)* Agreed.

RASHID And then I lifted off.

HALA In the dark?

RASHID That's the best time to fly.

RUND That's when I saw Rashid.

RASHID Then it was all sky. Slick, raw.

RUND He went over the wall in the glider.

FAWAZ Fuck. A glider.

RUND Yes, a glider.

HALA Cruising speed?

RUND It wasn't his speed.

FAWAZ He knew how to fly.

RASHID I did everything right.

DANNY T./RUND *(at the same time)* I saw what happened.

RUND Yes. He flew over the wall without a sound.

FAWAZ No one could glide like my brother.

HALA Did he stall in the air?

RUND There was no stall, Hala.

RASHID Damn it.

HALA He didn't have the speed.

RASHID Seventy kilometres.

FAWAZ Did he lose his speed?

RUND Stop it, Hala. It wasn't—

RASHID My speed.

FAWAZ He wouldn't make that kind of mistake.

DANNY T. He didn't make a mistake.

HALA He touched down?

RUND Yes.

DANNY T. Yes.

RASHID A precision spot landing—

FAWAZ —full flare.

HALA Then he got what he came for?

DANNY T. Yes. He got what he came for: the orchid.

RASHID The orchid. For my bride. I stole for Hala what was already ours.

RUND Then Rashid relaunched.

RASHID Full gas with between-the-teeth—

FAWAZ/RASHID *(together)* —clamp-type accelerator.

DANNY T. He started running. Long steps. Long steps.

HALA With a 10 kilometre headwind.

FAWAZ You looked for the lift, Rashid!

RASHID I got the lift!

HALA But he didn't get the lift.

FAWAZ Fuck.

RUND And then he began to fall.

HALA The wind wasn't right. He started to fall.

DANNY T. He started to fall.

RASHID Shit.

*At the same time:*

DANNY T. And then our soldiers shot him.

RUND And then their soldiers shot him.

*Some moments of silence.*

FAWAZ Well, I'll be damned. So Rashid almost made it.

RUND He almost made it.

RASHID I almost made it. Hala.

HALA *hears* RASHID *say her name. They suddenly see each other and speak directly to each other. There is a quiet joy in their meeting.*

You told me not to fly the glider, Hala. But I had to—

HALA —couldn't resist. I know. There were things I could not, could not—

RASHID —foresee. I needed to show you I could fly it. It's all right. I don't—

HALA —regret. Only that I was not—

HALA/RASHID *(together)* —with you.

HALA Our plans. Our wedding. Mine—

RASHID —and yours. It was almost a—

HALA/RASHID *(together)* —success.

HALA I wish we could—

RASHID —begin—

HALA/RASHID *(together)* —again.

HALA It was, always, my sweetheart—

RASHID My love, always, it was—

HALA/RASHID *(together)* You.

*RUND takes HALA's hand and they leave. RASHID watches HALA go.*

FAWAZ No. *(beat)* No. No. No. No. No. No. No. No. No. No. No. No. No. No. No. No. No.

*FAWAZ says this over and over, to himself, to DANNY T., to RASHID's death, to everything around him. DANNY T. and RASHID watch him. When FAWAZ is empty of "noes," he quits. Silence for some moments.*

DANNY T. Fawaz Al Haj. I saw your brother in the air. I saw his glider come over the wall.

RASHID Then why did you wait? / Why didn't you shoot me right then?

FAWAZ Why didn't you shoot him right then?

DANNY T. I'd been up all night with my charts. We were just about to start work to close the last wall section around Bethlehem in area three. I looked up from my office, which is my four-by-four. I looked up, and there he was: a man in mid-flight, floating down, something from another time. Something poured from the grace of one world into the next. I could not move. So, so . . . Extraordinary. Audacious. Yes. And I could not speak. I just watched him. And for the first time in so many, many years I wanted something else.

FAWAZ What did you want?

DANNY T. I wanted to be up there, in that peaceful sky. I wanted to defy gravity. I wanted to be. You.

*For the first time,* DANNY T. *looks at* RASHID *and sees him. But* RASHID *keeps his eyes on* FAWAZ *and nods his thanks.* FAWAZ *leaves.* RASHID *now looks at* DANNY T. *for the first time and they lock eyes. After some moments,* RASHID *exits.* DANNY T. *looks around; he is alone again.*

## SCENE EIGHT

MURAD *wears a pair of designer sunglasses; he's in a new "undercover" outfit.* MARYAM *is also wearing sunglasses. She studies* MURAD*'s glasses.*

MARYAM Ray-Ban or Police?

MURAD Klein. Calvin. Yours?

MARYAM Russian.

MURAD They can get you anything, those guys. I was an archaeologist. But I couldn't get a job. Now I'm security. Security, security, security.

MARYAM It's a growth industry. Can I try on your sunglasses?

MURAD Sure.

MARYAM *and* MURAD *exchange sunglasses.*

Not bad. Nice weight to them. Hey. Sky looks sort of. Black. With these on.

MARYAM Hmmm. Ground looks kind of bumpy. With these on. Big bumps. This how you see?

MURAD Hey. With these you look a foot smaller.

MARYAM Now you are a good metre taller!

MURAD I like this. You don't look like much trouble now. Hey, I'm looking for a little girl. Her name is Rund. Rund Barghouti.

MARYAM What do you want with her?

MURAD If you see her, tell her that security has located her school and it's still intact. Though not fully. It seems it was a 100 per cent until we halved it. Then we had to take another 24 per cent. But today she can have the rest, which is about 22 per cent and includes the toilet and art room. But while we can't give her 100 per cent of the 22 per cent that's left, we can give her 57 per cent of the 22 per cent that's left, which means of the toilet we may still have to take the plumbing and of the art room, we'll need the floor.

MARYAM So many pieces are missing. How to put the puzzle back together again? *(She begins to leave.)*

MURAD Hey!

*MURAD takes off his sunglasses. MARYAM and MURAD return each other's sunglasses.*

It was Humpty Dumpty who needed to be put back together again. After his fall.

MARYAM Yes, after his fall. From the wall. But when he fell, it wasn't his shell that broke into a thousand pieces. It was the ground beneath him.

*MARYAM sings and, in places, MURAD joins in. Before the song finishes they are both gone but we still hear them singing from offstage into the next scene.*

*Maryam's Song:*

*(sings)* Sleep, sleep my little one.
Tomorrow your father comes,
With a bag full of lemons.
Sleep, sleep, my little one.
Tomorrow your mother comes,
With a bundle of sticks.
Sleep, sleep, my little one.
You know when you wake,
You'll only keep waiting.
You'll always be waiting.

## SCENE NINE

*RUND runs in.*

RUND I found my school!

*We hear the SOLDIERS counting offstage. RUND listens to the counting then speaks to DANNY T. and the audience.*

I'm sorry I'm late. I ran into some *(spells quickly)* O-B-S-T-R-U-C-T-I-O-N-S. What? So this is not spelling class. Is it music? Or dance?

All right.

*RUND dances a traditional Palestinian dance in time with the SOLDIER's counting. Then the SOLDIERS enter. Suddenly, many SOLDIERS appear. DANNY T. joins them. They perform their twenty-one shoot-to-kill positions. The count is part of the dance. RUND begins to mimic the twenty-one positions back to the SOLDIERS as she sings.*

*(sings)* If I'm standing in the path of the wall as you
Build it, soldier, tell me, will it cut me in two?
Will one of my arms and one of my legs sit in class
And do maths and the other arm and leg play in the grass
By the swings? But where will my head go, I'm losing track,

Which side of the wall? How will my pieces find their way back?
And how can there be the other side of Bethlehem,
When there is only one, only one Bethlehem?

*RUND and the SOLDIERS stop dancing.*

*(to DANNY T.)* Wow. I did great. How many is that?

DANNY T. That's twenty-one.

RUND Twenty-one what?

DANNY T. Twenty-one shoot-to-kill positions.

RUND Do I get a star?

*In response, the SOLDIERS, now in various shoot-to-kill positions, raise their guns, aiming at RUND. She takes a couple of steps backwards, but doesn't flinch. She stares hard back at them.*

I can see. You. Can you. See me?

*Then after some moments, DANNY T. touches each soldier on the shoulder and they lower their guns one by one and exit. DANNY T. and RUND lock eyes. She exits.*

## SCENE TEN

*With a simple tape measure, HALA is taking measurements of the ground. And the air. She hums a similar tune as MARYAM sang. After some moments, FAWAZ appears. HALA stops measuring and they regard each other.*

HALA How tall are you?

FAWAZ Not as tall as my brother. Was.

HALA I heard you buckled up. Called ahead for a no-carb meal and flew back across the ocean.

FAWAZ Hala.

HALA I'd say you just miss six feet.

FAWAZ Why did you build the glider?

HALA Because I could.

FAWAZ You knew Rashid was crazy about those things.

HALA Of course. That's why I built it.

FAWAZ Rashid said as a kid he was always falling. He didn't mean falling as in falling down. It was something inside him that kept giving way. I think while he lived here with you he stopped falling.

HALA Mister Al Haj, it's too late for sentiment. I have objects to measure. Go away.

FAWAZ You made a mistake, Hala. I'm six feet tall exactly. Go ahead. Measure me. Maybe you got it wrong.

*HALA approaches FAWAZ with the measuring tape and eyes him. Then she kneels down and measures him, all the way up from his feet to his head, careful not to touch.*

Bingo.

HALA I still love Rashid.

FAWAZ So do I. *(beat)* How about my shoulders, straight across.

HALA Thirty-one inches. I will always miss him. *(She measures his shoulders.)*

FAWAZ So will I.

HALA Twenty-nine and a half.

FAWAZ Not even close. You're out of practice. My neck, around.

HALA Fourteen inches. *(She measures.)* Bingo.

FAWAZ My face.

HALA Eight. *(She measures.)* Rashid will always be with me.

FAWAZ My eyes, corner to corner. And with me. I wish I'd known him better.

*HALA measures, slowly, now letting the tape touch FAWAZ's skin, finding his face with the tape measure.*

My mouth.

HALA Open or closed?

FAWAZ *(uncertain)* However you want it.

*HALA measures FAWAZ's mouth. Then suddenly, almost accidentally, they kiss with the tape measure between their mouths. She breaks the kiss off.*

Could we try that again?

HALA Not now. I'm in mourning. And I have classes to prepare for. Adding to this, I'm building something new in my basement. Don't you have a plane to catch?

FAWAZ Lost my suitcase. Makes it hard to travel.

HALA It might not work out, Fawaz.

*FAWAZ and HALA regard each other some moments.*

FAWAZ Did you know that to get into my brother's room when we were kids you had to go down on your hands and knees?

HALA No. *(beat)* I didn't.

FAWAZ It was that crowded. I think even he was embarrassed by it.

*RASHID appears just as a model glider drops down from above and hangs over their heads.*

He had forty-seven model gliders hanging from his bedroom ceiling. It was crazy. No, it was fucking amazing. And so was he. I was lucky he stayed around as long as he did.

*FAWAZ and HALA are both looking up. RASHID is on his knees, looking up.*

You know, Rashid used to say—

RASHID — Fawaz. When I'm up in that glider, there is no plan. And all of it's possible. Up in that glider, there's just—

ALL — Wide open space.

*The stage grows darker as many gliders appear and hang over them. FAWAZ, HALA, and RASHID continue to watch the small gliders that begin to glow in the dark like many tiny stars. RUND appears, stands close behind RASHID, and watches the gliders, too. She makes the buzzing noise of the glider's motors. RASHID joins her in this sound. Slowly the room fills with this noise until it is deafening.*

*Then sudden, complete silence.*

*Blackout.*

# REFLECTIONS ON *TWENTY-ONE POSITIONS: A CARTOGRAPHIC DREAM OF THE MIDDLE EAST*

### INSPIRATION, CHALLENGES, AND EXPERIENCES IN WRITING AND PRODUCING THE PLAY

In a recent talk on life in occupied Palestine, Abdelfattah told the audience that one of the ways foreigners can participate in non-violent resistance to the occupation is to declare upon entering Israeli Immigration that they have come to visit Palestine. To say it: Palestine. At first, whenever foreigners announced they had come to visit Palestine, they were taken aside for questioning but were eventually allowed into Israel. For the past two years, however, they are almost always prohibited from entering the country.

Behind this petty act of refusing entrance lies the long, brutal history of denying Palestinians their identity and right to statehood. The United States has, of course, aided and abetted this project of "disappearing" an entire people. Instrumental in this long process of ethnic cleansing is the illegal and inhuman separation wall. The genesis of *Twenty-One Positions* is complex, but one of the central intentions of the play is to keep the issues surrounding Palestine and the Palestinian people visible.

In 2003 when Guthrie Theater's literary manager, Michael Dixon, asked a group of American writers to propose international plays, Naomi suggested we collaborate on writing a new play centred on the wall. Condemned by the International Court of Justice, the three-metre high, 422-mile long "Security Fence" cuts across the UN-recognized Green Line, cuts through villages, cuts off water resources and farmland, and makes life and travel for Palestinians at best difficult and at times impossible. In a word, it incarcerates. (Gaza is more thoroughly imprisoned by a barrier policed by both Israel and Egypt.)

In order to represent onstage the grotesque incision of this wall on Palestine, we knew we also needed to show both concrete and imaginary ways Palestinians circumvent and undermine the wall. Our theatrical action against the wall began in researching how it permeates every aspect of social and economic life for Palestinians and how they resist its carceral force.

We found a number of news stories in our research that helped focus our story. We learned, for instance, that some Palestinian resistance fighters crossed barriers into Israel on hang-gliders, and that Israel carried out "Operation Geophyte," the painstaking process of protecting and transplanting plants and bulbs during the building of the transnational highway. A highway for Israelis only.

The unusual nature of our three-person collaborative process also created a completely different perspective than one offered by a single playwright. One of our agreements in the writing of *Twenty-One Positions* was non-ownership. Rather than a singular authorial voice, the playwrights' voices fused and blended in a process of layering, re-visioning, and re-envisioning. *Twenty-One Positions,* we hope, challenges division, occupation, and oppression, in its practise of writing across borders and with its power of a collective imagination. It is in that spirit that we hope it continues its journey through the world.

## GLOSSARY

*All translations are from standard usage unless noted otherwise.*

| | |
|---|---|
| **ahlan** | Welcome |
| **Aliyah** | To make Aliyah is the process of Jewish people moving to Israel, but can also refer to going up to the Rima to read the Torah. |
| **ammu** | Uncle |
| **ayeee** | The beginning of a traditional wedding rhyme, often followed by a group zaghareet or ululation. |
| **Azhkenazi** | Jews who originated in Eastern Europe. |
| **baba** | Father |
| **baklava** | A sweet pastry containing nuts. |
| **bas** | Stop |
| **ben zonah** | Son of a bitch |
| **boychick** | An affectionate term for a young boy. |
| **dabke** | Traditional Palestinian step-dancing. |
| **e'ezifu** | Play |
| **Eid al-Fitr** | The festival and feast which marks the end of the Ramadan month of fasting. |

| | |
|---|---|
| **Eze yofi** | How's it going? |
| **falafel** | A deep-fried ball of ground chickpeas and spices. |
| **fedayeen** | Palestinian militants or guerrillas of a nationalist orientation. |
| **gatkes** | Underwear |
| **habibi/ habibti** | Darling |
| **hayati** | My heart |
| **helweh** | Sweet |
| **hijab** | A traditional headscarf worn by Muslim women, covering their hair, neck, and shoulders. |
| **Inshallah** | God willing |
| **kanafah** | A Palestinian cheese pastry. |
| **keffiyeh** | A traditional headdress worn by Arab men. Wearing a checkered black and white keffiyeh over the shoulders is a symbol of solidarity with the Palestinian cause. |
| **khalas** | Enough |
| **khalto** | Auntie |
| **kibbutznik** | Someone who lives in an Israeli communal settlement, typically a farm. |
| **kippah** | A brimless cap, usually made of cloth, worn by Orthodox Jews. |
| **kteer** | Very |
| **la** | No |
| **losamaht** | Please |

| | |
|---|---|
| **ma'amoul** | A cookie stuffed with dates and nuts. |
| **makloubeh** | A Palestinian dish with rice and meat. |
| **manaqeesh** | A popular Levantine food consisting of dough topped with thyme, cheese, or ground meat. |
| **maramia** | A tea made with sage leaves. |
| **mashallah** | An expression of praise and joy. |
| **matzo** | An unleavened flatbread that forms an integral element of the Passover festival. |
| **merhaba** | A common Palestinian greeting. |
| **mezuzah** | A piece of parchment inscribed with specified Hebrew verses from the Torah. |
| **muezzin** | A chosen person at the mosque who leads the call to service and prayers. |
| **omri** | Sweetheart, darling |
| **quahweh** | Coffee |
| **radiovka** | A traditional Czech beret. |
| **rugelach** | A Jewish pastry of Ashkenazic origin. |
| **schnozz** | A long nose. |
| **sharmouta** | Slut, whore |
| **shay bil n'ana** | Mint tea. |
| **shisha** | A water pipe for smoking. |
| **shmuck** | Prick (vulgar for penis) |
| **shofar** | An ancient musical horn used for Jewish religious purposes. |

| | |
|---|---|
| **shtetl** | A village. |
| **shukran** | Thank you |
| **Shu mallak** | What the fuck? |
| **tali** | Come |
| **tallis** | A Jewish prayer shawl. |
| **taraboosh** | A brimless felt cap, usually red, with a silk tassel. Worn by some Middle Eastern men, especially in the early 1900s. |
| **tayeb** | Fine |
| **tochas** | Buttocks |
| **umi** | Mother |
| **walla** | Really? |
| **ya albi** | A term of endearment. |
| **ya allah** | Oh, God! |
| **yaba** | Papa |
| **yallah** | Come on, hurry |
| **yallah shabab** | Let's go, guys! |
| **ya sater** | A Gazan expression used by men to announce their arrival. |
| **Yerusha-layim** | Jerusalem Day, an Israeli national holiday. |
| **yoni** | Vagina, womb |
| **za'atar** | A Middle Eastern herb blend. |
| **zaghroot** | A joyful sound traditionally made by Middle Eastern women at weddings. |

## ABOUT THE CONTRIBUTORS

Abdelfattah AbuSrour is a writer/actor/director from Bethlehem. He has performed and directed plays in Palestine, Europe, and the US, including *Waiting for Rain, We Are the Children of the Camp,* and *Handala,* adapted from Naji al-Ali's cartoons. *Far Away from a Village Close By* won first prize in the Deir Yassin Remembered Festival in London. In 2014, he directed *The Diary of Anne Frank* for Burning Coal Theatre Company in Raleigh, NC. AbuSrour is a recipient of the Ashoka Fellowship and Synergos' Arab World Social Innovator Award. In 1998, he co-founded the Alrowwad Cultural and Theatre Center for Children in the Aida refugee camp in Bethlehem.

Natasha Greenblatt is from Toronto, Canada. She is a writer, actor, and maker of theatre, television, and film. A graduate of the National Theatre School of Canada, Natasha has acted in plays across Canada and the United States. She wrote, acted in, and co-produced the short film *Flush*. Her play, *The Peace Maker,* was part of the 2013 Next Stage Theatre Festival.

Karen Hartman held the Playwrights' Center's McKnight National Residency and Commission for a nationally recognized playwright in the US. *Goliath,* about the 2005 Gaza pullout, won the Dorothy Silver New Play Prize, and underlies a new work *Gaza Rehearsal*. Hartman's works include: *Roz and Ray* (Edgerton New Play Prize), *The Book of Joseph, Project Dawn, Gum, Leah's Train, Going Gone* (NEA New Play Grant), *Girl Under Grain* (Best Drama in NY Fringe), *Wild Kate, ALICE: Tales of a Curious Girl* (music by Gina Leishman), *Troy Women,* and *MotherBone,* score by Graham Reynolds (Frederick Loewe Award for New Musical Theater). Hartman's work has been supported by the Rockefeller

Foundation at Bellagio, the NEA, the Sustainable Arts Foundation, the Helen Merrill Foundation, a Hodder Fellowship, a Jerome Fellowship, and a Fulbright Scholarship to Jerusalem. She has written for both *The New York Times* and *The Washington Post*. An alumna of New Dramatists and long-time New Yorker, Hartman is now Senior Artist in Residence at the University of Washington School of Drama. Visit her at www.karenhartman.org.

Ismail Khalidi's plays include *Truth Serum Blues* (Pangea World Theater), *Foot, Final Status, Tennis in Nablus* (Alliance Theatre), and a co-adaptation of *Returning to Haifa*. He is the co-editor, with Naomi Wallace, of *Inside/Outside: Six Plays from Palestine and the Diaspora* (Theatre Communications Group, 2015). His writing has appeared in *Mizna, Guernica, The Nation, American Theatre, The Daily Beast*, and *Remezcla*. Khalidi received his MFA in Dramatic Writing from NYU's Tisch School of the Arts. Born in Beirut and raised in the US, he resides in Chile, where he is an artist-in-residence at Teatro Amal.

Hannah Khalil is an award-winning Palestinian-Irish writer whose stage plays include *Ring* (winner of Soho Theatre's Westminster Prize), *Leaving Home, Plan D* (nominated for the Meyer-Whitworth Award), *Bitterenders* (winner of Sandpit Arts' Bulbul 2013), and *The Worst Cook in the West Bank*. Hannah's radio plays include *Last of the Pearl Fishers* and *The Deportation Room*, both for BBC Radio 4. Hannah's latest work includes a production of *Scenes from 68* Years* at the Arcola Theatre, London, in April 2016.

Arthur Milner was Resident Playwright at Ottawa's Great Canadian Theatre Company from 1984 to 1991, and then Artistic Director until 1995. He has taught theatre at Concordia and Carleton Universities, and at Algonquin College and the National Theatre School, and has worked as a dramaturge at the Manitoba Association of Playwrights, the Banff Playwrights Colony, and Playwrights' Workshop Montréal. His most recent play, *Getting to Room Temperature*, premiered at the Undercurrents Festival in Ottawa in February 2016. Other published plays include *1997; Zero Hour; Learning to Live with Personal Growth; It's Not a Country, It's Winter; Crusader of the World;* and *Joan Henry, the Musical* (with Allen Cole and Estelle Shook). He lives with his wife, theatre director Jennifer Brewin, in Val-des-Monts, Quebec.

Stephen Orlov is an award-winning dramatist whose plays have been showcased in such major theatre centres as Montreal, Chicago, and London. They include *Isolated Incident* (with Rahul Varma), *Salaam-Shalom*, *Bow Ties*, *Sperm Count*, and *Freeze*, his box office hit at Montreal's Centaur Theatre Company, published by Guernica Editions, 2016. Stephen also teaches master classes on scriptwriting for theatre and film, most recently for the Saint Lucia National Arts Festival and the Osher Institute at Dartmouth College. He served on the boards of the Playwrights Guild of Canada and Playwrights Canada Press, and he is a member of the inaugural playwrights unit of Infinithéâtre. He is writing *Birthmark*, the sequel to *Sperm Count*. Boston-born, Stephen resides in Montreal with his wife, cellist Karen Kaderavek.

Samah Sabawi is a Palestinian-Australian-Canadian playwright and poet. Her plays *Cries from the Land* and *Three Wishes* had successful runs in Canada, and *Tales of a City by the Sea* enjoyed a sold-out world premiere run at Melbourne's La Mama Theatre in Australia, an Arabic premiere at the Alrowwad Cultural and Theatre Society in Palestine, and was selected for the Victorian Certificate of Education Drama and Theatre Studies Playlist, 2016. Sabawi's poems feature in anthologies including *With Our Eyes Wide Open* (West End Press, 2014), *Gaza Unsilenced* (Just World Books, 2015), and *I remember my name* (novum publishing, 2016). In 2016 Sabawi received an Australian Postgraduate Award to undertake a PhD by creative project at Victoria University.

Lisa Schlesinger is a recipient of the NEA/TCG Theatre Residency Program for Playwrights Award, winner of the BBC International Radio Playwriting Competition, and a USA Artist Fellowship finalist. She has received commissions from the Guthrie Theater and Ensemble Studio Theatre, the BBC, and fellowships from the NEA, CEC International, and the Alfred P. Sloan Foundation. Her plays include *In the Wake of the Graybow Riots*, *Celestial Bodies*, *Rock Ends Ahead*, *The Bones of Danny Winston*, and *Iphigenia: Fragments from an Excavation*, a theatre/film collaboration. Lisa's work has been published in *The New York Times*, *American Theatre*, and *PAJ: A Journal of Performance and Art*.

Betty Shamieh is a Palestinian-American playwright and was named a UNESCO Young Artist for Intercultural Dialogue in 2011. Her off-Broadway premieres are *The Black Eyed* (New York Theatre Workshop) and *Roar* (The New Group). Her recent European productions in translation include *Again and Against* (Playhouse Teater, Stockholm), *The Black Eyed* (Fournos Theatre, Athens), and *Territories*

(European Capitals of Culture Festival). A graduate of Harvard College and the Yale School of Drama, Shamieh was selected as a Clifton Visiting Artist at Harvard in 2004 and named as a Playwriting Fellow at Harvard University's Radcliffe Institute for Advanced Studies in 2006. Her works have been translated into seven languages. Visit her at www.bettyshamieh.com.

Naomi Wallace is an Obie Award–winning playwright from Kentucky. Her plays—produced in the United Kingdom, Europe, the United States, and the Middle East—include *In the Heart of America, Slaughter City, One Flea Spare, The Trestle at Pope Lick Creek, Things of Dry Hours, The Fever Chart, And I And Silence,* and *The Liquid Plain.* In 2009, *One Flea Spare* was incorporated into the permanent repertoire of the French national theatre, the Comédie-Française. Wallace is also a recipient of the MacArthur Fellowship and the 2012 Horton Foote Award. In 2013 she received the Windham–Campbell Prize for Drama. In 2015 she received an American Academy Arts and Letters Award in Literature.

First edition: October 2016. Second printing: June 2024.
Printed and bound in Canada by Imprimerie Gauvin Ltée, Gatineau

*Cover design by: Christine Mangosing // CMANGO Design*

PLAYWRIGHTS
CANADA PRESS

202-269 Richmond St. W.
Toronto, ON
M5V 1X1

416.703.0013
info@playwrightscanada.com
playwrightscanada.com